Praise for Toland's research

"In *American Hero, Kansas Heritage: Years, 1865-1890*, Clyde Toland has meticu and realities of a fascinating and charmed from the age of two, Funston, like many of his generation—William Allen White, Vernon L. Kellogg—was destined to make a difference. In this first volume, Clyde Toland traces a Midwestern life in all its facets: family culture, educational opportunities, religious influences, the landscape—including weather, fire, even grasshopper invasions—employment, and recreation, including formative expeditions to the Colorado mountains. All of these prepared a Kansas boy to become a man of daring actions: the fearless, scrapping national figure who was General Frederick Funston. Toland's affection for detail, his deep mining of the public and private record, his clear-eyed analysis, his clean hand in the writing, and finally his affection for Funston and the Southeast Kansas that shaped him, all make this book valuable, and not only to those studying Funston, but to those who want to understand the Midwest and the America of the 19th and early 20th centuries."

—**Thomas Fox Averill**, founder of Thomas Fox Averill Kansas Studies Collection, Mabee Library, Washburn University of Topeka.

"In *American Hero, Kansas Heritage: Frederick Funston's Early Years, 1865-1890*, by Clyde W. Toland, we have the first of three volumes on the life of Frederick Funston. No one has done more to preserve the legacy of Frederick Funston than Toland, an attorney and native of Allen County, Kansas, where Funston lived during his early years. As Toland notes, in early 1917, Major General Frederick Funston commanded men who would later become known to all Americans: Dwight D. Eisenhower, George Patton, Douglas MacArthur, and John J. Pershing. Funston's premature death in that year meant that he would not command the American Expeditionary Force when the United States entered World War I. Had he not died so unexpectedly, Kansans would have commanded American forces in the two great wars of the 20th century.

"What we have in the first volume of Toland's trilogy is the meticulous reconstruction of the world in which Funston came of age, focusing on southeast Kansas in the last half of the 19th century. There is a detailed account of the Funston farm, the schools he attended, family and friends, the church, prairie fires, winter storms, a grasshopper plague, crime in that era including lynchings, even the appearance of President Rutherford B. Hayes at the Neosho Valley District Fair in 1879. From his time as a schoolmaster, through his Iola High School years, and his time at the State University (K.U), from which he, along with William White, did not graduate, we learn of the early experiences that forged a spirit of adventure, fearlessness, and independence that served Funston well for the remainder of his life."

—**Ramon Powers** served as Executive Director of the Kansas State Historical Society from 1988-2002.

"This first volume of ***Becoming Frederick Funston Trilogy*** is a thoroughly researched and referenced look at the family history and boyhood days of Kansan Major General Frederick Funston. But it is also a wonderful glimpse of life on the frontier during the early settlement of Kansas as it became a territory and later a state during very turbulent times. Funston's remarkable work ethic and sense of adventure are clearly based in his childhood upbringing during these times. This work also chronicles how his days at the State University of Kansas (now the University of Kansas) not only influenced the direction of his life and career, but also resulted in lasting relationships with well-known classmates such as William Allen White (Pulitzer Prize winning journalist and editor) and Herbert S. Hadley (future Governor of Missouri)."

—**Douglas Girod, MD**, Chancellor, University of Kansas

"In this meticulously researched first volume of the Frederick Funston trilogy, you not only learn about a genuine American Hero, you also learn about life on the prairie in the last half of the 19th Century. This is a fascinating tale of the many influences on a young Fred Funston as he navigated his character developing years. Thanks to Clyde Toland, we learn how Fred developed great physical strength, a spirit of adventure and a love for the out of doors. These traits led him on a path to a much-respected general and war hero, mourned by thousands nationally upon his sudden death."

—**Richard B. Myers**, President, Kansas State University
General, USAF, Ret.

Additional endorsements appear on the back cover from:

General David Petraeus, US Army (Ret.), former Commander of the Surge in Iraq, US Central Command, and Coalition Forces in Afghanistan and former Director of the CIA

Jarrett Robinson, BA History, MS International Relations, student of Frederick Funston's life for thirty years

American Hero, Kansas Heritage:
Frederick Funston's Early Years, 1865-1890

Volume One

of

Becoming Frederick Funston Trilogy:
A Tale of "cool courage, iron endurance, and gallant daring"

Clyde W. Toland

Flint Hills Publishing

American Hero, Kansas Heritage:
Frederick Funston's Early Years, 1865-1890

Volume One of ***Becoming Frederick Funston Trilogy: A Tale of "cool courage, iron endurance, and gallant daring"***

Cover and Book Design by Carol Yoho

Editorial Oversight, Thomas Fox Averill

This book was made possible by the Thomas Fox Averill Kansas Studies Collection, and through the generous support of the Washburn University Center for Kansas Studies.

Flint Hills Publishing
www.flinthillspublishing.com

Printed in the U.S.A.

ISBN 978-1-953583-30-7

Library of Congress Control Number application pending.

Fred Funston Cover Photo (1889): "No better picture of Funston anywhere is extant... He often set out alone for a day's hunting or fishing, accoutered as he is here. Note the gun, the bedroll, the tin cup."
—William Allen "Billy" White

Becoming Frederick Funston Trilogy
A Tale of "cool courage, iron endurance, and gallant daring"

This trilogy tells the story of the coming of age of Frederick Funston, the future famous United States Army Major General and American hero at his death in 1917. At age thirty-two, he discovered who he was, and the course of the balance of his life was set. In the process of self-discovery, he lived a fascinating life of adventure, and that life, and certain of the times in which he lived it, are told in this trilogy.

Volume One: ***American Hero, Kansas Heritage: Frederick Funston's Early Years, 1865-1890***

Volume Two: ***Heat and Ice: Frederick Funston's Exploration of Death Valley, Alaska, and the British Northwest Territory, 1891-1894***

Volume Three: ***"Yankee Hero": Frederick Funston, Expedicionario in the Cuban Liberation Army, 1896-1897***

The **Becoming Frederick Funston Trilogy** has forty chapters. The biblical number forty generally symbolizes a period of testing, and these chapters tell, in part, the testing of Frederick Funston in the formative years of his life.

The research and writing of this trilogy were done over a period of twenty-four years (1995-2019). The available time to research and write was the controlling factor. If there are any inconsistencies or errors in style throughout this trilogy, they have persisted despite my best efforts to eradicate them. My apologies for any such inconsistencies or errors.

About the Author

Clyde W. Toland received a BA in history in 1969 from the University of Kansas, and in 1971 a MA in history from the University of Wisconsin-Madison. He received his JD from the University of Kansas in 1975. He is a member of Phi Beta Kappa and the Order of the Coif. Mr. Toland is a semi-retired lawyer in Iola, Kansas.

As a grade school student, he became fascinated by his local Allen County, Kansas, history and by Frederick Funston's early adventurous life in Death Valley, Alaska, the British Northwest Territory, and Cuba. For more than thirty-five years, he has been a student of Funston's life. As president of the Allen County Historical Society, Inc., in Iola, Kansas, he was the driving force in the successful move in 1994 of Frederick Funston's rural childhood home to the Iola town square and in its subsequent restoration and opening as a museum in 1995. He did the research and writing for most of the eleven exhibits in the Funston Museum and Visitors' Center, which opened in 1997 next door to the Funston Home Museum.

Mr. Toland founded the Buster Keaton Celebration, a nationally known humanities event held annually in Iola, Kansas, from 1993 through 2017. He served as co-chair of the Keaton Celebration Committee for the first five celebrations, and continued as a committee member through the 2005 celebration. He is a member of the committee which revived the Buster Keaton Celebration on September 24 and 25, 2021.

At age fifteen he became a Life Member of both the Allen County Historical Society, Inc., and the Kansas State Historical Society. Mr. Toland and United States Senator Nancy Kassebaum Baker in 1996 were the two first recipients of the Alumni Distinguished Achievement Award from the College of Liberal Arts and Sciences of the University of Kansas.

For
Nancy, my wife

Our children and their spouses:
David and Beth
Andrew and Anna
Elizabeth and Bart

Our grandchildren:
Caroline
William
Charlotte
Isaac

"History is the essence of innumerable biographies."

—**Thomas Carlyle**
(1795-1881)

***

"Facts are stubborn things, and whatever may be our wishes,
our inclinations, or the dictates of our passions, they cannot
alter the state of facts and evidence."

—**John Adams**
(1735-1826)

***

"Frederick Funston was a national hero and the object of
great national affection."

—*Miami Herald* editorial
on Funston's death

Table of Contents and
Chronology of Funston's Early Years

Table of Contents, *continued* →

Table of Contents, *continued*

Notes follow each chapter, and, in the case of Chapters Five and Six, follow each subchapter.

CHAPTER ONE

A Charmed Life

He has always been full of adventure...

> —Edward H. Funston, describing his son Frederick
> in a letter (1901)[1]

If in ages to come the mythology of Kansas should be written, Funston would figure as the unconquerable warrior, who bore a charmed life.

> —"Colonel Funston," newspaper editorial (1899)[2]

From the hell of Death Valley, California, in 1891:

I have seen men fall on the field of battle like stalks of corn under the mower's scythe...but never have I suffered or seen suffering such as that I underwent in two days when I rode alone in Death Valley.

To the deadly waters of Miles Cañon on the Yukon River in the British Northwest Territory two years later:

By frantic paddling we kept in the middle and off from the cañon walls. The sensation was akin to that of riding a bucking broncho.

To the bloody battlefields of the Cuban Revolution in 1897:

I saw a dark object coming toward me. Involuntarily I threw my hands to my eyes. There was a dull explosion...[3]

Such was the adventurous early life of Frederick Funston. A stunned nation was to mourn his unexpected death a mere twenty years later in 1917. "When the news of General Funston's death was flashed across the country, from the President to the humblest citizen we were shocked and stunned, and said surely a great man has fallen among us..."[4] As a Major General of the United States Army, "the little General" held the highest filled rank at his death at age fifty-one in February of 1917, and was the commanding officer of men whose names would later become household words—Lieut. Dwight D. Eisenhower, Lieut. George Marshall, Lieut.

1

George Patton, Capt. Douglas MacArthur, and Major General John J. Pershing. To Pershing, not Funston, would go the command of the American Expeditionary Force when the United States entered World War I two months after Funston's death.

Prior to entering military service, Funston's civilian careers had been many and variegated: farmer, country schoolteacher, university student, journalist, ticket collector on the Santa Fe Railway, field botanist in the hellish heat of Death Valley and later in the Arctic cold of Alaska and the British Northwest Territory, lecturer, magazine writer, and guerrilla soldier in Cuba fighting against Spanish rule. In contrast, Frederick Funston's United States military career was to last nineteen years, starting in 1898 when, as Colonel of the "fighting" Twentieth Kansas Volunteer Infantry, he commanded his troops in the Philippines at the time of the 1899 "Philippine Insurrection" or "Philippine-American War" or simply "Philippine War." His bravery and skill were rewarded by a Medal of Honor at the age of thirty-four, and because of his spectacular capture in 1901 of the rebel Filipino leader Emilio Aguinaldo, Funston was transferred by order of President William McKinley from the volunteer army to the regular army and awarded the rank of Brigadier General. At age thirty-two he had been a civilian, and now, at age thirty-five, he had attained the exalted rank of Brigadier General in the United States Army.

Thereafter a career Army man, Funston again acquired national fame in 1906, this time as "the man who saved San Francisco" because of his work during and in the aftermath of the great earthquake and fire that ravaged that city. "[H]is genius and manhood brought order out of confusion, confidence out of fear, and much comfort in our distress."[5] In 1914, after successfully serving as the military governor of United States' occupied Vera Cruz, Mexico, Funston was promoted to Major General. Always modest, Funston thereafter resisted efforts by his friends to have him advanced to a higher rank, which would result in his outranking all other army officers. He wrote to his United States senator: "I have reached the highest rank possible in the army and can do my work better because I can do it fearlessly, knowing that I have nothing to gain and nothing to lose, so long as I do right...I would rather leave things as they are than to obtain advancement at the cost of humiliating the other major generals of the army, several of whom are my warmest personal friends."[6]

Funston's unexpected death occurred at the end of one of his most valuable services to his country—maintaining the peace along the nearly 2,000-mile border between the United States and Mexico during the political troubles between those two countries from 1915 to 1917. As the commander of the Southern Department, Funston commanded approximately 150,000 soldiers, including both federal troops and National Guardsmen from throughout the country who had been federalized and brought to the Mexican border for service. This force constituted the largest U.S. Army since the time of the Civil War some fifty years earlier. As commander of an entire theater of operations, Funston pioneered in the future pattern of high-level military command.[7]

Throughout his career for Uncle Sam, Frederick Funston's daring actions inspired his troops. "We would go to hell behind him."[8] The words of several of his soldiers from the battlefields in the Philippines capture why Funston was such an inspiration to his troops. "Our little colonel is a daisy. He is not afraid of anything. He was out here on his horse the other day and the sharp-shooters began firing at him, but instead of running away he turned his horse and took his field glass and looked all around, trying to locate the shots, at the same time saying: 'Those fellows would just as soon shoot a man as not.'" Another soldier, Funston's cousin, Burt Mitchell, wrote at the time: "It was my first experience under fire, and when the bullets began to drop all around, my legs began to shake and my natural inclination was to dodge, but when I saw Fred riding up and down behind the firing line, as if on dress parade, it seemed to give us all confidence and we braced to the work wonderfully." A third soldier noted "that in one of the regiment's fights Colonel Funston was on foot and 'kept running up and down the line patting us boys on the back and telling us to give the rebels hell.'" Sergeant C.L. Sampson summarized Funston's stature with his troops: "Colonel Funston, or 'Scrapping Fred,' as he is called, has proven himself to be the bravest officer in the line and one that the boys will follow through 'fire or water.' When the fire is the hottest he moves about unflinchingly and waves Mausers [bullets] aside as flies. He has found a place in the hearts of all of his men and if he leads [,] the regiment 'will drive the hosts into the sea.'"[9]

Funston had a "kindly solicitude" for his men. In February of 1900 on a search mission in the Philippines, a party of twenty soldiers became separated from the rest of the company. One of the seventeen privates, George Monroe, later wrote: "We had been letting the horses down the side of the mountain by ropes. We were all very tired and half starved. I was feeling so badly [sic] at nightfall that I was in dread of being put on guard. Funston was the most cheerful man in the party, and he made me grateful for life that night." The 34-year-old Funston told the privates to turn in and sleep for the night, and Funston and the other two officers split the guard duty. "There were seventeen privates in that camp next morning that were ready to lay down their lives for that little general," wrote Monroe.[10]

But Funston was never one to bask in praise. At the huge 1899 welcome home from the Philippine war celebration held for the soldiers of the Twentieth Kansas at Convention Hall in Kansas City, Funston, "in a clear voice that carried well over the great hall and was easily heard in the farthest balconies ...," responded to the adoring crowd of 7,500: "'I am not a hero. (Cries of 'Who is, then?') I don't feel like one. Just an officer, is all I am, who has been very fortunate because the officers and men under him have never failed to follow when he went somewhere. I know that it has been my lot to receive the major portion of the honor that belongs to the men. I give them three-fourths and claim only a share of the rest.'"[11]

Idolized by his soldiers and the public as "the little General" and "the little guy," Funston lacked typical heroic physical stature. Unlike Hollywood's hero Indiana Jones, as portrayed by six feet, one inch tall Harrison Ford, Funston stood a mere five feet, four inches in height and generally weighed a scant 120 pounds. That Funston was able to lead such a physically demanding and rigorous life is a testament to his courage, perseverance, intelligence, resourcefulness, physical strength, and sheer grit.

On the evening of February 19, 1917, 51-year-old Major General Frederick Funston and a hunting friend, Roy Miller, Mayor of Corpus Christi, Texas, dined together at the St. Anthony Hotel in San Antonio. Funston was in the best of spirits and said that he had never felt better in his life. Neither man knew that death had marked Funston for its own. Following dinner, they sat on a divan in the Peacock Alley section of the hotel. "Naturally the General's presence attracted much attention, not only on account of his own great personal popularity, but because of the apparent eminence [sic] of our entry into the World War" wrote Miller years later. Funston, the father of four and a lover of children, played briefly with 6-year-old Inez Silverberg of Des Moines, Iowa, and then, after she left, the two men listened to the hotel orchestra play Strauss's "The Blue Danube Waltz." Funston remarked, "You know, there is no music so sweet as the old tunes." His head fell forward; his body slumped; and death from a heart attack was almost immediate and practically painless.[12]

Funston's unexpected death was headlined in newspapers throughout the country. "Gen. Frederick Funston Mustered Out by Death," one newspaper noted, while another recognized a higher power: "Great Commander Quickly Summons Funston."[13] President Woodrow Wilson wrote a personal letter of condolence to Funston's widow, Eda.[14] Major General Funston's premature death was attributed to the stress of the tremendous responsibilities that he had shouldered since 1915 commanding the United States military forces on the American-Mexican border. "Regular army officers have said that General Funston gave his life to his country as surely as did any American soldier who died in battle. For the tremendous work of commanding 150,000 soldiers, about 100,000 of them practically untrained and unlearned in regular army customs, of disposing those troops along 2,000 miles of treacherous border, of listening to the disputes between regulars and militiamen, of organizing and then reorganizing, of conferring with Mexican generals, was a job that kept the general at his desk, continuously…"[15]

Funston's death brought outpourings of grief from the American people. The first person to be so honored, he lay in state in the Alamo, Texas' sacred cradle of liberty, where in three hours his body was viewed by more than 10,000 people.[16] Many of them had "an eye in which sparkled a tear."[17] The Alamo was nearly filled with flowers, and these reflected Funston's popularity, which extended to all classes. "Costly floral pieces were side by side with the simple tributes of humble workmen, who, hats in hand and with bowed heads, filed into the building."[18] Funston's body next lay in state in the rotunda of the new city hall of his beloved San Francisco ("City Bows At Bier Of Her Dead Hero"[19]). During Funston's funeral service at the Presbyterian Church, his pastor prayed "for the bereaved family, for the American people, who had lost a great leader, for President Wilson, deprived of an able lieutenant, and for the Nation as a whole, facing a future full of uncertainties."

Major General Funston was laid to rest in San Francisco in the cemetery at the Army's military fort, the Presidio, next to the body of his 7-year-old son, Arthur MacArthur Funston, namesake of Funston's commanding officer in the Philippines. The big guns of the Presidio boomed thirteen times in final tribute. All street traffic ceased throughout San Francisco, and for two minutes men stood with bared heads in honor of "the beloved officer."[20] Not bad for a Kansas farm boy who had never attended West Point.

Today, a man who had appeared destined to be long remembered is largely forgotten. Just as World War I swept away the monarchies of the principal defeated nations, it also swept Funston from public memory. Funston, the hero before the country's entry into the war, had been replaced by his subordinate and the war's eventual hero, General John J. Pershing. When Funston's name surfaces today, it is frequently as the subject of controversy, specifically for his role as a military officer in the United States' conquest of the Philippines during the "Philippine Insurrection" or "Philippine-American War" or the "Philippine War" and the subsequent guerrilla warfare which did not officially end until July 4, 1902. Although an Army officer and not a political leader, Colonel, and later Brigadier General, Funston was never bashful about publicly condemning opponents of the war. He was articulate and his language was colorful, all of which made good copy for the American press.

These characteristics also made him a lightning rod for criticism by vocal opponents of the war. This role has continued posthumously with modern day critics of this long-ago war, a war which resulted in U.S. acquisition of the Philippine Islands as part of an overseas empire. Funston's view of the anti-imperialists, as the war's opponents were popularly known, is easily understandable, since he believed that domestic criticism of the war effort encouraged the Filipinos to continue their fight against the United States. The result, in Funston's view, was the unnecessary deaths of American soldiers. In a famous 1902 speech to the Lotos Club of New York City, the "little General" averred as follows: "All of those men who have fallen since January, 1900, have died not because the Filipinos really had much heart in fighting against us, but because they were kept up by a lot of misinformed and misguided people here in the United States. (Applause and cries of 'That's right.') It is perfectly proper for us to have all sorts of opinions about the advisability of holding the Philippine Islands...but, for heaven's sake, let us keep those opinions to ourselves until the sovereignty of the United States has been established over every square inch of those islands, and then let us get together and pull hair and fight the thing out among ourselves." The crowd cheered Funston's words, and applauded at length.[21] This logical accusation of aiding the enemy by domestic criticism of the war effort probably has occurred in nearly every war fought by the United States.

With his customary vigorous and graphic language, Funston proceeded in the same speech to infuriate the war's critics—and his own—when he proposed this treatment of them: "[T]here are a great many men in the United States who have done more harm with their mouths, than these men did with the Krag-Jorgensen rifles that they carried to the enemy [two American soldiers who had deserted to the enemy and who had afterward been captured and executed as traitors].... I would rather see any one of these men hanged—hanged for treason, charged for giving aid and comfort to the enemy—than see the humblest soldier in the United States Army lying dead on the field of battle."[22] Strong language, indeed, but reflective of an impassioned commander who valued his soldiers' lives above all else.

Funston even incurred the wrath of author Mark Twain. He was also a leading anti-imperialist who vilified Funston because of his daring capture of Twain's hero, Aguinaldo, the leader of the Filipino resistance to United States' rule of the Philippines. In his sarcastic diatribe, "A Defence of General Funston," Twain excused Funston's conduct "because his conscience leaked out through one of his pores when he was little..."[23] Hiding in his remote jungle headquarters at Palanan, Aguinaldo had been surprised and captured by a small force of fewer than one hundred men commanded by Funston. To accomplish this feat Funston and four other American soldiers had pretended to be prisoners of war of Filipinos who were loyal to the United States, and who, in turn, pretended to be reinforcements for Aguinaldo's army.

Aguinaldo later admitted his surprise. "We were all stunned by General Funston's temerity in appearing at Palanan in the way he did...I was never before in such a position, and it was certainly one of the most remarkable captures in history... I never thought I could be captured in such a way... General Funston is a remarkable man to have planned my capture in the way he did. I hope I may always number him among my friends."[24] The captured Aguinaldo, President of the Philippine Republic and commander of its army, in the hours after his capture took two surprising actions. He wrote a complimentary letter about his capture to his captor, General Funston.[25] And he insisted that his photograph be taken with Funston standing next to him.[26] Aguinaldo acknowledged to one of his captors, "I should never have believed it that I could be deceived in this manner. I would not have dared to do such a thing."[27]

That Aguinaldo was stunned by Funston's audacious action is hardly surprising. Not only was the element of surprise successfully maintained by the Americans and their native allies, the actual trek to Palanan involved incredible physical hardships for Funston and his men. The small American force had been landed by the U.S. gunboat *Vicksburg* on the remote eastern coast of the Philippine island of Luzon. Their initial twenty-five mile march through the jungle was to the town of Casiguran where the expedition members successfully fooled the natives, loyal to Aguinaldo, as to their true identities.

After a two-day stay there, the American force, taking with them a small quantity of cracked corn for food, started on a ninety-mile march to Palanan. "The country is rough and uninhabited, and provisions could not be secured. The party ate small shell fish, but were almost starved. Wading swift rivers, climbing precipitous mountains and penetrating dense jungles, they marched seven days and nights..." until they were only eight miles from Palanan.[28] They were so weak at this point that only by sending a request to Aguinaldo for food, which he granted, were they sustained. Pushing on to Palanan, and revealing their true identities at an opportune moment, Funston's men surprised and captured the 32-year-old Aguinaldo in his own headquarters. "The transaction was brilliant in conception and faultless in execution" wrote Funston's commanding officer, General Arthur MacArthur. "All credit must go to Funston, who under the supervision of Gen. Wheaton, organized and conducted the expedition from start to finish."[29]

Theodore Roosevelt, hero of the Spanish-American War and serving as Vice President of the United States, wrote Funston an extraordinary congratulatory letter. In the initial sentence, Roosevelt averred that "[t]his is no perfunctory or formal letter of congratulation." He then complimented "[m]y dear General" with these words: "I take pride in this crowning exploit of a career filled with feats of cool courage, iron endurance and gallant daring, because you have added your name to the honor roll of American worthies." Near the end of the two-plus page, typed letter, the national military hero "Teddy" Roosevelt, who was seven years Funston's senior, paid him the ultimate compliment. After speculating that "it is always possible that [the United States] may find ourselves pitted against a big military power where we shall need to develop fighting material at the very outset," Roosevelt offered that "if that day is not too far distant I shall hope to be serving under or along side of you."[30]

The magnitude of Funston's accomplishment is apparent when one realizes that Aguinaldo's position was comparable to that of William McKinley, the then-President of the United States and Commander in Chief of its military forces. One can imagine the devastating political and military effect on the United States if the roles had been reversed and President McKinley, while at home in the White House, had been surprised and captured by the Filipinos.

In 1982, eighty-one years after this extraordinary feat of physical endurance by Funston and his men, a small group of Americans retraced Funston's route. Even with an enormous amount of foodstuffs, modern equipment, and the benefit of being in better shape than Funston's group, these latter day adventurers were worn out by the rugged terrain.[31] That the nearly starved and exhausted Funston party succeeded in its objective at Palanan is a wonder, and this success undoubtedly re-enforced Funston's belief that he was invulnerable and led a charmed life.[32]

As Aguinaldo had hoped, the former enemies did become friends, a friendship that meant so much to Aguinaldo that, nearly a quarter century after Funston's death, Aguinaldo sent his nephew to Iola, Kansas, to see the nearby small farmhouse that was Funston's home during his first thirty-two years.[33] Years later, Funston's grandson, Captain Frederick Funston III, a United States Air Force fighter pilot stationed at Clark Air Base in the Philippines, and his wife, Greta, visited Aguinaldo and his wife in their home. The elderly Aguinaldo told them, "I'm glad your grandfather captured me or I might have been killed."[34]

A twist on the Frederick Funston-Emilio Aguinaldo relationship, though posthumous in the case of Funston, was the joint attendance at West Point of their sons and namesakes, Frederick Funston Jr. and Emilio Aguinaldo Jr. This "Second Generation" was photographed shaking hands at the time of their West Point entrance as plebes in 1923. Frederick Jr., had the honor of being appointed to the military academy by the President of the United States, Warren G. Harding. General Leonard Wood, Governor General of the Philippines, appointed the junior Aguinaldo. The two young men had not previously met.[35]

Of his capture, Aguinaldo volunteered that he "would not have dared to do such a thing." And yet Frederick Funston dared and succeeded. How did a 35-year-old man from the heart of the United States—the prairie state of Kansas—become the remarkable man and American hero that his archenemy so greatly admired? The answer is a coming-of-age story, since it was not until Frederick Funston was 32 years old that he knew fully who he was. His Kansas heritage is a significant part of Funston's story, and is the subject of this first volume of *Becoming Frederick Funston Trilogy.*

FUNSTON FUNERAL CORTEGE REACHES THE ALAMO

Body of Frederick Funston lying in state, City Hall of San Fancisco, California

Chapter One Notes—*A Charmed Life*

1. Elihu S. Williams, "Gen. Fred Funston," *The Buckeye*, Troy, Ohio, April 4, 1901. Williams was a friend of Frederick Funston's father, and quoted Fred's father's description of Fred made in a letter to Williams (Frederick Funston Papers at Kansas State Historical Society, hereafter FFP) (Archives Division, Kansas State Historical Society).

2. "Colonel Funston," unidentified 1899 newspaper (editorial) (*Wilder Stevens Metcalf and Frederick Funston With The Twentieth Kansas In The Philippines During The Spanish–American War*) (scrapbook of newspaper clippings, Spencer Research Library, University of Kansas).

3. The three brief quotations are from, respectively, (1) "Funston, Brig. Gen., U.S.V.," *The Kansas City Star*, May 7, 1899 (FFP); (2) Frederick Funston, "Over The Chilkoot Pass To The Yukon," *Scribner's Magazine*, November 1896; and (3) "Fred Funston Tells Of Cuba," *Topeka Daily Capital*, March 4, 1898.

4. "Body Is Buried In National Cemetery," *The San Francisco Examiner*, February 25, 1917 (Eckdall Scrapbook IV, 19). Includes the Reverend William Kirk Guthrie's funeral sermon.

5. "Body Is Buried In National Cemetery," *The San Francisco Examiner*, February 25, 1917.

6. "Funston Opposed Effort To Advance Him By Law," *The Topeka Daily Capital*, February 26, 1917. The quotation is reprinted from a letter written by Funston to United States Senator Charles Curtis on August 17, 1916.

7. John B.B. Trussell, Jr., "The Man destiny just missed," *Military Review*, June 1973, 59. Trussell was a retired U.S. Army Colonel, and, as such, was qualified to assess Funston's pioneer role.

8. "He Pounded Them," unidentified and undated 1899 newspaper (reprint from "Topics in K.C. Journal") (Frederick Funston Papers on microfilm at the Kansas State Historical Society, hereafter FFP Micro).

9. "Kansas Topics," *The Kansas City Journal*, March 31, 1899 (FFP Micro). Excerpts from letters from several soldiers.

10. "Funston As Sentinel," *The Iola Daily Register*, May 6, 1901. Story of Private George Monroe of Hutchinson, Kansas, when he was with Company C, Thirty-fourth Infantry. "And as for nerve—well, he was one solid bunch of it. I have seen him standing in an exposed position when it was fairly blue [with bullets] around him. He paid less attention to bullets than he did to mosquitoes."

11. "Reception At The Hall," *The Kansas City Journal*, November 11, 1899 (FFP Micro).

12. Roy Miller to David Potter, January 29, 1932 (FFP). See also "Attack Follows Dinner Party and End Comes Almost Instantaneously," unidentified San Antonio, Texas, newspaper with presumed date of February 20, 1917 (FFP Micro).

    Funston had suffered from heart problems for several years. He also had gained significant weight, and to combat this, his physician had Funston take up cigarette smoking (Ella (Funston) Eckdall to Frank F. Eckdall, May 19, 1928). Courtesy of Deborah (Eckdall) Helmken. Smoking helped suppress the appetite and was advertised as the "Modern Way to Diet" (Linda Simon, *Lost Girls — The Invention of the Flapper* (London: Reaktion Books Ltd, 2017), 206). When Fred visited his sister, Ella (Funston) Eckdall, at her Emporia, Kansas, home, she refused to allow her famous brother to smoke inside her house. She banished him to the porch to smoke, where he was visible to passersby. Despite his requests to smoke inside, Ella refused to permit it (Telephone conversation on January 2, 2017, of author with Ellen (Lees) Stolte, a granddaughter of Ella (Funston) Eckdall).

    Inez Silverberg (1911-2006), under her married name of Inez Asher, was a novelist and radio and television writer.

13. "Gen. Frederick Funston Mustered Out By Death," unidentified and undated newspaper (FFP Micro); "Great Commander Quickly Summons Funston," unidentified and undated newspaper (untitled scrapbook on Funston, Iola Public Library, Iola, Kansas).

14. "President Pays Tribute to Gallantry, Devotion and Patriotism of Funston," *The San Antonio Express*, February 20, 1917 (Eckdall Scrapbook II, 179). Wilson's letter, as corrected by examination of the original letter in FFP:
     "My dear Mrs. Funston: May I not tell you with what genuine grief I have learned of the death of your distinguished husband? I feel confident that I am expressing the feeling of the whole country when I say that we have lost in him an officer of unusual gallantry, capacity and loyal devotion to the interests of the country. He has repeatedly in the very recent months proved his ability to handle situations of unusual delicacy and difficulty with discretion and success.
     "May I not express my warm personal sympathy for you in your irreparable loss?
     "Cordially and sincerely yours, Woodrow Wilson."

15. "Major-General Funston," unidentified newspaper dated March 10, 1917 which appears to quote from *The New York Times* (FFP Micro). Funston himself described the stress that he was under: "I stayed up all night, too; not one night, but many. I called for soldiers and I got only men, thousands and thousands of them, but not armies. They had to be put into brigades and divisions and regiments one day, and unscrambled and put together on paper the next day as a new batch came in. They had to be fed and clothed, and equipped and trained, and some of them had to be petted, but we didn't do much of that. I didn't stay up to hear the news. I stayed up with a tremendous job of getting armies down where something would happen to them; or, with luck, where something would happen to the other side" ("Revered On The Border," *The New York Times*, February 20, 1917).

16. "Report Of Custodian Of The Alamo," dated April 18, 1917, contained in a publication *Daughters Of The Republic of Texas*, 28 (no other identifying information on copy of the pages in FFP). According to this source, Funston was "very fond" of the Alamo. The local firemen draped the flower-filled interior of the Alamo in black, and several arc lights were installed. "There was only a prayer said by an old army chaplain—his voice tearful and broken."

17. "Alamo Thronged To Pay Last Honors For General Funston," unidentified San Antonio, Texas, newspaper, with presumed date of February 21, 1917 (FFP Micro).

18. "Funston's Body To Rest At Presidio," *The Kansas City Journal*, February 21, 1917 (FFP Micro).

19. "City Bows At Bier of Her Dead Hero," unidentified San Francisco newspaper with presumed date of February 24, 1917 (FFP Micro). "In silence the people filed into the City Hall, paused to gaze with sorrowful eyes upon the scene, then moved past the casket and out into the street again, with tear-marred vision. This endless procession moved ever on, paying the city's impressive tribute to the dead... No one minded the rain. There seemed to be something appropriate about it—it was as though Heaven were weeping in sympathy with the city's sorrow" ("All San Francisco Mourns Over Gen. Funston's Body," *The San Francisco Examiner*, February 24, 1917).

20. See Appendix A for the account of Funston's funeral and burial as reported in *The San Francisco Examiner*, February 25, 1917. Appendix A also contains the letter of Funston's cousin, Maude Minrow, who was in San Antonio at the time of Funston's death. For "the beloved officer," see "Funston Laid To Rest At Presido," unidentified San Francisco newspaper with presumed date of February 24, 1917 (FPP Micro).
     On February 28, 1917, after the burial of Frederick Funston, Kansas Governor Arthur Capper wrote to Funston's widow, Eda B. Funston, and made a "suggestion"

12

that she declined: "There is a very general desire among our people that the body of General Funston should be brought to Kansas and laid to rest in a mausoleum to be erected by the state on Mount Oread (State University hill) at Lawrence" (FFP).

21. "What the Little General Said in New York," *The Topeka State Journal*, March 14, 1902 (*Frederick Funston: Adventurer, Explorer, and Soldier*, scrapbook, Spencer Research Library, University of Kansas). Complete text of speech on March 8,1902, at Lotos Club, New York City, before more than 300 members.

22. "What the Little General Said in New York," *The Topeka State Journal*, March 14, 1902.

23. Mark Twain, "A Defence of General Funston," *The North American Review*, Vol. CLXXIV (May 1902), 621. Twain had taken a totally different tack three years earlier with the 25-year-old Winston Churchill, future Prime Minister of Great Britain, on the occasion in 1899 of introducing him to an audience in Boston, Massachusetts. Great Britain was then engaged in its own war—the Boer War—in South Africa against the native populace, a war that was unpopular with Churchill's American audience. In introducing Churchill prior to his speech about the British point of view in this war, Twain said, in part, the following: "although he and I do not agree as to the righteousness of the South African war, that's not of the least consequence, for people who are worth anything never do agree" ("'This is a very great country my dear Jack...,'" Richard M. Langworth, *Finest Hour*, Autumn 1999), 35.

Men such as Funston were not the only objects of Twain's venom. He attacked famed author Jane Austen: "Every time I read 'Pride and Prejudice,' I want to dig her up and hit her over the skull with her own shin-bone" (Alexander Theroux, "A Nasty Way With Words," *Wall Street Journal*, November 20, 2009; review of *Poisoned Pens*, edited by Gary Dexter).

24. Harry Steele Morrison, "Aguinaldo Tells of His Capture," unidentified and undated newspaper article (FFP). This interview occurred shortly after Aguinaldo's capture and subsequent return to Manila on March 28, 1901.

25. David Potter, *Frederick Funston: A First Class Fighting Man: A Biography*, 226 (manuscript) (David Potter Manuscripts; 1950s, Manuscripts Division, Department of Rare Books and Special Collections, Princeton University Library).

26. David Haward Bain, *Sitting in Darkness: Americans in the Philippines* (Boston: Houghton Mifflin Company, 1984), 370.

27. Bain, *Sitting in Darkness: Americans in the Philippines*, 370.

28. "Gen. Funston Tells How the Capture Was Made," unidentified newspaper article with dateline of Manila, March 28 (*Frederick Funston: Adventurer, Explorer, and Soldier*).

29. "MacArthur Gives Credit," *Leavenworth Times*, March 29, 1901 (*Frederick Funston: Adventurer, Explorer, and Soldier*).

30. Theodore Roosevelt to Brig. Genl. Frederick C. [sic] Funston, Oyster Bay, N.Y., March 30, 1901 (FFP). Bain, see note 31 below, at 135 stated that this letter is hand-written, but examination of the original in the FFP reveals that it is typewritten.

31. David Haward Bain, "Manifest Destiny's man of the hour: Frederick Funston," *Smithsonian*, May 1989, 135.

32. Frank Funston Eckdall (1907-2000), nephew of Frederick Funston, in conversation with the author in 1993. From his mother, Ella (Funston) Eckdall, Eckdall had learned much about his famous uncle, who was his mother's brother. Frederick Funston was not the only member of his family who believed that he led a charmed life. In a newspaper interview with his parents in May 1901 after he had captured Aguinaldo, Fred's mother, Ann (Mitchell) Funston, stated, "He will come back to us, too. I'm sure he will." The interview continued as follows:

"He seems to lead a charmed life," it was suggested.

"'Yes, you know,' said Mrs. Funston, 'that the Greeks fought under the shield of their favorite god. Well, I'm not a pagan, but I have a belief in the Christianized version of that doctrine of the incidents [sic: ancients], and I hope to see the boy back. I wish he were here now'" ("Would Make His Son A Senator," unidentified newspaper of May 1901 (FFP Micro)).

On July 22, 1905, Fred barely escaped death in California, when an electric streetcar crashed into the carriage in which he and two other officers were riding. They jumped from the vehicle, and Fred had his left hand severely bruised. The streetcar was going at a slow rate of speed and had its gong sounding, yet the driver of the Funston carriage "attempted to turn across the track when the car was almost upon him" ("Funston Hurt," *The Iola Daily Register*, July 22, 1905).

Fred's parents offered their assessments of this potentially fatal collision. His father, Edward H. Funston, said, "Fred was always lucky. He always came out on top. You can't hurt him." Fred's mother "said that it was simply another case of a marvelous escape. 'He has had so many though,' said she, 'that I always expect them. People have often asked me if I do not worry about him, but I don't. I always feel that he will come out all right. I suppose though, that when his time comes he will go, but I don't worry'" ("Funston Makes Comment," *The Iola Daily Register*, July 22, 1905).

One reason Fred's mother never worried about him was that he had told her that "before his exploits, he always considered several plans, also several ways to avoid tragedy, if the[y] didn't develop as planned. Later, he said that, while his capture of Aguinaldo was successful, he thought it was too dangerous because too many other people were involved. He and the other Americans always had to guard and watch the Philippinos [sic] to see that something they said or did, would reveal their situation. So, he said that if he had it to do over, he would use another plan. (I wonder what it was, but do not know)" (Lida (Eckdall) Lees to Jarrett Robinson, July 7, 1991; Lida was the granddaughter of Ann (Mitchell) Funston, and daughter of Ella (Funston) Eckdall). Courtesy of Jarrett Robinson and Ellen (Lees) Stolte.

33. "Filipino Speaker Here Yesterday, Nephew of One-Time Funston Foe," *The Iola Register*, Nov. 6, 1941. In a 1932 letter to David Potter, whom Eda Funston had retained to write her husband's biography, Emilio Aguinaldo closed with this request: "Kindly convey to Mrs. Funston my remembrance and best wishes" (E. Aguinaldo to Capt. David Potter, July 11, 1932) (FFP Micro).

34. Hal Drake, "Aguinaldo Lived to See His Dreams Come True," *Pacific Stars and Stripes* (photocopy of undated article in my possession). In telephone conversation with Greta Funston on January 9, 2003, she confirmed to me Aguinaldo's quotation. She stated that Aguinaldo had no resentment about his capture, and that he had no hard feelings against Fred III's grandfather. She further stated that Aguinaldo had malaria and Fred Funston, his captor, got medical treatment for him.

Frederick Funston III's nickname was "Freddie" but he went by another nickname in the family—Tod, which had been given to him by his mother based on a character she liked in a book called *Water Babies*. In his fighter squadron, he was called "Fearless Freddie." Greta said that her husband was "very, very modest about his grandfather." She summarized the three generations of Funston men as General Fred, Colonel Fred (his son), and then the youngest Fred, who was Captain Fred. All three died of heart attacks, with Fred III dying at thirty-four. His father, Frederick Jr., was fifty-two at his death, and his grandfather, fifty-one. Part of the foregoing information was furnished by Greta to me in an earlier telephone visit on August 27, 2001. After the birth of Fred III in 1929, he was known in army circles as the "Little General" (Eckdall Scrapbook II, 220).

35. "Funston and Aguinaldo—The Second Generation," *The Kansas City Star*, July 6, 1923 (Eckdall Scrapbook II, 225).

CHAPTER TWO

Myth and Reality

Myth, noun – Any fictitious or imaginary story, explanation, person, or thing.

Reality, noun – A person, entity, or event that is actual.

—*The American Heritage Dictionary of the English Language*

"One of [Funston's] assignments on this [Kansas City] [news]paper was to cover an Indian outbreak in Southwest Kansas and in order to do this the 23-year-old reporter traveled with the troops and even took an active part in the fighting."[1] A typical Fred Funston dangerous experience? Yes. But is it true? No.

In the years after Funston's death, his only sister, Ella (Funston) Eckdall (1873-1964), compiled four scrapbooks of newspaper clippings about her famous brother. On occasion, she made handwritten notes next to various articles, and next to that portion of the 1936 article about Funston's life containing the above quotation, she wrote only one word— "wrong." For extra emphasis, she X'ed out the offending sentence.

Funston's adventures were frequently so unbelievable that it is hardly surprising that there exist apocryphal adventures in addition to the real ones. Unfortunately, at times, it is impossible to determine which adventures are mythical and which are real. In this book, I have omitted any stories that I believe are myths, and have included only the ones I believe to be true. When I have been unable to prove or disprove an account, inclusion has been my policy. I shall hereafter usually refer to Funston as Fred, the name customarily used by his family and friends.

In recounting Fred's early life, not only is there the occasional question of myth or reality, there is the additional problem that, in numerous published works, the chronology of much of the first thirty-two years of his life is confused, and, at times, impossible. A typical example is found in David Haward Bain's *Sitting in Darkness*, where he asserts that, after Fred graduated from Iola High School in Iola, Kansas, in a year not stated, he took the examination for admission to West Point Military Academy and was unsuccessful. Then, according to this chronology, being "dispirited," Fred taught five months at a rural school, following which he enrolled in a business college. Quickly deciding that this was not his calling, he enrolled as a student for the 1886 fall semester at the State University in Lawrence, Kansas.[2] This sequence of events is simply not accurate. Additionally, since Fred graduated from Iola High School in May of 1886, and entered the State University less than four months later, the foregoing chronology of multiple events is not merely incorrect, it is impossible timewise.[3]

The reality is that in May of 1884, while Fred was enrolled in the business college in Lawrence, he took the West Point examination. Being unsuccessful, he sometime thereafter, but no later than late August of the same year, left the business college, and in September of 1884 began teaching one four-month term at the rural schoolhouse popularly known as "Stoney Lonesome." One term was enough for Fred, and thus, in the fall of 1885, he entered the senior class at Iola High School from which he graduated the following May.[4]

At times, the mind reels at the cornucopia of factual misstatements in much of the literature about Fred's early life. To seek out all such errors and then rebut them one by one would be a tedious task, indeed. Instead, the correct record of his early life set out in the remainder of this book, based upon the primary materials cited, effectively rebuts some of these erroneous assertions. Some assertions, however, are so egregious, or so silly, in their distortion of the record that they will be duly noted to correct affirmatively those incorrect details of Fred's life. Essential in accurately telling the story of Fred's first thirty-two years, the years covered by this trilogy, are contemporary sources, notably various newspapers. These newspapers, especially *The Iola Register*, with their frequent brief references to Fred, are the principal tool to straighten out the prior confused and incorrect published chronologies of his early life, and, at last, set the record straight more than a century later.

Other contemporary accounts aid in fleshing out the details of those first thirty-two years. Fred's parents, the subject of several newspaper interviews at their farm home, provide particularly interesting and informative details about their famous son. The Funston family, however, did not appreciate some of the newspaper correspondents from New York: "Some of those small brained correspondents from N.Y. who used to come to our home to ascertain some facts as to Fred's parentage & and [sic] who were always received by my father in a most courteous manner insisted upon offending the first rules of a gentleman, by criticizing the host and hostess, their home, circumstances, & in order to make their stories readable enough to secure for themselves no doubt a much needed meal ticket. Had they been sufficiently qualified to write upon the subject, they would have found that their host was a real gentleman, a scholar and one of the best known and most respected men of Kansas."[5] Thus complained Fred's only sister, Ella (Funston) Eckdall.

After Fred's death in 1917, Ella lit the torch of preserving and publicizing the record of her brother's life of accomplishments. Ella is a worthy source of information through her writings concerning Fred's life, including her letters, her account of the Funston family and their home in *The Funston Homestead* (1949), and the scrapbooks that she compiled about Fred's life.[6] Even Ella, however, and perhaps because she was eight years Fred's junior, can, and does, make occasional mistakes in the chronology of his early life. For example, in a 1925 letter to Fred's widow, Eda Funston, she mistakenly stated that Fred taught country school after graduating from high school instead of the reverse, and that Fred attended business college after graduating from high school, which is also incorrect.[7] In addition to her own writings, Ella assisted Eda Funston in compiling information on her husband's life in order that his biography could be written and published.[8] As a part of this compilation, Eda wrote, in her own handwriting, a brief chronological sketch of her husband's life.[9]

Ella (Funston) Eckdall's recollections of Fred as a person and of various episodes of his life are invaluable in understanding him. In like fashion, the remembrances of several of his contemporaries are also helpful in learning about Fred's experiences, though these reminiscences are, at times, equally deficient as far as accurate chronology is concerned. This is probably attributable to their being written years after the events in question. Even Fred himself, later in life, might have had to think for a minute before being able to recount accurately the sequence of events of his early life.

Charles F. Scott (1860-1938), who was five years older than Fred and known as Charlie Scott, is another important contemporary source. Although living as a boy in the same rural neighborhood as the Funstons did after they settled in 1868 near Carlyle, Kansas, the Scott family about six years later moved to the nearby town of Iola. Fred and Charlie Scott became better acquainted when Fred entered Iola High School and Scott was editor of *The Iola Register* newspaper. After Charlie married Fred's former high school classmate, May Ewing, in 1893, the two men became "such intimate and firm friends."[10]

After Fred's capture of Aguinaldo in March of 1901, Scott, by then a United States congressman at large for Kansas, wrote a sketch of the famous general's life for *The Independent* of April 11, 1901. Scott had previously written for a Topeka newspaper in 1898 a sketch titled "Remarkable Career of a Kansas Boy."[11] Charlie also delivered one of the two eulogies at the memorial service held in the Kansas House of Representatives following Fred's death in 1917.[12]

The other eulogy that day was delivered by Charles S. Gleed (1856-1920). A prominent Kansas business leader, Charlie Gleed, as he was known, had become friends with Fred when the former was a regent for the State University of Kansas and the latter was a student there. After Fred first acquired national fame in the spring of 1899, Gleed had written a sketch of Funston's life aptly titled "Romance And Reality In A Single Life. Gen. Frederick Funston."[13] Like Scott, Gleed provides insights into Fred's early life and character.

As a further result of Fred's fame in the spring of 1901 following his capture of Aguinaldo, another friend published a biographical sketch. "Funston: A Product of Kansas" was authored by James H. Canfield (1847-1909) and published in *The American Monthly Review of Reviews* in May 1901. Canfield had been one of Fred's professors at the State University of Kansas and had formed with him there a "most delightful comradeship." Canfield wrote knowledgeably about Fred's years as a student there, and Ella (Funston) Eckdall regarded this article, with the exception of one minor detail, as "so true to life and is so good a description of him in his school days that it is worth keeping."[14]

William Allen White (1868-1944), the famous and Pulitzer Prize-winning editor of the *Emporia* (Kansas) *Gazette*, is an oft-quoted source of information about Fred Funston. This is hardly surprising, since White and Fred had begun a close friendship during their first year at the State University of Kansas in 1886-1887, a friendship terminated only by Fred's death more than thirty years later. White was always "Billy" to Fred. Their intimate friendship and the resulting insights Billy had into Fred's life are not the only reasons he is a highly popular source of information about Fred. White's own fame is partially responsible, but a key factor is that he is so quotable. As a journalist, White developed a flair for writing, and provided graphic descriptions of Fred's adventures and personality. Unfortunately, at times he gets the chronology of Fred's early life wrong. More importantly, however, he is not always accurate in his comments about his friend's life, including being guilty of exaggeration, perhaps in order to tell what he regarded as a better story about his famous friend.

White's first published story about Fred, "Frederick Funston's Alaskan Trip," appeared in *Harper's Weekly* on May 25, 1895. This laudatory account contained White's assessment that has been frequently quoted: "Nothing was said of his going, and no bugles were sounded upon his return. Yet for continual hardship, unceasing danger, and uninterrupted adventure, probably this trip has not been excelled by any other on the American continent in this century."[15] Four years later Fred Funston was a household name, and Billy White was busy in that spring of 1899 providing his reminiscences and analysis of his now nationally famous friend. At the end of April of that year, the *New York Sun* detailed Funston's life, including quoting White, and this article was reprinted the following day by *The New York Times* under the headline, "Daring Little Col. Funston."[16]

The next month, *The St. Louis Republic* published White's article, "The Hero Of The Philippines." The deck, the three lines immediately below the headline, promised not simply an accurate account but "the First Really Accurate and Striking Story of the One Really Great Man Developed by the Land Battles of Manilla."[17] In reality, there are factual errors, two of which are particularly surprising: one, that Fred entered the State University of Kansas in 1885 instead of 1886, as was the case, and, two, that his intermittent college career spanned five years instead of the four that it actually did. Billy surely would have known the difference in view of their close friendship which began in 1886 in their first year as students together at the State University. Perhaps White thought the exaggerated number of years was more impressive to the reader than the correct number.

On the day before the publication of White's article in the Sunday Magazine Section of *The St. Louis Republic*, a second article by him about his close friend had appeared in *Harper's Weekly*. Billy was later to discover that Fred was angered by part of what White had written in this story. Titled simply "Gen. Frederick Funston," in his introductory paragraph, White wrote what, at least to the reader today, seems to be some rather silly statements explaining that the "key to the character of Frederick Funston" is that "he has never passed a period when he thought the second time about the dirt on his clothes."[18]

In the faraway Philippine Islands, Fred, by then a Brigadier General of Volunteers, at some point read White's article. His friend's words did not sit well with Fred, who wrote a strongly worded objection to Billy's story and to the public reminiscing that Billy had been doing about some of Fred's adventures during his days as a student at the State University of Kansas and while working on the Santa Fe Railway. By letter dated July 1, 1899, at San Fernando, Luzon, in the Philippine Islands, Fred wrote to his old friend, signing his letter with one of his college nicknames:

> My dear Billy
>
> I got your cable about magazine article but did not reply right away because I wanted to hear particulars by mail. It is not a good idea for me to just now break into the magazines.
>
> I want for the sake of public opinion to be mighty careful what I do. After I am mustered out which will probably be before long it will be different. For God's sake Billy take a different tack in the things you are writing about me or <u>dont</u> [sic: usage throughout] <u>write anything</u>. You will simply do me up. That Harper's thing with

its dirty stuff paragraph and a lot of uncouth language you put into my mouth simply does <u>me</u> up with the kind of people whose opinion I value. And then raking up the old rows of my college and train collector days was bad, awfully bad. I want those things <u>forgotten</u>, and <u>forgotten</u> hard. I dont care a damn for the admiration of the mob that likes those things. For the Lord's sake don't show me up as a boor who can't use English properly and who eats with a knife just to get good stuff.

I know your heart is in the right place Old Man and you mean all right but for God's sake, <u>dont dont</u> write "yellow" stuff about me.

I dont want to be Senator I <u>dont</u> want to be governor. I <u>dont</u> want to be banqueted and lionized. I wish the damned papers would let up on [me]. I feel like a fool. My love to Mrs. Sally.

Lovingly,
Gric[19]

Billy White's response to this letter came the following month in letter form. The original of this response likely did not long survive in the Philippines, but White kept carbon copies of his typed letters. Although the blue type of the carbon of White's letter is so faded in places as to be totally illegible, enough of the letter is legible to get the drift of Billy's response to his friend's criticisms. The beginning and concluding paragraphs, with blanks for those words that are illegible, are as follows:

My Dear _____,
You are a good boy, and as you say of <u>me</u>, you mean well; but you are several thousand miles from Deer Creek, and your head isn't working. You are all right when you are alone; there is not a clearer eye on God's footstool than yours when you are away from the maddening throngs, ignoble strife; but down there in the Phillipines [sic] you seem to have absorbed the point of view of the regular army man who is a poor, benighted heathen about most things of this world, even if he is a first class fighting man.

...

I have made these remarks my son, in sorrow and not in anger. I have not intended to wound you, but rather to open your eyes to what seemed to me to be some important facts. I do not want you to get mad about this [two words illegible]. I did not get mad when you suggested that I would lie to sell [a few words illegible] get mad when you [one word illegible] my _____ffles [?] _____ we will call it "horse and horse," and [one word illegible] we will always be to each other "Billie and Timmy" [about ten words illegible.]

Sincerely yours,[20]

Whether Fred, known as Timmy in the college fraternity that he and Billy belonged to, responded to him is unknown, but their close friendship continued.

That White's 1899 *Harper's Weekly* article upset Fred greatly, and even publicly, is shown by a *Collier's Weekly* article published in late 1899 upon the return from the Philippines of Funston and his Twentieth Kansas Volunteers. Written by the famous war correspondent, Frederick Palmer (1873-1958), this complimentary account of Funston and his troops concluded with this assessment:

> Seasoned soldier and adventurer as he is, he takes his lionizing in good part. Only one thing, so far, has ruffled his temper. That was when William Allen White, his Kansas countryman who put the famous question, "What is the matter with Kansas?" charged him with being a sloven in his dress. In his appreciation of Funston, White wrote: "Many a heroic deed in this world has been left undone because it would soil a shirt, but with Funston the deed, not the shirt, has ever been of primary importance. Throughout his life it has been of more importance to him to accomplish his ends than to keep his cuffs clean."
>
> As a regimental commander with whom it has been a point of pride to keep his regiment up to the utmost notch of cleanliness, General Funston objects to this characterization. To use his own word he considers it a "grind."[21]

Fred clearly was not pleased with his close friend.

Throughout all of this, Fred reacted modestly to his newly acquired national fame in that summer of 1899. A special correspondent of the *Globe-Democrat* newspaper reported from the Philippine Islands in June of that year as follows:

> The quantity of mail that a new hero receives is enormous, ranging as it does, through letters of congratulation from personal friends, autograph hunters, would-be political advisers and enterprising manufacturers of cigars who seek permission to trade on his name and fame. Quantities of clippings from the press come, and are eagerly read, but when the praise takes on a hue too roseate in tint, he bursts out impatiently with: "If they would only not say such extravagant things." ...
>
> Warm sincere letters from friends have given him, of course, great pleasure; but it is the letters from children, and of those there have been many, that make him most demonstrative.[22]

In May 1901, after Fred's capture of Aguinaldo, *The Saturday Evening Post* published White's "Funston—the Man from Kansas," and featured on

the front cover a sketch of Fred in the foreground with several of his soldiers in the background. This article complimented Fred profusely, but,
as usual, there are chronological and other errors in it. The colorful language is great, describing General Funston as "a dynamic knight–errant
of great voltage, with a nimble wit and a cavalier's courage." Although
Billy had asserted in *The St. Louis Republic* that Fred's intermittent college career had spanned five years instead of the four that it actually did,
White now lengthened that five years to six in *The Saturday Evening
Post* article.[23] In 1896, William Allen White himself had become nationally prominent as the editor of the *Emporia Gazette* because of his editorial attack on the Populist political movement. Thus, his 1899 and 1901
published accounts about Fred carried a clout with the reader that would
otherwise have been lacking.

This error, and additional ones, appeared many years later in White's
Autobiography. Published posthumously in 1946 and awarded a Pulitzer
Prize the following year, this work is frequently cited as authoritative as
to details of Frederick Funston's life, particularly as to his college years.
This is hardly surprising in view of the intimate White-Funston friendship, but all who rely on it as non-fiction would do well to heed White's
warning at the start of the book: "This Autobiography...is necessarily fiction. The fact that names, dates, and places seem to correspond with such
things that may have occurred in real life does not guarantee the truth of
these stories.... I wish to warn the reader not to confuse this story with
reality."[24]

White's characterization of Fred outraged the latter's sister, Ella
(Funston) Eckdall, who drafted and typed a stinging six-page rebuttal,
which began as follows: "[T]he author has taken the unlicensed liberty of
defaming the good name and character of one of Kansas's most respected
and most honored sons.—Gen. Frederick Funston. In this Autobiography
the author resorts to the most extravagant exaggeration and distortion
of facts regarding the life of Gen. Funston, both in college and in later
years."[25] Whether this rebuttal was ever published is unknown to me,
but in view of the appearance of the rebuttal as if it is in a draft form, it
is doubtful that such publication occurred. Since the most salient points
of White's description of Fred pertained to his college years and shortly
thereafter, analysis of White's "facts" and of Ella's rebuttal will be de-
ferred to the later chapters on Fred's collegiate years.

In the meantime, the reader should know that William Allen White
and his wife, Sallie, and Ella Eckdall and her prominent physician husband, Frank A. Eckdall, all lived for many years in the Kansas town
of Emporia, population 14,067 in 1930.[26] According to Ella's son, Frank
Funston Eckdall (1907-2000), the Whites and Eckdalls did not have
much association, each having "their own lives," but they were "a little

more than acquaintances," since White made "a big deal" out of being a close friend of Funston. This was White's "privilege" and this "probably helped General Funston."[27] I concur and believe that White and Funston were two intimate friends who both subsequently became famous, and hence their friendship redounded to their mutual benefit.

Frederick Funston himself is the last significant contemporary source about his own life. Unfortunately, because of his modesty and self-deprecating humor, apparently straight forward remarks by him are sometimes not true. For example, a fellow member of the Death Valley Expedition of 1891 later reported that Funston was concerned about a sudden rainfall which filled a valley but only to the depth of about six inches. Fred was quoted as saying to his companion, "Coville, doesn't that water worry you? It worries me like sin!"[28] As a joke, this remark rings true, but only as a joke. As a child on the family farm, Fred swam in the best swimming holes in nearby Deer Creek; as a soldier in 1899 he swam the Bag Bag River in the Philippine Islands. The latter feat was memorialized in a special cheer for him upon the hero's return to Topeka, Kansas:

> Who can swim?
> Who can swim?
> Funston, Funston,
> Biff, bing, bim![29]

Another example of Fred's frequent minimization of his talent, knowledge and skills was his claim prior to the Death Valley Expedition that his knowledge of botany "scarcely enabled him to distinguish a pansy from a sunflower."[30] In reality, as a child Fred read books about botany, and as a student at the State University of Kansas he not only studied botany as an academic course, but was sent on field trips by his professor, Francis Snow, to collect botanical specimens.[31]

An 1899 newspaper article, "The Making of Brigadier Funston," succinctly and accurately characterized this self-deprecating part of Fred's personality: "One trait of General Funston is to tell stories on himself that tend to belittle his real qualities; whereas if one seeks to learn of his heroic exploits he might as well interview a tombstone as to question Funston."[32] Thus, Frederick Funston as a candid source about his own strengths and weaknesses is of little assistance, but his autobiographical writings do help to disclose the quiddity of his personality. Hence, the story of the formative first thirty-two years (1865-1897) of his life is primarily told through letters and articles written by Fred himself.

Fred's letters are invaluable, since they are not filtered by hindsight. His letters are also invaluable, since even the best of memories can fade over time, and facts and feelings can be misremembered or even forgotten. His several published articles about his adventures, all written within no more than four years of their respective occurrences, have the concreteness of the recently lived account, though they are inevitably subject to the influence of hindsight. Additionally, Fred's letters and articles provide an intimacy with him not otherwise available, particularly with regard to his feelings on personal subjects. Fred was a skilled writer, utilizing vivid descriptions and crisp prose, spiced with self-deprecating humor. There is no substitute for quoting extensively his letters and articles no matter how well they be paraphrased.

Fred's letters and articles from and about Death Valley, Alaska and the British Northwest Territory, and the writings of other members of the 1891 Death Valley Expedition, all quoted in the next volume, are a rich contribution to the literature of the American West. Fred's letters as a soldier from Cuba, quoted in volume three, shine a fascinating light on details of the fight by the Cubans to liberate their island from centuries of oppression by Spain. These letters also show his evolution from the impassioned idealist, determined to help boot Spain from that war-torn island, to the seasoned, battle-scarred, war-weary veteran.

The repository for most of Fred Funston's letters and copies of some of his articles, and the essential source of primary and secondary information about Fred, is the Frederick Funston Papers located at the Kansas State Historical Society in Topeka. This collection was made primarily by Eda Funston, Fred's widow, and David Potter, whom she hired to write the biography of Fred's life. There are actually two collections under this title, one consisting of original documents which have to be examined in person, and the other of microfilmed documents. The two collections overlap some, but since they are not identical, researchers must review both or otherwise much valuable information will be missed. To distinguish between the two collections in the notes, the original materials are cited as FFP and the ones on microfilm as FFP Micro. Another important source, though subject to the influence of hindsight, is Fred's *Memories of Two Wars: Cuban and Philippine Experiences*, published in 1911.

In addition to correcting the chronological record of Fred's early life, his personality and character are aspects of his story that cry out for an accurate characterization. Through the years much has been made of the obvious fact that Fred's father with his six feet, two inch, 200-plus pound frame, towered over his adult son's slim five feet, four inch, 120 pound body. Since Fred's father was a skilled talker and a dominant personality with a "foghorn" voice, various authors have concluded he also towered psychologically over his son to the latter's disadvantage. Thomas Crouch, who did admirable ground-breaking biographical work on Funston, in 1974 described Fred as he grew up as "more taciturn, less outgoing" than his father and preferring the written word to the spoken word.[33] David Haward Bain in *Sitting in Darkness* in 1984 stated that Fred "had been a taciturn child in the face of a father who loved to talk, lecture, debate." Fred was to find his voice only when he attended college, according to Bain.[34]

Mark Carnes in his 1998 article "Little Colonel Funston" even asserted that Fred had a "stark lust for martial glory."[35] This arose from a fear that he did not measure up, in part because of his small physical stature and, in part, because his father, with his physical size and strong personality, "had set so daunting a standard" for Fred.[36] In other words, Fred suffered from a Napoleonic complex. Carnes concluded that Fred's so-called martial-glory lust "disconcerted those who chose to look closely," and then immediately quoted none other than—Mark Twain![37] And the quotation? Of course, it's the oh-so-quotable excuse: "because his conscience leaked out through one of his pores when he was little..." The facts that Twain was a leading anti-imperialist, a virulent Funston critic, and anything but an objective observer of Funston are omitted.

Although various authors have jumped to the above conclusions, their collective leap falls woefully short of the truth. The description of the overawed young boy and his lifetime struggle to escape from his father's shadow provides a psychologically simple explanation of Fred's personality, but it is wrong. Although Fred's personality and character will be discussed in more detail later in this book, suffice it to say now that, according to the historical record, Fred was the only one of his father's six children who was not in awe of him; Fred's droll observations as a youth precipitated roaring laughter from the senior Funston; and in the rural school he attended, Fred bubbled over with fun and was full of various practical jokes.[38] In high school "he was always gay, full of pranks, fond of practical jokes with a rare gift for narrating his own experiences, particularly when a humorous turn could be given to them."[39] "It was this rare combination of a sense of humor, along with his innate modesty, that was one of his greatest charms."[40]

After reading in the subsequent pages of this trilogy about Fred's early life of adventure, you may be interested to read about the details of the balance of his life—the last nineteen years before his pre-mature death at age fifty-one. Hence, a word of warning is in order: Beware the poisonous tree and its fruit. The poisonous tree is the 1982 book *"Benevolent Assimilation": The American Conquest of the Philippines, 1899-1903* by Stuart Creighton Miller (1927-2010). Although this may appear, at first blush, to be a history of the Philippine War, it is not. Instead, it is a study of the climate of opinion in the United States about the war. This study contains various unproved allegations of misconduct by Fred Funston during the war, and, using this work, these allegations have been repeated as fact by various authors since then. These subsequent secondary sources are the fruit of Miller's poisonous tree. When challenged by a Funston scholar in 2003 about a particular allegation of misconduct by Fred Funston contained in *"Benevolent Assimilation,"* Miller responded that he had accepted "at face value" newspaper reports and editorials and did not check the "veracity" of "stories of less than civilized behavior on both sides." Miller's interest, he wrote, was in the climate of opinion in the United States "based on both fact and fiction..." If he had been writing a military history or Funston's biography, Miller "would have investigated in great detail...."[41]

Unfortunately for Fred Funston, the disastrous consequence of Miller's non-verification approach has been that unproved allegations against him made by the anti-war critics more than a century ago are being repeated many years later as fact. Fred's reputation has suffered accordingly. When there is an allegation of misconduct against Fred, I encourage you always to check a book's notes. If *"Benevolent Assimilation"* is the sole source cited, you can safely conclude that the allegation has not been verified from other sources, and thus you can treat it as unproved.

Chapter Two Notes—*Myth and Reality*

1. Herbert E. Smith, "Fighting Fred," *Foreign Service*, January 1936 (Eckdall Scrapbook II, 162). This story may have been copied from the one in "That Red-Headed Soldier From [balance of headline missing]," *The Sunday Times Herald*, Chicago, April 16, 1899 (FFP).

2. David Haward Bain, *Sitting in Darkness: Americans in the Philippines* (Boston: Houghton Mifflin Company, 1984), 16-17.

3. "Commencement," *The Iola Register*, May 21, 1886. Frederick Funston is listed as a graduate. Iola High School records also confirm his graduation in 1886.

4. See Chapters Seven, Eight, and Nine.

5. Ella (Funston) Eckdall to Eda B. Funston, October 25, 1925 (FFP).

6. Ella (Funston) Eckdall to Eda B. Funston, October 25, 1925, for an example of her letters.

7. Ella (Funston) Eckdall to Eda B. Funston, October 25, 1925.

8. Eda Funston arranged with a Captain David Potter to write Fred's biography. The completed manuscript is at the Princeton University Library in its Department of Rare Books and Special Collections. According to Funston's son, Frederick Jr., no publisher was interested in the book (Alan Stewart to Ella (Funston) Eckdall, May 1, 1954) (FFP Micro).

9. Eda B. Funston, "Notes on Frederick Funston" (FFP Micro).

10. Chas. F. Scott to Mrs. Frederick Funston, December 29, 1924 (FFP).

11. Chas. F. Scott, "Remarkable Career of a Kansas Boy," *Mail and Breeze* (about March 20, 1898) (FFP).

12. Charles F. Scott, eulogy, "Report of Select Committee," *Journal of the House*, Hall of the House of Representatives, Topeka, Kansas, February 26, 1917 (FFP).

13. Charles S. Gleed, eulogy, "Report of Select Committee," *Journal of the House*, Hall of the House of Representatives, Topeka, Kansas, February 26, 1917 (FFP). Charles S. Gleed, "Romance And Reality In A Single Life. Gen. Frederick Funston," *The Cosmopolitan Illustrated Monthly Magazine*, July 1899.

14. Ella (Funston) Eckdall to Eda B. Funston, October 25, 1925 (FFP).

15. William Allen White, "Frederick Funston's Alaskan Trip," *Harper's Weekly*, May 25, 1895. For examples of the use of this quotation, see biographical sketch of Funston (title not given) in *Chicago Tribune*, Sunday, May 2, 1914 (FFP), and see Bain, note 2, who cited this quotation at 36-37.

16. "Daring Little Col. Funston," *The New York Times*, April 30, 1899.

17. William Allen White, "The Hero Of The Philippines," *The St. Louis Republic Magazine Section*, May 21, 1899. Photocopy at Allen County Historical Society, Inc. This article, *without attribution to White* and with only nominal changes, was reprinted at least twice. One reprint was in an unidentified newspaper under the headline "Kansas's Lively Hero" (FFP). Louis Stanley Young and Henry Davenport Northrop reprinted it in their *Life and Heroic Deeds of Admiral Dewey* (Philadelphia: Globe Publishing Co., 1899), 341-347.

18. William Allen White, "Gen. Frederick Funston," *Harper's Weekly*, May 20, 1899. See Appendix B for the complete first two paragraphs of this article.

19. The history behind this letter subsequent to its receipt by White is of interest. According to Frank Funston Eckdall (1907-2000), nephew of Fred Funston, in conver-

sation with this author about 1993 and repeated by him in later years, following White's death in 1944, his widow called Eckdall's mother, the General's sister, Ella (Funston) Eckdall, and fellow resident of Emporia, Kansas, and asked if she would like to have this letter written by her brother. Ella accepted. This letter appears in FFP Micro.

20. William Allen White, *Letter Book*, B1, pt.1, June 27, 1899 – Dec. 22, 1899 (on spine it reads Vol. 1, Pt. 1 – Series B), 82 (*Letter Books*, container B1, pt. 1, William Allen White Papers, Manuscript Division, Library of Congress, Washington, D.C.). See Appendix B for the complete letter.

21. [Frederick Palmer,] "The Return of Funston and the Kansas Volunteers," *Collier's Weekly*, November 4, 1899. Although Palmer is not credited as the author, his biographer, Nathan Haverstock, in his *Fifty Years at the Front: The Life of War Correspondent Frederick Palmer* (Washington: Brassey's, 1996), 282, credited Palmer with this article.

    Fred Funston was not the only person displeased with White's article. A friend, perhaps from college days, wrote Fred on June (July?) 11, 1899, about White's allegation that the cause of Fred's success was "indifference to dress, untidiness and a predilection for dirt. I read only the first ten or fifteen lines of the article and it made me so angry that I threw the paper down in disgust and labeled William Allen White—well your vocabulary is larger than mine." Unknown (signature illegible) to General Frederick Funston (FFP Micro).

22. "How They Left Him," *The Iola Daily Register*, Iola, Kansas, August 18, 1899. This article was noted as "Special correspondence in the Globe-Democrat" and was datelined San Fernando, Luzon, P.I., June 26 (Eckdall Scrapbook II, 101).

23. William Allen White, "Funston—the Man from Kansas," *The Saturday Evening Post*, May 18, 1901.

24. William Allen White, *The Autobiography of William Allen White* (New York: The Macmillan Company, 1946), np.

25. Original draft in possession of the late Frank Funston Eckdall (photocopy in the possession of this author).

26. *Kansas Facts* (Topeka, Kansas: Charles P. Beebe Pub Co., 1931), Vol III, 85.

27. Telephone conversation of Frank Funston Eckdall and author, February 21, 1999.

28. William E. Johnson, "The Making of Brigadier Funston," *The New Voice*, May 13, 1899 (FFP). Johnson quoted T.S. Palmer of the Death Valley Expedition for Funston's "swimming" remark.

29. "In Kansas City Forty Years Ago." [Nov. 7, 1899], presumably *Kansas City Star* (Eckdall Scrapbook II, 71).

    After a friend of Funston sent him a newspaper clipping that alleged that he could not swim, Fred responded to his friend: "The officer of whom you spoke is undoubtedly one of those small souled creatures who, never having the courage to do anything themselves, take a sort of puppish delight in deprecating the laurels won by other men. His statement that he heard me say that I never swam a river in the Philippines, and that in fact I couldn't swim, is a lie out of the whole cloth" ("More from Funston," unknown newspaper, Minneapolis, Minn., December 30 [1899]) (*Wilder Stevens Metcalf and Frederick Funston With The Twentieth Kansas In The Philippines During The Spanish-American War*) (scrapbook of newspaper clippings, Spencer Research Library, University of Kansas).

30. Johnson, "The Making of Brigadier Funston."

31. See Chapter Thirteen.

3 2. Johnson, "The Making of Brigadier Funston."

33. Thomas W. Crouch, "Frederick Funston of Kansas: His Formative Years, 1865-1891," *The Kansas Historical Quarterly*, Summer 1974, 184.

34. Bain, *Sitting in Darkness*, 19.

35. Mark C. Carnes, "Little Colonel Funston," *American Heritage*, September 1998, 60.

36. Carnes, "Little Colonel Funston," 56.

37. Carnes, "Little Colonel Funston," 60.

38. See Chapter Five.

39. Chas. F. Scott to Mrs. Frederick Funston, December 29, 1924 (FFP).

40. Charles F. Scott, eulogy, "Report of Select Committee," *Journal of the House*, Hall of the House of Representatives, Topeka, Kansas, February 26, 1917 (FFP).

41. Stuart Creighton Miller to Jarrett Robinson, January 5, 2004 (e-mail). Courtesy of Jarrett Robinson.

CHAPTER THREE

Heroic Ancestry

If your descent is from heroic sires, Show in your life a remnant of their fires.

—Nicholas Boileau-Despreaux (1636-1711)

In the spring of 1899, Frederick Funston was nationally famous. He had swum the Bag Bag River in the Philippines in the war with the natives of those islands. Under enemy fire he had led his troops in the raft crossing of the Rio Grande de la Pampanga River, and they had then driven the Filipino soldiers from their trenches. For this feat, Fred Funston and two of his soldiers received the coveted Medal of Honor, and Fred was promoted from Colonel to Brigadier General in the volunteer army.

This newfound fame brought metropolitan reporters to the Allen County, Kansas, farm home of Fred's parents, Edward Hogue Funston and Ann Eliza Funston. These reporters were eager to learn more about the new hero. One reporter was from *The Chicago Sunday Tribune*. In a lengthy account of his visit with the famous "dare-devil" general's parents titled "Fred Funston's Restless Life of Adventure," the reporter queried Ann and Edward about the source of Fred's fighting ability:

"It would seem as if General Funston was a fighter by hereditary right?" it was suggested.

"O, yes," said his father. "He gets his fighting blood from his mother."

"You were a soldier and come of the fighting race?"

"Yes, but his mother is Irish, too, with a fighting heritage from Daniel Boone's family. No, he gets his fighting blood from his mother's side."[1]

There truly was a lot of fighting blood on the distaff side of Fred's pedigree. One great-grandfather, Pomroy Mitchell, was a soldier of the Revolutionary War, as was another great-grandfather, Philip Sweigert (also spelled Swigert). Pomroy Mitchell had two sons, John and Archibald, who fought in the War of 1812, and two other sons, Charles and Anderson, who fought in the Mexican War. Anderson gave his life in the battle of Mexico City.[2]

30

Although not a soldier herself, one of the more interesting of Fred Funston's maternal ancestors is his great-grandmother, Margaret Van Meter (or Metre), who, as a widow, married, as her second husband, Pomroy Mitchell. Born on the Yadkin River in North Carolina in 1769, she was purportedly a cousin of the famous frontiersman and explorer, Daniel Boone.[3] Hence, the Boone connection. According to one of her grandsons who knew her, she was a "remarkable woman" of "bright mind, and fine memory."[4] As a child, she lived within the sound of the Revolutionary War Battle of Kings Mountain in which her father and at least one brother participated.[5] Margaret's family migrated at one point to Boonesborough in Kentucky and was there when it was attacked by Indians in 1778.[6]

Margaret's first husband was a man named Neal, who soon died. A widow with one child when she married Pomroy Mitchell, she many years later, after his death, married one McClure.[7] In 1807, Margaret and Pomroy Mitchell emigrated from Culpepper County, Virginia, where their children had all been born, to the new state of Ohio.[8] They settled on a farm three miles east of the town of New Carlisle, Clark County, which is located in western Ohio. There they raised a family of six sons and one daughter.[9] New Carlisle was to become the birthplace of their great-grandson, Fred Funston, some fifty-eight years later. It was Margaret's "delight, in her old age" before her death in 1848 to gather her grandchildren around her and tell of the "dangers trials and hardships" of early pioneer days.[10] Her daughter-in-law, Elizabeth (Sweigert) Mitchell, also listened to these stories, and she passed them to her grandson, Fred Funston, during his boyhood.[11]

Margaret holds two particular distinctions. First, not only did she purport to be a cousin of Daniel Boone, she also, according to family history, was a cousin of Meriwether Lewis of the Lewis and Clark expedition fame. As to her putative relationship to such eminent explorers, its validity is unknown to this author. Nevertheless, the Funston family believed in this consanguineal relationship at a time when it undoubtedly impressed, and, perhaps, inspired young Fred Funston.[12]

The other particular distinction that Margaret holds, though she did not live to see it happen, is that she had thirty-one grandsons who fought for the Union during the Civil War.[13] Another source claims that there were only thirty grandsons, but even those thirty had an aggregate military service of sixty years.[14] The military career of six grandsons is of particular interest and relevance. Four grandsons, who were brothers, served in the 16th Ohio Battery, to-wit: Captain James A. Mitchell, Lieutenant Newton Mitchell, and Pomroy and Bartly Mitchell, non-commissioned officers. Also serving in that battery were their cousins, bugler James Mitchell and Asa Mitchell. Asa Mitchell's sister, Ann Eliza Mitchell, shortly after the start of the Civil War married Edward Hogue Funston, and they were to become the parents of Fred Funston. To round out the family connection, Edward Funston himself served as a Lieutenant in the same battery. Thus, six Mitchells and their near relative by marriage, Edward Funston, served in combat together.[15]

The 16th Ohio Battery originated with James A. Mitchell, who raised the company, which was enrolled into service on August 20, 1861, and then mustered in the following September 5. Captain Mitchell was 37 years old and a lawyer when the call for troops came. The company saw service in Arkansas, and though it went out with 166 men, it had lost over eighty by sickness and death by early 1863. After being filled up by detailed men, the company, in the spring of 1863, joined the army opposite Vicksburg, Mississippi, which was then besieged by Union forces. Now a part of the 1st Brigade, 12th Division, 13th Army Corps, Army of West Tennessee, the 16th Ohio Battery crossed the Mississippi River on the day and night of April 30.

The 16th Ohio quickly participated in several battles, including that of Champion's Hill. The 16th Battery was placed in the front line of battle and was charged upon by the enemy in overwhelming numbers. "Our supports were crushed and beaten back, but the Captain [James A. Mitchell], the personification of calm, cool bravery, sitting on his horse, held his position until he fell, pierced through the left breast by a ball. Our line was forced back. He was mortally wounded and fell into the hands of the enemy. The ground was retaken and fought over five times, until after about six hours of desperate battling the enemy was crushed and driven in disastrous defeat from the field." His men found Captain Mitchell near where he had fallen; he died the next morning, May 17, and was buried temporarily on the battlefield.[16] Forty-five out of every one hundred men of the division of which the 16th Ohio was a part were killed or wounded in the Champion's Hill battle, but this defeat of the enemy, with its breaching of the outer defenses, led to the ultimate capture of Vicksburg on July 4.[17] There definitely was heroic ancestry on Fred Funston's maternal side.

Fred's paternal ancestry was considerably less adventuresome and heroic from a military standpoint, with the exception of Fred's father, Edward Hoge (sometimes spelled by him as Hogue) Funston.[18] Born on September 16, 1836, on a farm in Clark County, Ohio, Edward was the grandson of Paul Funston, a native of the County of Donegal, Ireland, who migrated with his wife, Ann (Johnson) Funston, to the United States. Family tradition claimed that Paul Funston's father was a British Army officer, possibly a Scotsman, who had gone with the army to the north of Ireland.

This early Funston family was Protestant, and, again according to family tradition, suffered severely at the hands of the Irish Catholics. On one occasion the family was compelled in the "dead of night" to flee to save their lives by means of crossing a stream in a small boat. Paul and Ann Funston migrated to the United States in 1806, bringing with them their children, including a son Frederick, who had been born six years earlier in 1800. They soon settled on a farm near Paris, Kentucky, and, about five years later, moved to a farm near Donnelsville, Ohio.[19] Paul Funston lived to an advanced age, not dying until October 15, 1839, at the age of ninety.[20]

According to his grandson, Edward Funston, Paul "was tall and straight and possessed of a full share of self respect or pride. He was well educated for one of his day…he was a constant and careful reader and I have heard said that he could repeat whole passages of scripture without prompting." Paul must have been a man of vitality even in his old age. "[I]n his old days he would sometimes ride his old horse Bally ten miles to tell some one that he had done a 'filthy trade' though it was perhaps none of his business." His death was ultimately the result of an infection that had originated in one of his big toes. His tombstone cites Job XIX, Chapter 26 ("And though after my skin worms destroy this body, yet in my flesh shall I see God."). Paul and Ann's son, Frederick, and his wife, Julia (Stafford) Funston, cared in their home for his parents in their last years. Ann died at age sixty-five on April 30, 1825, after being an invalid in a chair for seventeen years. Despite her long confinement, this "frail little being" retained "her courageous spirit and her Christian faith to the end." In appreciation for the care rendered to himself and his wife, Paul, in his will, devised the family farm to their son, Frederick.[21]

Alas, Frederick Funston was to enjoy ownership for only a year before dying accidentally. On October 29, 1840, Frederick walked to a nearby farm where a cider press was located. While two of his sons drove a wagon load of apples that were on hand, Frederick cut across the fields to the press. At the cider press, one of its beams slipped, and Frederick, who was standing directly below, was struck on "the crown of the head," the blow killing him instantly. Edward Funston later wrote: "Young as I was I fully realized what happened. I can distinctly see in my memory to this day the house and yard filled with sympathizing neighbors." After Frederick's funeral, his seven children were seated around the coffin in an old-fashioned wagon, on which they rode to the graveyard. Julia was apparently so distraught that she was unable to attend her husband's service.

Fatherless at age four, Edward Funston many years later described his father Frederick as strong and vigorous, weighing perhaps 230 pounds, and standing perhaps six feet, one inch tall. He was "kind hearted and generous even to a fault." Frederick was a Whig and a strong supporter of General William Henry Harrison in the presidential election of 1840, which occurred just a few days after Frederick's death. Interestingly, Frederick "took special interest in military affairs and was a lieutenant in a company of militia. It is said that he was a very fine conversationalist and a most welcome guest at dinner parties...no man appeared to better advantage on horseback than he."[22] The future famous General Frederick Funston was named for this militarily inclined grandfather.

Edward Funston, at maturity six two in height and weighing over 200 pounds, rivaled his father in stature. Accompanying this large physical presence was an equally impressive loud voice, which resulted in his being called during his political career "Foghorn" Funston. Edward's voice was so impressive that in 1991, eighty years after his death, an elderly, former neighbor remembered Edward thusly: "He lived up to his name—Foghorn Funston. He had the deepest voice. You knew he was there." This former neighbor also described Edward as "pretty self-important."[23] His size and voice were such that, even at age sixty-two, he was described by one newspaper reporter as "gigantic in stature" and with a "stentorian voice that is famous in Kansas politics."[24]

Edward was a self-made man. "He was reared on a farm as a farmer and shared with his brothers and sisters hardships and privations that none but the poor know of." Completing his common school education at the age of thirteen, he hired himself to a neighboring Clark County, Ohio, farmer for six dollars per month, and, being large for his age, Edward was "compelled to do a man's work." Edward returned to his home at the end of the season and attended school during the winter. He did this for three years until he qualified to enter the Linden Hill Academy at New Carlisle. He boarded at a farmer's house and paid his way by chopping cord-wood in the mornings, evenings, and on Saturdays.[25] "Ed," as he was known to his classmates at Linden Hill and later in life, was described by a former classmate as "a large over-grown boy" at age sixteen, and "energetic and enthusiastic in his studies, but at all times ready for a fight or frolic as the occasion required."[26]

Completing his studies, Ed Funston taught at a country school in Hopewell, Indiana, before the Civil War.[27] With his earnings he was able to enter Marietta College in Marietta, Ohio, where he remained two years.[28] Like thousands of other young men, the call to arms at the outbreak of the Civil War in April of 1861 interrupted Ed's schooling. He left Marietta College, never to return as a student. Twenty-eight years later, however, his alma mater awarded him an honorary Master of Arts degree. This degree was belatedly conferred upon Funston by the Board of Trustees of the institution. By then, Ed had long been a resident of Allen County, Kansas, living on the farm near Iola, and the award of this degree was applauded by Charlie Scott, editor of the local *Iola Register*, who noted that Ed "has retained through all of his later years the taste for study and for reading the best books, imbibed within its walls, and he now has one of the most complete private libraries to be found in this part of the State—and he knows every book in it." Charlie Scott commended this action as "a merited reward upon one who has been all his life a student and who is now a scholar of unusual attainments."[29]

Ed had become a U.S. congressman by then, and even such a gracious act as the belated bestowing in 1889 of the MA degree on the Union Army veteran was more than congressman Funston's then-political enemies could endure. *The Iola Register* noted the "distressing effect" that this act had upon the "Aristoi of Lawrence," where the State University of Kansas is located. The Aristoi had based its opposition to Funston on the assumption that "he was uncultured and illiterate and was therefore not a representative of gentlemen who like themselves breakfasted on Homer and dined on Plato and supped on Virgil." Now, according to *The Iola Register*, for these individuals to find that "this same despised Funston, this illiterate farmer" was their peer "breaks their hearts."[30]

Although Ed's course of studies was interrupted and terminated by his enlistment in the service of the Union Army, his courtship of the beautiful Ann Eliza Mitchell was not only not terminated, it was probably accelerated to fruition. On September 4, 1861, the day before he was mustered into service, Lieutenant Edward Funston, nearly twenty-five years of age, wed the 18-year-old Miss Mitchell, popularly known as Lida Mitchell. By the name of Lida she will be referred to in this book. The wedding took place at the Mitchell House in New Carlisle, the two-story hotel owned by her late father, who had died in 1859, and apparently still operated by Lida's mother. "Our best wishes attend the Lieutenant and his bride," noted *The Springfield* (Ohio) *Republic* two days later.[31]

Lida had been born on March 28, 1843, on a farm near Charleston, Miami County, Ohio, which adjoins Clark County. A few years later her family moved to New Carlisle.[32] "Mrs. Funston was educated in the common schools and at Linden Hill Academy... She received a good musical education, and was popular and pretty. She is small in size, and weighs not over 90 lbs..."[33] According to her daughter, Ella, Lida, in height, was five feet, two inches.[34] But, according to her granddaughter and namesake, Lida (Eckdall) Lees, Lida was only four feet, eleven inches and wore a size-one shoe.[35] Although Lida bore eight children, she retained "to the end of her life a girlish slenderness."[36] Lida Funston was quite musical, singing and playing the guitar and the piano.[37]

The physical and personality contrasts between Frederick Funston's parents were marked throughout their lives. *The Chicago Sunday Tribune* reporter who had queried Ed and Lida in 1899 about their famous son's fighting ability described them:

One would never think it to look at the gentle, sweet-faced, fragile little woman [age fifty-six], the mother of the dare-devil soldier of Malolos, that she had bequeathed to him the spirit that prompted him to deeds of fame. She is so small that one is impelled to notice the slightness of her figure when she stands alone. When she stands beside her husband [age sixty-two] the figures of the two form a striking contrast. He is six feet and two inches in height, and weighs 225 pounds. The contrast is in more respects striking. She is retiring and silent. He is brusque and loud-spoken. She is yielding and timid; he is aggressive and a fighter.[38]

The reporter noted the unhappiness of the Funston family with how they had been portrayed by Eastern newspapers as "rude and uncouth, and the elders [Lida and Ed] as decrepit and unsophisticated."[39] The *Tribune* reporter found the situation to be the opposite:

Happily, it is true that they are industrious and have the honest simplicity of the health-giving surroundings of the farm. Mr. Funston works on the farm and his dress at work is suitable to the labor. His hands are hard and his face is tanned with the sun, but he is none the less a student and a lover of books. When he comes in out of the field to receive a visitor in his home he is beaming with the air of hospitality. One begins to like his homespun clothes out of a liking for the easy manner in which he convinces one he is welcome.

When one has sat with him in his little study and listened to him talking for an hour he wishes he had homespun clothes also, with their unstarched shirt open at the collar instead of the silly primpins dictated by artificial whims. His hair is gray, but he is rugged and strong, and his ponderous frame is active. Mrs. Funston is a neat little person in a well-fitting gown and of correct speech. She certainly does not look old enough to be the mother of a Brigadier General...[40]

From this attractive couple Fred Funston was to inherit certain physical and personality traits, and they became a part of his own unique makeup.

Entering the Union Army as a 2nd Lieutenant, Ed had attained the rank of 1st Lieutenant by the time his service ended nearly four years later in August of 1865.[41] As a member of the 16th Ohio Battery during the siege of Vicksburg in 1863, Ed was ordered to silence a battery in front of the breastworks since it was damaging the Union forces. He replied that it had been in vain for his guns to reach the Confederate battery, since he could not lower his guns sufficiently to hit the battery. In response, his superior officer told him either to silence the offending battery or someone else would be sent with another battery to do so. Unwilling to give up, Ed had one of his cannons dragged over the Union breastworks out where the enemy's fire could reach it, and then "calmly proceeded to stand the rebel guns on end and silence them."[42] More than thirty years later Ed's son, Fred, followed suit in Cuba during the revolution against Spanish rule, and placed his cannon within reach of the enemy's fire. A Spanish officer later recalled: "Why, the little devil hauled his guns up so close that they scorched our eyebrows."[43]

In the subsequent Red River campaign in Louisiana that fall of 1863, word was sent to Ed from the front lines that the battery was nearly out of ammunition and would soon have to retire as a result. "Funston selected his men, loaded wagons with ammunition, and headed the dashing relief expedition to the front, riding through a shower of bullets and not stopping until he delivered the goods right on the firing lines."[44] Despite Ed's claim that his son Fred's fighting ability was a maternal inheritance, clearly Ed himself set a good example of the bravery and resourcefulness that Fred Funston was to exhibit throughout his own life. Following Fred's death, his brothers, Pogue and Aldo, recalled that as a child Fred read everything of a military nature that he could get his hands on, and that, if he was not reading, "he was at his father's knee, having him recount the tales of the war through which he had just passed."[45]

Ed had not had a furlough or leave of absence since November 1861, or been home since then, and thus on January 15, 1865, more than three years later, he wrote from camp in Louisiana to his superior requesting a thirty-day furlough in his home state of Ohio.[46] The furlough was granted for January and February, and he returned home to Lida in New Carlisle. Their first child, Frederick Funston, was born nine months later on November 9, 1865. By that time, the Civil War was over, and Ed, following his muster out on August 2, 1865, at Camp Chase, Ohio, had returned to New Carlisle to his pregnant wife.[47]

Chapter Three Notes—*Heroic Ancestry*

1. "Fred Funston's Restless Life of Adventure," *The Chicago Sunday Tribune*, May 7, 1899. This belief that Fred's "military tendencies" were inherited from his maternal ancestors was concurred in by one of his cousins, A.H. Mitchell, in a letter printed in the *Indianapolis Journal* (see quotation of this letter in letter of S. Gordon Smyth to Frederick Funston, July 31, 1909 (FFP)).

2. Smyth letter. Smyth apparently was a genealogist working on a history of the Mitchell and Van Meter families.

3. Pomroy Mitchell to Fred Funston and Burton J. Mitchell, August 20, 1909 (FFP). This Pomroy Mitchell was a grandson of Margaret (Van Meter) Mitchell through her son, Archibald, and Pomroy was a first cousin of Fred Funston's mother.

4. Pomroy Mitchell to Fred Funston and Burton J. Mitchell, August 20, 1909.

5. Pomroy Mitchell to Fred Funston and Burton J. Mitchell, August 20, 1909.

6. Pomroy Mitchell to Fred Funston and Burton J. Mitchell, August 20, 1909.

7. Pomroy Mitchell to Fred Funston and Burton J. Mitchell, August 20, 1909.

8. Pomroy Mitchell to Fred Funston and Burton J. Mitchell, August 20, 1909.

9. Elihu S. Williams, "Gen. Fred Funston," *The Buckeye*, Troy, Ohio, April 4, 1901 (FFP).

10. Pomroy Mitchell to Fred Funston and Burton J. Mitchell, August 20, 1909.

11. "Memorandum" (a typed one-page biographical sketch of Pomroy and Margaret Mitchell) (FFP).

12. Margaret (Van Meter) Mitchell herself told of her relationship to Boone and Lewis (Pomroy Mitchell to Fred Funston and Burton J. Mitchell, August 20, 1909). See also in FFP a handwritten one-page statement, originally composed by John Mitchell, which states that Margaret was a "niece" of Daniel Boone and a "full cousin" of Meriwether Lewis, whose "maternal grandfather was a Sweigert who was also in the Revolutionary War." Since Lewis' mother was of the Meriwether family, this last assertion as to the relationship is obviously incorrect. I have not attempted to prove or disprove Margaret's purported relationship to two such famous men, since its existence is not essential to the story of Fred Funston's life. The key is what Fred Funston was told, and how it may have influenced him to emulate such daring explorers.

13. Pomroy Mitchell to Fred Funston and Burton J. Mitchell, August 20, 1909.

14. A.H. Mitchell letter (see note 1).

15. Pomroy Mitchell to Fred Funston and Burton J. Mitchell, August 20, 1909.

16. Biographical sketch of Capt. James A. Mitchell read at an anniversary reunion of Mitchell Post No. 45, Grand Army of the Republic (post is named for him) (FPP). Mitchell's body, after the end of the war, was reburied near Louisville, Ohio.

17. Biographical sketch of Capt. James A. Mitchell. Unable to attend in 1889 the sixth annual reunion of the surviving members of the 16th Ohio Battery, Ed Funston wrote a letter to his former comrades, which read, in part: "There is no body of men on this green earth that I would rather meet than the old comrades of the 16th battery." He offered this assessment of them: "Coming as they did from the best families of their localities, many of them were well educated and well raised. One would naturally suppose they would be difficult subjects to discipline into the duties of a soldier, but strange to say, my observation was that the better educated and the better raised, the better the soldier" ("The 16th Battery Boys," unknown newspaper and unknown date; Funston Political Scrapbooks).

18. Ella (Funston) Eckdall to Eda B. Funston, October 25, 1925 (FFP).

19. Handwritten, undated document with the last page or pages missing telling of the Funston family history (FFP). Someone, other than the writer of this document, has noted on the document that it was apparently written by one of Edward Funston's sisters. This is incorrect, in my opinion, since (1) the document appears to be written in Edward's handwriting, and (2) it states that the writer was "but little more than 3 years of age when [Paul] died" in 1839, and four years of age when Frederick Funston died in 1840. Edward Funston was born on September 16, 1836, and, according to author Stanley Steele Funston (see next note), and, according to Paul's tombstone, Paul died in October 1839. Thus, Edward Funston was the writer of this document.

20. The various sources do not agree as to the date of Paul's birth. See Stanley Steele Funston's *Paul Calvin Funston and Some of His Descendants, Including Major General Fredrick* [sic] *Funston and His Family* (Cedar Rapids, Iowa, by author, 2002) (copy at Allen County Historical Society, Inc.) for date of birth of 1744, and the document cited at note 19 for date of birth of 1748. The inscription on his cemetery marker states that he "departed this life October 15, 1839, age 90 years. Job XIX, Chap. 26" (see next note), and I have accepted this for Paul's age at death.

21. See the document at note 19 above for all information about Paul and Frederick and Julia Funston, except Paul's, Frederick's, and Ann's dates of death and Ann's invalid condition are from Ella (Funston) Eckdall, "Nearly-forgotten, Neglected Cemetery Forms Burial Place of Early Pioneers of County," *The Sun*, Springfield, Ohio, May 28, 1932 (FFP). Ella Eckdall personally visited the graves of Paul, Ann, and Frederick; copied the data from their tombstones; and wrote a story about her trip of exploration.

22. See document at note 19 for all information, except Frederick's status as a Whig, which is from "James S. Funston," *Portrait And Biographical Album of Washington County, Iowa* (Chicago: Acme Publishing Company, 1887), 459.

23. Interview of 97-year-old Edwin "Ed" Kelly (1894-1996) by the author on December 22, 1991. A widower, Ed was living, alone, on his family farm six miles north and a half-mile west of Iola, Kansas. This farm was near the Funston farm.

24. Ode C. Nichols, "Funston, From Babyhood to Present Day as His Mother Knows Him," *The World*, May 21, 1899 (FFP).

25. *Southern Kansas Horticulturalist*, Vol I–No. XI (March Number) [1896] (published at Iola, Kansas, by E.S. Davis, and edited by L. M. Pancoast). An "Extra Edition" devoted to the life and career of the Hon. E. H. Funston, "a successful farmer and horticulturalist" (biographical sketch on page 1). Photocopy at Allen County Historical Society, Inc.

26. Elihu S. Williams, "Gen. Fred Funston," *The Buckeye*, Troy, Ohio, April 4, 1901 (FFP).

27. Ella Funston Eckdall, *The Funston Homestead* (Emporia, Kansas: Raymond Lees, 1949), 2.

28. *Southern Kansas Horticulturalist*, Vol I–No. XI (March Number) [1896].

29. "Mr. Funston Honored," *The Iola Register*, Iola, Kansas, July 12, 1889.

30. "Editorial Note," *The Iola Register*, Iola, Kansas, July 26, 1889.

31. Ella (Funston) Eckdall to Eda B. Funston, October 25, 1925 (FFP). Included with this letter is a biographical sketch of Ann Eliza (Mitchell) Funston prepared by Ella (Funston) Eckdall, her daughter.

32. Ella (Funston) Eckdall to Eda B. Funston, October 25, 1925.

33. Williams, "Gen. Fred Funston."

34. Eckdall, *The Funston Homestead*, 29.

35. Sandy Funston booklet of materials. Page titled Ann Eliza Mitchell. Copy at Allen County Historical Society, Inc.

36. "Mrs. E.H. Funston is Dead," *The Iola Daily Register*, Iola, Kansas, April 27, 1917.

37. Sandy Funston booklet of materials.

38. "Fred Funston's Restless Life of Adventure," *The Chicago Sunday Tribune*, May 7, 1899 (FFP). Edwin (Ed) Kelly (see note 23) in 1991 described Lida Funston: "But his wife was kind of timid. She didn't never do anything out of the way."

39. "Fred Funston's Restless Life of Adventure," *The Chicago Sunday Tribune*, May 7, 1899.

40. "Fred Funston's Restless Life of Adventure," *The Chicago Sunday Tribune*, May 7, 1899.

41. Stanley Steele Funston, *Paul Calvin Funston and Some of His Descendants*. See note 20.

42. "Elder Funston Some Fighter," *The Iola Daily Register*, May 8, 1914. Interview with local citizen W.H. McClure, who had known Edward Funston in New Carlisle, Ohio, and who had migrated to Allen County, Kansas, at Funston's encouragement.

43. Charles F. Scott, "Frederick Funston," *The Independent*, April 11, 1901.

44. "Elder Funston Some Fighter."

45. "Death of Funston Shocks Community," *The Iola Daily Register*, Iola, Kansas, February 20, 1917.

46. Sandy Funston booklet of materials. Letter dated Jan. 15th 1865 at Greenville Louisiana, to Colonel Geo. B. Drake, A.A. Gen. Dept. of the Gulf (a typed copy of the original letter contained in Funston's Civil War Service file in Washington, D.C.).

47. "Statement of the Military Record of Edward H. Funston" (loose document in Funston Political Scrapbooks). Copy at Allen County Historical Society, Inc.

CHAPTER FOUR

The New Land

Go West, young man!

—Slogan popularized by journalist Horace Greeley
(1811-1873)

Ad Astra per Aspera
("To the stars through difficulties")

—The motto of the state of Kansas, which was referred to by
various contemporary writers describing Fred Funston

Late in 1867, 31-year-old Ed Funston stepped from a stagecoach at the Covert Inn located a short distance south of the village of Carlyle in southeastern Kansas. To his great surprise and pleasure, the inn keeper was an old acquaintance, John Covert, formerly of Hopewell, Indiana. As a schoolteacher in Hopewell before the Civil War, Ed had lived with the Covert family. Like many former soldiers following the close of the Civil War two years before, Ed was seeking a new home in the largely unsettled west. Traveling first to Wyandotte in northeastern Kansas, but being unimpressed with conditions there, he journeyed south to Allen County, to the village of Carlyle.[1]

The first years of Allen County's existence reflect two historical events, one peculiar to the newly formed Territory of Kansas and the other common to much of the settlement of the middle and western parts of the United States. The first event—the bloody struggle between the pro- and anti-slavery forces over whether the new territory was to become a slave or a free state—caused Kansas to be known as "bleeding Kansas." The Kansas-Nebraska Act of 1854, which established the new territory, provided the doctrine of "popular sovereignty," which was the right of resident voters to decide whether slavery would be allowed or prohibited in the territory.[2] Each side encouraged its supporters to settle in the new territory. The settled portion of the territory along the eastern border of Kansas Territory, which adjoined the slave state of Missouri, soon became a battleground with pro-slavery "border ruffians" and "bushwhackers" from Missouri clashing with the anti-slavery "jayhawkers" from Kansas. The very name of Allen County reflects this struggle, since the

41

pro-slavery territorial legislature in 1855 named it in honor of William Allen, a proponent of popular sovereignty.[3] Because of his big, powerful voice, Allen, a former United States senator from Ohio (1837-1849), was popularly known as "Fog-Horn Bill Allen."[4]

The early settlement of Allen County was along the Neosho River, which flows through the western side of the county, and the resulting Valley of the Neosho was separated by broad and uninhabited prairies from the counties on the east and north where the dispute over slavery was the greatest. Although avoiding the bloody struggle of much of the rest of the territory, the first settlers of Allen County were still divided into pro- and anti-slavery factions. In the spring of 1855, a party of pro-slavery men from Fort Scott, the nearest town located about forty miles to the east, laid out the first town in the county on the high ground east of the Neosho River and near the mouth of Elm Creek.[5]

The new settlement bore the mellifluous name of Cofachique, pronounced Coffychee, which sometimes was spelled Cofachiqui, and was named in honor of a legendary Indian princess, Cofachiqui.[6] The young princess was the chief of her tribe, and had the misfortune to be the object of the greed of the sixteenth century Spanish conquistador, Hernando DeSoto, on his three-year search for gold in what is now the southeastern United States. Welcoming DeSoto and his soldiers with friendliness, the princess took her long string of pearls, which were as large as hazelnuts and which coiled three times around her neck and fell to her waist, and personally suspended them around DeSoto's neck. Ultimately, Cofachiqui realized the greed of the conquistadors, and though they made her a prisoner, she successfully escaped from DeSoto's grasp.[7]

The entire population of the town of Cofachique was pro-slavery.[8] A company of pro-slavery men from Alabama and Georgia used Cofachique as their headquarters, and from there, in 1856, they spread "terror" among the free-staters of the Neosho Valley. Malarial fever cut the southerners' work short when several of the men became ill, and after the death of one, the remainder left the county.[9]

At its height, Cofachique was a town of considerable importance. Designated the county seat in 1855 by the pro-slavery territorial legislature, it had 400 or 500 inhabitants and had more business transactions than any other town in the southern part of the territory.[10] By 1859, however, both Cofachique's dominance and actual existence had ended. The townsite lacked easily available well water, but probably more important to its demise was the enmity toward it by the anti-slavery majority of the settlers in the county. "[C]onceived in sin and born in iniquity...," Cofachique could not long survive. The founding of the town of Humboldt in 1857 on the east bank of the Neosho River about five miles south of Cofachique and, thus, in the southern part of the county, provided an opportunity in early 1859 for the, by now, anti-slavery territorial legisla-ture to remove the county seat from Cofachique to Humboldt.[11]

This removal symbolizes the other historical event which was common in pioneer settlement—the struggle between communities for the prize of the county seat. A county seat town was more than a seat of justice. County seat status brought increased population, business, influence, and money among various benefits. The loss of the designation of county seat could result in the very disappearance of the loser, as was the case with Cofachique.

Humboldt's status as the county seat under the 1859 law was only tem-porary, since at any general election the county seat designation could be changed to another community.[12] In that same year of 1859 another new town, Iola, was founded a couple of miles northeast of Cofachique. The following year saw an electoral contest between Humboldt and Iola for the county seat designation, and this election, in the words of a Humboldt supporter, was won by the former "by dint of doing some good voting," (a polite way of acknowledging ballot stuffing by the Humboldt support-ers).[13] The Civil War soon followed, and Humboldt, as a bastion of Union supporters, was sacked by forces loyal to the Confederacy in September of 1861, and then burned the next month in a second raid.[14]

The people of Iola and the inhabitants of the northern part of the coun-ty remained unhappy about Humboldt's continued hold on the prize, and, by copying the strategy of Humboldt supporters when they had utilized the territorial legislature to remove the county seat from Cofachique to Humboldt, the Iola proponents ultimately prevailed. In 1865, they con-vinced the state legislature to transfer a strip of land from the south part of the county to the adjoining Neosho County.[15] With this strip went many of Humboldt's supporters, and, at the next county seat election in May of 1865, Iola received 243 votes while Humboldt received only two (thirty-seven votes went to two other towns).[16] Although Iola secured the coveted status, for the next couple of decades a rebuilt Humboldt pos-sessed a larger population than Iola.[17] The rivalry between the two towns continued for years. Although Humboldt's "theft" of the county seat from Cofachique is little remembered more than 150 years later, many Hum-boldt residents to this day have not forgotten that Iola allegedly stole the county seat from them (personal experience of this author, an Iola resident).

When Ed Funston arrived at Carlyle in late 1867 and found a near-by farm that he wished to purchase, he was not alone in selecting Al-len County as a new home. The years 1867 through 1869 witnessed the county's "big immigration." The educated Funston was not atypical of these new settlers, since "the old settlers saw with astonishment a new and more enterprising race seizing upon all the fair unoccupied spots, bringing with them all the habits of an old and cultivated society, and looked upon school-houses, churches and public improvements springing up with the rapidity of magic...There are more educated men than usually fall to the lot of new communities. Music is cultivated to a surprising extent."[18]

In the words of an out-of-state observer, J.H. Beadle, in 1871, this period of the "big immigration" constituted the "modern age," which was the second of the two eras of settlement of Allen County and the surrounding area. The "modern age" was in contrast to the earlier "mythical" and "heroic" age starting with the initial white settlements in 1855. In addition to the troubles of "bleeding Kansas," these pioneer settlers experienced the "dry season" of 1860-1861 when the drought was so severe that the resulting dry bed of the Neosho River was used regularly as a public road from the town of Neosho Falls, a few miles upstream from Iola, all the way down to Humboldt, a few miles below Iola. "The settlers contended successively against short crops, no crops, Indian thieves and all devouring grasshoppers."[19] Then came the four years of the Civil War, and "the whole section [southern Kansas] went back ten years."[20] Now, all of that was past, and the "modern age" had begun.

Beadle roamed Allen County for ten days in 1871.[21] This visit was part of his travels through "that vast region between the Mississippi and the Pacific" Ocean.[22] Beadle viewed Allen County as "the great agricultural center and leading county of southern Kansas."[23] Consequently, he wrote, in detail, of its favorable agricultural features. He praised the rich soil of the county for its production of corn, wheat, oats, potatoes, turnips, wild strawberries, grapes, gooseberries, peaches, and apples. He noted that raising cattle, and then selling them, was highly profitable. Oats were the "money crop" of Allen County due to stock raising and to sales to those living in Indian Territory south of Kansas.[24]

In characterizing the people of Allen County, Beadle observed that, as to alcohol, they were more temperate than the residents of the average county in his home state of Indiana. In the towns, the standard drink was whiskey, known commonly as "stone fence," "forty-rod," and "tarantula juice." Whiskey was regarded as the only drink for men.[25]

"Deducting something of western swagger and a great deal of local exaggeration," Beadle wrote, "the southern Kansian is really a first-rate fellow; frank, generous, and with ideas expanded by change and experience, he is a good fellow to travel with and a desirable neighbor."[26] Residents, however, were prone to exaggerate all aspects of Kansas. There never was "so rich, great, and prosperous a region"; in a year, town lots are sure to double in price; "a man's children will grow fat by mere contact with the soil, and his wife return to the beauty of her youth..."; and the health benefits were life sustaining and restoring. An old resident of

Deer Creek, near which Ed Funston settled, "had lived so long, life was a burden (to his heirs probably), and yet the country was so healthy he could not die." He returned to Illinois, where he died, but he had stipulated that his burial was to be on his Kansas farm. "But such were the life-giving properties of this soil that when laid in it animation returned to his limbs, his heart resumed its pulsations, and the incorrigible centenarian walked forth in renewed health, to the disgust of his heirs and the confusion of those who had doubts about Kansas."[27] In extolling the virtues of Allen County, Beadle put his money where his mouth was. After seeing other Kansas counties, Beadle in 1873 purchased a farm a few miles east of Iola where he fitted up a home for himself.[28]

The dominant geographical feature of Allen County and of all of eastern Kansas and eastern Nebraska was the rolling prairie. The extended view of the limitless prairie must have been a sight to behold. In 1869, one observer described this scene of beauty:

> The most perfect display of the prairie is found in the eastern parts of Kansas and Nebraska. It is no exaggeration to pronounce this region, as left by the hand of Nature, the most beautiful country in its landscape upon the face of the earth. Here the forest is restricted to narrow fringes along the rivers and streams, the courses of which are thus defined as far as the eye can reach, whilst all between is a broad expanse of meadow-lands, carpeted with the richest verdure and wearing the appearance of artistically-graded lawns. They are familiarly called the rolling prairies, because the land rises and falls in gentle swells, which attain an elevation of thirty feet, more or less, and descend again to the original level, within the distance of one or more miles. The crest-lines of these motionless waves of land intersect each other at every conceivable angle, the effect of which is to bring into view the most extended landscape, and to show the dark green foliage of the forest trees skirting the streams in pleasing contrast with the light green of the prairie grasses...[29]

The prairie grass was several feet tall, and another observer, traveling in 1857 in unsettled Johnson County about ninety miles north and east of Allen County, described the grass as a "miniature forest. In some of the wet lowlands it rose above our heads and completely hid us from each other, when a few yards apart, though we were mounted on tall steeds."[30]

Upon this vast rolling prairie, the Allen County pioneers had established two settlements near the farm that Ed Funston was to select for himself and his family. The settlement of Carlyle was possibly named for the Scottish historian Thomas Carlyle.[31] It is located about 1¼ miles from the Funston farm by road, though a lesser distance as the crow flies by walking northeast across the intervening fields. In the spring and summer of 1858, several Presbyterian families from Parke and Johnson Counties, Indiana, arrived to establish a village on two quarter sections of land, but they soon decided that they did not want a town and divided their town site into farms.[32] Although there was to be no town, there developed the small settlement of Carlyle, consisting of a church, schoolhouse, and a few other buildings, and this settlement was described in 1876 as "one of the most thrifty and substantial in the county."[33]

Not until long after Fred Funston had grown up and left the family farm did Carlyle become a settlement of any significance. The impetus was the location there of a cement plant, and, during the brief boom years of 1909–1913, the town had a population of nearly 600 people, before declining to a village again.[34] In 1896, this village was so unprepossessing that, when a reporter came from Kansas City, Missouri, to the Funston farm to interview Fred's parents, he lamented that "the sight of [Carlyle], even on a balmy sunshiny day, is depressing…[there are] four buildings which, with a small, dazzlingly white church, comprise the town of Carlyle."[35]

The other settlement was Iola. Located about five miles south of the Funston farm, the county seat was the nearest commercial center for the Funston family. Iola, named for local resident Iola Colborn, had been laid out by its founders near the confluence of two streams, the Neosho River, approximately one mile west, and Elm Creek less than one-half mile south of the new town. "It might almost be said that Iola is situated upon an island, for, with the river upon the west, Elm Creek upon the south, Rock Creek [about 1½ miles] upon the east, and Deer Creek [about three miles] upon the north, all of which are within view, it is, during a great portion of the year, surrounded with water."[36] This island location fostered the belief among early inhabitants that they were safe from tornadoes, since they would not skip over water.[37] This belief was unfounded, and its speciousness was devastatingly shown on February 28, 1918, when Iola was struck by a tornado, which caused major damage.[38]

Although the names of the creeks on three sides of this "island" represented the natural world—elm trees, rocks, and deer—the name of the river on the west side—the Neosho—originated much earlier with the American Indian. A journal entry of a member of an 1825 Santa Fe Trail survey team mentioned the Nee Osho River. "Ne" means water; "osho" means "stream in" or "stream with water in it." Although pronounced Nē-o-sho, Kansas pioneers, presumably including some in Allen County, preferred the derisive spelling and pronunciation of Noshow during the occasional times when the river was dry in the summer.[39]

Although Iola was located on the gently rolling prairie, an unusual natural feature rose up one-half mile south of the new town. On the south verge of Elm Creek was a "beautiful mound," at the western base of which ran the stagecoach road south to Humboldt. In October of 1861, Iola's approximately 150 residents had seen the pillar of fire rising from the burning town of Humboldt, which had been torched by the rebel forces. On this mound a watch was then stationed "and kept anxious vigil through that long night expecting each moment to hear the tramp of marching hosts."[40] Most of Iola's inhabitants fled, and the eponymous Iola Colborn, then 29 years old, and another young woman, their husbands gone to war, loaded their household goods into a wagon, and, without any assistance, hauled them to safety across the Neosho River.[41] Fortunately for the small town, this night of terror passed without the appearance of the Confederate forces, which had departed to the south from Humboldt.

The magnificence of the view from atop this beautiful mound was enthusiastically noted by a traveler in 1869:

> From the top of this mound as grand a sight is to be had as ever feasted the gaze of mortal man; and some irreverent fellows have emphatically asserted to me that this Iola mound is the one on which Satan tempted the Saviour...I don't know whether they thought I was verdant enough to believe their story or not, but as they did not produce any well defined historical statistics, or data to back up their assertions, I give it for what it is worth. But this aside: I don't think that mount afforded a grander view than this one. From that one Satan pointed out a vast country, and the cattle grazing on many hills. The same sight is to be had from this one...[42]

Although Christ may not have been tempted on top of this mound, undoubtedly mortal man was tempted at the large stone brewery at the base of the mound on the Elm Creek side. The same traveler noted that "it is a magnificent location." The recently erected brewery, owned by an Englishman named Roberts, was "embowered in as pretty a grove as ever grew, and the proprietor has a splendid chance to build vaults by taking out the bowels of the mound. Then he'd have no occasion for ice to cool his beer; while the grove would be a splendid place for a beer garden, and Sunday picnics for the *Liberals*."[43]

At the start of the Civil War, Iola's population had been about 150 persons, but with the four years of war there was no growth. Following the close of the war in 1865, the town grew steadily as immigrants arrived, and, in 1870, it was incorporated as a city.[44] In that year, Iola's population was approximately 1,000 persons.[45] Its population reached 1783 persons in 1888.[46] But Iola was only "a country village, a fairly good trading point but nothing more" during Fred's years growing up in Allen County.[47]

Described as "a straggling frontier village" in its early years, Iola had available many of the typical businesses and professional people of frontier towns.[48] The city in 1873 contained these businesses, "manufactories," societies, churches, and professions: five dry goods, two furniture, two boot and shoe, two drug, two millinery, two hardware, one book, six grocery, one "exclusively Clothing establishment," one bakery, one saddle and harness, one photographer, two jewelry, one real estate and insurance, two dentists, one bank, one flouring mill, three liveries, one lumber yard, three blacksmith shops, two barber shops, two meat markets, two confectionery, three hotels, two agricultural implement houses, one distillery, one grain and coal dealer, two nurseries, the Masonic Lodge and the Odd Fellows, three churches (Baptist Society, Presbyterian, and Methodist Episcopal Society), four clergymen, seven lawyers, and six physicians.[49] Perhaps these six physicians found practicing their healing arts in the small town more lucrative than a Dr. Teagarden had anticipated four years earlier. After purchasing a new house with the intent of practicing his profession in Iola, "he visited our graveyard, found only three or four graves that had been made within a year, concluded that Iola was no place for a doctor, and left."[50]

Although a small community, Iola was visited in November of 1871 by the former slave and famous abolitionist, Sojourner Truth. Her appearance and her lectures were part of her Kansas petition campaign for the federal government to set aside land in the western part of the United States for "the African race." The local *Neosho Valley Register* described her as "an old African lady aged 83 years who had been a slave in the State of New York for 40 years..."[51] In reality, though her date of birth is unknown, she was probably closer to 74 years old.[52] *The Register* editor paid Truth high compliment: "Sojourner is a woman of no education, but has an excellent brain and has seen a great deal of the world and talked with a great many smart men, consequently has gathered and retained a host of good ideas, which makes her lectures quite interesting."[53]

Upon his arrival in Allen County in late 1867, Ed Funston lodged with the Cozine family near Carlyle until he found a suitable farm to purchase. He selected one adjoining the Cozine farm on the north.[54] The purchase closed on January 13, 1868, when he paid $1,200 to the farm's owners, John and Sarah Iddings.[55] At 162.69 acres, the farm contained slightly more than the standard quarter section of 160 acres, and on it was located a 1½ story shack with a gabled roof and dormer window. Inside were three low-ceilinged rooms, an attic, and a native stone chimney. A cottonwood was the only tree visible. Ed had misgivings about the suitability of this primitive structure for his family, and with the aid of the neighborhood schoolteacher, James W. MacDonald, he added a "summer kitchen" on the back of the house.[56]

Traveling by train, Lida Funston set out from New Carlisle, Ohio, in the spring of 1868 to join her husband in Kansas. With her, she brought

2-year-old Fred and the baby, James Burton Funston, known as Burt. Tucked into her handbag were her travel instructions: "From Kansas City, go to Lorence [sic: Lawrence] and change cars for Ottawa, and then take the stage for Carlyle." In addition to her children, Lida brought her "extensive wardrobe of silks, hoop skirts, poke bonnets, Dolman coats, Sable furs and a green 'watered silk' opera cape."[57]

Attired in her Ohio finery, Lida must have found the approximate fifty-mile stagecoach trip from Ottawa to Carlyle an ordeal. The saving grace may have been the stage drivers, most of whom had been drivers on the old Santa Fe Trail. Polite, accommodating, and possessed of a sense of humor, these drivers "were particularly chivalrous to women."[58] A pretty young woman with two small children would have been a worthy object of their chivalry.

The Southern Kansas Stage Company had both its supporters and detractors. One Iola supporter and passenger acknowledged in 1870 that a seat on a stage meant only a six-inch by eight-inch space with four inches of leg room, which would appear to be impossible, but he did not complain about this extremely small area upon which to sit.[59] Other passengers on the S.K. Stage Company were not so supportive. The year after Lida's 1868 stage trip between Ottawa and Carlyle, located about five miles north of Iola, a disgusted passenger described the overloaded coach on his Ottawa to Iola trip. Of the seventeen passengers, there were "[n]ine grown persons and four children inside, four on the outside—three with the driver—one on the boot—holding for dear life to the baggage straps, and in that uncomfortable and dangerous position riding over the rough roads all night." This particular passenger was on the boot, and "speaks feelingly regarding the comforts of that position." Four other passengers were left behind for lack of space.[60]

The Ottawa to Iola trip of fifty-five miles lasted twelve hours over dirt roads, and, as one passenger noted on another trip, "If any body is in love with Kansas staging when the mud is limitless and as adhesive as glue, let him love on. We did not get up much of a flame between Ottawa and Iola."[61] Travelers found that the roughness of the road threatened "not only serious injury to our vehicle, but no small inconvenience to ourselves."[62] Otherwise silent passengers on one trip made themselves known by "sundry oaths as they were bumped against the standards of the coach when driven over a stone or stump."[63]

About a mile from a town, the stage driver reached into the boot at the front of the coach, removed the postilion horn, and "began to blow loud and lusty fanfares signaling the approach of mail and express together with 'the latest news from the outside world.'"[64] Whether Lida and her small sons' arrival at the agricultural settlement of Carlyle one spring day in 1868 was trumpeted in this fashion is unknown, but the warmth of their welcome, upon their arrival, by their husband and father can be well imagined.

Although the wide expanse of "softest green" made the prairies "a joy forever," a viewer's judgment was heavily influenced by the season.[65] That same year of 1867 when Ed Funston arrived in Allen County, another Ohio family traveling by a Concord coach to Humboldt had a decidedly less favorable impression of their new home county. The newcomers arrived on a January morning filled with a drizzly rain. "[T]he geographical features of the earth's surface of Kansas with its uninhabited, barren and unproductive appearance, the noticeable lack of trees, gave to mother, brother, and myself a feeling that can only be adequately described as one of sadness."[66]

Lida Funston was more fortunate, arriving in Allen County in early spring when "[t]he prairies were awakening from their long winter's sleep..."[67] One attraction of the prairies was the blue, purple, and yellow flowers interspersed in the green of the prairie grass. "Sometimes over hundreds of acres these blossoms predominate, making the earth blue or yellow instead of green. In spring bloom the flowers of modest, delicate hues; those of deep, gorgeous color flame in late summer and early autumn."[68] Even with the nascent beauty of the open prairie, one wonders, however, what Lida thought when she first saw the naked shack. But she, Ed, and the children stayed. The new land was theirs.

1st Lieutenant
Edward Hogue Funston

Ann Eliza (Mitchell) Funston
(1861)

The Funston Homestead (1861)

Funston Museum Complex, Iola, KS (2018)

Lifesize statue of Fred Funston, Funston Museum and Visitors' Center
Funston Homestead (restored to 1890s-early 1900s period)

Chapter Four Notes—*The New Land*

1. Ella Funston Eckdall, *The Funston Homestead* (Emporia, Kansas: Raymond Lees, 1949), 2-3.

2. Robert W. Richmond, *Kansas: A Land of Contrasts* (Saint Charles, Missouri: Forum Press, 1974), 62.

3. Charles R. Tuttle, *A New Centennial History of The State of Kansas* (Madison, Wisc.: Inter-State Book Company, 1876), 581.

4. "For Your Scrap Book" [The Story of Allen County], *The Iola Register*, January 8, 1897.

5. William G. Cutler, *History of the State of Kansas* (Chicago: A.T. Andreas, 1883), 668.

6. Cyrus R. Rice, "Experiences of a Pioneer Missionary," *Collections of the Kansas State Historical Society, 1913-1914*, Vol. XIII (Topeka, Kansas, 1915), 298.

7. Norman B. Wood, *Lives of Famous Indian Chiefs* (Aurora, Ill.: American Indian Historical Publishing Company, 1906), 21-38.

8. S. H. West, *Life and Times of S. H. West* (LeRoy, Ill.: S.H. West, 1908), 52. West visited Cofachique at this time.

9. Rice, "Experiences of a Pioneer Missionary."

10. "Editorial History of Allen County, Kansas," *Neosho Valley Register*, May 5, 1869.

11. "Editorial History of Allen County, Kansas," *Neosho Valley Register*, May 5, 1869.

12. *General Laws of the Territory of Kansas* (Lawrence, K.T.: Herald of Freedom Steam Press, 1859), Ch. XLIX, 366 (approved February 4, 1859).

13. Watson Stewart, "Sketches of Early History in the Settlement of Humboldt & Allen Co., Kan.," *Humboldt Union*, July 15, 1876.

14. Cutler, *History of the State of Kansas*, 672.

15. Stewart, "Sketches of Early History."

16. Cutler, *History of the State of Kansas*, 671.

17. Cutler, *History of the State of Kansas*, 667. Humboldt's population in 1880 was 1,542 while Iola's was 1,096. In 1870, Humboldt's was 1,202, and though Cutler does not give Iola's population for that year, it was calculated at 1,000 by a visitor ("Down the Neosho Valley, Kansas," *Neosho Valley Register*, March 25, 1870).

18. J. H. Beadle, *The Undeveloped West, OR, Five Years in the Territories* (Philadelphia: National Publishing Company, 1873), 210.

19. Beadle, *The Undeveloped West*, 209.

20. Beadle, *The Undeveloped West*, 210.

21. Beadle, *The Undeveloped West*, 207.

22. Beadle, *The Undeveloped West*, title page.

23. Beadle, *The Undeveloped West*, 206-207.

24. Beadle, *The Undeveloped West*, 225-228.

25. Beadle, *The Undeveloped West*, 227.

26. Beadle, *The Undeveloped West*, 222-223.

27. Beadle, *The Undeveloped West*, 223-224.

28. *Neosho Valley Register*, May 10, 1873, and "Rockville, Parke Co., Ind." letter, *Neosho Valley Register*, June 7, 1873.

29. D. W. Wilder, *The Annals of Kansas New Edition, 1541-1885* (Topeka: T. Dwight Thacher, Kansas Publishing House, 1886), 505 (quoting a paper by Lewis H. Morgan on Indian Migrations published in *The North American Review*, Vol. CIX, 401-402).

30. Albert D. Richardson, *Beyond the Mississippi* (Hartford, Conn.: American Publishing Company, 1867), 79. *The Iola Register* of September 18, 1875, carried this report in the "Local Department": "The tallest wild grass we have seen is a bunch at John Francis & Co's.—it measures eight feet. Some of our farmers say they can furnish specimens that will beat that two feet. Get such things ready for exhibition at the county fair."

31. John Rydjord, *Kansas Place-Names* (Norman, Okla.: University of Oklahoma Press, 1972), 161. According to Rydjord's book, another possible source for the name "Carlyle" was Adda S. Adams, who allegedly inserted a penknife into a book at a page where the name Carlyle appeared. This would be impossible, since she was not born until 1869.

32. John W. Scott, "Historical Sketch of Allen County," *The Iola Register*, July 8, 1876.

33. John W. Scott, "Historical Sketch of Allen County," *The Iola Register*, July 8, 1876.

34. "History of Carlyle, Kansas" (typed manuscript written in 1982 but with no author stated). Allen County Historical Society, Inc.

35. "A Kansas Cuban Soldier," *The Iola Register*, December 25, 1896 (reprint from *The Kansas City Star*).

36. "Iola, The County Seat of Allen County," *Neosho Valley Register*, April 21, 1869. Another 1869 description of Iola as almost an island is as follows: "The location is almost an island one, being surrounded with living streams of clear water—the Neosho on the west, Elm creek on the south, Rock creek on the east, and Deer creek on the north —each stream fringed with timber, making it a really romantic and admirable town site" (Perambulator, "Letter From Iola," *Neosho Valley Register*, August 11, 1869). Although the Neosho River, Elm Creek, Rock Creek, and Deer Creek were visible from Iola in 1869, with the growth of timber and buildings over the prairie, such a view became extinct.

37. The author's father, Stanley E. Toland (1907-1995). Although not a native of Iola, he moved there in 1932 to begin a 62-year practice of law. He was keenly interested in local history and learned much about it from "old timers."

38. Mickey and Emerson Lynn, *The Annals of Iola and Allen County 1868-1945* (Iola, Kansas: The Iola Register, 2000), Vol. One, 542 (*The Iola Daily Register*, February 28, 1918, entry).

39. Sondra Van Meter McCoy and Jan Hults, *1001 Kansas Place Names* (Lawrence: University Press of Kansas, 1989), 140-141 ("Neosho County").

40. Annie A. Apple, "Reminiscences of Pioneer Days in Allen County," *The Club Member* (Topeka, Kansas, November 1908), 1.

41. "How It Came To Be Iola," *The Iola Daily Register*, May 20, 1904.

42. Perambulator, "Letter From Iola," *Neosho Valley Register*, August 11, 1869.

43. Perambulator, "Letter From Iola," *Neosho Valley Register*, August 11, 1869.

44. Cutler, *History of the State of Kansas*, 676.

45. "Down the Neosho Valley, Kansas," *Neosho Valley Register*, March 25, 1870.

46. L. Wallace Duncan and Chas. F. Scott, *History of Allen and Woodson Counties Kansas* (Iola, Kansas: Iola Register, Printers and Binders, 1901), 82.

47. L. Wallace Duncan and Chas. F. Scott, *History of Allen and Woodson Counties*, 76.

48. Obituary of William H. McClure, *The Iola Daily Register*, December 15, 1916. This description of Iola is for the year 1874, when McClure moved there.

49. "The City of Iola," *Neosho Valley Register*, January 18, 1873.
    An unusual business was the Iola Mineral Well. In 1872 an attempt, southwest of Iola, to locate coal began. In the process of drilling, "a jet of gas and water was struck, which afterward proved of value for its medicinal and curative properties." In 1874, the well and six acres were purchased by R. W. Acers and Nelson F. Acers (pronounced Acres), who "made many improvements, opened a hotel, built cottages, and bath-rooms...," and thus created "a summer resort, which is visited by hundreds of individuals annually, and the water is said to possess curative properties equal to Eureka, or Hot Springs of Arkansas." The temperature of the water was 61°, and the principal component was chloride of sodium (Cutler, *History of the State of Kansas*, 676-677).

50. *Neosho Valley Register*, October 20, 1869.

51. "Local Department," *Neosho Valley Register*, November. 9, 1871.

52. Jacqueline Bernard, *Journey Toward Freedom: The Story of Sojourner Truth* (New York: W.W. Norton and Company, 1967), 3.

53. *Neosho Valley Register*, November 9, 1871.

54. Eckdall, *The Funston Homestead*, 3.

55. John T. Iddings et ux. to Edward H. Funston, Deed dated January 13, 1868, Record Book C, 344 (Office of Register of Deeds, Allen County, Kansas).

56. Eckdall, *The Funston Homestead*, 3.

57. Eckdall, *The Funston Homestead*, 3.

58. J. H. Andrews, "Old Cofachique," *The Humboldt Union*, May 5, 1927.

59. Henry W. Talcott, "On The Stage," *Neosho Valley Register*, August 3, 1870.

60. "The Stage Company," *Neosho Valley Register* October 27, 1869.

61. "Trip to Iola," *Neosho Valley Register*, March 24, 1869 (reprint from *Ottawa Republic*).

62. "From Lawrence Southward," *Neosho Valley Register*, March 17, 1869.

63. Talcott, "On The Stage."

64. Andrews, "Old Cofachique."

65. Richardson, *Beyond the Mississippi*, 328.

66. Andrews, "Old Cofachique."

67. Eckdall, *The Funston Homestead*, 5.

68. Richardson, *Beyond the Mississippi*, 34.

CHAPTER FIVE

Childhood: 1865–1883

You know father always said that Fred was a very cheerful boy and that he performed his duties and tasks at home without complaint. He seemed to get so much happiness and enjoyment out of life.

—Ella (Funston) Eckdall to Eda B. Funston,
October 25, 1925[1]

Introduction

Frederick Funston was born under the outstretched wings of an eagle, an auspicious beginning for the future Major General, whose cap proudly bore this feathered emblem of the United States. His birth occurred on November 9, 1865, a Thursday, in an upstairs room of the Mitchell House, the hotel established by his maternal grandparents in New Carlisle, Ohio, and from the topmost pinnacle of which a golden eagle for many years displayed its outstretched wings.[2] Likely, the bell in the hotel's belfry tower pealed the happy news of baby Fred's birth.[3]

The Holy Bible owned by Fred's parents, Ed and Lida Funston, contains the record of Fred's birth. Published in 1866, perhaps the Funstons purchased this Bible that same year. In the "Family Record" section of this Bible, Ed has written in his strong handwriting: "Frederick Funston Born Novem 9' 1865." At times during Fred's life, and subsequent to his death, the middle initials of "C" and "N" have been attributed to him. In truth, Fred had no middle name or initial. The "Family Record" then continues, in Ed's handwriting, with the record of the births of Fred's seven younger siblings.[4] It is not surprising that Fred was named for his paternal grandfather. Ed undoubtedly took pleasure in naming his first-born for his own father, who had died at forty when Ed was only four years old.

The first two-plus years of his life Fred spent in New Carlisle. Whether the Funston family lived in the Mitchell House is unknown, though likely they did, since it would have been an economical place for them to stay. Although his grandfather, James Mitchell, was deceased, his grandmother, Elizabeth (Sweigert) Mitchell, was still living and, apparently, still owned the Mitchell House. Also unknown is how Ed earned a living for the next two years before traveling to Kansas in the fall of 1867, seeking a new home for himself, Lida, and their two sons, Fred and baby Burt. Perhaps Ed made his living as a nurseryman selling trees throughout the area.[5]

Fred's national fame in 1899, during the war in the Philippines, resulted in the discovery by the news media of his "old nurse." Amanda Looney, commonly known as "Aunty" Looney, was living in Springfield, Ohio, which is not far from Fred's birthplace of New Carlisle. "She is the proudest woman in the city because her 'boy, Freddy,' is being talked of by the whole world for his brilliant and fearless work in the Philippines. She took care of him when the family lived at New Carlisle. She says that when he was quite small he showed unusual ability for a child. He was a good boy, but full of life and grit."[6]

The foregoing newspaper account described Amanda Looney as a cook for Captain Russell O. Twist of Ed Funston's 16th Ohio Battery, but the 1906 history of the 16th described her as a "colored laundress" who was married to Jacob Tyler, "colored cook." After the war ended, Jacob was mustered out with the battery. He and Amanda moved to Springfield, Ohio, where he subsequently died, and she married one Looney. The 1906 history of the 16th notes that, though she was never mustered into the service of the United States, she "rendered faithful service to the members of the battery in many ways."[7] Ed Funston brought Amanda to New Carlisle to care for "Freddy."[8]

The only other story of Fred's babyhood comes from his mother in the 1899 interview with the reporter for *The Chicago Sunday Tribune*. In that interview with Fred's parents, the reporter noted that "[s]ometimes Mrs. Funston talks of her boy, but not to strangers. To those she knows best she talks not much either." In response to the reporter's question about Fred's early life, "she hesitated and yielded slowly, still hesitating. But she is proud of him. She can't conceal that, though it seems as if she tries hard to do it. She shudders at the thought of notoriety." She went on to explain her famous son's point of view: "'Fred doesn't want to be talked about so much,' she said. 'He did nothing but what he felt he should do, and why should people wish to make it so much a public matter?'"

As to Fred's childhood, she did share these memories:

> "There was nothing remarkable about him as a child. He was never dangerously ill. He never had any narrow escapes as a child, and he never had anything happen to him of an extraordinary sort. It is true, he was bright in his earliest years."
>
> A smile stole over her face as she paused. Some reminiscences had come to her.
>
> "Fred was only two years old when we moved from Ohio to this farm. That was in 1867 [sic], shortly after Mr. Funston returned from the war. Well, as we were coming on the train, Fred would look out of the car window and try to read the names of the station signs on the

depots. The other people in the car were greatly surprised that such a little fellow could name the letters on the signs."

And that was the only babyhood incident she recalled.[9]

The desire of the news media for stories about Fred's early life was likely even greater in 1901 after his capture of Aguinaldo. Ed and Lida Funston refused, however, to invent stories about their famous son, as was noted in a 1901 news story: "Mr. and Mrs. Funston refused to gratify a prying New York yellow journal by relating apocryphal anecdotes of their son Fred's boyhood. They deserve the thanks of society for refusing to allow their son's fame to be used in an advertising scheme for a morbid newspaper."[10]

Allen County, Kansas, though unique as all counties are in the details of its life, is a part of the larger historical theme of settlement of the ever westward-moving frontier in nineteenth-century United States. Let us turn to the details of Fred's childhood and to those details of the world in which this childhood was spent.

Exterior view of Fred Funston's birthplace, New Carlisle, Ohio
("X" marks the birth room)

Baby Fred Funston

Fred Funston Age 2 Years, 3 months

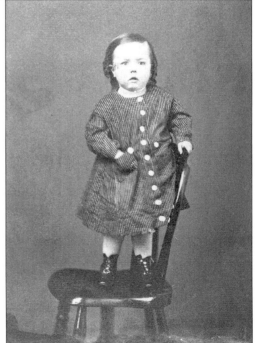

Chapter Five Notes—*Introduction*

1. Ella (Funston) Eckdall to Eda B. Funston, October 25, 1925 (FFP).

2. Ella (Funston) Eckdall to Eda B. Funston, October 25, 1925 (FFP). This golden eagle was in the possession of Eda Funston and her family at that time. The exact date the golden eagle was mounted on the building is unknown, but, presumably, it was there in 1865.

3. "New Carlisle Inn Affords Historic Memories To Be Transformed Into Interesting Reading," unidentified and undated clipping from a New Carlisle, Ohio, newspaper (Eckdall Scrapbook II, 1). The Mitchell House was located on the northwest corner of the public square (same article). Known as the New Carlisle Inn, it was torn down in 1936 and replaced by a gas station ("'Gas' Station Will Replace Stage Coach Inn," *Columbus Sunday Dispatch*, February 23, 1936) (Eckdall Scrapbook II, 3).

   An early stagecoach road was known as the Dayton-Bellfontain Road. In 1828, John Hay built in New Carlisle a stagecoach inn at the intersection of this stagecoach road and another one. The two-story building was built of native stone and timbers, had walnut woodwork, and the doors and windows were roughly made. There was a "long narrow stairway in the front hall [which] opened on one side into an office; on the other into a parlor with a large colonial fireplace and a bar at the end of the room. A commodious dining room and a number of sleeping rooms accommodated the many guests."

   In the early 1840s, James and Elizabeth Mitchell purchased the Hay Inn and renamed it "The Mitchell House." Since James was "a straight-laced prohibitionist, [he] closed the bar and forbade any intoxicating liquors." "Under the supervision of the Mitchells, with their children, Asa, Frances, and Lida, the Hotel became the social center of the town. [Elizabeth] was a generous hostess. There were children's parties, young folks' dances, old folks' quilting-bees and church socials accompanied with delicious vianda from the well-stocked Hotel larder." [Ella (Funston) Eckdall,] "The New Carlisle Inn," unpublished manuscript (two pages, balance missing). Copy in my possession.

4. The Funstons' Bible is located at the Allen County Historical Society, Inc.

5. Ella Funston Eckdall, *The Funston Homestead* (Emporia, Kansas: Raymond Lees, 1949), 7. Ella does not state when Ed traveled for a nursery house in Rochester, New York, but it apparently was before he came to Kansas, and in the chronology of his life, the two years after the Civil War would be the most likely time. Date of James Burton (Burt) Funston's birth is from the Funstons' Bible.

6. "Nurse of a Hero," *The Lima News*, Lima, Ohio, June 23, 1899 (reprint from *St. Louis Globe–Democrat*).

   Lida Funston's brother, Asa Mitchell, wrote about his five-month-old nephew: "'Freddy' is all the rage now I suppose. Ill [sic] bet he will be a spoiled 'younen' if there ever was one. Tell Lida to lick him for me if he needs it" (Asa N. Mitchell to Elizabeth (Sweigert) Mitchell, April 21, 1866). Courtesy of Deborah (Eckdall) Helmken.

7. *History of the Sixteenth Battery of Ohio Volunteer Light Artillery U.S.A.*, no publisher, 1906, 187.

8. "Nurse of a Hero."

9. "Fred Funston's Restless Life of Adventure," *The Chicago Sunday Tribune*, May 7, 1899 (FFP).

10. Unidentified newspaper clipping dated April 4, 1901, in Gilson Files on Frederick Funston. Lyon County History Center & Historical Society, Emporia, Kansas.

Farming and Stock Raising

The immediate and great concern of new Kansas farmer Ed Funston in 1868 was to plant and raise a crop. Spring was the time "when the farmers who expect to make farming pay must devote their whole time and energy for the next eight months to putting in crops, keeping down the weeds, repairing the old or making new fence, harvesting the crops and preparing a good, safe place to receive the grain after it has been raised and gathered."[1] For farming to pay, all of these steps were essential.

Deep plowing of eight or ten inches, and not simply top plowing of only two or three inches, was better. After the seed had been planted and then had sprouted, the plants needed to be weeded and tended to. The fields themselves needed to be fenced to keep out roaming cattle. Once the grain crop was harvested, the need was for safe and dry storage of the grain in buildings, not "emptied into rail pens and covered with straw...," as would otherwise be the case.[2] Thus, the work of the early farmer involved not just the crop itself from planting to harvest, but also the construction of fences, and then keeping them in repair, and the construction of storage buildings. "The fact is a man to make farming pay must devote his whole time to it, the same as any other business man that succeeds."[3]

None of this was easy for the early farmer. Ed and Lida's daughter, Ella (Funston) Eckdall, described this challenging situation many years later: "Times were unbelievably hard in the 60's and 70's, as all pioneer families know. There were few labor-saving machines and much work was done by hand. Men walked behind their plows which required firm hands to guide them through the stubborn sod. Father planted corn, hill by hill, with a hand-manipulated dropper and husked the crop by hand; he cut his wheat with a cradle scythe and threshed it with a primitive machine. He stacked his hay in the fields as balers were at that time unknown."[4]

Since successful farming was labor intensive, Ed naturally used the help of his two small sons, Fred and Burt, even before they were old enough and strong enough to guide the horse-drawn plow. The two boys were stationed at opposite ends of Ed's fields so that he could plow his furrows straight.[5] Then, as the boys matured, they helped with the farm work. Fred and Burt plowed corn, one holding the plow handle and guiding the plow while the other was riding and guiding the horse, "Old Nell." When they reached the end of a row, Burt enjoyed listening to Fred tell him a story that he had read. In exchange, Burt let Fred take Burt's turn riding "Old Nell."[6] At times, Fred took a book from his shirtfront and read to Burt, or if Fred did not have a book, he would declaim the rhetorical monologue "Spartacus to the Gladiators at Capua" or recite a half canto of Sir Walter Scott's *Lady of the Lake*.[7] At harvest, Fred was able to feed wheat so swiftly into the separator of the threshing machine that the wheat choked it up.[8]

The hard, physical work required of a farm boy benefited Fred. As one contemporary journalist wrote in 1899, "General Funston is a typical Kansas boy. Reared to manhood on a Kansas farm, his nature partakes of the sturdy strength of Kansas climate... He has harbored his strength. The only excesses he ever knew were those of hard work. As he followed the plow day after day, he was but tempering his muscles and building up an endurance that would enable him to withstand the fatigues of later life. Although small in stature, he has a magnificent physique. He can withstand hardships and exertions under which many a larger man would succumb."[9]

Fred was diligent in plowing corn and hoeing potatoes, and even when he was grown and attending the state university, he helped on the farm during vacation periods.[10] By 1884, Kansas was becoming known as the Sunflower State, and in 1903 the sunflower became the state flower. Charlie Scott, having spent his early boyhood on a farm near Carlyle, offered his firsthand testimony about the sunflower in *The Iola Register*: "[W]hen we hear the word 'sunflower,' our mind always goes back to the time when, as a 'bare-foot farmer's boy,' we were compelled to spend weary, weary days in the cornfield chopping down the overtopping weeds with a corn knife, and somehow we can't get up any great amount of enthusiasm for these 'gay emblems of our greatness.'"[11] Farm work was never done. On the occasion of a sighting of the Aurora Borealis at Carlyle in April 1882, the Carlyle correspondent for *The Iola Register* observed that "the farmers in this vicinity find little time for 'star gazing;' nothing but work, work from morning till night is to be thought of."[12]

Ed also utilized hired labor. According to the 1870 federal census, the Funston household included 23-year-old William McDonald, a white "Farm Laborer" who owned personal property valued at two dollars.[13] Ed reported no wages, including board, in the 1875 Kansas agricultural census. Perhaps Fred, age nine, and Burt, age seven, provided all of the extra labor needed.[14] In the 1880 federal census, Fred, age fourteen, and Burt, age twelve, are described as "help on farm." No occupation is shown for their younger brother, Pogue, age eight, since he was under the age of ten, but, undoubtedly, he helped also on the farm to the extent possible.[15] Ella (Funston) Eckdall, in the context of describing an 1877 event, noted that there were "colored help," John and Angeline Campbell, who had a son, Lutie.[16] In 1885, Ed reported $200 in wages, including board, for the year ending March 1, 1885.[17] In the same Kansas census, Fred, age nineteen, was listed as "Teacher."[18] Although he had last taught at the beginning of 1885, he apparently still regarded himself as a teacher. He, undoubtedly, helped with the farm operation while living at home.

As the first years passed, Ed concluded that he had made a mistake when he had purchased his farm. It was not the farm itself that was the

error, but the fact that he had used nearly all of his money in its purchase. In later years, he frequently told of this experience in the hope
that others would not make the same mistake. By investing all of his
capital, "[i]t left him cramped for means with which to improve the land
and strike out more successfully. His advice is that, by all means, a man
should guard most strictly against getting land crazy and land poor. Not
over one-third of a man's means, he says, should be invested."[19] As a way
of supplementing his income, Ed resumed his earlier occupation of tree
salesman by traveling as a salesman for a Quincy, Illinois, tree nursery.[20]
As an agent, he visited towns along the route of the Kansas Pacific railroad.[21]

For ten years (1868-1878) Ed was a grain farmer. The earliest settlers
in Allen County had primarily grown subsistence crops and raised cattle
on the "luxuriant growth of blue stem and other grasses." Once the county's population started to grow with new settlers following the arrival of
railroads in Allen County in 1870, the production of farm crops became
the county's main agricultural pursuit. The principal crops grown in this
time period were corn, oats, wheat, and hay. Corn was the dominant crop
during the years that Fred Funston was at home. In 1879, about 81,000
acres of Allen County land were used for crop production, with 45,809
acres planted to corn; 4,960 acres to oats; 4,886 acres to wheat; and 24,636
acres to hay and forage crops, which included clover and alfalfa. The federal census of 1880 reported 1,520 farms in the county, with an average
size of 144 acres, of which 77.6 acres were classed as improved land.[22]

What part did Ed Funston's farm play in these larger statistics? At
162.69 acres of land, the Funston farm was slightly larger than the average size farm of 144 acres in 1880.[23] The 1875 and 1885 Kansas censuses
contain agricultural production schedules, which document the details
of Ed's farm operation. In the 1875 Kansas agricultural census, Ed reported two acres of rye sown in the fall of 1874, and, as sown or planted
in 1875, twenty acres of corn, eight acres of oats, one acre of sorghum,
and fifteen acres of flax. Ten years later, according to the 1885 Kansas
agricultural census, for the category of crops sown or planted and to be
sown or planted in the spring of 1885, there were forty acres of corn, fifteen acres of oats, one acre of Irish potatoes, and ten acres of "Millet and
Hungarian." He had three hundred bushels of corn on hand, and three
bushels of wheat on hand on March 1, 1885, and had ten tons of tame hay
and twenty tons of prairie hay cut in 1884. For the year ending March 1,
1885, Ed had on hand one hundred pounds of butter.

In 1885, Ed had in "cultivation and under fence" all 160 acres of land.
Eighty acres were in prairie grass. His fences consisted of three types:
forty rods of board fence; 480 rods of hedge; and 480 rods of wire fence.
For livestock as of March 1, 1885, Ed owned nine horses, six milch cows,

and five "other cattle." He had fifty head of swine. During that year ending March 1, 1885, Ed had fattened or slaughtered, or sold for slaughter,
animals with a value of $250. Ed's orchard amply included these fruit
bearing trees: two hundred apple, six pear, six peach, six plum, and six
cherry. He also had fifty nonbearing apple trees. His farm, including improvements, was valued at $4,000. His farming implements and machin-
ery were valued at $90.[24]

Ed had netted little from his ten years as a grain farmer. He had thus
decided, about 1878, to add a more profitable operation, and securing
a fair-sized loan, started raising cattle. Within ten years he had from
cattle sales the capital with which he thereafter operated.[25] A couple of
local newspaper reports shed some light on Ed's cattle operation. In 1883,
"Mr. E. H. Funston began to feed a carload of five steers last Monday."[26]
In 1884, Ed was elected to Congress, and, in December of 1888, the local newspaper recognized this status in reprinting a story from another
newspaper: "While E.H. Funston was at home taking his vacation from
Congress, he drove twenty-seven hogs to the rail-road himself, and received $369.20 for them. This shows Mr. Funston's great versatility. One
day driving hogs along a muddy road and the next hieing away to Washington to make a speech. — *State Journal*."[27]

Ed's active involvement in the hard work of farming, even when he
had become a U.S. congressman, was noted by *The Iola Register* in March
of 1885: "Hon. E.H. Funston and lady are looking quite hearty after their
winter at the Capital. The Honorable takes to the cornfield just as though
he had not been to Congress, and shows 'the boys' how to gather corn and
'whispers' to them to 'come on.'"[28]

Ed neither shirked hard work nor let his prominent social status interfere with his helping those in need. The editor of the *LaCygne* (Kansas) *Journal* newspaper was well acquainted with Ed, and recounted this
story in an 1894 editorial: "He is a man of the people and his acts of kindness and sympathy come so direct from the heart that no one can doubt
their integrity. Once while walking along the road with him we overtook
a neighbor with his wagon stuck in the mud. Mr. Funston looked the situation over, took off his coat, and said, 'Barber, you boost on that wheel
and I will boost on this one.' He then gathered hold of the wheel that
was deepest in the mud and the wagon came out on solid ground. The
congressman was as well plastered with mud as if he had just closed a
campaign against fusion and the devil, except it did not smell as rank,
coming as it did only from a hog wallow."[29] That was not the only time
Ed's helping a neighbor was publicly recognized. In February of 1877,
The Iola Register noted that "W.C. Adams, up on Deer Creek, lost his
smokehouse last Monday. Mr. Funston happened to be near, and saved
Mr. A's bacon."[30]

Ed farmed nearly to the end of his life in 1911. Even in 1896, when he was sixty, he was still physically impressive and still farming. A newspaper reporter described him accordingly: "He is a giant. His big head is fitted for a short nose, under which is a white mustache cropped close and quite young and jaunty looking. Wholesome, big-voiced and bundering [sic] is Farmer Funston, with a welcome for a newspaper man learned in Washington. If he doesn't look like Stanley, the African explorer he looks like pictures of him. He was clad in a mixed dark gray suit of cloths [sic] and a pair of cowhid [sic] boots that came halfway up his calves. On his shoulder was a handful of broken straw and hayseed. 'I've been looking after the cows,' he explained without the asking. 'I plowed yesterday, but I'm not very good afoot any more.'"[31]

Three years later, in the 1899 *Chicago Sunday Tribune* interview, the reporter noted that "[s]ince the completion of his last term in Congress a few years ago [1894] he is back on the farm looking after things there just the same as if he had never known the glamour of life at the nation's capital and had never felt the flattery of power in the assembly of lawmakers. He was called 'Farmer' Funston when he was first elected, and he has never lost the blunt honesty of a farmer since."[32]

Chapter Five Notes, continued—*Farming and Stock Raising*

1. "Farming," *Neosho Valley Register*, March 22, 1873.

2. "Farming."

3. "Farming."

4. Ella Funston Eckdall, *The Funston Homestead* (Emporia, Kansas: Raymond Lees, 1949), 9.

5. Eckdall, *The Funston Homestead*, 9.

6. Ella (Funston) Eckdall to Eda B. Funston, October 25, 1925 (FFP).

7. David Potter, *Frederick Funston: A First Class Fighting Man: A Biography*, 7 (manuscript) (David Potter Manuscripts; 1950s, Manuscripts Division, Department of Rare Books and Special Collections, Princeton University Library).

8. Photograph with caption and brief text, *The Kansas City Star*, May 19,1907.

9. R. M. Ruggles, "Leaves From The Diary of Gen. Funston's Eventful Life," unknown newspaper, datelined May 11 [1899] (FFP).

10. "Fred Funston's Restless Life of Adventure," *The Chicago Sunday Tribune*, May 7, 1899 (FFP).

11. "Editorial Notes," *The Iola Register*, September 26, 1884.

12. "Carlyle Letter," *The Iola Register*, April 28, 1882.

13. 1870 United States Census, Schedule 1, Deer Creek Township, Allen County, Kansas.

14. 1875 Kansas Census, Schedule 2, Productions of Agriculture, Deer Creek Township, Allen County, Kansas.

15. 1880 United States Census, Schedule 1, Deer Creek Township, Allen County, Kansas.

16. Eckdall, *The Funston Homestead*, 15.

17. 1885 Kansas Census, Schedule 2, Productions of Agriculture, no township designated, Allen County, Kansas. This is Deer Creek Township, however, since the Funstons and their neighbors are listed.

18. 1885 Kansas Census, Schedule 1, Inhabitants, no township designated, Allen County, Kansas. This is Deer Creek Township, however, since the Funstons and their neighbors are listed.

19. Brief biographical sketch of Edward H. Funston in the *American Agriculturalist*; the issue is not identified, but it apparently was published in 1889 (Funston Political Scrapbooks at Allen County Historical Society, Inc.).

20. "Here and There," *Fort Scott Weekly Monitor*, January 24, 1878.

21. *The Fort Scott Daily Monitor*, November 13, 1877.

22. W.I. Watkins and W. H. Metzger and J. R. Latta, *Soil Survey Allen County Kansas* (United States Department of Agriculture Bureau of Chemistry and Soils: Series 1935, No. 2. Issued November 1938), 6-7.

23. John T. Iddings et ux. to Edward H. Funston, Deed dated January 13, 1868, Record Book C, 344 (Office of Register of Deeds, Allen County, Kansas)

24. 1875 Kansas Census, Schedule 2, Productions of Agriculture, Deer Creek Township, Allen County, Kansas.

    1885 Kansas Census, Schedule 2, Productions of Agriculture, no township designated, Allen County, Kansas. This is Deer Creek Township, however, since the Funstons and their neighbors are listed.

25. Brief biographical sketch of Edward H. Funston.

26. "Carlyle Correspondence," *The Iola Register*, September 21, 1883.

27. "Local Matters," *The Iola Register*, December 7, 1888.

28. "Carlyle Correspondence," *The Iola Register*, March 27, 1885.

29. "Editorial Notes," *The Iola Register*, March 30, 1894 (reprint from *LaCygne Journal*).

30. *The Iola Register*, February 10, 1877.

31. "A Kansas Cuban Soldier," *The Iola Register*, December 25, 1896 (reprint from *The Kansas City Star*).

32. "Fred Funston's Restless Life of Adventure."

Expanding the Farm

On the day in January of 1868 when Ed Funston purchased the quarter section upland prairie farm from John Iddings, he also purchased from Iddings a separate, approximately five-acre, tract of land. The purchase price was $75. Although this small tract was primarily situated on the north side of the Neosho River, it also included in its boundaries the river itself to its south bank.[1]

Why would Ed want such a tract, particularly since it was located, as the crow flies, about three miles southwest of his farm? This tract was known as a woodlot, an area consisting of native trees which had developed in response to the soil and climatic conditions.[2] With Ed's woodlot located next to the river, there was a source of water to nourish the trees, and the trees were also more likely to survive the prairie fires on the generally treeless prairie. By owning a woodlot, Ed had his own source for timber with which he could make fence posts and additions to his small house, and he also had a source of fuel to heat his home.

More than seventeen years later, on June 3, 1885, Ed expanded the size of his farm by nearly fifty percent when he purchased from his friends and neighbors, C.A. and Emma Cozine, two tracts of real estate for $2,200. The Cozines owned a quarter section of land immediately south of Ed's quarter section, and they sold to him the east half (eighty acres). This left the Cozines with the west eighty acres, which is located next to the north-south road along which both the Cozines and the Funstons lived. The second tract Ed purchased that day adjoins the newly purchased eighty acres on its south boundary, and then extends south to the north bank of Deer Creek.[3] With this small tract bordering a source of water, Ed had a woodlot far closer to his home. Nearly three years later, he sold for $100, a profit of $25, the woodlot that he had purchased from Iddings.[4] The Iddings woodlot had well served its purpose of supplying timber for the Funstons for twenty years. The practical value of a woodlot was not to be underestimated.

Ed had paid cash for his original farm, the quarter section that he had purchased in 1868, and did the same for the woodlot purchased at the same time. As a result, these two tracts were initially free of a mortgage. As discussed in the prior subchapter, the early years of approximately 1868-1878 were financially challenging ones for grain farmer Ed Funston. By April of 1874, he found it necessary to mortgage the south half of his quarter section. This was a clever strategy, since his house was located on the north half of the quarter section. Thus, should Ed be unable to pay off his mortgage, he would lose half of his land, but not the half on which his home was situated. He followed this same strategy for nearly twenty years.

The 1874 mortgage on this tract was in the sum of $500 at 10% interest and was for five years.[5] This mortgage was paid in February of 1880, apparently in part by Ed's mortgaging again the same real estate for five years. The new mortgage amount was $350 at 9% interest. Ed had been elected to Congress the prior year, and likely a part of his annual salary of $5,000 (more than $100,000 in 2018 dollars) went toward payment of the mortgage, which was paid and released on January 27, 1885.[6] It was later that same year that Ed purchased for $2,200 the eighty-acre tract and woodlot from the Cozines. This was a cash purchase, free of mortgage, and presumably made possible by Ed's congressional salary.

Ed was to serve in Congress for ten years (1884-1894), and annually received his handsome $5,000 salary. Thus, it is not surprising that Ed was mortgage-free for more than four years, but, surprisingly, in August of 1889 he mortgaged the Cozine eighty acres for $2,020 at 10% interest. Analysis of the mortgage records from 1889 until Ed's death in 1911 leads to a dismaying conclusion—Ed's land was mortgaged most of this time period. The details of these mortgages are provided in the notes. For a prosperous farmer to be in this situation is mystifying, since for the first five years of this period he had the benefit of his congressional salary. I wonder if Ed was like the individual who inherits a large sum of money, and then adopts an expensive lifestyle which he is unable to continue. Ed not only added numerous buildings to his farm after his election to Congress, he likely enjoyed a more lavish lifestyle than before, a lifestyle appropriate for a United States congressman.

Even after leaving Congress in 1894, he may have continued a lifestyle that his farm income could only partially sustain, thus necessitating the incurrence of substantial debt at times. Another possible explanation is that he sent five of his six children to college, a significant expense for him. There could be additional or different reasons, but, whatever the reason, Ed's income was exceeded by his expenses.

In the probate of Ed's estate in 1911, the original quarter section that he had purchased for $1,200 in 1868, and had subsequently improved by adding numerous buildings, was valued at $4,860. It was subject to debt of $1,000. The Cozine eighty acres, purchased in 1885 for nearly $2,200, was valued at $2,000. It was subject to debt of $1,300. The two-acre woodlot was valued at $40.[7] The total value of all of Ed's real estate was thus $6,900, and it had a total indebtedness of $2,300 against it.

Chapter Five Notes, continued—*Expanding the Farm*

1. John T. Iddings et ux. to Edward H. Funston, Deed dated January 13, 1868, Record Book C, 345 (Office of Register of Deeds, Allen County, Kansas).

2. Lloyd F. Smith, "Farm Woodlot Management in Kansas" (Manhattan, Kansas: Kansas State College of Agriculture and Applied Science, Agricultural Experiment Station, Department of Horticulture, October 1940, Circular 201), 1.

3. C. A. Cozine et ux. to E. H. Funston, Warranty Deed dated June 3, 1885, Deed Record 4, 355 (Office of Register of Deeds, Allen County, Kansas). The eighty acres is described as the east half of the southwest quarter of Section 2, Township 24, Range 18.

4. E. H. Funston et ux. to Stephen Trine, Warranty Deed dated February 10, 1888, Deed Record 8, 204 (Office of Register of Deeds, Allen County, Kansas).

5. Edward H. Funston et ux. to George L. Thompson, Mortgage dated April 8, 1874, Mortgage Book C, 365 (Office of Register of Deeds, Allen County, Kansas).

6. Edward H. Funston et ux. to Langdon G. Morgan, Mortgage dated February 2, 1880, Mortgage Book F, 594 (Office of Register of Deeds, Allen County, Kansas).

7. In the Matter of E. H. Funston, Deceased, Case No. 1810, Probate Court of Allen County, Kansas (Office of the Clerk of the District Court of Allen County, Kansas).

Details of 1889-1910 Mortgages

The $2,020 August of 1889 mortgage on the Cozine eighty acres was due in six months.[1] This was paid in March of 1890 when Ed mortgaged both the usual south half of his quarter section (the part where his house was not located) and the Cozine eighty acres for $1,100 at 6% interest.[2] This five-year mortgage was paid in full when due in 1895, and the Funston land remained mortgage-free for two years. Then, in January of 1897, Ed mortgaged for the first time the north half of the quarter section, thus mortgaging his home. Only the north half was subject to this mortgage, which was for $500 at 8½% interest for five years.[3] Why Ed would put his home at risk of loss by mortgaging this part of his quarter section is impossible to determine. He could have easily mortgaged, instead, the other part of the quarter section. Two months later, in March of 1897, Ed mortgaged the Cozine eighty acres for $500 at 8% interest for five years.[4] Both of these mortgages were paid when due in early 1902.

Less than two months later, in May of 1902, Ed mortgaged the Cozine eighty acres to his son, Frederick Funston, for $1,400 at 6% interest for three years. This was paid in March of 1904 prior to maturity.[5] A year after the mortgage to his son Fred, Ed mortgaged in February of 1903 the south half of the quarter section, thus reviving his strategy of never mortgaging the land where his house was situated. This mortgage was for $1,500 (interest rate not stated in recorded mortgage) and was due in five years.[6] It was paid when due in 1908 by the execution of a new mortgage to the same mortgagee and for the same principal sum of $1,500.00 (interest rate not stated in recorded mortgage).[7] The maturity date of this mortgage is not stated in the mortgage, but it was outstanding at the date of Ed's death in September of 1911. The unpaid balance was $1,000.[8]

The Cozine eighty acres, free of mortgage since 1902, was subject to two final mortgages in Ed's lifetime, the first being one he granted in June of 1910 for $1,300 at 6% interest and due in seven years.[9] The same day, and to the same mortgagee, Ed mortgaged the Cozine eighty acres for $91 for seven years (interest rate not stated in recorded mortgage).[10] Both of these mortgages were outstanding at the time of Ed's death in September of 1911, and the unpaid balance was $1,300.[11]

Chapter Five Notes, continued—*Details of 1889-1910 Mortgages*

1. E. H. Funston et ux. to Bank of Allen County, Iola, Kansas, Mortgage dated August 2, 1889, Mortgage Book U, 50 (Office of the Register of Deeds, Allen County, Kansas).

2. Edward H. Funston et ux. to The Connecticut Mutual Life Insurance Company of Hartford, Connecticut, Mortgage dated March 10, 1890, Mortgage Book X, 600 (Office of Register of Deeds, Allen County, Kansas).

3. Edward H. Funston et ux. to William Merchant, Mortgage dated January 21, 1897, Mortgage Book 7, 308 (Office of Register of Deeds, Allen County, Kansas).

4. E. H. Funston et ux. to Frederick Hinzie, Mortgage dated March 27, 1897, Mortgage Book 7, 342 (Office of Register of Deeds, Allen County, Kansas).

5. E. H. Funston et ux. to Frederick Funston, Mortgage dated May 1, 1902, Mortgage Book 24, 159 (Office of Register of Deeds, Allen County, Kansas).

6. Edward H. Funston et ux. to M. L. Brewster, Mortgage dated February 14, 1903, Mortgage Book 23, 413 (Office of Register of Deeds, Allen County, Kansas).

7. Edward H. Funston et ux. to M. L. Brewster, Mortgage dated February 12, 1908, Mortgage Book 40, 26 (Office of Register of Deeds, Allen County, Kansas).

8. In the Matter of E. H. Funston, Deceased, Case No. 1810, Probate Court of Allen County, Kansas (Office of the Clerk of the District Court of Allen County, Kansas).

9. Edward H. Funston et ux. to The Merriam Mortgage Company, Mortgage dated June 23, 1910, Mortgage Book 38, 184 (Office of Register of Deeds, Allen County, Kansas).

10. Edward H. Funston et ux. to The Merriam Mortgage Company, Mortgage dated June 23, 1910, Mortgage Book 38, 185 (Office of Register of Deeds, Allen County, Kansas).

11. In the Matter of E. H. Funston, Deceased, Case No. 1810, Probate Court of Allen County, Kansas (Office of the Clerk of the District Court of Allen County, Kansas).

Expanding the Family

Fred was to be the oldest of eight children born to Ed and Lida Funston. After Fred and the two-year younger Burt, born August 24, 1867, the third child was born in September of 1869 and died the day after birth. A baby girl, she was unnamed. Lida soon became pregnant again, and gave birth on July 28, 1870, to a baby boy, who lived about two months before dying on October 2, 1870. He, too, was unnamed. The little babies were buried in the neighborhood cemetery, which was known as the Vezie Cemetery from its location on the farm owned by the Vezie family.

The fifth child, Pogue Warwick Funston, was born July 9, 1871. The only daughter to survive infancy was Ella, who was born two years later, on December 13, 1873. There was then a gap of more than three years before Aldo Funston was born on May 6, 1877. The eighth, and final child, was born a decade later, on December 4, 1887, when Lida was 44 years old (Advanced Maternal Age in today's parlance). He was named Edward Hogue Funston Jr. in honor of his father.[1] Edward Sr. was in Washington, D.C., at the time of the birth, but came home "to make the acquaintance of the heir that had been born to him three weeks ago."[2]

Ed had a soft spot in his heart for children. In 1892, as a U.S. congressman and a member of the House committee on immigration, he toured New York's Ellis Island, a place of arrival of immigrants to the United States. Included in his party was an interpreter. In one room of the processing facility was a family that likely would be sent home. As noted by a Democratic newspaper, *Paola* (Kansas) *Spirit*, what occurred next showed that Ed "has a good deal of the milk of human kindness in his make up…"

There were several children in the family, the youngest a girl of four. The mother had been taken away from them sick with typhus. With the aid of the interpreter Mr. Funston talked with the children. They were very poor and as they told of the hard time they had had they began to cry. The little girl was moaning for her mother.

The Congressman could not stand it. He took the little thing up in his arms and before he could comfort her there were tears in his eyes. Then he drew his wallet, put the little girl down and began distributing $2 bills. He gave one to every member of the family from the father down to the 4-year-old. Then he straightened up to his full six feet and his heavy voice was husky as he said: "I'm not used to this. I've got some children of my own. I can't stand it to see these little things crying for their mother."[3]

At this time, Ed's youngest son, Edward Jr., was only 4 years old.

Ed, who had largely acquired his own education, both formal and informal, was concerned that his children have a good education. "He was insistent in urging an education upon his children and sent five of us to college, he placed the best of books for us in his library and held the highest ideals before us to which we were to strive to attain,"[4] remembered Ella (Funston) Eckdall. Ed's library was extensive and a great blessing for all of his children. In the words of his grandson, Frank Funston Eckdall, "Grandfather had the finest library in the county, stocked with the classics of the day (Carlyle's *French Revolution*, the Federalist papers, *Chitty's Blackstone*, Macauley's *Essays*, Plutarch's *Lives*, complete poems of Shelley, Burns, Cowper, Campbell, and Moore; and, of course, a set of Waverley novels and Dickens). Fred read all of them and borrowed others."[5]

There were various activities in the Carlyle neighborhood that the Funston family members attended. Ed Funston helped supervise the preparations for the 1872 celebration of the Fourth of July in the grove near the crossing of Deer Creek.[6] About 2,000 people attended that year's celebration, which included reading of the Declaration of Independence, band music, a picnic, and vocal music. The celebration concluded with those present singing "Old Hundred" accompanied by the band. That evening there were fireworks and a dance in Iola.[7] At the time of the 1876 centennial celebration of the Fourth of July, Ed participated in a more important capacity. He gave the response to one of fourteen toasts, the toast being titled, appropriately for him, "The Plow Anvil and Loom." The words of this toast were the following:

"'Go till the ground'—said God to man—
'Subdue the earth, it shall be thine.'"
"And the tinkle of the anvil, first of the village sounds was heard."
"Swift flies the shuttle."[8]

Unfortunately, Ed's response was not reported in the local newspaper. This centennial celebration was a huge one that began in Iola by the firing of cannon and the ringing of bells. "[E]arly in the forenoon the people began to arrive in town from all directions. They came in wagons and on horseback, singly and in delegations, and our streets were soon crowded with men, women and children..." The actual exercises, including a picnic and the toasts, occurred in a grove on the banks of Elm Creek south of town. A display of fireworks in the evening ended the celebration of our nation's centennial.[9] Presumably Ed, Lida, 10-year-old Fred, and the younger siblings all participated in and enjoyed the celebration.

Perhaps the Funston family also attended a unique event in March of 1877: "A novel supper came off in Deer Creek township last Wednesday evening. The folks divided into two squads, for a general rat hunt, and the party which brought in the fewest rat tails paid for the supper. The victorious party, by an 'honest count,' came out just 131 ahead. A total of 2,269 rats were killed. And so ended the first rat-tail supper that we ever heard of."[10]

Unfortunately, there appears to be no record of the types of social activities that the Funston children indulged in. Likely, they were the same as, or at least similar to, those that Angelo Scott was aware of in the Carlyle neighborhood until 1874 when, at age seventeen, he and the other members of the Scott family moved to Iola. "If it was a large party, groups of young men would go by farm wagon to the homes of their several girls, pick them up, and then converge at the place of entertainment. It might be a candy-pulling if it was in deep winter; or it might be charades and other word games; or it might be something more hilarious in which a bit of kissing was possible, and very popular." The girls wore hoods in the winter, and the boys "wore hand-me-downs and at these parties high collars."[11]

Chapter Five Notes, continued—*Expanding the Family*

1. All of this information is from The Holy Bible which belonged to Ed and Lida Funston, and which is described in the Introduction to this Chapter Five. The unnamed baby girl was born on September 14, 1869, and died on September 15, 1869.

2. "Personals," *The Iola Register*, December 23, 1887.

3. "Funston's Big Heart," *The Iola Register*, March 18, 1892.

4. Ella (Funston) Eckdall to Eda B. Funston, October 25, 1925 (FFP).

5. Frank F. Eckdall, "'Fighting' Fred Funston of Kansas," *The Kansas Historical Quarterly*, Vol. XXII, No. l (Spring, 1956), 78.

   This is Eckdall's speech at the annual meeting of the Kansas State Historical Society on October 18, 1955, at which time he presented to the State of Kansas the deed to the Funston homestead from Funston family members, particularly his mother, Ella (Funston) Eckdall. She had paid about $3,000 to restore the Funston house.

   The property was thereafter known as the Funston Memorial State Park and was managed for the state by the Kansas State Historical Society until 1994, at which time ownership of the house, contents, and four outbuildings was transferred to Frank F. Eckdall and his daughter, Deborah (Eckdall) Helmken, who then transferred the house, contents, and two outbuildings to the Allen County Historical Society, Inc., Iola, Kansas. The Society moved, in 1994, the house and the two outbuildings (three-hole privy and store house) to the Iola town square, and then restored the house. It has been open to the public as the Funston Home Museum since 1995.

6. "The Celebration," *Neosho Valley Reporter*, June 22, 1872.

7. "Programme for the 4th," *Neosho Valley Register*, June 29, 1872, and "The Fourth," *Neosho Valley Register*, July 6, 1872.

8. "Fourth of July Toasts," *The Iola Register*, June 24, 1876. An interesting celebration occurred in September of that year. "The celebration by the colored folks of our county of the anniversary of the Emancipation Proclamation in the grove near Iola last Friday [September 22], was not so well attended by the white folks as it would have been had not the fair been in progress. They concluded, however, that to postpone the celebration would be like having a Fourth of July celebration in June" ("Local Department," *The Iola Register*, Saturday, September 23, 1876). September 22, 1862, was the date of issuance of the preliminary Emancipation Proclamation.

9. "The Centennial Fourth at Iola," *The Iola Register*, July 8, 1876.

10. *The Iola Register*, March 24, 1877.

11. Angelo C. Scott, *A Boyhood in Old Carlyle* (Oklahoma City, 1940), 25-26.

Expanding the House

As previously related, when Ed Funston purchased in 1868 the Allen County quarter section, the only improvement on this farm was "a mere shack" of three low-ceilinged rooms and an attic with a dormer window. Before Lida, young Fred, and baby Burt arrived, Ed had added to the back of the house a "summer kitchen."[1] There were only these four rooms when Fred was a boy,"[2] and they were used as a sitting room, a dining room, a bedroom for the parents, and the "summer kitchen."[3] This last room was probably used year-round for culinary purposes. The attic room with its dormer window was the bedroom of the children, presumably including the only daughter, Ella.

By 1877, there were four sons and one daughter, and as the family grew, other rooms were added to the house. Ella (Funston) Eckdall described these additions: "Despite the lean years that followed this great destruction of crops [by the grasshopper plague in 1874], Father managed with small remunerations from his political activities, to make a few additions to his house. By the addition of two rooms on the north—a 'parlor' and 'spare bedroom'—and a porch across the entire west front, it met the needs of his growing family."[4] Ella's description is inadequate. Above the new parlor were constructed two bedrooms—one for Ed and Lida and one for Ella. Although her bedroom was only about eight feet by seven and a half feet, Ella must have been thrilled to have her own room and privacy!

No room in the Funston house was large. The parlor was 14½-feet deep by about 12½-feet wide. The sitting room was eventually divided into two rooms, a sitting room 14½-feet deep by about 10-feet wide, and a study and library for Ed, 14½-feet deep by 6-feet wide.[5] In 1875, a five feet, four inch-wide bay window facing the south was added to the library, and thus Ed, seated in his large desk chair, could sit at his desk and look south at the yard of his house and at his fields. The sitting room and library were connected by a five feet, four inch-wide opening hung with portieres.[6]

It is unknown exactly when the two-story addition on the north consisting of the parlor and two bedrooms upstairs was constructed. Likely, it was in 1883 when Ed was serving as president pro tempore of the Kansas Senate. The Carlyle correspondent for *The Iola Register* noted in the May 18, 1883, issue that Ed was "improving his dwelling with a new addition."[7] The same correspondent several weeks later made this compliment: "It looks quite tony at Senator Funston's since his new house has been completed."[8] Although it was not a new house, the large, two-story addition and porch across the entire front of the house dramatically changed the house's appearance.

The last addition to the house was the "spare bedroom," which was located behind the parlor. This addition appears to have been constructed in the summer of 1885. By then, Ed was in his second year as a United States congressman and thus received a $5,000 annual salary. The Carlyle correspondent reported accordingly: "Hon. E. H. Funston has built an addition to his large barn, and is building an addition to his house. His farm now presents a fine appearance."[9]

Ella (Funston) Eckdall later recorded the details of the improvement of the Funston farm. As Ed "received more substantial returns from public office, he made more extensive improvements. He built a large barn with a floored driveway, an ample loft for hay, stalls for his horses—Fanny, Pete, Dan, Panic, Doll and the pony, Tom—harness and machine rooms. Additional buildings were grain cribs, chicken houses, a carriage shed, an ice house, a stone smokehouse where country hams were cured over hickory log fires, and an outdoor cellar or storm cave, with a store room above it."[10] Ed built so many buildings that, in the fall of 1885, *The Iola Register* observed that "Hon. E. H. Funston has been building so many barns, wood sheds and other farm buildings lately that his neighbors refer to his place as 'Funston's town.' We presume he must be adding another block to it as we saw him riding out of town on a load of lumber Tuesday."[11]

Ella (Funston) Eckdall described these other improvements to "Funston's town":

> In the yard adjoining us on the south, he built [in 1887] a tenant house and barn where the man lived who tended the garden and yard. His large farm gates were carpenter-made—no makeshift affairs—and painted white like all the buildings. Fences were built about the farm and ponds located at convenient spots. Cattle were in well-built corrals and "porkers" were in feed lots about the barn. Labor was now plentiful and a great part of the farm work was delegated to "hired help." Neatly kept flower beds, square and star shaped, filled with gay tulips and peonies, decorated the front lawn and lent life and color to the sombre gray cedars. Large red tubs holding blooming plants, often from the neighboring greenhouse, graced either side of the yard.
>
> Close beside the house was a deep well in which was "the old oaken bucket, the iron-bound bucket, the moss-covered bucket which hung in the well." Over this was built a small pagoda-like structure that kept the water refreshingly cool as it was hauled up to the curb by pulley and rope.
>
> A large cast iron dinner bell mounted on a tall cedar post stood at the far end of the back porch. It was rung regularly at eleven-thirty to call the men in from the fields to their dinner. The work hors-

es, sensing the fact that the call of this bell meant "quitting time," stopped wherever they were in the fields to be taken to the barn for their corn and oats. Not only our horses but those of the neighbors as well, formed the same habit, and the mules on the old Cain farm a mile away, voiced their hearty approval of the noon hour call with long, sonorous brays. [Visitors today to the Funston Home Museum ring this same bell.]

Another innovation of Father's was the introduction of a "stile block" at the front gate. Having witnessed several disastrous attempts by ladies to climb into the high wagons of that day, Father decided to assist them by means of a stepping stone. Getting into a wagon was an undignified performance for one who esteemed herself a lady, and no one less than a trapeze performer could have qualified for such a feat. Mounting from the ground, she placed her left foot upon the hub of the wheel, her right foot upon the narrow step (if any) that projected from beneath the wagon bed, swung herself upward in a curve, in the hope of landing right side up inside the bed. If by any chance she missed her goal, she was left clinging helplessly to the side of the wagon, or else whirling around the hub in a vain effort to gain a foothold upon the ground. Such spectacular acts did not conform to the conventional standards of pioneer ladies. Father's "stile block" required but a step from stone to vehicle. With the accompanying hitching post, a horse stood close beside the stile block while its lady rider edged into her red plush sidesaddle.[12]

Ed's improvements to his prairie farm were not limited to structures. In the early years after he and his family settled there, he took an interest in landscaping. As a younger man he had once traveled for a nursery house in Rochester, New York, and thus was personally knowledgeable about the varieties of trees. Ella (Funston) Eckdall, a talented writer like her brother, Fred, described the results of Ed's application of this knowledge:

> About his home he planted cedars, elms, cottonwoods, maples and poplars, some of which became veritable giants. As a background for the house, he planted an orchard of a thousand fruit trees. He knew well the choice varieties of fruit... In the springtime when all these apple trees opened their delicate pink blossoms with those of the bright pink cherries, the snowy plums and the rosy Indian peach, it was a sight to behold. Nothing surpassed their beauty and fragrance. In time, this orchard produced wagon loads of fruit which Father freely gave away. A small cider press furnished our family with pure, sweet cider, superior in quality to any produced in recent years. Mother recalled that when this orchard was young,

an occasional deer bounded through it.

Against the south line of the front yard, Father planted two Transcendent crab trees, for both shade and fruit, a prolific red cherry tree, purple lilac bushes, a gay trumpet vine and a yellow-throated honeysuckle. These were balanced on the opposite side of the yard by Cottonwood trees, spicy-scented Currant bushes and snow-white Bridal Wreaths. Against the house were the pink Prairie Queen and the bluish Baltimore Belle roses. On either side of the back door were two immense bushes of that old favorite, the pink-petaled Cabbage rose... All this shrubbery was set in a wide bluegrass lawn confined on three sides by a white picket fence and on the front [next to the road], by a closely clipped Osage Orange hedge.

...

Along the north and west limits of the farm, Father planted an Osage Orange hedge which was always trimmed to a low height. For three successive summers he hauled water from the Deer Creek, a mile distant, to promote its growth through the dry seasons.[13]

Ed's accomplishments with his home and farm were impressive. In 1874, when Ed was a member of the Kansas House of Representatives, the editor of a Humboldt newspaper stopped at Ed's farm. He reported to his readers about this visit: "On our return we visited, for the first time, the farm of Hon. C. [sic] H. Funston, and had a few moments' chat with him. Mr. Funston has reason to be happy in the possession of a splendid farm, in a high state of cultivation—the result of his own energy and thrift—an interesting family, an excellent library of standard works, an enviable State reputation, and the respect of his neighbors. He ought to be happy, and we believe he is."[14]

Eleven years later, in 1885, when Ed was now a United States congressman, a journalist from Lawrence visited Ed at his home, and then wrote a descriptive account titled "A Man of the People," which read, in part, as follows:

But it is when you have entered the house that you catch the most pleasing glimpses of Mr. Funston's manner of life. The distractions of a public career have not yet, and never will, make him a disintegral part of his family. The charm of happy domestic environment and the congenial companionship of his little household seem to be indispensible [sic] conditions of his existence, thus furnishing proof of the truth that in the highest state of social development the family constitutes the unit of society in fact as well as in theory.

When one enters the house he becomes at once conscious of that air of comfort, harmony and good taste that marks the high tide of our civilization; the point from which its waves begin to recede towards barbarism, reaching their lowest ebb in the garish gaudery of the vulgar rich.[15]

This comfortable prairie farmhouse served as the base from which Ed Funston successfully accomplished his political ambitions. That Ed had political ambition is unsurprising. He was intelligent, articulate, well read, and lived in a new state, where there was room for a newly arrived political hopeful to compete in the electoral process. Ed, like many of his fellow inhabitants of Kansas, arrived in the years immediately following the end of the Civil War, the years in which Kansas was being settled and developed. Just as farmer Ed had broken the prairie sod on his farm, politician Ed broke into the ranks of government officialdom.

Ed started his political career at a high level—running for state office as Representative from the 47th District in the Kansas Legislature. The 47th District consisted of five Allen County townships: Geneva, Deer Creek, Osage, Iola, and Elm, and the balance of the county composed the 48th District. Subject to the decision of the "Republican Convention," Ed announced his candidacy in the September 28, 1872, issue of the *Neosho Valley Register*,[16] the predecessor of *The Iola Register*. Ed came out of the Republican County Central Committee meeting of October 8, 1872, the nominee for Representative of the 47th District.[17]

The still simmering controversy over the 1865 removal of the county seat from Humboldt to Iola soon became a part of the election campaign. Ed's Democratic opponent, Nelson F. Acers (pronounced Acres), charged that if Ed were elected, he would work in the Legislature to have the county seat returned to Humboldt, a charge meant to upset voters in Iola and in the northern part of the county, which comprised the 47th District. In a letter in response, which was published in the October 26, 1872, Iola newspaper, Ed denounced this and another allegation as "unmitigated falsehoods," stating emphatically: "If sent to the Legislature this winter I will oppose with all my strength any movement tending toward the removal of the county seat...."[18] At the election held on November 5, 1872, Ed prevailed by a majority of 108 votes, 500 to 392.[19]

Ed was re-elected at the 1873 and 1874 elections. The Salina, Kansas, *Journal* paid him these compliments in August of 1874: "He is a man of excellent good sense and with abilities far above the average. He is a clear, logical and forcible speaker, about the best of those who appeared on the floor of the House last winter."[20] At the organization of the Legislature in January of 1875, Ed was accorded the high honor of being elected Speaker of the House of Representatives. The reasons behind this election were articulated by *The Commonwealth* newspaper:

> Mr. Funston came to Topeka a very raw recruit, entirely uninformed as to the business of legislation, and without any parliamen-

tary knowledge or experience whatever. He has grown very rapidly in all practical information as well in the esteem of all having occasion or opportunity to observe the working of the legislature. He has acquired considerable skill as a forcible debater, has learned to discern with ease and precision the merits or defects of any bill, and to convey that information to his fellow members briefly and perspicuously. These are no small acquirements for a man of Mr. Funston's limited experience. But it is chiefly in his notable ability to preside with dignity, discretion and fairness that the wisdom of his choice is demonstrated.[21]

At the close of the legislative session, Ed "was highly complimented by both Republicans and Democrats for the faithful and impartial manner in which he had discharged his duties as Speaker of the House."[22]

Ed apparently did not seek re-election as Representative. After an absence of nearly five years from the legislative halls in Topeka, he threw his hat into the political ring again, but this time for an even higher position—Senator from the 17th District, which consisted of Allen and Anderson Counties. At the Republican delegate convention on August 25, 1880, Ed received twenty of the possible twenty-three votes, and thus was declared the party's nominee.[23]

On Wednesday, October 20, 1880, a "grand Republican demonstration" was held in Iola. Present were Governor John P. St. John and United States Senator Preston B. Plumb. Undoubtedly, also present was state senatorial candidate Ed Funston, and, likely, members of his family, including Fred. "All afternoon the people from the different townships came pouring into town and at five o'clock the streets were crowded with the surging mass of humanity." Over four hundred torches had been made, and these were distributed at the train depot to those designated to carry them. By 7:30 p.m. the procession, including the local band, marched from the depot to the large town square, going down Washington Avenue and then over on Madison Avenue, and then north around the public square. The procession was formed in double columns, and "[n]ot the least attractive feature of the march was the mounted horsemen nearly two hundred strong. The march was continued for nearly an hour and was confessedly the best thing in that line ever attempted," claimed the Republican *Iola Register*. Speeches were then given at a stand set up on the southwest corner of the public square. More than a thousand people were present. At the close three cheers went up for Republican presidential candidate James A. Garfield and vice presidential candidate Chester A. Arthur.[24]

Ed was handily and impressively elected Senator at the election the next month. Out of a total of 4,380 votes, he lacked only thirty-six votes from having a thousand vote majority. Ed received 2,672 votes and his opponent, 1,708 votes.[25] The following January of 1881, Ed was accorded a high honor—election as the president pro tempore of the Kansas Senate. Since he was only a first term senator, this election is particularly impressive. A biographical sketch of Ed at this time noted these qualities: "Mr. Funston is one of the strongest members of the senate. He exhibits rare powers as a parliamentarian and is a forcible speaker."[26] Although Ed's term as a Senator was four years, he was not to complete it, as we shall see later.

Ed Funston loved to entertain,[27] and thus the Funston home served as the venue through the years for many social events. Some were on a large scale. Some involved young people, including, undoubtedly, children of the Funston household. In January of 1883 during Fred's seventeenth year, *The Iola Register* reported an "enjoyable" evening party of young people at Senator Funston's residence.[28]

In the spring of 1885, Lida Funston hosted a supper for the benefit of the Ladies' Missionary Society of the Presbyterian Church. A "mite of ten cents" was expected from each attendee.[29] On the evening of June 30 of that same year, Ed, Lida, and family were surprised by the arrival of about ninety uninvited guests, all members of Iola's McCook Post of the Grand Army of the Republic, the organization of the Union veterans of the Civil War. According to *The Iola Register*, "The visit was an entire surprise to Mr. Funston and his family, but that did not hinder them from making their guests feel entirely at home, and all who were fortunate enough to be there report a most pleasant time."[30] As the *Register's* Carlyle reporter noted, "The fireworks, supper and the hospitality of E. H. and family, seemed to be appreciated by all present."[31] One wonders who furnished the supper for the ninety guests; presumably, they brought it with them.

The Funstons were not only generous to Ed's former comrades in arms, they also were generous and hospitable to a young man who had grown up in the Carlyle neighborhood before attending the State University in Lawrence. In the fall of 1885, E. F. Caldwell and his bride, née Viola McFarland, were wed in Lawrence, and then came to his old Carlyle home where his father still lived. "Mr. Funston took advantage of their visit to the groom's old home, to extend to the young couple his characteristic hospitality," reported Charlie Scott. "Those, who have experienced that hospitality, will know that nothing was left undone by the host and hostess that could contribute to the enjoyment of the company. Mr. and Mrs. Funston have a faculty, possessed by few, of making their guests feel perfectly at home, and on this evening they succeeded fully as well as usual."[32]

The Funstons were once again the subject of a surprise party at their own home in the spring of 1887. It was "quite a success."[33] Several weeks later the young ladies of the Carlyle Presbyterian Church held a "crazy tea" at the "Hon. Funston's." In describing the upcoming "crazy tea," the Carlyle reporter wrote that it would be "a performance which certainly deserves the name given. As we understand it, it is to be a crazy supper put into crazy looking dishes, upon a crazy table, to be eaten by crazy people dressed in crazy costumes, and so on indefinitely. The young ladies wish to get a new church organ, and they know how to get up an entertainment that will attract everybody."[34] In 1890, Lida hosted a carpet rag bee in her home at which twenty pounds of rags were sewn.[35]

The Funstons were amazingly hospitable. One day in the summer of 1895, they hosted twenty-two guests from Iola, and former Governor and Mrs. D. W. Finney from the town of Neosho Falls. It was "an old-fashioned country dinner," and "[o]f course there was a fine time, and of course everybody enjoyed it and was glad to be there."[36]

The most extraordinary surprise celebration at the Funston home occurred on March 28, 1901, the day that word reached Iola, and the rest of the country, that Fred had captured Aguinaldo. The account in *The Iola Daily Record* of this celebration at the Funston home is so descriptive that it is reprinted in full here, except rather than quoting the *Record's* paraphrase of Ed Funston's "little talk," the verbatim text of the "little talk" in Charlie Scott's *The Iola Daily Register* is inserted into the account below:

All the busses and several carriage loads of people went out to the home of ex-Congressman Funston's last evening to help the old folks celebrate the good news received yesterday of Gen. Funston's capture of Aguinaldo. They were headed by the band and when they arrived at the homestead Mr. Funston must have thought that a band of escaped insurgents had come to avenge themselves on him for his son's acts. Finally convinced that they meant no harm he invited them [inside] in his hospitable way. They all availed themselves of the invitation and soon the house was filled with people in all the stages of enthusiasm.

The entire lower floor was thrown open to the crowd. In one room the band was stationed playing patriotic airs while the rest of the visitors ranged themselves in other rooms and gave vent to their enthusiasm in all conceivable ways.

Soon Chas. Gardner was found and he was escorted to the piano where he gave the crowd, "Don't you make them Goo-Goo eyes at me," "She is my Filipino Lady" and other popular songs. By this time the crowd was ripe for a speech and finally after repeated calls Mr. Funston gave them a little talk.

"My friends and neighbors: I am sure that your presence here tonight is exceedingly agreeable to myself and wife. This is the proudest day in our lives. And when I say that I do not forget my own life, which has not been without its own successes. But when the sun is setting low in the life of a parent, nothing brings such deep and unmixed joy to the heart as honors to one's child.

"And I will say for Fred that he has always been a good son. I do not mean that he has lived a life prescribed by his mother and myself but that there has been no little meanness in his life, his ideals have always been high. His associates have been picked for their virtues and he has sought to accomplish something in the world, something worth doing, not something merely that would bring notoriety. I know the boy's character thoroughly—he was born in my family—and I say he was always a good boy. The success which has crowned his work I think might well teach a lesson to young men, to have an aim in life and make that aim high.

"And so this glorious news comes to us and is doubly welcome. It is welcome to us because it has brought acknowledgement from you, his neighbors, and from the people of his State and country that you are proud of him. And further it is welcome because it comes on the happy birthday of his little mother, who today celebrates her fifty-eighth year."

After a cheer for the general, the family and everything they could think of they bid them good night and departed.[37]

Chapter Five Notes, continued—*Expanding the House*

1. Ella Funston Eckdall, *The Funston Homestead* (Emporia, Kansas: Raymond Lees, 1949), 3.

2. Ode C. Nichols, "Funston, From Babyhood to Present Day as His Mother Knows Him," *The World*, May 21, 1899. Nichols had been a Lieutenant in Troop M., First Volunteer Cavalry (Rough Riders) (FFP).

3. Untitled one page writing by Ella (Funston) Eckdall listing the original four rooms and describing the furniture in various rooms (Eckdall miscellaneous material donated in 2004). Allen County Historical Society, Inc.

4. Eckdall, *The Funston Homestead*, 11.

5. Scale diagram of the first and second floors of the Funston Home prepared while the house was owned by the Kansas State Historical Society. Copy at the Allen County Historical Society, Inc.

6. Scale diagram of the first and second floors of the Funston Home prepared while the house was owned by the Kansas State Historical Society. Copy at the Allen County Historical Society, Inc.

   The portieres reference in the chapter text is based on the fashion in which Ella (Funston) Eckdall restored the house before giving it to the State of Kansas. In 1994-1995, when the Funston house was restored as a museum in Iola, Kansas, these portieres were in poor shape, and thus were replaced by a set owned by the Allen County Historical Society, Inc. This set came originally from the large home of Iola pioneer merchant, A. W. Beck, at 606 East Street, Iola, Kansas.

   The description of Ed in his chair is the logical conclusion from the placement of his desk and chair in his study in the Funston Home Museum (this placement was originally made by Ella (Funston) Eckdall).

7. "Carlyle Correspondence," *The Iola Register*, May 18, 1883.

8. "Carlyle Correspondence," *The Iola Register*, June 22, 1883.

9. "Carlyle Correspondence," *The Iola Register*, August 7, 1885. While the Funston house was still "up in the air" from its move on July 28, 1994, to the Iola town square, I asked the workers to inspect from below the parlor portion and the "spare bedroom" portion. They advised that the latter had clearly been completed later than the former. Thus, the 1885 addition must be of the "spare bedroom."

10. Eckdall, *The Funston Homestead*, 11-12.

11. "Local Matters," *The Iola Register*, October 30, 1885.

12. Eckdall, *The Funston Homestead*, 12-13. The date of construction of the tenant house comes from "Carlyle Correspondence," *The Iola Register*, August 19, 1887.

13. Eckdall, The Funston Homestead, 7-8.

14. "Geneva," *The Rural Kansan*, July 1874 (Vol. I, No. 9), 279. This was published at Humboldt, Kansas, by D. B. Emmert, editor and publisher. A bound volume of issues, from October 1873 to November 1874, is at the Iola Public Library, Iola, Kansas.

15. "A Man of the People," *The Lawrence Daily Journal*, October 4, 1885.

16. E. H. Funston's response to published letter to him, *Neosho Valley Register*, September 28, 1872.

17. "Proceedings Of Republican Central Committee," *Neosho Valley Register*, October 12, 1872.

18. Letter to "Editor Register" from E. H. Funston, *Neosho Valley Register*, October 26, 1872.

19. "Official Vote of Allen County," *Neosho Valley Register*, November 16, 1872.

20. "Unjust," *Neosho Valley Register*, August 1, 1874 (reprint from Salina *Journal* editorial).

21. "The Working of a Caucus," *The Commonwealth* [Topeka, Kansas], January 13, 1875.

22. *The Iola Register*, March 13, 1875.

23. "Senatorial Convention," *The Iola Register*, September 3, 1880.

24. "The Grand Rally," *The Iola Register*, October 22, 1880.

25. *The Iola Register*, December 5, 1880.

26. "Hon. E. H. Funston" sketch in "Biographical Sketches of Senators and Representatives of the Kansas Legislature of 1881," *The Daily Capital*, March 3, 1881 (FFP).

27. Frank Funston Eckdall (1907-2000), nephew of Frederick Funston, in conversation with this author.

28. "Carlyle Cuts," *The Iola Register*, January 26, 1883.

29. "Carlyle Correspondence," *The Iola Register*, April 11, 1885.

30. "Local Matters," *The Iola Register*, July 3, 1885.

31. "Carlyle Correspondence," *The Iola Register*, July 3, 1885.

32. "Local Matters," *The Iola Register*, October 30, 1885. Unfortunately, Viola Caldwell died less than two years later, leaving her husband and an 8-month-old baby ("Local Matters," *The Iola Register*, August 5, 1887).

33. "Carlyle Correspondence," *The Iola Register*, April 1, 1887.

34. "Carlyle Correspondence," *The Iola Register*, May 6 and May 13, 1887.

35. "Carlyle Siftings," *The Iola Register*, May 9, 1890.

36. "The Week's News," *The Iola Register*, July 5, 1895. Editor Charlie Scott attended and wrote the account.

37. "Helped Them Celebrate," *The Iola Daily Record*. March 23, 1899, is written above this article in Ella (Funston) Eckdall's handwriting, but this cannot be correct (FFP Micro). "At The Funston Home," *The Iola Daily Register*, March 29, 1901.

   The piano belonged to Lida Funston and was hauled from Kansas City by ox team to the farm after the Funstons settled there. This oversized piece of furniture in the tiny sitting room caused comment among the neighbors, one of whom commented, "That's the biggest sewing machine I've ever seed [sic]" (Eckdall, *The Funston Homestead*, 6).

Fred's Personality

"Funston, From Babyhood to Present Day as His Mother Knows Him" is the account in *The World* newspaper of an extensive interview in May of 1899 with Lida Funston. It provides significant detail about the childhood and personality of Ed and Lida's oldest child, Fred, then age thirty-three. The interviewer, Ode C. Nichols, a young man residing in Iola, had, the prior year, served as a "Rough Rider" with Colonel Teddy Roosevelt in the Spanish-American War.

Nichols met Lida at the Funston farmhouse, which he described as "completely bowered in young trees and shrubs." There, "a gentle-faced lady with a low voice and the sweetest smile imaginable told me all about her boy..." She was "the quiet little mother of the quiet little hero of the Philippines." Lida recalled how Fred as a little boy picked out the ABCs on the signs as he traveled by train from Ohio to Kansas. She then elaborated on her memories of his childhood:

"I don't see why there is so much talk about him. He's only a soldier who has done his duty. No, he was not a remarkable boy. He helped about the farm when he got big enough and—yes, I can remember that he was always and forever whistling—except once when a bee stung his upper lip. If Fred didn't whistle he was ill.

Fred wasn't the brightest boy in school, nor was he by any means at the bottom of his classes. What he learned he remembered well. His greatest delight was to get a little time off from his work to go fishing or swimming in Deer Creek.

The little white schoolhouse down there, just on the edge of the timber belt—that's where he went. He never fought with the other boys, was never punished by his teachers. He was fond of reading, especially books on natural history, botany, mining, agriculture—very few novels. He was interested in accounts of wars.

Since he was sixteen, Fred has always subscribed to some humorous publication. He loves a joke, but seldom makes one....

In all his school days, he never stood either at the top or bottom of his class. He was very quiet, and did not have much to do with the girls. I've been told that he never studied more than he had to. He bought a good many books and we have some here."[1]

In the early years, after the Funstons arrived on the farm in 1868, the prairie land was a range for cattle, which were allowed to roam freely. "Great herds of long-horned, wild-eyed cattle ranged the prairies. Often the cattle would come in great droves past the house, and Mrs. Funston would gather in her babies and lock the doors, terrified by the creatures with such signature horns."[2]

Under Kansas law, the farmer was required to build a fence to keep neighboring ranchers' cattle out of the farmer's crops. The underlying factor behind this law was the determination of who would have to bear the expenses of fence building—the farmer to keep his neighbor's livestock out of the farmer's fields, or the rancher to keep his livestock penned in and thus away from the farmer's crops. The law at the time placed the financial responsibility on the farmer. In the Herd Law of 1872, however, Kansas provided the option for each county to decide whether it would have a herd law. Adoption of a herd law would require the rancher to build the fence. Allen County never adopted this law, and thus the building of fences continued to be the responsibility of the farmer.[3] Ed Funston's cows were among those roaming the prairie in search of food:

> Fred was the cowboy of the family. Sometimes he would have to go for miles to find the little herd and drive them home in the evening for milking. Off he would go, whistling, through the wild prairie grass, which was many inches higher than his head, to find the cows and bring them home. Often night would fall and the whistling boy would still be away in search of the cows. On these occasions his mother would become apprehensive and to still her fears the future Congressman would go in search of his son.
>
> "One day," said his father, "while Fred was looking for the cows darkness came and I went to find him. I knew he had gone off toward Lije Lowe's place and I went in that direction. I had gone a mile when I heard a cowbell. I listened and recognized the bell, and I knew by the regular tinkle of it that the cows were on a steady march home and that Fred was with them. I waited and soon I heard his whistling tune."[4]

In the interview with both of Fred's parents by *The Chicago Sunday Tribune* reporter in May 1899, this conversation between them occurred:

> "He was always whistling," said his mother, "whenever he was at work or going anywhere."
>
> "Yes, and I wouldn't give a snap," said his father, "for a boy who didn't whistle and who wasn't freckled."
>
> "But Fred was not freckled much."
>
> "No, but he made up for it by whistling more."[5]

Some believed that there was more to whistling than the act itself. "Whistling as an Indication of Character" was the title of an article in the October 23, 1875, issue of *The Iola Register*:

> An old farmer once said to us that he would not have a hired man on his farm who did not habitually whistle. He always hired whistlers. Said he never knew a whistling laborer to find fault with

his food, his bed, or complain of any little extra work he was asked to perform. Such a man was generally kind to children and to animals in his care... He never knew a whistling hired man to kick or beat a cow or drive her on the run into a stable. He had noticed that the sheep he fed in the yard and shed gathered around him as he whistled, without fear.

He never employed a whistler who was not thoughtful and economical. That this farmer's philosophy is generally correct is true. A cheerful, hopeful, buoyant man is sure to get through this life more smoothly and with less friction than one of those chaps with acute angles and rasp like sides to their characters.[6]

Fred's whistling went with his cheerfulness. According to his sister Ella, "You know father always said that Fred was a very cheerful boy and that he performed his duties and tasks at home without complaint. He seemed to get so much happiness and enjoyment out of life."[7] One day when Ella was a small child, Fred invited her to go fishing with him. When they reached the top of the meadow, which was about halfway to their destination of Deer Creek, Ella realized that Fred had said nothing to her. Fred, barefooted and with his overalls rolled up to his knees, did not talk, since he "was swelled up almost enough to burst just whistling, whistling all the way."[8]

Fred's love of swimming was an important part of his life. "Fred Funston used to say that the finest swimming place on earth was in the shadow of the big maples where Deer Creek winds near to the Maple Grove schoolhouse."[9] This was where Fred learned to swim. "It is rated the last testing place of a swimmer's skill. It is deep and currentless, and it has a swirling eddy at the lower end of the 'hole.' Fred Funston could swim through this eddy on his back, and he could dive halfway across the widest part of the hole."[10] Interestingly, he did not swim with the broad, slow strokes of the "sailor fashion," but instead swam with the quick, nervous, jerky strokes of "dog fashion." And yet Fred was clearly a strong swimmer. As William Allen White recalled, "Full many times and oft, has the Colonel stood above the ice houses on the Kaw, near Lawrence, clad in the evening sunset glow, and after taking precaution against cramps, has plunged into the raging flood and dashed over to the sand bar."[11]

Fred had a muscular strength and agility that stood him in good stead. But he was not to be the only future famous Allen Countian who gained his strength and endurance from the hard work of farming. Legendary baseball great and Hall of Fame member Walter "The Big Train" Johnson was born on a Neosho River bottom farm between Iola and Humboldt in 1887, and he attributed his tremendous strength and endurance to the hard work of the farm and the wholesome outdoor life he experienced.[12]

Swimmers would have been nude, but apparently that did not cause a problem. Likely, the Deer Creek swimming hole was sufficiently secluded that the swimmers were not visible to passersby. Such was not the case with those who crossed Elm Creek at the ford southeast of Iola. The author of a letter to the editor of *The Iola Register* in June of 1878 complained: "[O]f late, I almost invariably find from one to a dozen naked boys playing in the water or on the banks of the creek, many of whom are old enough to be ashamed of such public indecency. Last Sabbath, persons traveling this road to attend church in Iola, found the creek full of these nude bathers... If it cannot be stopped by law, I would, through the columns of your paper, ask the parents of your town to see to it that their boys may not thus disgrace them."[13]

Fred was also a fisherman. Allegedly, he caught more catfish in Deer Creek than any other boy in Carlyle Township (formed out of Deer Creek Township). "He would go to a place on the bank of Deer Creek with one pocket filled with fishhooks, another filled with bait, and a book under his arm and stay till sundown," remembered Lida, who spoke of Fred's fishing prowess to the reporter in 1899: "'He always came home with a large string of fish,' said his mother, smiling. 'He had more patience than the other boys when he went fishing.'"[14]

Lida had said in her interview that Fred "never fought with the other boys," but that does not appear to have been the case. Perhaps she was unaware of this aspect of her son's life or, if aware, chose to ignore it. In the account in *The Chicago Sunday Tribune* containing the interview of both parents, that reporter noted that Fred had a great interest in trading for old revolvers. Other young men in Carlyle Township envied Fred and his rather odd collection—odd because "[m]any of them were old and rusty and broken and had the peculiarity of letting all the chambers off whenever one was fired." According to this reporter, none of the young men of the township "says that Fred Funston ever developed any bloodthirsty inclinations by reason of his armament." Furthermore, they characterized Fred as follows:

> These same young men will unhesitatingly bear testimony that Fred Funston was never quarrelsome and never sought unfair advantage in a fight. But he would fight. He was small, but he was wiry, and although he would now and then get licked he would fight again.
>
> One day he went to Iola with his father. Because he lived outside the confines of the little town the town boys called him "a country jake" and waited for a chance to give him a thrashing. After some maneuvering they caught him away from his father and surrounded him. He was smaller than any of his assailants, but he didn't

cry for quarter. He dodged into the street and got a stone and stood off the crowd until a benevolent citizen came along and ordered an armistice.[15]

Fred himself provided evidence of his fighting when he was a student at Maple Grove School. In 1893, he noted that "some fifteen years ago, I was considered a pretty fair sprinter, especially when I got more than I could handle in a fist fight..."[16]

Ella (Funston) Eckdall wrote about another incident: "If Father had one besetting sin, it was in constantly extolling the virtues of his own brood—not that he really believed it himself but as a spur to further efforts." On one occasion, when Fred and Burt were young, Lida's brother, Asa Mitchell of Ohio, was visiting at the Funston farm. "Father just about exhausted his vocabulary of laudable terms in describing the extraordinary qualities of his offspring. Drawing himself up to his full height and swelling with pride, he said, 'Asa, come with me, I want to show you my two fine boys, Fred and Burt, how faithfully they work in the fields from morn 'till night, never once resting until the job is finished.'" When they reached the field, to Ed's horror "[t]here in the field stood an idle team of horses with the reins down, while the 'two fine sons,' obscured in a whirlwind of dust, were slugging it out in a free-for-all, knock-down fight. Father's face was red as he walked slowly homeward, and his boastful pride somewhat deflated, but he still contended that these were two of the 'finest of sons.'"[17]

Fred was a voracious reader, as noted by his mother. Fred first read the books in his father's library, including *The Boyhood of Great Men* by J. G. Edgar, and then borrowed books from neighbors, including a Mrs. Cummings. She lent Fred the book *Cook's Voyage Around the World.* As Burt Funston recalled, however, this was the first book that Fred "read through" and that he was a very young boy at the time.[18] He also borrowed books from William Alexander Johnson, an attorney who lived in Garnett, twenty-five miles to the north, but who, as legal counsel, appeared at times in the courts at Iola. Johnson had one of the finest law libraries in Kansas.[19] Perhaps Fred had some interest at one time in studying the law.

After Fred's death, his brothers, Burt and Pogue, recalled that the chief feature of Fred's childhood was that he was always reading. He read history and adventure. If he was not reading, then he was at his father's knee hearing the tales of the war in which Ed had fought. Fred also read everything that he could obtain of a military nature.[20] Fred's drawings as a child were always of soldiers, cannons, and deer.[21] *The Chicago Sunday Tribune* reporter described Fred's actions when plowing his father's fields: "He used to carry a book hid in the bosom of his hickory shirt when he went to the fields to plow. He never was known to neglect the plowing, but when it was time to give the horses a rest he would open his book to read."[22]

The extent of Fred's reading is amazing, since it included all of his father's library and his neighbors' books. He read at home, at work in the fields, and at play fishing. According to *The Chicago Sunday Tribune* reporter in 1899, Fred "devoted so much time to reading that his father sought to divert him from books. He used to call him 'my little newspaper crank [enthusiast].'" The reporter further noted that "[f]or a long while the little room that serves as a library was kept locked to keep Fred from the books."[23] The library, however, has no door to it, just a broad open doorway with portieres. Thus, the room would not have been locked, but Fred may have been forbidden access to Ed's extensive library located there. Fred was allowed, however, to read the newspapers that came to the Funston home. This would be logical, since that would keep Fred abreast of the events of the larger world, and thus help to make him a well-informed young man which, presumably, his educated parents would have desired. This had an interesting consequence:

> His father received the Congressional Record, and for lack of room on the shelves they were stowed under Fred's bed. His father never supposed he would find anything [to] interest him, or that any boy on earth would read the Congressional Record. He didn't know this until he was elected to Congress [in 1884]. His election was to fill an unexpired term made vacant in December. The election was not held until February. A question was raised as to when the pay of Congressman-elect Funston would begin. The lawyers in Iola were talking about it, but nobody could decide the question. It was one of importance, as a salary of $5,000 a year would naturally be to any farmer. One day the family was discussing the question at the dinner table.
>
> "Why, pa, your pay begins in December," said Fred.
>
> "What time in December?" asked his father, who doubted the decision of the question that had stumped Lawyer Foust and the other authorities of Iola.
>
> "The date of your predecessor's death," said the youth.
>
> "How do you know that?"
>
> "I read in the Congressional Record: the decision of a case exactly like yours."
>
> The number of the Record was pulled out from under the bed and the decision was found and the Congressman-elect went to bed happy that night.[24]

In 1899, Ed Funston described his eldest son in these words: "The only extraordinary thing about Fred that I know of was his willingness to do all the farm work and get down to study when the farm work was done. He always had a great fondness for books and newspapers. He was away up on statistics and helped me along in my Congressional campaign." Ed also noted on another occasion that "he was never a bad boy, but never got into much trouble on account of being too good."[25]

At some point in his life, perhaps as a child but more likely as an adult, Fred learned to multi-task, as it is known today. While in his "apartments" at a Kansas City hotel in 1899 prior to attending a celebratory dinner in honor of the Twentieth Kansas, Fred "gave an exhibition of his Napoleonic way of doing a dozen things at once. While a barber trimmed his beard he dictated a letter, received telegrams and cards, dispatched bellboys on errands, talked to a group of friends that surrounded him and gave an interview to a newspaper man." He had had a very busy day, and concern was expressed that he "would be nearly worn out." Fred responded: "You can't wear me out... I am not easily tired."[26]

Fred's sister, Ella, provided insight into his love of nature during his childhood. On one occasion, Fred called to her attention the "brilliancy" of a redbird's scarlet coat and the loveliness of its singing. On another occasion, when Ella was going to pluck one of her mother's radiant tulips, Fred stopped her hand, saying "Don't pluck it, for you take it's [sic] life and it dies."[27]

On a Sunday afternoon in the spring of 1870, 4-year-old Fred and his father wandered over the meadows to the woodlands by Deer Creek. After wading in the water, Fred pulled a living cottonwood sapling from the soft sand along the creek bank. He took it home as a memento of the day's adventure, and planted it near the house. A pious old Presbyterian neighbor, "Uncle Jimmy" Caldwell, observed the sapling, and, shaking his finger, predicted that the little tree would not grow because it had been planted on a Sunday. In reality, the tree grew to be a magnificent specimen, which survived until at least the late 1930s.[28]

Fred's love of flowers was lifelong. When he was stationed at Fort Leavenworth, Kansas, his and Eda's home was surrounded with flower beds and flowering shrubs. When he had time, he worked in the flower beds and watered the flowers himself. He was especially fond of tulips.[29] Fred grew plants in the basement of their home wherever he and Eda lived, and then brought them upstairs to blossom.[30] After Fred's death, a Funston Memorial Day was held at the old Funston homestead as a part of a state encampment of Spanish War veterans and auxiliaries. In front of the house was a cross of flowers. Fred's widow, Eda, wrote at that time to the veterans of Fred's Twentieth Kansas Volunteers: "The cross of flowers is more appropriate perhaps than you realize for Gen. Funston loved flowers. Wherever we were stationed we always had a garden to which he gave his personal attention."[31] Fred's interest was greater than raising only flowers. When he was stationed at St. Louis, Eda laughingly noted in an interview shortly after they moved there, "The General thinks he is going to cultivate vegetables and raise chickens next summer."[32]

Fred appears to have been utterly daring at times: "'I remember,' said Mr. [E. F.] Caldwell, 'that when we were both boys we used to catch a wild calf, I would hold it and [Fred] would get on. As soon as he was on I would hand him the calf's tail and the greatest show on earth was small beside what followed.'"[33] What a colorful example of both Fred's physical strength and fearlessness.

In February of 1874, when Fred was eight years old, Iola's *Neosho Valley Register* reported this news:

> A story is in circulation that there is a panther in the woods south of town, that he has killed pigs, and we believe a calf or two, and has been heard to cry and scream like a woman, beside doing many more things that would have a tendency to frighten children. Some of our Nimrods having heard this story determined to go for this child-frightener; so on last Friday all the old muskets were got out and greased and away they went, with powder in their pouch and blood in their eye—don't know whether they had anything else in their flask or not. They roamed around a good portion of the day, found the track of something that resembled a half-grown dog, followed it awhile, and returned home convinced that the panther talked about is nothing more than a wildcat, catamount or lynx. Whatever the thing may be, it is still at large, and persons who have a big brood of chickens should teach them to roost high, and besides small boys should be kept at home in the evening.[34]

This panther story apparently inspired Fred's friend, Roy Fetherngill, and two other neighbor boys to "tell tall tales of a panther that haunted the Deer Creek woods."[35] Ella (Funston) Eckdall told what happened next:

> Fred and Burt, who scoffed at such wild stories and boasted of their fearlessness of this savage creature, shouldered their guns one evening at dusk and made for the woods. Knowing the plans of the two boys to investigate for themselves, the three neighbor boys concealed themselves in a high tree in the woods and awaited the arrival of Fred and Burt. When the two boys were well within the woods, the boys in the tree let out the most blood-curdling cries, so that Fred and Burt, terror stricken, took to their heels and made for home at lightening [sic] speed, not waiting for further proof. They leaped over fences, fearing to look behind lest the furious beast might be upon them at any moment. In his great haste Burt

dropped his gun, but feared to retrace his steps until some days later. When they reached home and had recovered their breath and senses, they were troubled as to what would be their father's reaction to their late return—10 p.m., when they had promised to be back much earlier. They decided that the corn crib would be the safest refuge until their father's wrath had turned to anxiety, when they would emerge as heroes and relate their narrow escape from the jaws of an angry beast.[36]

Neighbor girl Adda Adams recalled more than seventy-five years later this panther incident: "I remember Fred telling about the blood-curdling cries in the woods, at school the next day. He said the cries sounded like a woman was screaming from being dragged through briers by her hair."[37] A couple of years later a wiser and fearless Fred had a very different hunting adventure:

> When 10 years of age Funston organized the small boys of Iola for a coon hunt. The larger boys of the neighborhood heard of the project and being sore because they were not invited determined to break up the expedition.
>
> Accordingly, when the youngsters had ventured into the dark forest and were beating about for the quarry, all of a sudden, right near them, there arose a terrific din, the noise of wild animals snarling, fighting tearing each other to pieces. The sound was blood curdling and the 10 year-old hunters did not stop to investigate. They fled; every mothers boy of them, except one.
>
> Ten-year-old Fred Funston stood in his tracks and bringing his light rifle to his shoulder began firing away, with might and main, at the direction of the sounds. The noise stopped as suddenly as it had begun and a dozen badly scared big boys went pounding pell-mell away from Fred Funston's bullets. Thereafter no attempt was ever made to scare or deter him.[38]

Although Fred was to be fearless as a soldier, that did not mean that he was not nervous before a battle. He described his mental and physical conditions candidly: "I always had the nervous jim-jams before I went into a fight, and I always had nervous prostration after it was over." After one battle in the Philippines, "Col. Funston fell, completely prostrated from the exertion and the exciting experiences he had undergone," wrote Charlie Scott, who compared Fred to "the blooded horse that runs until it drops!"[39]

In telling in *The Funston Homestead* the account about the panther, Ella introduced it as "one of my brother, [sic] Fred's stories." Undoubtedly, Fred enjoyed telling and re-telling this story even though it did not put him in the best light since he and Burt had fled from the putative panther. Ella does not mention the second incident where Fred dramatically took charge of the situation. Presumably, she had heard Fred tell this story, but, in view of Fred's modesty and self-deprecating humor, he likely told it infrequently, at best. The first story of the panther, but not the second story, would be in the category that Charlie Scott described when he wrote that Fred had "a rare gift for narrating his own experiences, particularly when a humorous twist could be given to them."[40]

The Funston home was tobacco-and-alcohol-free. In 1871, when Ed was 35 years old, a doctor told Ed that smoking had given him heart trouble. Ed was "man enough to never touch it once afterward." He had such a great willpower that he continued to carry tobacco in his pocket and thus could smell it. He did this "to show himself that he was master of himself," recalled his daughter, Ella. As for Fred, he did not take up smoking until the last couple of years of his life.[41] Presumably, the members of Ed's family did not smoke in view of his attitude on the subject.

Ed was one of the first politicians in Kansas to espouse the cause of prohibition.[42] Its goal was to prohibit the use of intoxicating liquors by Kansans, and such was the situation in the Funston household. In 1878, Republican prohibitionist John St. John was elected Kansas governor, and in November of 1880 a constitutional amendment prohibiting "the manufacture and sale of intoxicating liquors" was ratified by a majority of the voters. The Kansas legislature put some teeth into the amendment by making manufacturing alcohol a misdemeanor. This criminal penalty became effective on Sunday, May 1, 1881, and had consequences in Iola.[43] The brewery located at the foot of the large mound south of Elm Creek, then-owned by Dick Schindler, was still in business. On the night before the amendment's effective date, "[t]he men hauled kegs of beer to the top of the mound and celebrated all night."[44] *The Iola Register* reported that night's activities in these words: "There was a high old time at the brewery Saturday night, we are informed."[45]

Like other boys in the neighborhood, Fred apparently was mischievous at times. According to Ora Dunlap, a neighbor boy when Fred was growing up, Fred participated during the night in "pulling" the "large, sweet" watermelons raised by Garrett Brewster, who lived on a farm on the other side of Carlyle Township.[46]

As he matured, Fred changed one part of his personality. As a little boy, he had a "quick temper, which he later learned to curb, or control." On one occasion when Fred was in a hurry, he tripped on the rocker of a chair and retaliated by kicking the chair.[47] At some now unknown point, Fred mastered his temper.

An important part of Fred's life that his mother did not mention was hunting. In the words of Charlie Scott's brother, Angelo, hunting was "the king of sports" during his boyhood days in the Carlyle neighborhood.

"With the coming of the grain fields, the quail multiplied enormously, and the low-growing Osage-orange hedges which surrounded every farm gave them a favorite though precarious cover." Doves were "everywhere," but were not considered game birds so they were not shot. Cottontail rabbits were so numerous that they were a "nuisance."[48] The choicest game, however, was the prairie chicken. Their abundance in Allen County was great. In 1870, when three civil engineers involved in building the railroad through the county decided to go hunting, they shot "probably 12 dozen or more."

Angelo Scott described how to hunt prairie chickens:

> These birds were at their best for food when about three-fourths grown; they were a delicacy of the first order. But at that stage they could hardly be called game birds. They were found exclusively in the open prairie or in the grown-up stubblefields, and while they had a peculiar "shake" in flight, they always flew straight away, and anybody could bring them down.
>
> But when they were full grown and had separated into pairs and flew high and far, it took real marksmanship to stop that flight....
>
> At that adult stage, too, they frequented the corn-fields where the stalks [s]till stood, and it was exciting sport to stalk them from afar, first crouching stealthily along and then crawling on the stomach until the range was sure; then the lifting on the elbows and the quick discharge.[49]

About 1870, at age twelve and thirteen, Scott was allowed to go with his "older brothers and other 'big boys' on all-night rides through the woods on 'possum hunts. These were highlights in any boy's life."[50]

Fred hunted with a double barrel, muzzle-loading shotgun, the barrels of which were 32 ⅝-inches in length. Fred went hunting daily when one of his brothers was ill and required broth each day. Daily hunting was necessary since there was inadequate refrigeration to keep the meat fresh.[51] Perhaps the brother's illness was Burt's, when he was ill with a fever, and the Funstons' "old dog, Ring, parked himself beneath the sick boy's window, and voiced his grief in loud and mournful yowls throughout the night." This led a superstitious neighbor to say, "Mrs. Funston, when a dog howls beneath a sick person's window, that person will surely die."[52] Burt died in 1948 at age eighty-one.[53]

In the context of "all his school days," Fred's mother noted in her newspaper interview that "[h]e was very quiet, and did not have much to do with the girls." As for Fred's relationship with the girls at Maple Grove School, there appear, however, to have been two female classmates that Fred was romantically attracted to. In the account in *The Chicago Sunday Tribune* in May of 1899 which contained the interview with both of

Fred's parents, these affairs were described by the reporter as "gentle affairs of less mature years, but they were sufficient to be still remembered by those who knew the parties." Fred's first romantic interest was Gertie Christian, but ultimately she "failed to see the greatness that was in him, and she elected to go to the church sociables and parties thereabout with another..." Gertie was replaced in Fred's heart for awhile by Lizzie Shreck. She, too, passed from the scene. Both Gertie and Lizzie married other men.[54] One wonders if they ever regretted passing on Fred once he became nationally famous in 1899.

Lida had described her first born as "very quiet" in his school days at Maple Grove School. That may have been his general demeanor, but he possessed quite a sense of humor. One of his classmates, who became acquainted with Fred when the latter was 14-years-old, said that "Fred was recognized as a thorough student bubbling over with fun and full of all sorts of practical jokes. He always saw the funny side of any situation and was quick to analyze the situation."[55] Lida noted in her interview that since the time Fred was 16-years-old, "he had always subscribed to some humorous publication. He loves a joke, but seldom makes one." His jokes may have been infrequent, but his droll observations as a youth precipitated roaring laughter from his father.[56] Fred was the only one of the six Funston children who was not overawed by their father with his large physical size and equally large personality.[57]

In fact, Fred and Ed appear to have been similar in personality. Ed as a young schoolteacher in Hopewell, Indiana, "was fond of a joke and pranks generally."[58] His daughter Ella remembered that "he possessed a rare sense of humor, for no one enjoyed an amusing story or a witty joke more than he."[59] How nice for the father and son to share a sense of humor. They also both played the flute.[60] They undoubtedly had intellectually stimulating discussions about the content of various of the fine literature contained in Ed's library. As a cheerful, hardworking boy on the farm, Fred would have gained the admiration and appreciation of his equally hardworking father. Ed's pride in his sons, Fred and Burt, was noted in Ella's account of the fight between the two brothers in the field. Fred respected his father, in whom he often confided.[61]

Rather than feeling he was in his father's shadow, Fred was like many boys—he simply wanted to emulate his father with his many achievements and talents, which he admired. Fred's nephew, Frank Funston Eckdall (1907–2000), and I concur in this assessment. As Mr. Eckdall said when we spoke, "Fred realized his father's eminence and liked to be like him, like a son would be with a father."[62] Frank Funston Eckdall's sister, Lida (Eckdall) Lees (1906–1991), summarized the father–son relationship succinctly: "Despite the difference in size, he was never uneasy or awed by his large father and they were great friends, as well as father and son."[63] As children of Fred's sister Ella, Frank Funston Eckdall and Lida (Eckdall) Lees were in a position to know the nature of the père-fils relationship.

Fred was devoted to his mother. *The Chicago Sunday Tribune* reporter, in his 1899 interview of Ed and Lida, recorded this exchange between them:

> "Fred loves his mother," said the elder Funston. "He sent all of these things to her." [The house was "elaborately garnished...with furs, carvings, and curios from the many lands in which the soldier son has sought adventures."]
>
> "And to Ella," added Mrs. Funston.
>
> "Yes. All of his letters and telegrams are sent to his mother. He never sends me anything."
>
> "Why, he sent you a pair of sealskin gloves from Alaska," said Mrs. Funston.
>
> "That's so; he did, the rascal. I don't want him to send anything to me. I want him to keep on sending everything to his mother and loving his mother just as he does, so I can continue to think the more of him."[64]

Wherever Fred was, he wrote letters to his mother.[65] Almost all of Fred's letters to his parents which have survived are addressed solely to his mother. In a 1914 editorial titled "His Mother," the editor of an unidentified newspaper noted Fred's return to his maternal home after completing his military service in the United States' occupation of Vera Cruz, Mexico:

> The little woman of Iola was at the station when the train pulled in. That the short, thick-set man who sprang from the rear platform was the hero of Vera Cruz, the captor of Aguinaldo, and one of the most famous fighting men of modern times, didn't seem to count for much to the little woman who was waiting. She was looking only for Fred Funston—her boy.
>
> Funston spied her in the crowd of town's folk who had gathered to do him respectful homage. Deeds of valor were forgotten as he swept her into his arms. Major General Frederick Funston, U.S.A., was with his mother.
>
> The picture is compelling in the sweetness of its charm.
>
> And is there not a new–old philosophy behind the picture?
>
> Long ago 'twas said that "every great man had a mother"—and the inspired meaning of the epigram has never been disputed or misread. Another epigram, however, should travel as its correlary [sic], "No great man ever forgot his mother." And you'll find the second just as constant as the first.

"No great man ever forgot his mother."...
Funston but exemplified an universal truth.[66]

When Fred was injured in an automobile accident in San Francisco in 1905, Lida traveled there to see him. His father noted that "his son's injuries were not serious, but that 'mother just wanted to see her boy.'"[67] As a military commander, Fred was angered by the number of his soldiers who failed to write to their parents. He received letters from mothers asking about their sons. "Many a soldier boy has had a 'dressing down' for failing to write to his mother."[68] Fred allowed no one to interfere with his conversation with his mother when he was visiting with her at her home. On one occasion while he was there, he answered the phone to find a reporter who asked if General Funston was there. "Yes, I'm here and I'll not talk on the Mexican question. Five experts [newspapermen] tried it today and failed. I'm visiting with my mother and I don't want to be disturbed."[69]

Ed asserted that "[a]ll of Fred's good qualities he got from his mother."[70] Lida blushed when Ed said this. Ella (Funston) Eckdall summarized Lida's feelings for her first born: "She loved all of her children but she was very proud of Fred and she should have been as every mother should be of a worthy son."[71]

A final aspect of Fred's personality—his physical attributes. As with much else about him, completely erroneous information was published at times. In one newspaper article, he was described as having "very black eyes and very red hair."[72] What an image! But wrong on both points. His eyes were blue, according to his nephew, Frank Funston Eckdall, and niece, Lida (Eckdall) Lees.[73] Frank Eckdall described his uncle's hair as "reddish," not red. The "reddish" color was not a strong red, he said. A Kansas State University librarian described Fred as having "brown, wavy hair, blue eyes, and an intriguing laugh." David Potter, in the biography commissioned by Eda Funston, described Fred's hair as "reddish-brown" or chestnut.[74]

As for other physical characteristics as an adult, his hat size was 7¼ and his shoe size was a 7.[75] Interestingly, we know the exact dimensions of the shoes that he wore to capture Aguinaldo: 6 ⅛" high; 3 ⅝" wide; and 10" long. "The dimensions were obtained from the top of the high tops to the bottom of the heel, the widest portion of the sole and the length of the sole plus a slight overhang on the back of the heel."[76] One of Fred's college fraternity brothers noted that Fred "has remarkably small feet and hands..."[77] In *The Chicago Sunday Tribune* interview of 1899, the reporter commented that Fred "has hands and feet so small that the girls of Iola always envy him them."[78] According to Charlie Scott in 1899, Fred had "a chest girth of thirty-eight inches—plenty of room for lungs and other necessaries."[79] In view of his small physical stature, a 38-inch chest would be large. Another contemporary observed that Fred was "broad in the shoulders, slight in the waist, heavily hipped, short of stature..."[80]

Fred's most obvious physical characteristic was, of course, his short height—five feet, four inches.[81] His own attitude about this evolved over time. In 1888, when he was twenty-two, he was still sensitive about this fact, but, by 1898, according to Charlie Scott, "he has gotten bravely over it since..."[82] In the words of Fred's niece, Lida Lees, "Although Frederick wasn't tall, one of his friends said that he just didn't let it bother him. 'Just took it in his stride,' was what he said."[83] As to how Fred had "gotten bravely over" being sensitive about his short height, that is a tale to be told in the balance of our story of his adventurous early life. A telling image of Fred's short height after he became famous occurred when he was in a crowd of admirers: "Persons even though they be tall must stand on tiptoes to see him, because where Funston is there is a deep hole in the crowd as he is so much shorter than everyone else."[84]

As for Fred's weight, he weighed no more than one hundred twenty pounds until he was middle-aged.[85] The Omaha, Nebraska, *Bee* had this interesting take on Fred's weight in 1899: "Colonel Fred Funston is a small man, but his fighting weight is evidently in the neighborhood of a ton."[86] At the time of a huge welcome for the Twentieth Kansas soldiers in Kansas City in 1899, a reporter noted: "As Brigadier General Frederick Funston sat in a carriage that drew up in front of the Coates House yesterday, he was a living example of the fact that mere avoirdupois does not constitute dignity nor great stature a commanding mien. There was something about the little man—a determined set to the shoulders and a stern, serene look in the eye—that was suggestive of military precision and authority."[87]

Frank Funston Eckdall described his uncle Fred's voice as firm, "even with his sister" Ella. In pitch, it was neither high nor low.[88] In contrast, when fearless leader Fred fought in the Philippines and encouraged his fighting troops, "[h]e yelled louder than the bugler could blow."[89]

Our review of Fred's personality began with the newspaper account containing Ode C. Nichols' interview of Fred's mother. That article's conclusion is appropriate here:

> "Would you like to see Fred's room?" asked Mrs. Funston.
>
> I followed her to a neat little apartment whose walls are adorned with flower pictures, landscapes and drawings of birds. A prairie breeze swayed the delicate lace curtains.
>
> In the corners are walrus tusks and other Alaskan trophies. A friendly tree shreds the sun rays that fall through the window. A vine clings to the window-sill, a flower lifts its head outside to peep in.
>
> On the corner of an old-fashioned dresser hangs a straw hat stained from Cuban campaigns.

"This is Fred's room," said the mother of the little general, dropping her voice to a hushed tone, almost a whisper. "It's ready for the boy and his wife—waiting for them to come back."[90]

Chapter Five Notes, continued—*Fred's Personality*

1. Ode C. Nichols, "Funston, From Babyhood to Present Day as His Mother Knows Him," *The World*, May 21, 1899 (FFP). Nichols had been a Lieutenant in Troop M., First Volunteer Cavalry (Rough Riders).

2. "Fred Funston's Restless Life of Adventure," *The Chicago Sunday Tribune*, May 7, 1899 (FFP).

3. Alvin Peters, "Fences and Settlers," *The Law and Lawyers in Kansas* (Topeka, Kansas: Kansas State Historical Society, 1992), 16-20. Also, Alvin Peters, "Herd Laws in Kansas," graph showing "Adoption of Herd Law," 34. Emporia State University website esirc.emporia.edu

4. "Fred Funston's Restless Life of Adventure."

5. "Fred Funston's Restless Life of Adventure."

6. "Whistling as an Indication of Character," *The Iola Register*, October 23, 1875.

7. Ella (Funston) Eckdall to Eda B. Funston, October 25, 1925 (FFP).

8. Ella (Funston) Eckdall to Eda B. Funston, October 25, 1925 (FFP).

9. "Fred Funston's Restless Life of Adventure."

10. "Fred Funston's Restless Life of Adventure."

11. "Funston as a Swimmer," *The Lawrence Daily Journal*, May 1, 1899 (reprint of a William Allen White editorial in the *Emporia Gazette*). David Haward Bain, *Sitting in Darkness*, 15, claimed that Fred did "strenuous exercises" to develop his chest and shoulders, but I have not located the source for this assertion, which I question. Farm boy Fred did not need this extra to develop a powerful physique.

12. Henry W. Thomas, *Walter Johnson: Baseball's Big Train* (Washington, D.C.: Phenom Press, 1995), 3.

13. "Indecency," *The Iola Register*, June 15, 1878. This letter was signed "Grumbler."

14. "Fred Funston's Restless Life of Adventure."

15. "Fred Funston's Restless Life of Adventure."

16. "From Fred Funston," *The Iola Register*, August 25, 1893. This is Funston's letter dated May 28, 1893.

17. Ella Funston Eckdall, *The Funston Homestead* (Emporia, Kansas: Raymond Lees, 1949), 9-10.

18. Ella (Funston) Eckdall to Eda B. Funston, October 25, 1925 (FFP). Ella (Funston) Eckdall to Eda B. Funston, December 8, 1924, for Burt's recollection (FFP Micro).

19. Anderson County Historical Society, *Anderson County Kansas: Family Stories and History* (Salina, Kansas: KANLEN Printing & Advertising, 1989), 275 (biography of William Alexander Johnson).

20. "Death of Funston Shocks Community," *The Iola Daily Register*, February 20, 1917.

21. Lida (Eckdall) Lees to the author, October 4, 1966–yes, that is 1966!

22. "Fred Funston's Restless Life of Adventure."

23. "Fred Funston's Restless Life of Adventure."

24. "Fred Funston's Restless Life of Adventure."

25. For first quotation, see "Fighting Funston, Hero of Calumpit," *Santa Cruz Morning Sentinel*, October 20, 1899. The second quotation is from Charles S. Gleed, "Romance

And Reality In A Single Life. Gen. Frederick Funston," *The Cosmopolitan Illustrated Monthly Magazine*, July 1899.

26. "A Talk With Funston," *The Kansas City Journal*, November 11, 1899 (FFP Micro).

27. Ella (Funston) Eckdall to Eda B. Funston, October 25, 1925 (FFP).

28. Ella Funston Eckdall, "General Funston's Tree Still Watches Progress," *Topeka Capital*, September 5, 1937.

29. "Funstoniana," unknown newspaper, calculated date of February 20, 1917 (FFP).

30. Lida (Eckdall) Lees to Jarrett Robinson, July 21, 1991. Courtesy of Jarrett Robinson and Ellen (Lees) Stolte.

31. "A Touching Message From Mrs. Fred Funston," *Hutchinson News*, May 29, 1923.

32. No title and unknown newspaper with a calculated date of about 1907 (FFP).

33. "A Funston Story," *The Lawrence Daily World*, March 8, 1901. Caldwell was identified as "Postmaster Caldwell, and "it used to be charged that Mr. Caldwell got his start herding hogs for the father of the general." This is E. F. Caldwell who, with his bride, Viola, was feted at the Funston home by Ed and Lida Funston following their marriage (see "Expanding the House" section of Chapter Five).

34. *Neosho Valley Register*, February 14, 1874.

35. Eckdall, *The Funston Homestead*, 20.

36. Eckdall, *The Funston Homestead*, 20-21.

37. Adda B. Adams to Ella Eckdall, June 8, 1951. Adda was expressing her enjoyment in reading *The Funston Homestead* (Eckdall materials donated in 2004). Allen County Historical Society, Inc.

38. "Is Picuuresque [sic]," *The Iola Register*, November 26, 1906 (reprint of a lengthy biographical sketch of Fred Funston in the *Joplin Globe*).

39. "Frederick Funston," *The Iola Daily Register*, February 22, 1917 (editorial tribute by Charles F. Scott) (Kansas State Historical Society, *Frederick Funston Clippings*, Vol. 1) for Fred's quotation. "Brigadier General Funston," *The Iola Daily Register*, May 2, 1899 (editorial).

40. Charles F. Scott to Mrs. Frederick Funston, December 29, 1924 (FFP).

41. Ella (Funston) Eckdall to Frank Funston Eckdall, May 19, 1928. Courtesy of Deborah (Eckdall) Helmken. *The Iola Register* correspondent for the Osage area of Allen County in 1895 remembered the time, just "a few years since," when few smoked. "Now ninety-nine out of every one hundred smoke. Has the one left the fold, or have the ninety and nine gone astray? It is cigars, cigars, the spacious earth around. As Horace Greely said of cigars, 'Fire at one end and fool at the other" ("Osage Occurrences," *The Iola Register*, May 1, 1895).

42. Ella (Funston) Eckdall to Eda B. Funston, October 25, 1925 (FFP). Ed Funston was widely known as a teetotaler, and, thus, in 1892, while serving as a U.S. Congressman, Ed felt compelled to defend his reputation by sending the following telegram to the editor of *The Iola Register*, who then printed it in the newspaper: "The statement in the New York *Voice* that I was seen by its correspondent taking a drink in the House saloon is a lie." Charlie Scott editorialized that Ed "is so well known in Kansas as a total abstainer that the slanderous attack of the *Voice* will only make him friends" (*The Iola Register*, April 8, 1892).

43. "Prohibition," Kansapedia, Kansas Historical Society (www.kshs.org).

44. Ida (Weith) Faddis's handwritten notes in "Misc. Articles" at Allen County Historical Society, Inc. The Weith family lived across Elm Creek at that time, and Ida's mother told her this story.

45. "Local Matters," *The Iola Register*, May 6, 1881.

46. "Fred Funston's Restless Life of Adventure."

47. Lida (Eckdall) Lees to Jarrett Robinson, July 3, 1991.Courtesy of Jarrett Robinson and Ellen (Lees) Stolte.

48. Angelo C. Scott, *A Boyhood in Old Carlyle* (Oklahoma City, 1940), 9-10.

49. Scott, *A Boyhood in Old Carlyle*, 10. See also "A Chicken Hunt with the Ladies," *Neosho Valley Register*, August 10, 1871. The hunting of prairie chickens was "new to the ladies of Iola, but quite common to those of most other prairie countries..." The small group killed between twenty and thirty chickens, "and had lots of fun. The ladies... think chicken hunting delightful sport."

50. Scott, *A Boyhood in Old Carlyle*, 10.

51. Raymond E. Cooper to Frank Funston Eckdall, October 1, 1986. In conversation with Ella (Funston) Eckdall, Mr. Cooper learned from her the account of the illness of Fred's brother. Allen County Historical Society, Inc.

52. Eckdall, *The Funston Homestead*, 19.

53. Cemetery monument of J. Burton Funston, Funston family plot, Iola Cemetery, Iola, Kansas.

54. "Fred Funston's Restless Life of Adventure." Ella (Funston) Eckdall pasted a copy of parts of this article in one of the scrapbooks she made about Fred. The part telling about Gertie and Lizzie is not included. Why, I do not know (Eckdall Scrapbook III, 2).

55. "His Remarkable Career," unidentified newspaper and unknown date (untitled scrapbook of newspaper clippings about Frederick Funston at Iola Public Library, Iola, Kansas).

56. Alan J. Stewart, "Maj. – Gen. Fredrick [sic] Funston Brought Glory to Kansas With His Victories," *The Topeka Daily Capital Sunday Magazine*, March 13, 1955. Surviving members of the Funston family, notably Ella (Funston) Eckdall, assisted Stewart, who was writing a biography of Funston. If completed, apparently this was never published.

57. Stewart, "Maj. – Gen. Fredrick [sic] Funston Brought Glory to Kansas With His Victories."

58. "A Story About Funston," *The Iola Register*, January 12, 1894 (reprint from Franklin (Ind.) Republican). This was an interview with "Jos. V. Covert" in whose house Ed Funston had boarded while teaching in Franklin Township, Johnson County, Indiana, in School District No. 1. Sometimes the practical joke was played on the bachelor, Ed Funston. Covert one evening, while Ed was away, placed a "dummy" with a night cap on it in Ed's bed. Ed was "almost scared out of his wits" when he struck a light and discovered the occupant of his bed. "He hurried into Covert's room and gasped out: 'What woman is that you've put in my bed?' A burst of laughter revealed to him the whole business."

59. Ella (Funston) Eckdall to Eda B. Funston, October 25, 1925 (FFP).

60. This flute is on display at the Funston Home Museum, owned and operated by the

Allen County Historical Society, Inc. This flute is identified as having been played by both Ed and Fred Funston.

61. Stewart, "Maj. – Gen. Fredrick (sic) Funston Brought Glory to Kansas With His Victories."

62. Telephone visit of Frank Funston Eckdall and the author, December 18, 1998. Mr. Eckdall also noted that "everything was harmonious in the family—a proud family."

63. Lida (Eckdall) Lees to Jarrett Robinson, July 3, 1991. Courtesy of Jarrett Robinson and Ellen (Lees) Stolte. At Memorial Day ceremonies in Ottawa, Kansas, in 1901 soon after Fred Funston's capture of Aguinaldo, ex-congressman Ed Funston, the guest speaker, was introduced as "the father of Frederick Funston." Smiling, Ed responded: "It used to be said that great sons emanated from great fathers. It now appears that great fathers emanate from great sons" ("Was 'Funston Of Kansas,'" *The Kansas City Star*, February [day and year not shown]) (FFP).

64. "Fred Funston's Restless Life of Adventure."

65. Ella (Funston) Eckdall to Eda B. Funston, October 25, 1925 (FFP).

66. "His Mother," unidentified newspaper from the year 1914 (FFP Micro). Charlie Scott summarized the mother-son relationship after Fred's death: "For his mother he showed a genuine affection seldom displayed by men after they have wandered afar and have settled in homes of their own" ("Death of Funston Shocks Community," *The Iola Daily Register*, February 20, 1917).

67. "Just Wanted To See Her Boy," *The Iola Daily Register*, July 31, 1905 (quoting the *Kansas City Star*).

68. A typed sheet without title concerning Fred Funston's "soft and tender nature" (FFP).

69. "Always Devoted To His Mother," *Topeka Capital*, February 20, 1917 (Kansas State Historical Society, *Frederick Funston Clippings*, Vol.1).

70. "Fred Funston's Restless Life of Adventure."

71. Ella (Funston) Eckdall to Eda B. Funston, October 25, 1925 (FFP).

72. "Love and War," unidentified newspaper with dateline of "New York, Sunday, April 9, 1899" (part of this is in FFP and part in FFP Micro).

73. Telephone visit of Frank Funston Eckdall and the author, October 13, 1999. Lida (Eckdall) Lees to Jarrett Robinson, July 7, 1991. Lida Lees referred to Fred's eyes as "blue, rather aqua." Courtesy of Jarrett Robinson and Ellen (Lees) Stolte.

74. Telephone visit of Frank Funston Eckdall and the author, on October 13, 1999. "Emporia Girl, Niece of Funston, Writes of 'Incidents' in His Life," *Emporia Gazette*, October 9, 1928, for the librarian's description (Eckdall Scrapbook II, 105). David Potter, *Frederick Funston: A First Class Fighting Man: A Biography*, 13 (manuscript) (David Potter Manuscripts; 1950s, Manuscripts Division, Department of Rare Books and Special Collections, Princeton University Library).

75. Untitled article about Fred Funston among multiple front-page articles about the warm welcome in Kansas City for "Gen. Funston and Officers of the Twentieth," *The Kansas City Journal*, November 11, 1899 (FFP Micro).

76. Sarah Wood–Clark, Museum Registrar of the Kansas State Historical Society to the author, October 28, 1999. The Society owns these shoes.

77. Paul Wilkinson, "Frederick Funston In The Chapter," *The Scroll of Phi Delta Theta*, Vol. XXV, October 1900-June 1901, 430-431. Just how small were Fred's hands? I calculate a length of 6.15 inches based on extrapolation from a photograph of Fred's

hand. From another photograph, he appears to have had long fingers. Perhaps while the fingers were long, the rest of the hand was unusually small.

78. "Fred Funston's Restless Life of Adventure."

79. "A Kansas Cuban Soldier," *The Iola Register*, December 25, 1896 (reprint from *The Kansas City Star*).

80. "Colonel Fred Funston," *Post-Intelligencer*, May 7, 1899 (first part of newspaper title missing) (FFP Micro). This is a strange article. The unnamed writer stated that, ten years before, when he was seated in a Kansas City, Missouri, newspaper office, Fred Funston came to start his first newspaper job. The writer gave the date as the spring of 1889, which is clearly incorrect, since Fred was a student at the State University at that time. He started his Kansas City newspaper career in the fall of 1887. The chronology of Fred's life as set out in this article is confused, and it is a largely unsatisfactory article.

81. Fred Funston's height has been variously reported as 5'2", 5'3", 5'4", and 5'5". Confirmation that it was 5'4" comes from his sister, Ella (Funston) Eckdall. The Western Shade Cloth Co. issued *Pull*, a small magazine for the benefit of its "salesmen and saleswomen." In the April 1917 issue (Vol. I, No. 6) appeared "The Story of General Funston." In her copy, Ella Eckdall has made in ink various corrections, one of which was striking out the word "two" and replacing it with "4" in the phrase "barely five feet two inches tall with a round bullet head and a quiet well-poised demeanor." Allen County Historical Society, Inc.

82. Chas. F. Scott, "Remarkable Career of a Kansas Boy," *Mail and Breeze* (about March 20, 1898) (FFP).

83. Lida (Eckdall) Lees to Jarrett Robinson, July 3, 1991. Courtesy of Jarrett Robinson and Ellen (Lees) Stolte.

84. "The City's Famous Guests," an unidentified Kansas City newspaper, 1899 (*Wilder Stevens Metcalf and Frederick Funston With The Twentieth Kansas In The Philippines During The Spanish–American War*) (scrapbook of newspaper articles at Spencer Research Library, University of Kansas).

85. David Potter, *Frederick Funston: A First Class Fighting Man: A Biography*, 13 (manuscript) (David Potter Manuscripts; 1950s, Manuscripts Division, Department of Rare Books and Special Collections, Princeton University Library).

86. "Bouquets For Funston," undated and untitled newspaper containing quotation from Omaha *Bee* (FFP Micro).

87. "A Talk With Funston," *The Kansas City Journal*, November 11, 1899 (FFP Micro).

88. Telephone visit of Frank Funston Eckdall and the author, January 1997.

89. "Vivid Memories of Spanish War," *The Kansas City Star*, estimated date of 1964 (Homer M. Limbird Papers, Archives Division, Kansas State Historical Society). Quoted is Homer M. Limbird, who served in Funston's Twentieth Kansas Volunteers in the war in the Philippines.

90. Nichols, "Funston, From Babyhood to Present Day as His Mother Knows Him," This bedroom, I believe, was the one off the north end of the dining room. The only other bedroom on the first floor was the "spare bedroom" for guests, and the three bedrooms upstairs were for Fred's parents, brothers, and sister, respectively.

Maple Grove School

"Wherever the Christian religion has gained a foothold there it may be counted as certain that the cause of education is firmly entrenched," wrote an early Allen County historian. "The pioneers of Allen County lost no time in organizing school districts, building schoolhouses and employing teachers for the instruction of their children. In the beginning, as must necessarily be the case where the people are few in number and poor in purse, the schoolhouse was poor, (although it was usually the best house in the neighborhood), and rudely furnished, and the school term lasted but three or four months in the year."[1]

The school districts of Allen County, which eventually totaled more than eighty, were numbered in the order of their establishment. The first school district was at the town of Geneva, and the fifth was to become the school attended by the Funston children. Known as Maple Grove School, it was located roughly half-a-mile south of the Funston home. This was the second school district to be numbered 5, since "the former No. 5 had, for some years, been totally disorganized and that number lost from the list."[2] On June 1, 1867, a petition was presented to the County Superintendent of Public Instruction by thirteen residents living south of school district No. 2, which was known as "Old Carlyle." Its school building was located west of Carlyle just north of the Funston farm. The petition requested the erection of a new school district south of No. 2 to be located next to Deer Creek. Six days later, the petition was granted by the County Superintendent, and District No. 5, located on Deer Creek south of No. 2, was formed.[3]

This newly formed school district was an L-shaped rectangle 3½ miles east-west and 2 miles north-south except at the west end where it was 2 ½ miles north-south. Along the north line, it included the village of Carlyle itself, and the southern portion included lands on both sides of Deer Creek.[4] The school building, located on the same road that ran in front of the Funston home, was nearly in the center of the district, making it about equally situated for all of the families of the new district. The district acquired the one-acre site for this school building by purchasing it for one dollar from the Cozine family, the owners of the larger tract of land, which abutted on its north boundary the Funston farm. Transfer of title to the district was by deed dated February 20, 1869.[5]

School classes were held before this building was constructed, since on November 11, 1867, the County Superintendent visited the school and recorded in his journal: "Found the school well managed, and highly promising."[6] This was in contrast to the superintendent's visit to eight district schools the prior June: "Found these schools generally doing well, though several of them are in a very backward state, held in miserable cabins without accommodations for either Teachers or scholars."[7]

Five days after his visit to Maple Grove School (No. 5), the County Superintendent made his Annual Report for 1867 to the State Superintendent. This Annual Report provided statistics for all Allen County schools in 1867: 20 school districts and 1,128 children of school age, of which 583 were males and 545 were females. There were 35 "colored" children, 19 males and 16 females, and there were 354 white males enrolled and 327 white females enrolled, for a total of 681 students. The average time taught was 5.4 months. There were 24 teachers, 13 males and 11 females; male teachers' average monthly salary was $38, while the average monthly salary for females was $27; all teacher wages totaled $3,670.50. There were 16 schoolhouses, of which 6 were made of logs, 7 were framed, and 3 were of stone construction. The value of all schoolhouses was $11,057.74.[8]

At nearly five years of age, Fred Funston started school at Maple Grove in 1870. He stopped frequently, as he walked the half-mile down the road, to fight imaginary Indians and bears.[9] Whistling, he walked alone, since Burt was not old enough to accompany him. His mother later said, "He was never tardy at school. Never, from the first day. And he never missed a day at school."[10] Maple Grove School had thirty-four students, according to the Annual Report of August 16, 1870.[11] The boys and girls were separated by sex, the boys sitting on one side of the schoolroom and the girls on the other.[12]

Fred's first term of school likely was the winter term of 1870, and, in March 1871, there were forty children at Maple Grove.[13] On November 2, 1871, the County Superintendent visited several schoolhouses, including No. 5, where "at 3 o'clock delivered a lecture to a pretty full house. These schools were well attended & among the best in the county."[14] In March 1872, Maple Grove had forty-three students.[15] Ed Funston was actively involved in the affairs of the district, since he served as a district director, resigning from that position in December of 1872.[16]

Fred was a great reader, and had a memory that "was almost phenominal [sic]," according to his sister Ella.[17] As a little boy, he recited pieces at school, and, on one occasion, recalled Ella, he recited at a church social "an almost incredible number of pages" from Sir Walter Scott's epic, *The Lady of the Lake*.[18] In 1899, Fred's father stated that "[h]e can recite every word of it today."[19] Fred was the best speller in Maple Grove School.[20]

His first speech at Maple Grove was as follows:

> You'd scarce expect one of my age
> To speak in public on the stage;
> And if I chance to fall below
> Demosthenes or Cicero
> Don't view me with a critic's eye,

But pass my imperfections by.
Large streams from little fountain's [sic] flow,
Tall oaks from little acorns grow.[21]

Another poem that Fred recited was highly appropriate for the boy who was so interested in soldiers:

YOUNG SOLDIERS

Oh, were you ne'er a schoolboy,
　And did you never train,
And feel that swelling of the heart
　You ne'er can feel again?
Did you never meet, far down the street,
　With plumes and banners gay,
While the kettle, for the kettledrum,
　Played your march, march away?
It seems to me but yesterday,
　Nor scarce so long ago,
Since all our school their muskets took,
　To charge the fearful foe.
Our muskets were of cedar wood,
　With ramrods bright and new;
With bayonets forever set,
　And painted barrels, too.
We charged upon a flock of geese,
　And put them all to flight—
Except one sturdy gander
　That thought to show us fight.
But, ah! we knew a thing or two;
　Our captain wheeled the van;
We routed him, we scouted him,
　Nor lost a single man!
Our captain was as brave a lad
　As e'er commission bore;
And brightly shone his new tin sword;
　A paper cap he wore.
He led us up the steep hillside,
　Against the western wind,
While the cockerel plume that decked his head
　Streamed bravely out behind.
We shouldered arms, we carried arms,
　We charged the bayonet;
And woe unto the mullein stalk
　That in our course we met!

At two o'clock the roll we called,
  And till the close of day,
With fearless hearts, though tired limbs,
  We fought the mimic fray,—
Till the supper bell, from out the dell,
  Bade us march, march away.[22]

As a schoolboy, Fred enjoyed playing soldier. A classmate, Emma (Powell) Heath, many years later, in 1932, memorialized Maple Grove School in the form of a quilt. A picket fence, with the names of teachers and the year each taught school and covering the years of 1867 through 1931, serves as the border of this quilt. One of the quilt illustrations is of Fred Funston playing soldier. He is shown as "Brig. Gen." of the Twentieth Kansas, and his classmate troops are Norris Ball, Hayes Ball, Roy Fetherngill, and Merrill Winchester.[23] Fred's niece wrote, years later, that "he led the boys in skirmishes, or playing battles. Later, I heard an old neighbor tell that, 'Fred's side always won.'"[24]

On December 10, 1876, 11-year-old Fred wrote a letter to his maternal grandmother, Elizabeth Mitchell, in which he described, in part, his studies at Maple Grove:

Dear Grandma: I thought I would write you a letter today and tell you the news. We are having nice weather here now, but in November we had a snow storm 4 inches thick. Pogue and Ella have whooping cough. Besides that we are all well. Burt and I are going to schol [sic] now. Mr. McDonald is our teacher. We had 20 bushels of apples on our trees this year but we did not have but a few peaches. Burt and I planted some early potatoes this spring and raised 6 bushels and we sole [sic] them for 50 cents a bushel and so we have 1 dollar and a half a piece. Pogue and Ella are always asking when you are going to come here. At school I am studying in the fifth reder [sic] McGuffey's spelling. Grammar, Bay's second part arithmetic and Bays [sic] third part Arithmetic. In Bay's third part I am in simple interest which is half way through the book.

Write soon from your Grandson Frederick Funston[25]

End of the school year was the time for an entertainment. The one held on May 26, 1879, in a grove near Maple Grove School, called Colonel Goss' grove, was advertised as follows: "A general pic nic [sic] for all. Bring your baskets well stored and come early. The exercises will begin at ten o'clock. The young girls are requested to bring garland and flowers with them, and assist in crowning May Queen."[26]

In 1879, when Fred was fourteen, he was later described by a classmate as follows: "In the district school Fred was recognized as a thorough student bubbling over with fun and full of all sorts of practical jokes. He always saw the funny side of any situation and was quick to analyze the situation."[27] A complete list of the subjects that Fred studied does not exist, but, he and his schoolmate, Roy Fetherngill, obtained a textbook on the Spanish language and studied this on the side. Both were to benefit from acquiring a knowledge of Spanish, Fred in Cuba and the Philippines, and Roy in the Philippines where he worked for many years. Initially, he was a postmaster, then a builder of schoolhouses for the United States government besides owning forty acres, where he raised hemp, coffee, and cocoa.[28]

What kind of student was young Fred? The Maple Grove School records apparently no longer exist for the time period that Fred was a student there, but, thanks to five reports by his then-teacher over the course of two years, which were published in *The Iola Register*, one can gain insight into Fred the student. The answer to the question is a positive one.

In January 1880, when Fred was fourteen, his teacher was J. C. Gordon, who, in his report, described the school as "prospering." The enrollment was sixty-five, and the school board had now furnished the schoolhouse with blackboards, for which Gordon was "thankful."[29] For the month ending January 16, 1880, Fred was recognized with others for "regular attendance." On January 15 and 16, the scholars took an examination covering reading, spelling, arithmetic, geography, grammar, and history. Average scores ranged from a low of 50 to a high of 97. Fred scored 69, and his good friend, Roy Fetherngill, scored 67.[30]

For the next month, which ended on February 13, Fred was reported neither absent nor tardy. The average standing of each member of the "advanced class" based on a two-day examination was listed in the report. Fred excelled with an average of 93, which was higher than any other students'. Next highest score was 90, and the lowest was Burt Funston's 68. Roy Fetherngill's score was 82.[31]

The next time Fred's name appeared in a teacher's report is nearly two years later and was in the report for the month ending December 16, 1881, when there were 73 pupils, 36 of whom were males. Fred did not qualify for the roll of honor, which consisted of those who were neither absent nor tardy, and who were perfect in deportment. He was recognized, however, as perfect in deportment.[32]

For the next month, ending January 20, 1882, Fred was reported both "perfect in deportment" and being present every day.[33] The following month, ending February 17, he was perfect in deportment again, but apparently had been either absent or tardy, or both, since he did not make the roll of honor. This is the last time that school year of 1882 that Fred's name appeared on at least one of the two lists: perfect in deportment and roll of honor.[34] This is also the last record we have of Fred's academic and personal performance as a scholar at Maple Grove School.

At the end of the school year in May of 1882, a "pic nic [sic] and school convention" was held in the grove on the Fetherngill farm south of Deer Creek. Fred is not listed by name as one of those presenting the program, but perhaps he was one of the eleven unnamed boys making a "recitation."[35] In his report for the spring term ending on May 26, the teacher, J. W. Tulles, noted that the average tuition per month for each pupil was 96 cents. "As to deportment in the school, without scarcely an exception it has been very good. A double interest has been manifested by the pupils in their studies during the spring term, which has made duty seem an easy task."[36]

At the end of the school year in December of 1882, teacher Tulles expressed this hope: "Now that the farm work is about all done for the winter it is to be hoped that parents will send their children more regularly." School attendance in a farming community usually came second to helping on the farm. Pedagogue Tulles noted the school's festivity at the end of the year of 1882: "A Christmas tree, which was gotten up by the school, gladdened the hearts of the little folks, and also the older folks, last Saturday evening; many were the presents bestowed."[37]

Life was not all study at school. Fred enjoyed playing soldier with classmates. Angelo Scott, eight years older than Fred, attended "Old Carlyle" district, and recollected games that the students played there: "We were wild for the school ground sports, especially the ball games. We played one-old-cat and two-old-cat, and then graduated into 'townball,' the direct precursor of baseball. We made our own balls, of yarn, twine, and other ingredients, with something heavy to give them weight; and on these our mothers sewed deerskin covers in sections." These balls had a short lifespan, and, thus, sometimes solid rubber balls, which had been purchased at a store, were used. In winter, "furious snowball battles" were waged.[38]

On February 13, 1881, Fred wrote to his grandmother, Elizabeth Mitchell, about a trip that he and his brother Burt had taken to Topeka, the Kansas state capital. They visited their father who was there attending the Legislature. This letter shows Fred's and Burt's thoughtfulness and generosity toward their 7-year-old sister, Ella:

> Dear Grandma As I have not written to you for some time I thought I would write today and let you [hear] how we are getting along. Ma got a letter from yesterday [sic]. We are all well none of us have been sick this winter. I have been going to school this winter and am getting along very well with my studies. Last week Burt and I went to Topeka. We started on Friday and got back Wednesday. We had a fine time and saw a great many nice things. The best things in the State House are the collections of the State historical society

and Agriculture department. In the Historical society are a great many things connected with the early history of Kansas among them John Brown's revolver. In the agricultural department we saw all of the different kinds of birds animals and reptiles of Kansas stuffed among them a buffalo. While we were at Topeka there was a hard rain and the ice on the river broke. The ice was two feet thick and when it broke it carried away several bridges. On one large ice cake was a live hog. There is a Chinese laundry in Topeka and Burt and I went to see the Chinamen; their heads were all shaved except a small place on the middle where they have a long braid. While we were at Topeka Pa gave us a dollar to go to the minstrels but while we were in a jewelry store we saw some nice earrings so we bought a pair for a present for Ella. It is getting late so I must close.

From your grandson
Fred. Funston[39]

Maple Grove school building was apparently well maintained. In the words of an 1884 passerby: "[W]e judge from the neat condition of the building, fences and outhouses that the boys do not carry a hatchet to school to destroy the property, as has been done elsewhere."[40] This school building served a dual purpose as host of the Literary Society. Adda Adams, who attended it as a child, summarized succinctly the Literary's purpose: "The children sang, spoke pieces, or gave a dialogue. After a recess, the men had a debate."[41] In January of 1880, the Carlyle correspondent for *The Iola Register* trumpeted the success of the Maple Grove literary:

> Carlyle literary has passed silently away. Maple Grove literary prospering. The recitations, essays, declamations, select readings and music are good and improving each night. The question debated Wednesday night, *Res.*, that the United States ought to pay each soldier of the Union army a sum sufficient to make their pay equal to gold with 6 per cent. per annum was both interesting and exciting. The question for next Wednesday night, *Res.*, that the Indian Territory should be opened up for settlement on the conditions proposed in Senator Vest's bill. Not many literary societies can boast of a president who combines the rare ability, sound judgment and ripe experience as parliamentarian of President E. H. Funston. He is a man that has the confidence of the entire people of Deer Creek township.[42]

Two weeks later the same correspondent reported about both the Maple Grove and Carlyle literaries:

> Maple Grove literary society was well attended last Wednesday

night. The question chosen for debate next Wednesday evening is: *Res.* That capital has more influence than education.

The Carlyle society, no doubt becoming alarmed at the prosperous condition of the Maple Grove society have [sic] revived and show [sic] something of their [sic] former greatness in their exercises.[43]

The report a week later read as follows:

Literary Society of Maple Grove elected officers last Wednesday evening, re-electing those who have administered the affairs of the society successfully during the past eight weeks. The question for discussion the next evening, vis: *Res.,* That St. Domingo should have been purchased at the close of the late war and opened up for settlement according to the homestead and pre-emption laws of the United States, no one but the negroes being allowed to go there and they not allowed more than forty acres each.[44]

In December 1881, the "Carlyle News" column noted that the two literaries met on alternate Wednesday nights. "They are well attended and a great deal of pains taken to make the exercises entertaining and interesting."[45]

At times, the question landed closer to home. At a Maple Grove Literary, in January of 1887, the question for debate was "Resolved, That the county seat should not be removed from Iola." The Carlyle newspaper correspondent, "I. X. Pect.," observed, "We do not care much which side wins in debate but when it comes to application we do think the affirmative will win." The correspondent had previously noted that the "county seat question is all the rage now, in Carlyle, although there are few persons who advocate the removal and they who do will soon wear a woebegone expression of countenance, when it is settled in favor of Iola."[46]

In February 1883, the then-Carlyle correspondent, using the pen name "Lettuce C.," reported the continuing success of the literaries held at both school buildings, Maple Grove and Carlyle:

The literary at Maple Grove two weeks ago was quite a success, at least as far as numbers are concerned. Even standing room was at a premium, and many of us members of the frailer sex, pitied our stronger "gumbanions." Because of the lateness of the hour when the other literary exercises were over the debate on "Capital Punishment" was postponed for a week... The Carlyle society, we learn, had a good meeting on Friday week [sic]. The question for debate, "Resolved, That the United States should take forcible possession of the Isthmus of Panama," is said to have been ably handled and decision rendered by the judges in favor of the affirmative. But where the justice of taking what belongs to another from him comes in

Lettuce C fails to C.[47]

Angelo Scott, who attended the Carlyle Literary Society until 1874, provided this description:

> In memory I always associate its meetings with wintry nights, with snow, and with moonlight. I still can see, after the meetings, the wagons departing in every direction, clattering loudly over the frozen roads. Inside, the jam-packed audience revealed our people as they were, not in their Sunday best, but in their daily garb. As for the women, the hoop-skirt and sunbonnet era was passing out, though some still clung to these habiliments.
>
> The men still wore their masklike beards, and nearly all wore heavy boots, some pulled on over their trousers. These boots were the sole instruments of applause, and they thundered on the floor when some lucky performer made a hit.[48]

The Carlyle Literary Society had a weekly paper which Angelo Scott edited and named *The Weekly Outbreak*. He soon received suggestions that he should change the name to *The Weekly Insult.* [49]

Likely, Fred both attended, and participated, in these literaries. The only record found of his participation occurred in 1879, when he was thirteen, at the Carlyle Literary. At the March 18, 1879, literary, Fred gave a declamation. His father gave an address.[50] At times, some of those attending the literaries apparently became contentious. In December of 1882, three "young men" were charged in the local court "for creating a disturbance at the Maple Grove literary society." Two defendants pled guilty and were each fined one dollar and costs, for a total of $25.00. The case against the third defendant was dismissed."[51]

When Fred completed his schooling at Maple Grove is unknown. Like the other rural schools of Allen County, Maple Grove School was ungraded, meaning that there were no established grade levels. Without grade levels, there was no set time for completion of a scholar's studies. As noted above, Fred was still a student at the end of the school month ending February 17, 1882. Likely, the year of 1882 was Fred's final year. By then he was sixteen years old. His wife, Eda, later wrote that Fred attended until he was seventeen, which would be in November of 1882.[52] Charlie Scott in a 1901 biographical sketch of Fred described his Maple Grove experience: "He was quick in his books and ambitions to obtain an education; so at an early age he had mastered the course of study in the country school..."[53]

Two events of note occurred within a few years after Fred completed his studies at Maple Grove. First, with the year 1885-1886, the school became a graded school, and with the establishment of grade levels, there was a graduating class of five scholars in May 1886.[54] The "diplomas of graduation" were presented by the County Superintendent of Instruction after an "entertaining program" of songs, recitations, and dialogues. Only one other country school in Allen County had a graduating class that year. Prior to the program and graduation, there had been a bountiful dinner. A visitor that day graphically described this dinner: "Is it necessary for us to enlarge upon the merits of that dinner? We think not. We, and a hundred others did enlarge, then and there, several inches under its influence. Further, we feel entirely unable to do it justice, and that too would be unnecessary, since every one present seemed to feel it his bounden duty to see that justice to it should be done. And it was done."[55]

The second change after Fred had completed his studies at Maple Grove was that the school became known as North Maple Grove, because of the establishment southeast of Humboldt of another school known as Maple Grove. The latter school acquired the name South Maple Grove. In some secondary sources, Fred's first school is identified as North Maple Grove when, in reality, it was known only as Maple Grove during his years of attendance.[56]

Fred Funston Age 16 Years

Maple Grove School (1888)

Chapter Five Notes, continued—*Maple Grove School*

1. L. Wallace Duncan and Chas. F. Scott, *History of Allen and Woodson Counties Kansas* (Iola, Kansas: Iola Register, Printers and Binders, 1901), 60.

2. *Accounts and Transactions of County Superintendent of Public Instruction for Allen County*, Journal A, 65. These handwritten Journals A, B, and C are at the Allen County Historical Society, Inc.

3. *Accounts and Transactions*, Journal A, 64-65.

4. "Descriptions of School Districts Allen County Kansas," handwritten document located in Office of Register of Deeds, Allen County, Kansas. The actual legal description of School District No. 5 is as follows: Commencing at the North East corner of Section 1, Township 24, Range 18, thence running West 2½ miles; thence North one half mile; thence West one mile; thence South 2½ miles; thence East 3½ miles; thence North 2 miles to the place of beginning.

5. Deed dated February 20, 1869, Deed Book H, 36 (Office of the Register of Deeds, Allen County, Kansas). This is a tract 12 rods by 14 rods in Southwest Quarter of Section 2, Township 24, Range 18.

6. *Accounts and Transactions*, Journal A, 74.

7. *Accounts and Transactions*, Journal A, 66.

8. *Accounts and Transactions*, Journal A, 75.

9. Alan J. Stewart, "Funston Homestead Will Become Park," *The Topeka Daily Capital Sunday Magazine*, October 9, 1955. Adda Adams is quoted as the source for this information, except she stated the schoolhouse was a mile from the Funston home, when, in reality, it was only about a half-mile. Adda lived on the farm east of the Funston farm, and apparently was relying on what an older sister of hers had said. The older, unnamed sister may have observed little Fred Funston when he walked to school.

10. "Fred Funston's Restless Life of Adventure," *The Chicago Sunday Tribune*, May 7, 1899 (FFP).

11. *Accounts and Transactions*, Journal B, 48.

12. Stewart, "Funston Homestead Will Become Park."

13. *Accounts and Transactions*, Journal B, 86.

14. *Accounts and Transactions*, Journal C, 5.

15. *Accounts and Transactions*, Journal C, 26.

16. *Accounts and Transactions*, Journal C, 75.

17. Ella (Funston) Eckdall to Eda B. Funston, October 25, 1925 (FFP).

18. Ella (Funston) Eckdall to Eda B. Funston, October 25, 1925 (FFP).

19. "Fred Funston's Restless Life of Adventure."

20. "Fred Funston's Restless Life of Adventure."

21. Ella (Funston) Eckdall to Eda B. Funston, October 25, 1925 (FFP).

22. *McGuffey's Third Eclectic Reader*, Revised edition (New York: American Book Company, orig. 1879), 184. Fred's sister, Ella, is the source that Fred recited this poem. Ella (Funston) Eckdall to Eda B. Funston, October 25, 1925 (FFP).

23. This quilt is owned by the Allen County Historical Society, Inc. I do not believe that

the names of the teachers and the years they taught are always correct on this quilt.

24. Lida E. Lees to Jarrett Robinson, July 3, 1991. Lida E. Lees was the daughter of Ella (Funston) Eckdall. Courtesy of Jarrett Robinson and Ellen (Lees) Stolte, daughter of Lida (Eckdall) Lees.

25. In the FFP is a typescript by Frank Funston Eckdall, nephew of Frederick Funston, of two letters written by Fred Funston as a boy, one dated December 10, 1876 (mistyped as 1976) and the other dated February 13, 1881. Frank Eckdall owned the original letters. The letter dated December 10, 1876, is copied from this typescript. As to the other letter, see note 39.

26. "School Pic Nic," *The Iola Register*, May 19, 1877.

27. Newspaper clipping, no title, unidentified and undated newspaper (untitled scrapbook on Frederick Funston). Iola Public Library.

28. "Fourteen Years in Islands," *The Iola Daily Register*, July 2, 1913.

29. "North of Deer Creek," *The Iola Register*, January 30, 1880.

30. "School Report," *The Iola Register*, January 30, 1880.

31. "School Report," *The Iola Register*, February 20, 1880. See also *The Humboldt Union*, February 21, 1880 (school report for Dist. No. 5).

32. "School Report," *The Iola Register*, December 23, 1881.

33. "School Report," *The Iola Register*, January 27, 1882.

34. "School Report," *The Iola Register*, March 3, 1882.

35. "Pic Nic," *The Iola Register*, May 19, 1882.

36. "School Report," *The Iola Register*, June 16, 1882.

37. "Maple Grove School," *The Iola Register*, December 29, 1882.

38. Angelo C. Scott, *A Boyhood in Old Carlyle* (Oklahoma City, 1940), 12. Angelo C. Scott (1857-1949) had an impressive career, which included serving as president of Oklahoma A & M College (1895-1908), which later became Oklahoma State University. Copy at Allen County Historical Society, Inc.

39. The original of this letter, minus a small portion of the first sheet, which apparently came loose, is at the Allen County Historical Society, Inc. I have a photocopy of the complete letter from when Frank Funston Eckdall owned this letter and thus it was used for the text.

40. "Notes By The Way," *The Iola Register*, July 25, 1884.

41. Adda Sophronia Adams, *"Pioneering In Kansas"1869 David Caldwell Adams, wife Delilah Smick Adams, and family,* no publisher, no date, 8. This is a ten-page typed booklet. Copy at Iola Public Library. Angelo C. Scott, see note 38, wrote that the "great and drawing feature" of the Carlyle Literary Society was the debates (19).

42. "North of Deer Creek," *The Iola Register*, January 30, 1880.

43. "North of Deer Creek," *The Iola Register*, February 13, 1880.

44. "North of Deer Creek," *The Iola Register*, February 20, 1880.

45. "Carlyle News," *The Iola Register*, December 23, 1881.

46. "Carlyle Correspondence," *The Iola Register*, January 21, 1887.

47. "Carlyle Cuts," *The Iola Register*, February 23, 1883.

48. Scott, *A Boyhood in Old Carlyle*, 19. Scott wrote that he did not learn to applaud with his hands, as opposed to his boots, until he went to college.

49. Scott, *A Boyhood in Old Carlyle*, 19.

50. "Carlyle Literary," *The Iola Register*, March 14, 1879.

51. "Local Items," *The Iola Register*, December 22, 1882.

52. Eda B. Funston, "Notes on Frederick Funston" (FFP Micro).

53. Duncan and Scott, *History of Allen and Woodson Counties Kansas*, 519. Scott erroneously stated that Fred then entered the "High School at Iola from which he graduated in 1886." The year 1886 is correct, but Fred did not enter until the fall of 1885 after teaching at "Stoney Lonesome."

54. "Carlyle Correspondence," *The Iola Register*, June 11, 1886. One of the graduates was Emma Powell, who made the quilt described in the text.

55. "A School Picnic," *The Iola Register*, June 11, 1886. Letter to editor from "A Visitor."

56. The North Maple Grove School District lasted until 1960 when it was consolidated with the Carlyle School District ("Locals," *The Iola Register*, March 1, 1960).

    For the fall term of 1959, there were only six one-teacher schools in Allen County, down from approximately eighty at one time. There were also six, two-teacher schools that term ("Annual Teachers' Institute to Start Machinery for Rural School System," *The Iola Register*, August 18, 1959).

    The abandoned school building later burned as the result of a fire of unknown origin (Iola, Kansas, resident Margaret Robb, a former North Maple Grove pupil, in conversation with the author on July 8, 2013). In 2019, a mobile home occupies the site of the former school building.

Carlyle Presbyterian Church

"Among the pioneers of Allen County perhaps an unusual percentage were educated, Christian people, and among the very first of the things to which they turned their attention after providing for the immediate necessities of life was the organization of churches and schools," pointed out an early history of Allen County.[1] The Congregational Church at Geneva was the first to be regularly organized in the county in 1858.[2] Geneva was a small town located about two miles north and about four miles west of the Funston farmstead. Closer to the Funston home was the nearby Carlyle Presbyterian Church, which was organized in 1859, and which was probably the second organized church in Allen County.[3]

It will be recalled that the settlement of Carlyle had been founded in 1858 by Presbyterian families from Parke and Johnson Counties, Indiana. A Sabbath School and prayer meeting were organized, which met at different houses in the neighborhood. The actual establishment of the church occurred on June 25, 1859, at a meeting held in a little cabin. It is believed that this was the first Presbyterian Church organized south of the Kansas Valley.

The following summer, church members undertook the erection of a house of worship. On the advice of the stone mason, who was to erect the stone building, the stone was laid up dry. After the walls were erected, there was a violent storm, which demolished the structure. Rather than rebuilding, the church members erected a temporary structure. The resulting box-like structure cost $600.[4] Once established, the Carlyle Presbyterian Church was the center of the social and religious life of the community for miles around.[5]

The minister for a number of years, starting in 1860, was the Rev. E. K. Lynn who was described many years later by Charlie Scott's older brother, Angelo Scott, who was eight years older than Fred Funston:

> The first minister of this church of whom I have any recollection was the Reverend Ezekiel Kasad Lynn. That name predestined him to the ministry. He was a man of God if ever there was one, but how the burden of it bore him down! While he had a certain majesty of appearance, he was the saddest man I have ever seen—sad in appearance, in conversation, in fact, I do not remember to have seen him smile.
>
> His sermons consumed an hour and a half in delivery and sometimes more. Even his prayers were half an hour long, at least in my remembrance, and it was an ordeal to stand through them. He was, in fact, in the direct tradition of Jonathan Edwards and the other Puritan divines of New England. And yet, in spite of his stern and rockbound creed, he was the kindest and most gentle of men.

He must have been paid but a pitiful salary. There came one winter day when his entire flock arranged a "donation party" for the minister and his wife. They descended upon the surprised pair with the makings of a grand dinner and an enormous lot of provender for future needs; and then it developed that only that morning the half-famished couple had prayed on their knees for deliverance, for there was no longer a scrap of food in the house and no money to buy food with.[6]

The little church prospered modestly the first two years of Rev. Lynn's ministry, but by 1862 the Civil War was fully underway. An early church history tells what occurred next. "[T]his little church in far off Kansas felt the drain perhaps more seriously than older churches in the more densely peopled states." Fifteen members of the church entered the Union Army, being three out of every five of the male membership. The women of the church "took up the burdens, both temporal and spiritual, which the men laid down, and labored indoors and out, in their fields or in the church as the exigencies of the times required."[7] By the end of the war in 1865, the church "seemed about to be utterly destroyed." Many soldiers never returned. Various members of the church colonized churches in nearby towns: Iola and Neosho Falls in 1864, and Geneva in 1866. In September 1866, church membership had declined to twenty-seven, the original number of members.[8]

A post-war revival gradually occurred. "Valuable acquisitions were made in the settlement of excellent Presbyterian families from Hopewell and Park [sic] County, Indiana, from Ohio and Illinois, and by accessions from the surrounding community."[9] Included in their members were Ed and Lida Funston and their little family, who arrived from Ohio in 1868. On April 17, 1870, Lida was admitted to church membership after an examination. That same day, she and the two little boys, Fred and Burt, were baptized. Ed joined the church on February 25, 1876, after an examination.[10] Ed soon became an elder of the church, being installed in December of 1876, and serving until December 30, 1882.[11] He also served as a church trustee starting in 1880, and served for an unknown period of time.[12] His service to the Presbyterian faith included serving as a member of the official board of the nearby Geneva Presbyterian Academy.[13]

A growing congregation needed a larger and better structure. On May 10, 1874, the new church building, located a half mile south of the first church building, was dedicated.[14] At the close of the sermon "it was announced that it was necessary to raise thirteen hundred dollars to free the house of debt. Considering the stringency in money matters this seemed a large amount; many feared a failure. The attendance was not so large on account of the threatening aspect of the weather in the morning, but our neighbors went at the job as though they meant business."

Members of the congregation donated over $1,200. After a dinner served in the basement of the new building, the congregation reassembled, and "the entire sum was taken, and the pastor in a brief and appropriate service dedicated the house to the worship of God, *free of debt*."[15]

The *Neosho Valley Register* described the new house of worship:

> Our neighbors have done well. Their building is a plain but neat frame house with a stone basement costing the sum of three thousand four hundred dollars. Its plan is by no means free from objections, still it is a house creditable to the thrift and intelligence of the people of that community. It is built on a high eminence about one half mile northwest of the station, commanding one of the most beautiful and extensive rural views in Kansas. It is in fact "a city set on a hill," and it is founded on a "rock." You enter at the front door into the basement, and pass either to the right or left up a flight of stairs into the audience room. This room is furnished with very complete seats for about three hundred persons. The pulpit is on a platform raised two steps, while in the opposite end is a place for the organ and choir. In brief, it makes a very convenient and attractive auditorium. The basement is not completed. Doubtless this will be done in the course of time...[16]

Ella (Funston) Eckdall noted that the church building was silhouetted against the sky and could be seen for several miles on the treeless prairie.[17]

This was the building where Fred worshipped in his childhood and young adulthood, since it was used until 1890, when a new building was built on the edge of the little community of Carlyle.[18] Undoubtedly, it was in the Presbyterian Church services that Fred learned to sing the song which, a few years later, was a favorite when he was serving as a revolutionary soldier in Cuba—"Beulah Land."[19] Why this four-verse hymn so appealed to Fred is unknown. Perhaps it was the music, or perhaps the words, or both. The first of four verses is as follows:

> I've reached the land of corn and wine,
> And all its riches freely mine;
> Here shines undimmed one blissful day,
> For all my night has passed away.

Then comes the chorus:

> O Beulah Land, sweet Beulah Land,
> As on thy highest mount I stand,
> I look away, across the sea,
> Where mansions are prepared for me,
> And view the shining glory shore,

My heaven, my home for evermore.[20]

The new building, with its capacity for about three hundred worshipers, was not satisfactory in several ways. In the words of a person who had attended the church as a child, "The church was much too large. It had a full-sized basement to be used for Sunday School rooms. The basement was never finished because there was not money enough. The church was impossible to heat in cold weather."[21]

When Ella (Funston) Eckdall was about two or three years old, she refused to mind at a church service, and her mother took her to the basement where she gave her the only paddling she ever received. Fred, who was about ten or eleven years old and who was wearing short pants and a little coat, followed his mother and sister to the basement, where he marched back and forth, hands in his pockets, looking straight ahead, and whistling. Fred "stepped it off like a soldier."[22]

Ed Funston's paternal ancestors had been Presbyterians, and his mother's people were Methodists, but he joined the Presbyterian Church, the religious preference of his wife Lida's family, the Mitchells. Both Ed and Lida were deeply religious, and all of their six children were raised in the Presbyterian faith. Attendance at Sunday School and church was their regular practice. Sunday afternoons, Lida read to her young children stories from *Youth's Companion*. No work, except essential work, was done, not even by the hired help, who put on clean clothes. The children read; walked over the farm for exercise and pleasure; and took rides, but they did not visit neighbors. Iola friends occasionally called on the family. The boys were prohibited from playing ball and hunting.[23]

The Carlyle church annually set up a Christmas tree. In 1885, "G. Hopper," the Carlyle correspondent for *The Iola Register*, reported that "[t]he Christmas tree at the Presbyterian church, was quite a success. 'Everything was lovely, and the goose hung high,' at least it looked like a goose. Among the numerous presents one of President Cleveland's admirers put on a fine doll for his excellency. But the committee took it down. How sensitive some people are."[24]

Even when he was no longer living on the farm, Fred was long remembered at Christmas in the church he had attended since he was a little boy. "[F]or many years after Fred had left Carlyle," his sister Ella recalled, "there was always put on that tree a bag of candy for him."[25]

Chapter Five Notes, continued—*Carlyle Presbyterian Church*

1. L. Wallace Duncan and Chas. F. Scott, *History of Allen and Woodson Counties Kansas* (Iola, Kansas: *Iola Register*, Printers and Binders, 1901), 59.

2. Duncan and Scott, *History of Allen and Woodson Counties Kansas*, 59.

3. Duncan and Scott, *History of Allen and Woodson Counties Kansas*, 59.

4. J. W. Scott, "The History Of Carlyle And It's [sic] Church," *The Iola Daily Register*, February 10, 1925.

5. Angelo C. Scott, *A Boyhood in Old Carlyle* (Oklahoma City, 1940), 6. Angelo C. Scott (1857-1949) had an impressive career, which included serving as president of Oklahoma A & M College (1895-1908), which later became Oklahoma State University. Copy at Allen County Historical Society, Inc.

6. Scott, *A Boyhood in Old Carlyle*, 6.

7. Scott, "The History Of Carlyle And It's [sic] Church."

8. Scott, "The History Of Carlyle And It's [sic] Church."

9. Scott, "The History Of Carlyle And It's [sic] Church."

10. "Register of Communicants" in *Minutes of the Session, Presbyterian Church, Carlyle, Kansas*. The record of baptisms is handwritten and titled "Children Baptized." Lida is listed as "Eliza Funston Adult." The "Register of Communicants" does not list Fred Funston as a member. Carlyle Presbyterian Church, Carlyle, Kansas.

11. "The Register of Elders" in *Minutes of the Session, Presbyterian Church, Carlyle, Kansas*. Carlyle Presbyterian Church.

12. "Carlyle Items," *The Iola Register*, January 16, 1880.

13. "Geneva Jottings," *The Iola Register*, December 16, 1881.

14. "A Brief History of the Carlyle Church and Community." Three-page pamphlet apparently written in 1969. Copy at Allen County Historical Society, Inc.

15. "The Carlyle Presbyterian Church," *Neosho Valley Register*, May 16, 1874.

16. "The Carlyle Presbyterian Church," *Neosho Valley Register*, May 16, 1874.

17. Ella (Funston) Eckdall to Eda B. Funston, February 17, 1931 (FFP).

18. "A Brief History of the Carlyle Church and Community."

19. Arthur Royal Joyce, "New Stories of Funston's Exploits In Cuba," unknown newspaper, with a handwritten notation of 10-29-1917 (FFP).

20. Words taken from an old (title page missing) coverless, battered hymnal that I purchased for 25¢ at the Iola Public Library book sale on October 20, 2001.

21. Adda Sophronia Adams, *"Pioneering In Kansas" 1869 David Caldwell Adams, wife Delilah Smick Adams, and family*, no publisher, no date, 8. Ten-page typed booklet. Copy at Iola Public Library.

22. Ella (Funston) Eckdall to Eda B. Funston, February 17, 1931(FFP).

23. Ella (Funston) Eckdall to Eda B. Funston, February 17, 1931(FFP).

24. "Carlyle Correspondence," *The Iola Register*, January 1, 1886.

25. Ella (Funston) Eckdall to Eda B. Funston, February 17, 1931(FFP).

Transplanted Family and Friends

Although Ed and Lida had moved in 1868 far away from their Ohio roots, they undoubtedly maintained contact by mail with their relatives back home. *The Iola Register* noted two visits back home by the Funstons. On April 15, 1881, the newspaper's Carlyle reporter wrote that Lida would soon start on a trip to Ohio to visit relatives.[1] This trip would have been made by train. In November of 1884, the newspaper report was about the new U.S. congressman: "Hon. E. H. Funston and wife start for Washington Thursday night. They will stop a few days in Ohio to visit relatives. His farm will be left in the care of his son Bert [sic] and the household duties will be managed by his niece, Miss Julia Krug."[2]

Julia was one of Ed and Lida's relatives who had migrated to Kansas by the 1880s. She was born in Logansport, Indiana, in 1858, and was the daughter of Ed's sister, Sarah (Funston) Krug (1833-1861), who died when Julia was a small child. By 1884, Julia was in Kansas with the Funstons, and was still living with Ed and Lida at the time of the 1885 Kansas census.[3] By 1889, she had moved to Emporia, Kansas, about eighty miles from Iola, where she was married that year to Eugene Whitaker.[4]

Another of Ed's sisters was Eliza (Funston) Flory (1834-1909), who had married in 1859 Aaron Flory (1832-1893). In 1883, they moved from Indiana to Emporia. Perhaps Julia Krug had moved from the Funston household to the Flory household in Emporia before her 1889 marriage there. Emporia was the town to which Ed and Lida's daughter, Ella, would move upon her marriage to Dr. Frank A. Eckdall in 1904. It was while visiting her aunt and uncle that Ella had met Frank Eckdall, who practiced medicine in Emporia.[5]

Aaron Flory was a lawyer and Civil War veteran, attaining the rank of Lieutenant Colonel. His regiment was in active service for four years, but Colonel Flory was captured by the Confederates in April of 1864, and spent several months in a prison in Tyler, Texas.[6] His wife, Eliza, had not heard from him for almost a year, and, then, one day in the mail she received a walking cane, which included no explanation. Close examination revealed that she could screw the top free from one end, and there she found a crumpled letter from Aaron written in the Confederate prison. After nine months in this prison, the Colonel and another Union officer escaped and finally reached Union lines, "exhausted, ragged, and dirty."[7] Flory rejoined his regiment, and was mustered out at the end of the war with the rest of his regiment.[8] The "privations and sufferings" that the Colonel experienced in prison nearly ruined his health. He did practice law in Emporia after he and his family moved there in 1883, and died ten years later.[9] Undoubtedly, young Fred Funston was as interested in the Colonel's war stories as he was in his father's military exploits.

Lida (Mitchell) Funston was the youngest of the three Mitchell siblings. The only son was Asa Nelson Mitchell (1840-1917) who, though growing up a farm boy in Ohio, became, at an early age, a teacher in Kentucky before the Civil War. Like so many of the Mitchell clan and his new brother-in-law, Ed Funston, Asa joined the 16th Ohio Battery. On one occasion, he was personally commended by General U.S. Grant for bravery on the field of battle. After the war, Asa was initially a bank clerk, but then engaged in the tree nursery business until he and his family came to Allen County in March of 1889. For two years, the family lived in the neighborhood of Carlyle near the Funstons, and then moved to Iola in the spring of 1891. They eventually settled in an elegant home at 514 South Washington. Asa continued in the nursery business for some years before entering the real estate and insurance business.[10]

Asa and his wife, Frances, known as Fannie, had five children, two of whom died in infancy. Their oldest, Clifford Alice Mitchell, known as "Cliffie" to the family, was born in 1869. She was described in 1901 as "a lady whose intellectual and professional attainments have won her an enviable place in the confidence and respect of the people of Iola."[11] Cliffie served from 1893-1899 as principal of Iola High School, and, in 1899, at age thirty, she was elevated to the high position of City Superintendent of Schools at Iola. In her first four years, Iola schools experienced dramatic growth during the "Gas Boom." The district went from one school building to six; from twelve teachers to fifty-three; and from 500 pupils to nearly 2,500.[12] Cliffie's employment as superintendent, with its lucrative salary of $1,500 annually, came to an unexpected end in April of 1907, when she was 37 years old. Honoring the request of the school board, Cliffie did not apply for re-election as superintendent. The board's main reason was "that they wanted a man as superintendent." In making this request to her, "the board did not offer any criticism whatsoever of her work in the Iola schools in the past, but declared that her work was very satisfactory in every way." When Cliffie informed the teaching staff of the board's decision, there were tears in her own eyes and in those of many teachers.[13]

The school board of nearby Gas City was apparently more enlightened, at least in modern eyes, than their brethren in Iola. Less than a month after the Iola board's action, the Gas City board hired Cliffie as superintendent on the first ballot. She prevailed over six other candidates.[14] Cliffie served as superintendent for only one year, since the following year, at age thirty-nine, she wed for the first time and moved to Pittsburg, Kansas. Her husband, Allen H. Bushey, was Superintendent of Schools there, and was a widower with three children.[15] Two years later, at age forty-one, Cliffie gave birth to a son, who was, appropriately, named Mitchell.[16] Cliffie lived to age eighty-two, dying in 1951 from a heart attack suffered while visiting in the Emporia home of her cousin, Ella (Funston) Eckdall.[17]

The next of Asa and Fannie Mitchell's children, Burton Johnson Mitchell, who was known as Burt, was born in 1871, and like his first cousin, Fred Funston, was nationally known in 1901, since he was one of the American army officers who made the arduous trek to Palanan to capture Aguinaldo. Second Lieutenant Burt Mitchell served on the staff of General Frederick Funston, a fact noted in the news accounts at the time, but their familial relationship was not identified in most of the contemporary newspaper accounts this author has read. There was obviously a close relationship between the two cousins, probably dating back to their childhood and re-enforced after the Asa Mitchell family moved to Allen County in 1889, when Burt was 17 years old and Fred was twenty-three. When the Spanish-American War broke out in 1898, Burt joined the newly formed Twentieth Kansas of which Fred was the commander.[18]

The youngest of Asa and Fannie's three children was Florence Brownie Mitchell, born in 1882, and who, like her siblings, was born in New Carlisle, Ohio. The Asa and Fannie Mitchell family also included Asa's niece, Maude Minrow, the daughter of Asa Mitchell and Lida Funston's older sister, Mary Frances (Mitchell) Minrow (1837-1874), who had died as a young woman, leaving two small children.[19] At some subsequent point, Maude, who had been born in 1871, joined the household of Asa and Fannie and was raised as a sister with Florence, even though the two cousins were eleven years apart in age.[20] Maude earned a bachelor's degree from Kansas State Teachers College in Emporia, and a master's degree from Columbia University in New York City.[21] Never married, Maude for many years lived in Emporia, and served as Dean of Women for the Teachers College there.[22] Maude's only sibling, her brother, John Minrow, moved from Ohio to Emporia, and frequently visited Maude in Iola. John was a train dispatcher for the Santa Fe Railway in Emporia. Suffering from "weak lungs," he died unmarried and childless in 1903 at age 33.[23]

The most important of the family transplants from Ohio was undoubtedly Lida and Asa's mother, Elizabeth (Sweigert) Mitchell, who was the last of her immediate family to come to Allen County. Her husband, James Mitchell, died in 1859, and she apparently continued, after his death, to operate for some time the Mitchell House in New Carlisle. She made at least two visits to Allen County, the first in the summer of 1883 when she visited the Funstons, and then in the summer of 1889. Her son Asa and his family had moved to Allen County in March of 1889. Elizabeth, age seventy-nine, visited at that time both her daughter, Lida, and her son, Asa, and their families.[24] Perhaps not long thereafter she moved to Allen County, where she made her home in Iola with Asa and Fannie until her death there in 1894.[25] Elizabeth's granddaughter, Ella (Funston) Eckdall, recalled her many years later: "My earliest recollection of my grand-mother Mitchell are [sic] of seeing her sit daily by the window, a sincere and earnest figure, reading her Bible carefully and pointing to each word with her fore-finger as she whispered to herself, creating in my mind, as a mere child, the most profound reverence for that book."[26] Several years after Elizabeth's death, her aged younger sister, Rachel (Mitchell) Seal (1820-1906), moved to Iola in 1901 to live with her nephew, Asa, and his family. She died at Asa's home at age eighty-five in 1906. Her body, accompanied by Asa's wife Frances, was shipped by the Missouri Pacific Railroad to New Carlisle, her former home, for burial.[27]

Family members were not the only ones who followed Ed and Lida to Allen County. Their close friends, the McClure family of New Carlisle, did not wait long to migrate to the new land in that same year of 1868 sometime after the Funstons arrived there. James "Jim" McClure had been a comrade in arms with Ed in the 16th Ohio Battery. Jim's older brother, William McClure, rose to the rank of Captain in the 71st Regiment Ohio Volunteer Infantry during his four years of military service. William's daughter, Julia McClure, remembered many years later that Ed had written her father telling him that homesteads were plentiful in Allen County and that the land was good and urging him to move to Allen County.[28]

The McClure family move to Allen County included Jim, William and his wife, and the brothers' parents, Thomas and Sarah, with their two unmarried daughters. When they arrived by stagecoach at Carlyle, they walked to the Funston home a mile or so away. William and his wife and Thomas and Sarah and their daughters all settled on a farm in the Carlyle neighborhood, but Jim settled in Iola where he eventually became a businessman. Farming was not well suited for the rural McClures, so, in 1874, they all moved to Iola. William built a handsome home in 1882 on South Washington, and after Asa and Frances Mitchell and their children moved to Iola in 1891, they ultimately lived in an equally fine home across the street from the McClure home. William served Allen County as county treasurer, and Iola as postmaster during the administration of President Benjamin Harrison, and as its mayor for four years.[29] The prominence attained by the two New Carlisle products, Ed Funston and William McClure, was duly noted at the "Pioneer Day" celebration held in New Carlisle in 1892.[30] Allen County was definitely a beneficiary of the Funston and McClure 1868 migration from Ohio.

In 1910, a reunion of former classmates of Linden Hill Academy in New Carlisle was held in Iola at the home of Asa Mitchell. Time was also spent at Ed and Lida Funston's home. In addition to the Allen Countians, other former classmates still living in Ohio attended. They had all been classmates together in "the early morning of our life" at a time "when Linden was a very important factor in the affairs of the community, in the creation of public sentiments for the right, in political matters, as well as every moral uplifting influence that tended to purify and better society." The visitors from Ohio concluded, at the end of their visit, that "[t]he Ohio contingent at this place is pleasantly situated, have beautiful homes and we could see no reason why they should not be happy."[31]

Elizabeth (Sweigert) Mitchell
Maternal Grandmother of Fred Funston

Chapter Five Notes, continued—*Transplanted Family and Friends*

1. "Carlyle Reveries," *The Iola Register*, April 15, 1881.

2. "Carlyle Correspondence," *The Iola Register*, November 27, 1884. The impending trip was also noted in the "Personal" column.

3. 1885 Kansas State Census, township not identified on the census pages, but it is Deer Creek Township, Allen County, Kansas.

4. Information about Julia Krug in this chapter courtesy of Dale Funston, descendant of Edward and Lida Funston and a Funston family genealogist.

5. Mrs. F. A. Eckdall, "Civil War Soldier Escaped From Prison," *The Emporia Gazette*, May 30, 1961.

6. "Death of Colonel Flory," *The Emporia Gazette*, August 19, 1893.

7. Mrs. F. A. Eckdall, "Civil War Soldier Escaped From Prison."

8. "Death of Colonel Flory," *The Emporia Gazette*, August 19, 1893.

9. "Death of Colonel Flory," *The Emporia Gazette*, August 19, 1893.

10. "Asa N. Mitchell — Obituary," *The Iola Daily Register*, September 27, 1917. This obituary stated that the family arrived in Allen County, Kansas, in 1888, but the obituary of his wife, Frances Mitchell, in 1932 seems to be more accurate, when it stated precisely March 1889, and, then, that the move was two years later to Iola ("Funeral Held for Aged Iolan," *The Iola Daily Register*, November 12, 1932).

11. "Miss Clifford Mitchell presided over growth," *The Iola Register*, May 24, 1979.

12. "Miss Clifford Mitchell presided over growth," *The Iola Register*, May 24, 1979.

13. "Miss Mitchell Not To Be School Superintendent Longer," *The Iola Daily Register*, April 17, 1907.

14. "Gas City News Items," *The Iola Daily Register*, May 22, 1907.

15. "Mrs. Bushey Dies At Emporia," *The Iola Register*, April 27, 1951.

16. "Descendants of James Mitchell and Elizabeth Swigert" (family chart). Courtesy of Burton Bowlus, their great-grandson. He is named for his uncle, Burton Mitchell.

17. "Mrs. Bushey Dies At Emporia," *The Iola Register*, April 27, 1951.

18. "B. Mitchell, Aided Aguinaldo Capture," *The New York Times*, June 17, 1941. The *Times* mistakenly stated that when "he was 7 years old his family moved to Kansas." This is perhaps a typographical error, since Burt was seventeen when the move was made in 1889.

19. "The Gerber Family" (family chart compiled by Ella (Funston) Eckdall) (FFP).

20. Burton Bowlus, Florence's son, in conversation with the author.

21. "The Gerber Family" (family chart compiled by Ella (Funston) Eckdall) (FFP).

22. "Maude Minrow Dies in Emporia," *The Iola Register*, June 18, 1952. Maude is buried in the Mitchell and Minrow plot in the Iola Cemetery, Iola, Kansas, where her uncle and aunt, Asa (1840-1917) and Frances (1848-1932) Mitchell, are also buried.

23. "Death of Mr. John Minrow," *The Iola Daily Register*, August 1, 1903, and "The Gerber Family" (family chart compiled by Ella (Funston) Eckdall) (FFP). John Minrow is buried in the Mitchell and Minrow plot described at note 22.

24. "Local Matters," *The Iola Register*, June 22, 1883, and "Carlyle Notes," *The Iola Reg-

ister, July 5, 1889.

25. "Obituary," *The Iola Register*, July 27, 1894.

26. "The Gerber Family" (family chart compiled by Ella (Funston) Eckdall) (FFP).

27. "Death Of Mrs. Rachel Seal," *The Iola Daily Register*, November 26, 1906. The obituary described Rachel as the aunt of Mrs. E. H. Funston and Mrs. Fannie E. Mitchell. The latter is incorrect, since she was the aunt of Asa Mitchell, not his wife.

28. "An Iola landmark to disappear," *The Iola Register*, undated newspaper clipping. Allen County Historical Society, Inc. This was an interview with Julia McClure (1883-1972) at the time that her parents' Iola home, built in 1882, was being razed. Julia attributed Ed's invitation to come to Allen County to General Frederick Funston, which obviously is incorrect since he was a baby at that time. It clearly came from Ed Funston, her father's friend. She also gave as the year of arrival 1869, but 1868, as reported in her father's, uncle's, and grandparents' respective obituaries appears to be the correct year. Miss McClure was a lovely person, and annually, on Memorial Day, my parents, now both deceased, and, now, my family places flowers on her grave.

29. "Obituary" [Sarah L. McClure}, *The Iola Register*, April 13, 1888; "Thomas J. McClure," *The Iola Register*, October 5, 1894; "Obituary" [J. W. McClure], *The Iola Daily Register*, June 13, 1913; and "Captain William H. McClure," *The Iola Daily Register*, December 15, 1916.

30. "The Week's News," *The Iola Register,* September 2, 1892.

31. J. C. Williams, "Reminiscences of Linden Hill," *New Carlisle Sun*, unknown date in 1910. Typescript courtesy of William Berry.

White, Black, and Indian

Since its founding in 1855, Allen County's population has been predominately white. It was in this world that Fred Funston grew up. There had been a few Black families in Iola virtually from the time of its founding in 1859, but the concentrated area for the Black population was in Charlestown. Also spelled Charleston, this community was located on the west bank of the Neosho River across from Iola.

The primary source of information about Charlestown is the reminiscences in 1930 of Nancy Grubbs, a 90-year-old Black woman. Born in 1840, as a 22-year-old Mrs. Grubbs had come to the village of Iola in 1862 during the Civil War from the Indian Territory, now Oklahoma. She came with other former slaves as refugees from their Indian owners. Since she could neither read nor write, Mrs. Grubbs dictated her memories in the form of two letters, which were then published in *The Iola Daily Register*. All spellings, as they appeared in these published letters, have been retained in quoting from them.

Mrs. Grubbs soon left Iola for Charlestown across the Neosho River. She stated that the town was named for Charles Ross.

> The Creeks, Choctaws, Freedoms, (Freedmen), Seminoles all lived together in Charlestown. Granny Cowden [who had come from France] often visited us. One day Granny Cowden and a bunch of us were walking over to Iola and we ran across two men that were hanged beside the road. One had on a hat, the other a chew of tobacco in his mouth. Both were white. I don't know who was frightened the worse the dead men or us. Granny Cowden never stopped running until she reached Coffachique [sic]. Aunt Sally Todd (colored) was there, hollering more than anybody.
>
> Of all the hangings there were none but white men.[1]

Since 1855, apparently only white men have been lynched in Allen County.

Mrs. Grubbs described two of the Indian tribes:

> There were many witches among the Seminoles and Cohoctaws. Thursday night was their time to go out and witch. The head witch was named "Rock." During the Civil War Old Rock was killed and the rest of them went back to Arkansas. Then we didn't have anybody to guide us. The mother witch was Peggy Hilderbrand. Betsy Squirreltake was also a head witch and Peggy Oughtlifter and Sally Chicka, Celia Weaktea, Diana Coldweather, Towney Coldweather, Sally Strongcoffee, Betsy Storekeeper, Lacy Hawkins, Jack Rope, John Terrell, Clay Hare, Umble Soule, Jack Cocklin, John Kell, Willis Squirrelltake, Jess Sunday, Anderson Sunday. After they left we just wandered about and lost trace of them.[2]

These Indians apparently moved on, likely after the Civil War ended.

The population of Charlestown received a boost in 1871. The story of "Deacon" Albert Woodard's arrival in Allen County was told in the news story of his death:

> In 1871 a couple of white men came down from Kansas [to Tennessee]. As the "Deacon" once put it, they gathered up the "herd" of colored folks, about 40 in all, loaded them into horse-drawn wagons and started for Kansas. After 65 days of wearisome travel they reached Iola. The "Deacon" was the last of the group—which included Bird Kellar, his brother Duncan, "Frosty" Mason, Townsend, Dickerson and Smith—to die.
>
> The party from Tennessee settled just across the Neosho river west of Iola. The settlement was called Charleston. Its population was made up entirely of colored folks. Nothing but cabins—no stores or public buildings—existed there. Charleston is long since gone, and but few persons now living in Allen county will remember that it ever was.
>
> The colored folks lived by the sweat of their brow cutting up firewood for use in Iola homes.[3]

How long Charlestown lasted is unknown. It is now among the things that were.

Mrs. Grubbs died in 1931 at age ninety-one. Her death at the home of relatives in Vinita, Oklahoma, was front-page news in the *The Iola Daily Register* which noted: "Many Iolans remember the kindly, jovial-natured negro woman, who, during her residence here, worked in many homes. She was especially fond of children and those who were children then and under her motherly influence, remember her kindly and as a sincere friend."[4]

Several days later, Fred Funston's friend, editor Charlie Scott, published this apology: "The Register has learned with genuine regret that the children of the late Mrs. Nancy Grubbs and friends of the family were hurt by the heading run over the report of her death in last Friday's issue of the Register, which read: 'Old Iola Negress Dies in Ninety-First Year.' As the article following the heading showed, the Register held Mrs. Grubbs in the highest respect, as it does all the members of her fine family, and it regrets extremely if a hastily written headline conveyed any other impression."[5]

A long-time resident west of the Neosho River, C.L. Arnold, recalled after Mrs. Grubbs' death that she "is well and favorably remembered by the few survivors who lived on the West Side, when she lived at Charlestown, a few rods more than a half mile west, and an eighth of a mile north of the [Neosho] river bridge. In these early days the latch-string of welcome hung out to the grasp of Aunt Lucy, as we white young folks called her, to a degree as great as accorded to others bearing much higher marks of professional distinction."[6]

The Indian tribe most associated with Allen County is the Osage. The northern part of the county had been reserved for the New York Indian tribe, which never moved there, and the southern part was part of the lands which had been given to the Osage by treaty with the United States government.[7] In post-Civil War Allen County, the Osage were not hostile to the white settlers. There were also Indians there from some other tribes. These Indians on occasion visited the towns of Allen County. In 1868, the Iola newspaper *Allen County Courant* noted: "A number of Sac Indians were strolling about town last Sunday, apparently without any business. There seemed to be but precious little of the 'noble' left in them judging from appearances. These were the first Indian[s] that have been in town in several months, excepting those passing through."[8]

By about 1870, most of the Indians had sold their lands in Allen County and moved elsewhere. A few remained, as would be noted in the local newspaper. In the fall of 1876, *The Iola Register* reported two appearances in town: "Quite a number of Indians were strolling on our streets last Wednesday plying the usual vocation of the noble red man, begging."[9] A couple months later, the same newspaper noted that there were a few Indians in town.[10] Even as late as 1878, Indians visited Humboldt.[11] In June of 1876, a group of Indians irritated the editor of *The Iola Register*: "A number of Indians are reported to have been camping at the head of Deer Creek last week and hunting for deer. This should be prohibited. Indians have no right to do what the law prohibits the whites from doing. Last year a party of Indians killed a large number of deer on the head of the Marmaton and Deer Creek while the game law was in force. They should not be allowed to straggle through the country and kill game in violation of law, and we suggest to the people in the vicinity where they are in the habit of stopping that it would be well to give them a hint to 'move on.'"[12]

Although the local Indians were not hostile, there appears to have been local concern about what might happen with Indians in general. In 1868, the year the Funston family arrived in Allen County, there was much alarm in the state of Kansas. "The month of June, 1868, brought the biggest Indian scare that Kansans ever witnessed."[13] Indians ransacked farm houses and killed livestock in Marion County before the Cheyenne, led by Tall Bull, attacked the Kaw Indian reservation at Council Grove. The Cheyenne were driven off and headed westward. "Instantly the entire east-central portion of the state was aroused... Not knowing where the Indians would strike next, the suspense was terrible to the people in the region."[14] Undoubtedly, Allen County residents felt this fear. In August 1868 a band of approximately 200 Cheyenne went on the warpath.

Beginning in the Smoky Hill valley, the Cheyenne swept northward to the Saline, Solomon, and Republican valleys, and killed at least a dozen settlers; raped women; took others captive; and committed other depredations.[15] The Governor of Kansas called for five companies of cavalry to be raised to join with the U.S. Army in the fight against the Indians.[16] Iola, with an estimated population of 900, raised 130 volunteers who became a part of the 19th Kansas Volunteer Cavalry.[17] A fall and winter campaign resulted in the "complete subdual" of the Cheyenne, Arapahoe, Comanche, and Kiowa tribes.[18]

There were Indians in the neighborhood of Carlyle when it was founded in 1858. When the Robert and Emaline Jordan family arrived from Iowa in May of 1857, they settled on a farm two miles east of the future site of Carlyle. At the steep bank of the creek east of their house, Indians camped for five years and some for as long as ten years before moving south. These were Osage, Sac and Comanche. These Indians gave the whites "no serious trouble." The Osage camped in the timber and traded with the white men. They traded a pony for a sack of flour. Their tents were made of buffalo and bear hides, the latter being as soft as quilts. By going fifteen to twenty miles west of Iola, hunters killed as many buffaloes as they wanted, since thousands would travel north in the spring and south in the winter. Only the hindquarters were used for meat.[19]

Another early family in the Carlyle neighborhood was the Gilkesons. Dave Gilkeson reminisced many years later about what had happened to him as a boy:

> "I remember one time," Dave said, "shortly after we moved to Kansas in 1858, and had taken the old farm up by Carlyle. Mother was always scared the Indians would kidnap some of us, and whenever they stopped to beg for food she always gave them some. One day she sent me over to the Evans farm for something, and I started on the mile walk to what is now the county farm. I got about half way and saw a bunch of Indians riding down on me. I started running, but I couldn't make it back home. Two big greasy bucks overtook me and threw a stinking old blanket over my head. I fought, bit and kicked their shins, but they only laughed. The harder I fought the harder they laughed. They finally let me go, motioning to me to run back home. They didn't have to though. They probably wanted to have some fun," Dave continued, "or it may be the reason they let me go was because I was redheaded. Indians always liked redheaded people."[20]

With the close proximity of the Funston home to the road, the Funstons had their own encounters with the Indians. Ella (Funston) Eckdall described this relationship years later:

The presence of a lone Indian or of several riding single file or in wagons, along the road was no uncommon sight. Seldom did they molest the settlers except to order food and drink. From sheer fear of these husky warriors, and with due respect for the safety of their own scalps, no housewife ever ventured to refuse their demands. Mother related the following story of her first caller from the red man's tribe: Stopping at the farm home, the chief demanded his dinner, in sign language, and ate it in utter silence except for an occasional grunt of satisfaction. Graciously Mother passed him a tall compote of choice canned peaches from the home orchard, when to her great astonishment, he greedily devoured the entire contents of the dish. Mother, being one of those dainty individuals who always sipped her tea with her little finger held upright, and who at all times strictly adhered to her Ohio code of correct table manners, was left speechless at this breach of civilized etiquette. This was her first introduction to the crude ways of the American savage.

I recall as a child [she was born in December of 1873], seeing a dusty, covered wagon draw up at our front gate and unload an unbelievable number of redmen. Mother, terrified at this sight and being alone with my [two year older] brother Pogue and me, concealed us beneath her bed and cautioned us to be absolutely quiet. These unwelcome visitors investigated the premises and were particularly pleased at finding a bed of spring onions which they appropriated to their own use. The loss of the onion crop, my brother Burt's special contribution to the family table, caused him great grief and many tears.

The return of the Indians at any time caused more or less apprehension among the settlers, lest their mission might not be a friendly one. I recall one day in the summer of 1877, when the noonday sun beamed down fiercely upon the men returning from the fields, that there was an unusual hurrying and scurrying about the place as the men fed and watered their horses. There was excitement in the air as we hastened to the stile block beside the front gate. Father assembled all his family, including the colored help, John and Angeline Campbell and son "Lutie," to await developments. Off to the west along the Johnny Powell road, crept a long line of white-topped prairie schooners that met the trail at the crossroad north of our farm. When the caravan reached our house, they stopped for a drink of water at the well. Here we learned from the United States officers in charge, that they were transferring a tribe of savage Sioux Indians from Dakota to the Indian Territory—now Oklahoma.

The first wagon, an open one, contained a group of officers who were closely guarding the Sioux chief, who somewhere along the way had imbibed too much "fire-water" and had killed a man at Garnett, Kansas. They took no chances with this wily barbarian, and kept him chained to the wagon bed. On the outside of their wagon, in the dust and dirt, hung their supply of dried meat.

A husky squaw and her swarthy-hued daughter sunned themselves for a time, against our front gate post and seemed in no hurry to continue their journey. They were gaudily attired in the latest Sioux fashions—gay colored calicoes, strands of vari-colored beads, and bright beaded circlets about their heads. As I, a little girl, stood enraptured with the beauty of this savage splendor, I secretly resolved to surpass them some day with dazzling finery of my own.[21]

The Iola Register of June 9, 1877, reported the passage of Indians and wagons through Iola: "Last Monday afternoon about 150 Indians and 41 wagons passed through Iola on their way to the Indian Territory. They were of the Ponca tribe, who have heretofore been living in Dakota Territory, and were on their way to the Quapaw reservation in the Indian Nation. The balance of the tribe, numbering in all about 700, will soon follow. They were a nice looking outfit."[22] Except for the fact that the Indians are described as of the Ponca tribe rather than being Sioux, this news account appears to be about what Ella had described.

Ella (Funston) Eckdall concluded her remembrances of the local Indians with these words:

As children we were well tutored in the ways of these stealthy nomads. In going and coming from school, we carefully scanned the horizon from the Cozine hill, for the sight of any lone rider in the distance. If we were suspicious of the nature of the approaching stranger, we lost no time in taking refuge in a hole in the hedge at the foot of the Cozine hill, made for such emergencies by my brother, Aldo [born in 1877]. Scratches from thorns were nothing to the horrors of a scalping-knife. As the years passed and the settlers become [sic] more numerous, the Indians made fewer trips over the old trail until they finally ceased entirely.[23]

Chapter Five Notes, continued—*White, Black and Indian*

1. "Former Slave Tells Her Experiences in Old Iola," *The Iola Daily Register*, October 7, 1930. The second letter appeared in the December 6, 1930, issue under the headline "Nancy Grubbs Writes Second Installment."

2. "Former Slave Tells Her Experiences in Old Iola."

3. "'Deacon' Albert Woodard Goes To His Rest After Lifetime of Toil," *The Iola Daily Register*, February 24, 1930.

4. "Old Iola Nigress Dies In Ninety-First Year," *The Iola Daily Register*, February 12, 1931.

5. *The Iola Daily Register*, February 17, 1931.

6. "Neosho Vally and Union" (C.L. Arnold), *The Iola Daily Register*, February 20, 1931.

7. Signage in "The Native American Indians of Allen County" exhibit in the Allen County Museum of the Allen County Historical Society, Inc.

8. *Allen County Courant*, February 22, 1868.

9. *The Iola Register*, September 2, 1876.

10. *The Iola Register*, November 25, 1876.

11. "Humboldt Items," *The Iola Register*, January 5, 1878.

12. *The Iola Register*, June 24, 1876.

13. Marvin H. Garfield, "Defense of the Kansas Frontier 1868-1869," *Kansas Historical Quarterly*, Vol. 1, No. 5, 454.

14. Garfield, "Defense of the Kansas Frontier 1868-1869," 454.

15. Garfield, "Defense of the Kansas Frontier 1868-1869," 456.

16. Garfield, "Defense of the Kansas Frontier 1868-1869," 461.

17. *Centennial Edition, The Iola Register*, May 30, 1955, 2-B. This citation is of a one-sentence paragraph with no title; the year is mistakenly given as 1869 instead of 1868.

18. Garfield, "Defense of the Kansas Frontier 1868-1869," 451.

19. Reminiscences of Samuel G. Jordan as told to his nephew, R. O. Howard, on September 27, 1929, and then written by him in his own words. Courtesy of Scott Jordan.

20. Undated newspaper article apparently from *The Iola Register*. Allen County Historical Society, Inc.

21. Ella Funston Eckdall, *The Funston Homestead* (Emporia, Kansas: Raymond Lees, 1949), 14-16.

22. *The Iola Register*, June 9, 1877.

23. Eckdall, *The Funston Homestead*, 16.

CHAPTER SIX

Childhood: 1865–1883, continued

Prairie Fires and Winter Storms

Prairie fires were an integral part of the Kansas frontier. As one pioneer woman remembered, "They are a grand and sublime sight when spreading over a large tract, the tall grass waving with every breeze, now fiercely blazing, and now with undulating motion, looking indeed like a 'sea of flame,' when the fiery billows surge and dash forcefully; or when the winds are still, like an unruffled, quiet burning lake."[1]

Although a prairie fire may have been a sublime sight, the early settlers of Allen County likely focused more on the threat they posed to themselves and their property. This threat of destruction, and even death, was not limited to the open prairie. The towns were equally at risk. A large prairie fire south of Iola in February of 1868 devoured fences, orchards, barns, haystacks and wood piles, while a strong wind from the south impelled the fire toward Iola. Although protected somewhat by the about ninety-feet-wide Elm Creek one-half mile south of town, at least two or three times the fire leapt the water barrier, only to be stopped "by dint of hard effort."[2]

A prairie fire on the march was an awesome sight. A local reporter detailed one which occurred on November 18, 1873: "[A]bout ten o'clock a fire was seen coming over the hills north of [Iola] with fearful rapidity. The wind was blowing a perfect gale and the fire traveled at race horse speed...the wind, smoke, dust and cinders made such a cloud that it was nearly impossible for any person to live in, much less do any work, still nearly all the men in town turned out and showed their good will." This effort was successful to save some buildings north of town, and the northwest wind carried the fire to the east of Iola instead of into it.[3]

A description of an 1872 fight to save a farm home from a prairie fire several miles east of Iola was related many years later by a man who had been only about sixteen at the time of the fire:

> People living on the prairie now cannot possibly realize how dangerous the big prairie fires were in an early day.

141

I think it was in the late fall of 1872 or perhaps 1872 [sic] for a Sunday that we were just sitting down to turkey dinner when we smelled smoke and on looking out we saw an awful fire a mile or two south of us, and as the wind was blowing a gale from the south we at once realized that our hedge row would be of no avail in such a wind. The wind would carry the blaze along on top of the grass for 150 feet and the grass would catch there and jump another 150 feet. The huge fire would run as fast as the wind blew.

My sister had learned to put the harness on the horses and I was so excited she got the harness on her horse first. We hitched them to a plow and plowed a furrough to set a back [fire] of hay just south of it, and if the stack got on fire the stable would burn. The sparks from it could set the house on fire, and we would be completely burned out with no insurance.

We set a back fire and I noticed two men had back fire at the school house. Then our attention was taken up in keeping the back fire from jumping the furrow.

We did not have time to plow two furroughs, or to unhitch the horses, just let them stand behind the stable. Father, Mother, my sister and I worked in the intense heat and choking smoke until we were ready to drop from exhaustion, but it was no use, the fire got over the furrough and with the all out efforts we could not prevent it spreading to the stack. My mother brought a wash boiler of water that helped some, but it was no use. We could not stop it and were nearly exhausted. The intense heat from the main fire now reached us, and the smoke was unbearable. Father gave a moan and gave it up and the rest of us were just going to run when the two men from the school house jumped into the fire and with vigorous sweeps had it out. Just then a strange thing happened, the wind changed to the east and the fire burned to Iola and went out, or else the whole country for thirty miles north of us would have been burned. When the fire was over we found the young men, Henry Moore and Leonard Sutherland, and we were quick to acknowledge that if it had not been for them, we would have been burned out.

When we went into the house to finish our dinner we found everything covered with black ashes from the fire.

The next day parties went south to see who had put the fire out and found that it had jumped the Neosho River near where Erie is now and came from the Indian Territory [now Oklahoma]. We have experienced hundreds of prairie fires, but none in a forty-five mile gale like this one was.

...

Often the women and children were loaded into the wagon and driven to the creek where the timber protected them until the fires burnt out.

I remember one fire that was set by an Iola man throwing a cigar away just in front of where Clarence Stanley now lives. It was about noon and the old blacksmith invited Mr. Fletch Bissett who was getting some plow work done to go to dinner with him. While they were gone the fire burned the shop, the wagon the team was hitched to, and all the hair off the horses. It did not kill the horses but they were an awful sight.

It was on account of these destructive fires that there were no cotton-tail rabbits on the prairie in those days, or quails either.[4]

On at least one occasion, a prairie fire proved fatal to both man and beast. Several families of Osage Indians lived several miles to the north of the Funston farm. Whether it was before or after the arrival of the Funstons in 1868 is unknown, but an "old brave" who liked to ride across the prairie was caught in a big prairie fire that had started near Humboldt and then burned north across the prairie. Both the Indian and his pony perished in this fire in adjoining Anderson County just a few miles northeast of the Funston farm.[5]

All of these prairie fires illuminated the skyline at night. The fires in the spring were intentionally set to burn the dead grass; the ones in the fall were not.[6] *The Iola Register* in September of 1877 editorialized accordingly: "The present is a good time to guard against prairie fires. While the grass is green it can be mowed and afterwards burned in places where it is not possible to plow. There is nothing so dangerous as the annual fall fires that sweep over our country and it is from sheer neglect that damage is allowed to take place. Attend to this matter in time and our farmers will save by it every year hundreds of times the cost of their precaution. Don't forget it."[7] Such admonition was not always effective. In the spring of 1881, "[p]rairie fires are numerous. Scarcely anyone is thoroughly protected by fire brakes [sic] and we may have a serious fire some of these days. All should be very careful."[8]

In March of 1883, *The Iola Register*, under the heading of "Carlyle Cuts," carried this brief report: "On last Sabbath while at church our good people were startled by the smoke of a prairie fire, which obscured the sun. The wind was blowing furiously, and pieces of burnt grass were carried miles by it." Perhaps the Funston family was part of the congregation that day. This fire came from the north and was prevented from reaching Carlyle by "the efforts of the people who had gathered."[9]

All of this made an indelible impression on young Fred Funston. As a revolutionary soldier in Spanish Cuba years later, he wrote to a friend, "Say, old man, you ought to see a battle. There is the most infernal roar, as if all hell had broken loose and the smoke resembled that of the prairie fires that we used to have at home."[10] By 1897, prairie fires in Allen County were largely a thing of the past due to the settlement by farmers of most of the county, thus eliminating the wide-open prairie.

Prairie fires were not the only notable natural part of the world in which the Funstons had settled. Ella (Funston) Eckdall summarized this world well:

Not all was pleasant and balmy in Kansas in the 60's and 70's, for the climate was subject to extreme changes. The summer's heat was often unbearable, scorching every living thing that braved its burning rays. Nature seemed to be testing human endurance. The insect world alone, flourished and added to the misery of the farmer. The noisy cicada rejoiced from the tree tops as the sun beat down unmercifully upon the scorched fields of grain and the seared grass in the meadows; the grasshopper did his utmost to add to the gleeful destruction, as he hopped from one resin weed to another and snapped his wings in derision, as the farmer saw his crops wither and die.

The winters were bitter cold. Fierce winds swept over the bleak prairies and cruelly lashed the unprotected homes of the settlers. Frequently in the upland areas, long poles were placed against the houses to support them in the raging storms. For months the settlers were snow-bound, having no access to the outside world. At such times, the twinkling lights of the distant settlers gave them a feeling of companionship and nearness in their isolated homes.

The days were dreary and the nights long. Few living things ventured forth across the icy landscape. Down in the hollow of the Cottonwood slue, not far from our home, the shrill cry of the coyote on snowy nights, voiced the loneliness of the great white stretches and the gray owl from his secret bower, hooted a solemn warning to the little creatures of the night.[11] ["Any person who has never heard a wolf [coyote] howl in the night cannot possibly imagine how terrifying the sound is. The sound makes one think that it comes from the throat of a whole pack of wolves, and ends with such an awful series of short yelps that one thinks the whole pack is after him."[12]]

The snow storm of January 22 and 23, 1873, was memorable: "Wednesday night and throughout Thursday we were visited by the worst snow storm known in Southern Kansas. In some places the drifts were from five to seven feet high. Most of the trains on the L.L. & G.R.R. were snowed in. The cold was not severe at any time, although a strong north wind prevailed."[13] The editor of the *Neosho Valley Register* provided his readers a harrowing description of his train trip through this huge snowstorm:

On Wednesday of last week your "humble servant" in company with Geo. A. Bowlus left the classic shades of Iola at the dead hours of night for the then center of attraction, Topeka. The wind was howling, the snow flying and everybody shivering, yet that noble steed, "the iron horse" carried us along at good speed, passing the quiet little town of Carlyle and the far famed city of Colony in capital order, but when we reached the Lone Jack region six miles above Colony our "noble steed" grew faint and weary... so the cars were all detached from the panting engine and thus freed, it made the snow scatter worse than the wind if possible, and continued on its course for a mile and a half when it struck a snowbank that resisted its power, and one of man's noblest inventions of beauty and strength, in the language of railroad men was left "dead," nearly buried in the drifting snow. By the way, if the person who wrote "Beautiful Snow" had been in the cars which were stuck fast in a drift on the "raging prairie" six miles from anywhere for two days and nights, with but little fire and less to eat, with snow over head, under foot, and in fact filling the air so that one could not see more than a rod or two, with no prospect of getting relief for two or three days, all on account of the snow, they would probably have used some other adjective than "beautiful." Whether it would have changed the mind of the author of "Beautiful Snow" we know not, but are satisfied that those young ladies that breakfasted, dined and supped, on a biscuit and melted snow the first day, and on fried pork and frozen bread the next, did not feel much like calling the snow "beautiful." We are also quite sure that the young man who had sixty-six head of cattle freezing and starving in the cars, with no means of relief, didn't see any great amount of beauty in the thing... Now it might have been very romantic to some people to be snowbound for two days and nights on the Lone Jack, with scarcely anything to eat, and no place to lie down and rest, but we couldn't exactly see it; therefore, as soon as we discovered that there was no probability of the train being released on the second day and the storm having abated we took, "Walker's line" for Iola which carried us sixteen miles in about six hours and landed us safe and sound in the land of the free and the home of the brave.[14]

A February 22, 1873, letter to the editor from a Carlyle resident provided this perspective on the magnitude of the bad weather that winter: "The winter thus far, has been one of the severest. Old settlers say, it has been the severest we have seen in Kansas. I believe we have had about fifteen storms since the first of Dec.— up to this hour, mercury has been below zero sixteen times since the above date (at sunrise), and no lower than 22°."[15]

The local newspaper reported a subsequent major storm. In February of 1881, eight years later, there was another severe snowstorm in eastern Kansas, and a strong wind caused the snow to drift badly. "As usual, the railroads were soon compelled to abandon their trains... While less snow fell than in the great storm of 1873, the greater drift made it worse on the railroads."[16] A year later there was a sleet storm, the like of which "we have never witnessed..." since November of 1864. "Fruit trees, especially peaches, are badly injured in many orchards. Forest trees have been badly cut, and in town the damage to ornamental trees has been very severe. Twigs the size of a lead pencil bore ice an inch in diameter and the weight on trees and bushes must have been enormous. Business was almost entirely suspended the fore part of the week."[17]

Our story of Mother Nature in Allen County during Fred Funston's childhood concludes with an 1882 front-page news story about her at her most spectacular—an electrical storm:

It has been so common to remark after each storm this season that it was the worst one yet experienced, that we do not see how so tame an expression can answer for the electric storm of last Saturday night. At an early hour in the evening the clouds which had lined the northern horizon began to gather, while the muttering thunder and rising wind foretold a storm was coming. Visions of cyclones affrighted the timid and shelter was sought by all. About 8:30 the rain commenced, the wind blowing a gale. About ten the storm was at its height, the wind blowing strong and the rain pouring down. At this time, the electric fluid began to play in the wildest way imaginable, the reports of the thunderbolts being almost incessant. But it was about twelve before the electric phenomenon was at its best. For half an hour the surcharged atmosphere was a continual blaze, the reports being deafening in their power. A large percent of the lightning bolts undoubtedly sought the earth. A number of instances are reported this week. The accompanying rain was a rushing wall of water. Altogether it was an exciting storm and but few people went to sleep until after it abated.[18]

Chapter Six Notes, continued—*Prairie Fires and Winter Storms*

1. Sara T.L. Robinson, *Kansas; Its Interior and Exterior Life. Including a Full View of Its Settlement, Political History, Social Life, Climate, Soil, Productions, Scenery, Etc.* (Boston: Crosby, Nichols and Company, 1856), 95. The prairie fires described by Sara Robinson were not in Allen County.

2. "Prairie Fire," *The Allen County Courant*, February 22, 1868.

3. "Prairie Fire," *Neosho Valley Register*, November 22, 1873.

4. J.C. Norton, *Community Tales of Old.* This is a series of articles published in *The Moran Herald*, Moran, Kansas, under this title from February 17, 1927, to February 16, 1928. Typescript at Iola Public Library and Allen County Historical Society, Inc.

5. Olin Church, *Lone Elm Days*, no publisher, no date, 4.

6. "Carlyle Cuts," *The Iola Register*, March 30, 1883. See also *The Iola Register*, March 24, 1877.

7. "Local Notes," *The Iola Register*, September 8, 1877.

8. "Special Correspondence," *The Iola Register*, March 11, 1881.

9. "Carlyle Cuts," *The Iola Register*, March 30, 1883.

10. "Another Letter From Fred," *The Iola Register*, April 16, 1897. Letter is dated January 22, 1897.

11. Ella Funston Eckdall, *The Funston Homestead* (Emporia, Kansas: Raymond Lees, 1949), 6. Buildings in town were also vulnerable to being blown over by high winds. In the late 1860s, in Humboldt, Kansas, there were two very tall and narrow buildings known as Shanghi [sic] buildings. Four immense poles or timbers, two on each side, were braced against them. These poles, a foot in diameter and 50 or more feet long, "held these prairie skyscrapers intact while buildings of lesser height were twisted out of harmony with the compass" ("Humboldt Union," *The Humboldt Union.* March 23, 1922).

12. Norton, *Community Tales of Old.*

13. *Neosho Valley Register*, January 25, 1873.

14. "In A Snow Drift," *Neosho Valley Register*, February 1, 1873.

15. Letter from H. C. J., *Neosho Valley Register*, February 22, 1873.

16. "Local Matters," *Neosho Valley Register*, February 18, 1881.

17. "Local Matters," *Neosho Valley Register*, February 26, 1882.

18. *The Iola Register*, July 21, 1882.

Deer Creek

Although their home initially was small and modest, the Funstons generously shared with those in need. In the spring of 1869, Iola lawyer and newspaperman Henry W. Talcott, his wife, and two small children, traveling in a side-spring buggy, were caught in a torrential rain storm on a return trip to Iola from the town of Garnett, located about thirty miles north of Iola. Reaching the north side of bridgeless Deer Creek, now swollen by rainwater and impassable, the family traveled several miles, and beyond habitation, in an attempt to find a crossing. Unsuccessful, they had no choice but to return to the settled area of farm homes at a late hour to seek shelter, but "the four wet, hungry, tired and discouraged people," recalled Talcott, were "peremptorily refused" shelter at three large and comfortable farmhouses. Traveling on, they eventually reached "a little cottage" and explained their plight. "The large, rough looking man spoke kindly, suggested that he had little room, was not in the habit of entertaining strangers, but if we were willing to take such shelter as he had we were welcome, especially on account of the children." The man, Ed Funston, refused to accept any pay from his unexpected overnight guests.[1]

This incident highlights not only the xenodochy and decency of Ed Funston, but also one of the geographical challenges encountered by the early settlers of Allen County—the lack of bridges over the Neosho River west of Iola and over the county's creeks. When the water level was low in the creeks, it was not a significant problem for the settlers, since the creeks could be forded, though, even when the water level was low, treacherous little Deer Creek, about 1½ miles south of the Funston farm, presented a problem of its own. According to Ella (Funston) Eckdall, "In fair weather the dreamy sound of water trickling over the rock-bottomed ford [Edmundson's crossing] seemed inviting and harmless, and so it was, had it not been for its terrifying approach. When the front of the wagon nosed down the extremely steep bank, the far end of the [wagon] bed stood periously [sic] near a perpendicular angle, threatening an unpremeditated summersault [sic] to the opposite bank. When rain deluged the country it became a raging torrent impossible to cross at any point."[2]

When Deer Creek was impassable, the Funstons and their neighbors, living north of the creek, were barred from reaching the commercial center of Iola, about three miles south of the creek, where they traded. There were those, however, who did not let the bank-filled stream prevent their reaching Iola. In 1873, the Funstons' neighbor, J. W. Christian, started for town with his family, but on arriving at Deer Creek found the banks full. Christian told his wife that if she wanted to go to town, she would have to swim the stream. Mrs. Christian "asked if there would be any danger, he replied no. Then said she go ahead, and he did. They arrived in town, dripping wet, but good natured." The editor of the *Neosho Valley Register* then noted in this news report, "We rather admire their pluck in not allowing a little back water to stop them."[3]

Not all travelers were as fortunate. In late May 1882, shortly before the construction of the long-desired bridge over Deer Creek at Edmundson's crossing was completed,[4] D.R. Beatty of Iola and S. Bienenstock, a wool buyer from St. Louis, attempted from the north side to ford Deer Creek at Edmundson's crossing. Beatty, the buggy driver, misread the high-water mark sign as being four feet when it actually was six feet or over. "The crossing is a bad one, as just below the roadway deeper water commences at once. The stream was swollen by the previous rain and the water was running swiftly. As the team entered the stream they were soon swept away from the roadway and before either could be loosened one was drowned." Ultimately, Beatty, who had been thrown into the creek while attempting to get out of the buggy, was swept upon the south bank. Bienenstock clung to the buggy until it upset, and after being swept downstream, was able, by catching at some bushes along the stream, to pull himself out onto the north bank. A neighboring farmer kept him at the farmer's house overnight. The other horse was saved through the efforts of those living near Deer Creek. "It is considered almost miraculous that either of the parties escaped with their lives," the newspaper reported.[5] Others were not so fortunate in crossing Deer Creek. There were several drownings in ill-fated attempts to cross it several miles upstream at the crossing east of the town of Colony, located two miles north of the county line in adjoining Anderson County.[6]

With the construction of the bridge across Deer Creek at Edmundson's crossing in 1882, the Funstons and others in their neighborhood north of Deer Creek had the long-desired improved roadway to travel to Iola. The remaining problem was that the dirt roads themselves, everywhere in the county, were difficult to travel in bad weather. *The Iola Register* editorialized in January of 1878 that the condition of the public roads is "almost intolerable" due to a lack of proper work and drainage. "[T]he rains have mired the roads to such an extent that hauling is out of the question. Road overseers have a fine opportunity to display their abilities."[7]

The newspaper correctly noted in a separate editorial the economic importance of good roads to the county's residents. "Of course the roads are most of them passable, but there are very few but that have places that an empty wagon would be a good load for a team. The farmers, too, are an interested class. It is not to be expected that our roads will always be smooth and dry, but the terrible 'sloughs of despond' that we have been afflicted with for the past month might have been in better shape... Too little attention is paid to roads by our citizens... Every person is directly interested in the state of the roads. They enter largely into the 'bread and butter' conditions of town and country, and both are deeply interested in their being kept in as good shape as possible. Good roads are essential to the welfare and prosperity of all communities..."[8]

A letter to the editor later in 1878 noted that Iola was losing "a large amount of trade and business through their neglect of putting in repair the road west of town." Although there was a bridge over the Neosho River west of Iola beginning in 1872, the "horrible condition" of the road between the river and Iola resulted, the letter writer noted, in people living west of the river going either south to Humboldt or north to Neosho Falls to trade rather than directly across the river to Iola. "*Remember that Humboldt now has a free bridge*, and that people will go a number of miles out of their way to avoid bad roads."[9]

The 1882 bridge for vehicles, animals, and individuals was not the only one to cross Deer Creek. The *Neosho Valley Register*, of April 27, 1870, proclaimed this good news: "Work on the bridge over Deer creek is progressing finely, and we may expect to here [sic: hear] the snort of the Iron horse soon, now. Let her snort!"[10] The "iron horse" was the railroad train. The importance of the arrival of railroads in Allen County is not to be underestimated. "The railroads sped the arrival of new settlers; they provided the farmer with surer markets for his products; they enabled the merchant to replenish his stocks quickly when sales were brisk; they made industrial development possible."[11] The railroad also provided the inhabitants of Allen County, including the Funston family, easy travel to the larger world of the rest of Kansas and of the nation.

There were actually two railroads constructed through Allen County in the year of 1870. The Missouri Kansas and Texas, known as the Katy, entered Humboldt from the north on April 2. The Leavenworth, Lawrence and Galveston Railroad (LL&G) entered Iola from the north in early October and Humboldt ten days later.[12] Its arrival in Iola was announced with the newspaper headline "'Joy' To The World."[13] It was the LL&G, later merged with the Santa Fe, which crossed the newly constructed bridge over Deer Creek near Carlyle.

In a summary of improvements in Deer Creek Township in the last five or six months of 1870, the Deer Creek Township correspondent for the Iola newspaper *Kansas State Register* cited, appropriately, the most important one: "The first and greatest improvement I will note, is the completion of the Leavenworth, Lawrence & Galveston Railroad through Deer Creek Township, and we can now hear the whistle of the locomotive, as it nears our station called Carlyle. It is cheering indeed to know that we are on such a great line of railway, connecting us with Railroad North, East, and West; and who will deny the truism that with the forward movement of the railroad 'old things pass away and all things become new.'"[14]

Chapter Six Notes, continued—*Deer Creek*

1. H. W. Talcott, "Reminiscences of an Old Settler," *The Iola Register*, April 8, 1892.

2. Ella Funston Eckdall, *The Funston Homestead* (Emporia, Kansas: Raymond Lees, 1949), 24-25.

3. *Neosho Valley Register*, May 31, 1873.

4. "Personal," *The Iola Register*, June 16, 1882.

5. *The Iola Register*, June 2, 1882.

6. Olin Church, *Lone Elm Days*, no publisher, no date, 4.

7. *The Iola Register*, January 5, 1878.

8. "Exchange Local News," *The Iola Register*, January 5, 1878.

9. "Southern Kansas Correspondence," *The Iola Register*, July 13, 1878 (letter to editor from "B").

10. "Local Items," *Neosho Valley Register*, April 27, 1870.

11. "Railroads Open New Era In County: Dramatic Race To Border," *Centennial Edition, The Iola Register*, May 30, 1955.

12. "Railroads Open New Era In County: Dramatic Race To Border."

13. "'Joy' To The World," *Kansas State Register*, October 15, 1870.

14. "Correspondence," *Kansas State Register*, December 17, 1870

The Grasshopper Plague of 1874

A Humboldt resident vividly remembered, many years later, what happened the day the long-awaited grasshopper invasion descended upon Allen County:

> On an August afternoon in the year of 1874 we were setting type on the Union [newspaper]. It began to get dark though it was early afternoon and the sun was shining brightly. What could be the reason? It was hard to realize what was going on. Suddenly a few grasshoppers lit on the sill of our window. We took a look at them. Then we looked out and upward to ascertain what was the matter with the sun. We found out, for millions of grasshoppers had obscured it. We were "next" good and plenty then and realized we were in for another grasshopper devastation [there had been one in 1866]. As soon as they hit the ground they began to eat and they never quit until they had consumed everything green, even the green paint on the farm wagons. We have seen a wagon tongue completely covered with hoppers working on the grease and sweat accumulation.
>
> The grasshoppers came from the northwest, the Rocky Mountain region it is said. But it did not matter where they came from, they were here and eating everything the citizens could use as food and that was enough to know, for the time being, at least.
>
> What an appetite this breed of grasshoppers had. You could not walk without stepping on them for they were so thick upon the ground all could not get out of your way as you walked along the streets of Humboldt or as teams traveled the roads. There was but one topic of conversation—"grasshoppers."[1]

The grasshoppers also ate curtains at the windows of houses and the bed clothing on the beds.[2] The collective beating of the millions of grasshopper wings made a roar that drowned out all other sounds.[3]

At age ninety, an Iola resident many years later had equally vivid memories of this winged invasion:

> That was the year when a cloud such as no man had ever seen before came out of the northwest hiding the sun. It was millions of grasshoppers. They settled on the grass and fields and devoured every particle of green foliage in a matter of minutes.
>
> There had been little grain that dry summer. Cattle died in the pastures from starvation. Wells and springs were clogged with the dead insects. Trains stalled from the slime on the rails....

There was only one redeeming feature. The prairie chickens came in droves to feast on the grasshoppers. They were not only food for hungry stomachs. They were shot and trapped by the thousands and shipped east where there was a ready market for them.[4]

The Funston family did not escape this calamity. Ella (Funston) Eckdall recalled her mother's description of the devastation caused by the grasshoppers as "one of the most desolate scenes she had ever witnessed, and one never to be forgotten."[5]

The arrival of the grasshoppers in Allen County had been preceded by very hot weather. The *Neosho Valley Register* noted in mid-August that daily, for the prior two weeks, the temperature had been above 100°, with the highest being 108°.[6] As a result of this extreme heat, "[s]ome people are beginning to think that the cremation process is likely to take place before the funeral services. It's so hot."[7]

The *Neosho Valley Register* editorialized on August 29, 1874, about the arrival of the grasshoppers:

HERE THEY ARE

The grasshoppers have arrived, and are as hungry and saucy as a rebel soldier. They not only forage on everything eatable they can find, but light on one's nose and squirt tobacco juice in one's eyes. They're no respecter of person either, for they would just as soon insult a colonel, captain or city councilman as any other man. Their capacity for storing away green things is wonderful and after they have eaten up all the corn, peaches, apple [sic], etc., we expect they will commence on the candidates for office, but if this don't turn their stomachs and cause them to make wry faces they are tough, that's all.

But seriously, they are here, and there is no use of crying about it or giving up the ship. Our wheat and our crops, although not large, are secured: there is already enough grass put up to keep the stock through the winter, and more is being saved every day.... Our corn crop will be injured to some extent, but the dry weather has ripened it and a great portion of it is dry and hard, so they will not eat near as much of the ear as many anticipate. The stalk will be stripped of the blades no doubt where it has not been cut up, but the hard corn will not be very much injured. As considerable corn has already been cut up we do not look for a big loss in this article. Our fruit crop will probably suffer most, as but a small portion of our apples and peaches are ripe, and unless the pests leave us soon, we shall probably lose most of our fruit.

But taking the very worst view of the case we will still have enough to carry us through the winter. Of course the prospect isn't as pleasant as it might be, still it will do no good to get discouraged and give up; rather let us all take a philosophical view of the situation and make the most of it, hoping for something better another year.[8]

The grasshoppers stayed only a few days. The Iola newspaper reported on September 5 that "[t]he grasshoppers which have nearly all left have done much less damage than was expected."[9] In the end, there was not general suffering among Allen Countians, but there were numerous individual cases of want. In January of 1875, the Allen County commissioners called a public meeting of the citizenry to discuss the "great destitution in the county" and to see what relief measures could be taken. A total of $43 was collected at this meeting and distributed that same day pro rata to the townships, with one person from each township being appointed both to distribute aid obtained and to solicit additional aid.[10]

Aid also came from both outside the state, brought by the trains, and from the state relief committee.[11] Relief was in the form of both food and clothing, and *The Iola Register*, formerly the *Neosho Valley Register*, duly reported both what was received and where and to whom in the county it was distributed. For example, on January 22, 1875, five thousand pounds of flour and forty pairs of shoes were received from the State Grange Relief Agent at Topeka.[12] The Funstons do not appear in any of the published reports as recipients of food, clothing, or money. These reports were detailed. A four-day distribution of goods and provisions in February of 1875 included, for example, "Geo. L. Smith—six children—flour 100 pounds, hominy ¼ bushel, two coats" and "Widow Colten—two children—flour 100 pounds, hominy ½ bushel."[13] *The Iola Register* of February 6 reported, "We are informed that no one in the Carlyle neighborhood has applied for or wants aid, but that on South Deer Creek they have received some aid and are now having dances almost every night. They are happy."[14]

In Iola, the Allen County Commissioners rented a small frame building for use as an "aid depot." Charlie Scott remembered many years later "how the dejected farmers, driving scrawny horses, hitched often with rope harness to dilapidated wagons, used to drive up to that store through the dreary fall and winter of 1874 to have the little jag of 'aid,' as it was called, doled out to them, shamefacedly carrying home the few pounds of beans and corn meal and bacon that was to keep their families from starvation. That is what the old settlers mean when they talk about hard times!"[15]

One of those who was left in poverty after the devastation caused by the grasshoppers was a neighbor of the Funstons, a Quaker minister.

Ella (Funston) Eckdall recalled what the minister later told her: "He had absolutely nothing left but the prospect of a job in the Indian Territory [now Oklahoma]. He said to Father, 'We are now all poor alike. If I could borrow two dollars from you, I could make it to the Territory and take that job.' Father, with nothing in his own pockets but wishing to help him, set traps for quail, sold them and gave him the money. The minister walked the entire distance to the Territory, saved his money for expenses and secured the job."[16]

Before the grasshoppers departed in September 1874, they had laid their eggs in the ground. The spring of 1875 saw these eggs hatch. "Young grasshoppers are hatching out by the millions, and they are very partial to early vegetation."[17] For example, early cabbages were already harvested—by the grasshoppers.[18] These were discouraging times. "Quite a number of persons have lately said good bye to Kansas and, as they expressed it, returned to 'God's country' and their 'wife's relations,' and now everybody is anxious to say good bye to—the grasshoppers," noted *The Iola Register* at the beginning of May.[19]

In reminiscing many years later about the grasshoppers, Humboldt resident J. H. Andrews remembered that the farmer and "the city garden maker" were uncertain as to what would happen—would the eggs hatch and the grasshoppers wait for crops to grow in order to devour them, or would the grasshoppers "wing it out" as soon as they could fly? According to Andrews, the farmers and garden makers decided to wait until June to act. In the meantime, the plague of insects was almost unbelievable: "[T]he ground was covered with billions of young hoppers that would jump out of your way as best they could as you walked along the street. They would pile six inches high on either side of the walk and when you had walked a block of three hundred feet you could look back and see the path you had made. Take it from us, it was not encouraging. You would squash, crunch and crush hundreds of them under your feet as you walked along and it required a rather well behaved stomach to stand it. Weak stomachs had a hard time of it until they became organized to the situations."[20]

The grasshoppers continued to hang on. *The Iola Register* of May 29 reported their status: "The grasshoppers, contrary to all prophesies, hope and expectation are still with us, and in many parts of the country are doing considerable damage. Their wings develop very slowly, a fact which the grasshoppers seem quite indifferent about, although it is a matter of grave concern to the people upon whose fruit and growing crops they are feeding. Their wings are growing, however, and they will doubtless soon swing around the circle."[21] A week later the newspaper was triumphant. "During this week the grasshoppers by the millions could be seen up in the air. They are on the move, and it is generally believed that they will soon all be out of this country."[22] The newspaper also opined that "[t]he grasshoppers are flying away and the wet weather is killing the chinch bugs, but the worthless dogs about our town seem to be on the increase. We wish our city fathers would go for them with the same zeal they have displayed on the license question."[23]

Total victory was announced in the June 19 issue of *The Iola Register*: "For two or three weeks we had hoped to be able to make the announcement (and tell the truth) that the grasshoppers had all left us, but heretofore we have been unable to do so. Last week vast multitudes flew away, and during the first of this week they have all disappeared, so far as we can learn, throughout the county. At least the exceptions are so few that no further damage from them can be expected. Corn and garden vegetables that have been replanted are coming on again nicely, and if the season continues favorable will give an abundant yield."[24] The newspaper was prophetic. According to J. H. Andrews, "[c]rops were put in and the fall of 1875 saw Kansas raise the biggest crop of her existence."[25]

Chapter Six Notes, continued—*The Grasshopper Plague of 1874*

1. J. H. Andrews, "Grasshoppers," *The Humboldt Union*, August 21, 1930 (Clippings file on "Grasshoppers," Iola Public Library).

2. "First Special Session In Kansas Called In State's Darkest Year," unknown newspaper dated February 5, 1938 (Clippings file on "Grasshoppers," Iola Public Library).

3. "The Whole Nation Helped Kansas Survive Its Great Grasshopper Plague in 1874," unknown newspaper dated December 15, 1940 (Clippings file on "Grasshoppers," Iola Public Library).

4. "At 90 Al Hecox Clearly Pictures Iola of 1870's," *The Iola Register*, November 3, 1959.

5. Ella Funston Eckdall, *The Funston Homestead* (Emporia, Kansas: Raymond Lees, 1949), 11.

6. "Local Department," *Neosho Valley Register*, August 15, 1874.

7. "Local Department," *Neosho Valley Register*, August 8, 1874.

8. "Here They Are," *Neosho Valley Register*, August 29, 1874.

9. "Local Department," *Neosho Valley Register*, September 5, 1874.

10. "Relief Meeting," *The Iola Register*, January 16, 1875.

11. "About Destitution," *The Iola Register*, March 6, 1875. Letter by Robert Cook to "Editor Register."

12. "Relief Report," *The Iola Register*, March 6, 1875.

13. "Relief," *The Iola Register*, February 27, 1875.

14. "Local Department," *The Iola Register*, February 6, 1875.

15. L. Wallace Duncan and Chas. F. Scott, *History of Allen and Woodson Counties Kansas* (Iola, Kansas: Iola Register, Printers and Binders, 1901), 27-28.

16. Eckdall, *The Funston Homestead*, 11.

17. "Local Department," *The Iola Register*, April 24, 1875.

18. "Local Department," *The Iola Register*, April 24, 1875.

19. "Local Department," *The Iola Register*, May 1, 1875.

20. Andrews, "Grasshoppers."

21. "Local Department," *The Iola Register*, May 29, 1875.

22. "Local Department," *The Iola Register*, June 5, 1875.

23. "Local Department," *The Iola Register*, June 5, 1875.

24. "Local Department," *The Iola Register*, June 19, 1875.

25. Andrews, "Grasshoppers."

Early Day Crime, Jail Bonds, Jail Deliveries, and Lynchings

With the establishment of Allen County in 1855 as one of the first thirty-three counties of the new territory of Kansas, settlement brought with it crime. The earliest existing court files containing criminal records date from 1858. It is difficult to believe that there were no criminal prosecutions in the years between 1855 and 1858; these early files may have been lost or destroyed. A likely explanation for their disappearance is the destruction, in the early months of the Civil War, of the then county seat of Humboldt. As was described in a civil case filed some years later, "on or about the 21st of Oct. A.D. 1861, the County Seat of Allen County was pillaged and nearly distroyed [sic] by a rebel force and many of the court records either lost or distroyed [sic]."[1]

Of the extant criminal case files, few, if any, appear to be complete. Most files do not disclose the outcome of the proceeding as to whether the defendant was found guilty or not guilty. Thus, while we have a record of the types of criminal cases filed, no conclusions can be drawn as to how often the defendants were found guilty of their alleged crimes. A sample of these cases, plus one reported in a history of Allen County, follows here.

The cases filed in 1859 include one involving the murder of an Indian. The grand jury indictment found that the defendant, Henry Mitchell, "not haveing [sic] the fear of God before his eyes but being moved and seduce [sic] by the instigation of the devil with force and arms...on the twenty-first day of November A.D. 1858..." murdered by use of a Colt revolver "an Indian whose name is to the Grand Jurors unknown." The fact that the murder of an Indian, presumably by a white man, was prosecuted was probably an unusual occurrence. Another early murder involved a dispute over a land claim. In that case, the defendant admitted his guilt and claimed self-defense, but was never brought to trial.[2]

Another prosecution, this time on behalf of an Indian, occurred in 1861, when Laborn Kingston was charged with stealing a bald face sorrel horse, described as the property of an Osage Indian. The defendant confessed his guilt to the crime, and since no jail "has as yet been provided in said County of Allen," the defendant was ordered to be placed in the jail of Douglas County, more than seventy miles to the north.[3]

Many of the early cases, beginning in 1858, involved crimes against persons. The affidavit of B.W. Cowden gives this graphic description: "He jerked out a large Bowie knife and made at me saying he would cut my heart out if I opened my mouth...a[f]ter flourishing it over my head some time [he] stepped back and picked up the [double-barreled] gun and shot a dog that was standing saying at the same time if I opened my mouth he would blow the other load through me."[4] Isaac C. Parker was charged with assault and battery, having allegedly beaten his wife.[5] Abram Coleman was charged with assault with intent to commit robbery.[6] Leonard Fuqua and seven other men were charged with assault with deadly weapons. Fuqua was found guilty and was fined $10 by the jury; the jury found the other defendants not guilty.[7]

Men were not always the defendants, since, in 1863, the state prosecuted Amanda Sheppard. In that case, the complaining witness, Naomie Davis, alleged that on April 18, 1863, the defendant came at her with an eight-inch butcher knife and threatened to cut her entrails out.[8] In another case, which occurred in 1864, the defendant allegedly used a knife to stab and cut the person of Israel Wilson, "well nigh killing the same."[9]

As the theft of the Indian's horse illustrates, early crime was not limited to crimes against the person. In 1860, Oliver Cox was charged with petit larceny, having allegedly stolen one sack coat of the value of $8 from Levi L. Northrup.[10] Northrup operated a merchandise store in the town of Geneva in northwestern Allen County, and, ultimately, became a very wealthy Iola banker and landowner. Northrup found himself on the opposite side of the law in 1865 when he was twice charged with selling intoxicating liquor from a certain two-story building in Iola used by him as a merchandising house, without having a license to keep a grocery, dram shop, or tavern.[11]

In 1859, two men were charged with attempt to commit grand larceny involving the theft of a $30 cow.[12] Five years later, a saddle[13] and a prairie breaking plough worth $5 were stolen.[14] Three defendants in 1860 were charged with killing the widow Randall's domestic animals, one mare of the value of $125 and one horse of the value of $75.[15] The alleged theft of fifteen head of "neat cattle" in Geneva Township occurred in 1860, but the prisoner escaped on October 9, 1860, stopping the prosecution.[16]

In pioneer days, when a horse was an essential element of transportation as well as, at times, the difference between life and death on the sparsely settled prairies, the theft of a horse was a serious offense. On or about April 9, 1859, a man living on the Little Osage was robbed in the night of a horse and bridle, and also "a lot of chickens."[17] The judicial system was not always resorted to in matters of horse stealing, however. In April 1866, two alleged horse thieves were hanged near Humboldt. A contemporary newspaper account of the lynching noted that "[g]entry with horse stealing propensities are having rather a sorry time in Kansas."[18] The alleged participants in the "necktie party" were prosecuted for murder, but the existing file does not disclose the result.[19]

On another occasion, three unidentified men were found a mile south of Iola hanging by the neck from a barn's gable end. All three had their hands tied behind them, and there was a playing card on them stating "Horse Thieves." Several men were arrested; charged with first degree murder; and appeared for their preliminary hearing before a justice of the peace. Their defense counsel suggested that the three deceased had committed suicide, because, after stealing the horses, they had been stricken with remorse and hanged themselves! In reply, it was argued that suicide was impossible, since all three of the dead men had their hands tied behind them when they were hanged. The defendants were discharged by the justice of the peace for lack of evidence.[20]

The year of 1868, in which the Funston family settled in Allen County, was noteworthy for a hotly contested bond election to fund the building of a county jail in Iola. The proposal aggravated the never healed wound created three years earlier in May of 1865, when the county seat had been moved by popular vote from Humboldt to Iola. The need for a jail was a combination of public safety and practical economics. As early as 1860 an Allen County grand jury had found "that there is no jail in said Allen County and as a consequence criminals laugh at our inability to punish offenders or confine outlaws and instead of a place to safely keep offenders against the property persons & lives of our citizens they are boarded at an exorbitant expense of $9.00 per week at private & public houses rollicking & fattening at the Public expense and thus as it were encouraging crime in our midst..."[21]

The financial necessity of having a local jail became more pressing following the close of the Civil War in 1865. In the 3¼ years from April 1865 to July 1868, Allen County spent $2,526.65 to keep prisoners in jails elsewhere and for other related expenses. Those favoring the 1868 bond issue argued that the estimated $8,000 cost of constructing a jail would be a better expenditure of funds, not only to house local prisoners, but also those of five neighboring counties which lacked jails: Neosho, Labette, Woodson, Wilson, and Montgomery.[22] As is so often the case, history repeats itself. The identical argument for erecting a jail as a revenue source was adopted by the Allen County Commissioners more than 130 years later to justify the construction of a multi-million-dollar jail facility, which opened in Iola in 2004.

The simmering issue of returning the county seat to Humboldt from Iola quickly became entangled in the bond election debate with the circulation of a petition requesting the county commissioners to hold an election for the designation of Humboldt as the county seat; this request, if presented, was apparently not granted.[23] Parochial positions ruled. *The Humboldt Union* newspaper opposed the bonds and referred to those who had originated the idea as "Lunatics";[24] the Iola *Neosho Valley Register* favored the bonds, advocating three points: "Vote for the bonds and let justice be administered." "Vote for the bonds and save $10 Sheriff's fees and traveling expenses to and return from jail." And, "Vote for the bonds, build a jail and quit paying Douglas and Franklin counties $6 per week for keeping our prisoners, when we can board them for $2 per week at home."[25]

Election day dawned on August 15, 1868. The vote was much larger than usual.[26] Only adult males voted, since women were disenfranchised. Ed Funston, like the other eighty-six voters in Deer Creek Township, voted in favor of the bonds. A similar result occurred across the northern part of the county, including in Iola Township where the vote was 304 in favor and six against. As was to be expected, the vote in the southern part of the county was heavily against the bonds, including in Humboldt Township where 299 voted against the bond issue and only three voted in favor. Proponents of the bonds carried the day by a vote of 489 to 387, a majority of 102.[27] An editorial in the *Neosho Valley Register* noted that "[t]he good people of this county propose to have a jail. The inside 'fixins' will principally be furnished by Humboldt."[28] This latter remark presumably referred to the prisoners to be kept there. Prominent supporters of Humboldt quickly filed suit challenging the validity of the election, and requesting that it "be adjudged void in toto and set aside..."[29] The District Court dismissed the suit on the grounds that the plaintiffs had no legal right to sue, and, thus, trumpeted the *Neosho Valley Register*, the plaintiffs' case "fell blasted and withered, like seed sown upon stony ground."[30]

The firm of White and Hays erected the jail for $8,400, exclusive of finishing the upper story,[31] and the completed facility was accepted by the county on October 7, 1869.[32] The two story, yellow limestone building is thirty feet across and thirty-seven feet deep, and its exterior walls exceed two feet in thickness. This was the first jail in Kansas west of Fort Scott, forty miles to the east, and south of Ottawa, fifty miles to the north. A visitor to Iola the following March observed that the jail "is built of stone, has twelve cells, and constructed in a manner that will preclude the hope of escape."[33] This was wishful thinking. Four months later, on July 17, 1870, six prisoners escaped from the jail by sawing off two of the bars of the window grate. It was believed that jail visitors had furnished the necessary tools to the prisoners to break jail. This was to be the first of an embarrassingly large number of jail deliveries (i.e., escapes) during the ninety years that the jail served as a place of incarceration (1869-1959). Three of the prisoners chose to remain, and of the six who escaped, one was Peter Kelley, who was awaiting trial on the "Ladore outrage."[34]

Ladore was a small town located in Neosho County, which adjoins Allen County on the south. The town bore the reputation of being "as tough as they make'em," according to a man present at the time. "Whiskey was sold in nearly every house in the town. Vice and immorality flourished like a green bay tree. One day in May 1870 about noon seven hard-looking characters came into town. They commenced to fill up on tangleleg. That evening about dusk they began operations by knocking men down

and robbing them. As they were heavily armed, they soon had full possession of the town and had everything their own way during the night."

In the evening, they took control of a boarding house about a quarter
of a mile south of Ladore, and proceeded to engage in "deviltry" with the
three young girls residing there. The next morning, the citizens of the
town, aided by workmen who were building nearby a railroad, captured
six gang members, the seventh having been shot to death during the
night by the gang leader in a quarrel over the young girls. The remaining six were led in front of the girls, who identified five of them as their
assailants. By eleven o'clock that morning, five men hung lifeless on a
large projecting limb of a hackberry tree. About three o'clock, after both
the people of Ladore and of the surrounding country had viewed the five
men hanging on one limb, the bodies were buried in a large grave. "One
of the hanging party, who had more to say and do in the hanging business
than anyone else, stole the pants and boots off one of the dead men and
cleared out. Had he been caught there would have been one more orna-
ment on the hackberry tree." The seventh "hard-looking character" was
Peter Kelley, who was not recognized by the girls as having assaulted
them. A committee was appointed to investigate him, and their report
would determine whether Kelley would hang or be let loose. The committee decided to spare his life. "While we were investigating him the Sheriff from Iola drove in, and we turned him over to him. We had to work
to save him, as sixty determined men were waiting outside with a rope
ready and too willing to send him along with his partners."[35]

The *Neosho Valley Register*, with the headline of "HORRIBLE OUT-
RAGE" and several subheads, including "Whiskey And Lust Rampant,"
reported to its readers the Ladore outrage, including details learned from
the prisoner, Peter Kelley. At the end of this news story, the newspaper pronounced its judgment on the hanging: "The terrible vengance so
quickly taken may seem to some to be wrong, but when the foul nature
of the crime is considered, who shall say that it was not just?"[36] The next
month, the citizens of Allen County were to be aroused by a lynching in
their own county.

Buzzards had circled for a number of days over the farm of Elzy Dolson
in Cottage Grove Township in the southern part of Allen County. There
had been only a few buzzards the first day, but, as the days passed, their
number grew and these vultures were flying closer to the ground. Round
and round the given point they circled.[37] A young boy, Calvin Griffin, who
had lived with Dolson and his family, had disappeared several weeks
earlier. Some sources claimed that Griffin was an adopted son of Elzy
Dolson, but, according to Dolson's own statement, Griffin's father, William Griffin, had bound Calvin to him as an apprentice in the spring of
1869.[38] Dolson has been variously described as a Methodist class leader[39]

and as a Methodist minister.[40] Although he may have been a minister, he was also a farmer, living some five miles south by southwest of Humboldt in the vicinity of Stewart's lake.[41] He was described as having been well thought of in the Cottage Grove community, including his identification with church and Sunday school, but as possessing a rather uncontrollable temper, at least at times.[42] In 1870, at age thirty, Dolson stood six feet in height, and had red hair, gray eyes, and a dark complexion.[43]

The missing boy had, in fact, been killed by Dolson. According to Dolson's written statement at the time of his appearance for his preliminary hearing following his arrest, Calvin frequently lied, and Dolson had punished him for a particular falsehood involving the milking of cows. Dolson confessed that he had whipped the boy, and then Dolson described what occurred next: "I hadn't struck him but a few licks when he commenced to flounce around. I was sick and weak and couldn't hold him well. I turned in & laid him down on his back, put my foot on his neck and hit him two or three licks with the lash end of a whip. He began to flounce and I pushed my foot down on his throat and the boy laid still and didn't struggle any more."[44] Dolson became alarmed when he realized what had happened, and used camphor, to no avail, to try to revive him. Calvin died in a few minutes.[45]

Dolson decided to conceal his crime by hiding the body in an abandoned well on his farm, and then filled the well with sticks, stones, branches, leaves, chunks of wood, etc. He told those who inquired that the boy had run away, and, in the meantime, Dolson continued, as usual, going to church and teaching Sunday school. Many of the citizens of Cottage Grove were not convinced by Dolson's story that Calvin had left, not finding Dolson's demeanor totally convincing. Throughout the community, the whereabouts of young Griffin were the subject of conversation. The circling buzzards and their growing numbers over the Dolson farm aroused much suspicion, and, ultimately, a number of citizens determined to investigate the Dolson farm, knowing that when buzzards began to circle, it was because of the presence of carrion upon which they could feast. By getting directly below the circling buzzards, the citizens found the abandoned well, and, digging into it, discovered the decomposed body of young Calvin Griffin.[46]

An inquest upon the body was held on Sunday, June 26, 1870, at the farm, and the jury found that Dolson was "concerned in procuring the Death of the Said Calvin Griffin."[47] Dolson was immediately arrested and taken to Humboldt for a preliminary hearing that same day before the Justice of the Peace, William H. Andrews. Dolson was described upon his arrival at the Andrews' house as being abject and cast down. At the hearing the defendant waived examination and was ordered committed to the Allen County jail at Iola. A large crowd attended this preliminary hearing, and though in a sullen, ill-humored mood, the crowd gave no indication of the violence that was to come. The hour was late when the preliminary hearing ended, and since Justice Andrews feared violence, he decided to keep the prisoner in a secure place at Humboldt, and then to take him to Iola the next morning.[48] The following day, Justice Andrews decided to go with the constable when he took the prisoner to jail in Iola. A two-horse farm wagon conveyed the prisoner, seated upon a board placed across the rear end of the wagon box, while the Justice of Peace and the constable sat on the seat in front. The trip to Iola was uneventful, and Dolson was imprisoned in the new county jail.

About midnight that night, June 27, there was a heavy pounding on the back door of the Rosenthal and Critzer Clothing Store located on the southwest corner of the square in Humboldt. A young brother of the owner worked at the store and slept there at night. He was awakened by the pounding and greatly scared by it. He stayed in bed, but the pounding grew louder and more determined. He got up and went to the door, and, upon reaching it, asked, "What do you want?" The response was, "Have you any rope? We are going to hang a man." The young man nearly collapsed from fear, but, in response to the demands from the mob, he unlocked the door and conducted the "committee" to a warehouse a short distance to the rear where they purchased the rope. Returning from the warehouse, he saw on Eighth Street as many as five hundred horsemen who took the rope and immediately headed north.[49]

Although the chronology is not totally clear, apparently that same night there was a knock on the door of the new jail in Iola. Both the Deputy Sheriff, J.H. Walters, and the Sheriff, John Harris, were sleeping downstairs. The deputy was awakened by the knock, and in response to his inquiry through the closed door, was advised that the man knocking had a prisoner from Neosho County, whom he wished to deliver for safekeeping to the Allen County Jail. The deputy awakened Sheriff Harris who opened the door. Three men rushed suddenly into the hall followed by "a host of associates" who seized the two officers. A revolver was placed at the sheriff's head, and it was demanded that Dolson be delivered to them so that they might hang the "S—of a B—." Sheriff Harris flatly refused and attempted to persuade the mob to cease what they were doing. The response was that they were going to have Dolson's life, even if it cost Harris's and his deputy's lives.

Again, demand was made upon the sheriff that the prisoner be delivered to the mob, and a second time Harris refused their demands, and declared that he would not deliver to them the prisoner. A third time the surrender of the prisoner was demanded or else the sheriff would lose his life. Harris for the third time refused, this time answering they could have his life, but not his integrity. The mob attacked the sheriff at this point, throwing him to the floor, and choking him while demanding the keys to Dolson's cell. Harris responded that he did not have the keys. At this point, Deputy Walters was similarly attacked, but the mob, finding that neither officer would obey, wrestled the cell keys from Deputy Walters.

Rather than the mob's unlocking the cell door themselves, Harris and Walters were ordered to unlock the cell, but they refused to do so. A mob member then proceeded to release Dolson. He was taken outside, gagged, and dragged on the ground, with a rope about his neck, to a wagon waiting outside the jail. The mob and their prisoner disappeared into the night, heading south toward Elm Creek. The darkness of the night made it impossible for the authorities to discover their course, but it was presumed that Dolson had been hung in the timber of Elm Creek.[50] His lifeless body was later found hanging in a deserted house on the old abandoned townsite of Cofachique.[51] Only one man was ever charged in connection with Dolson's lynching, and he was acquitted by a jury.[52]

The editor of the *Neosho Valley Register* was careful to note in the account of the lynching, under the headline of "Judge Lynch Again!" that "this mob was composed of men not known to Iola, and that the people of Iola, with one accord, no matter what may be their peculiar religious or moral predelictions [sic], denounce the act as a wicked, unjust and diabolical outrage, and will do everything in their power to bring the offenders to justice." The following week, under the title of "Lynch Is A Poor Judge," the *Neosho Valley Register* soundly condemned Judge Lynch, who, it noted, is "more appropriately called mob, or unlawful assemblage of scoundrels and murderers."[53] Interestingly, the editor of the newspaper was Henry W. Talcott, who was the same editor who had been much more forgiving of those who had hanged the five men at Ladore the month before. This was also the same Henry W. Talcott to whom Ed Funston had been so hospitable the year before when Ed provided Talcott and his family shelter in the storm. The Dolson lynching appears to have been the last lynching in Allen County. As the frontier disappeared there, so did this form of frontier justice.

Chapter Six Notes, continued—*Early Day Crime, Jail Bonds, Jail Deliveries, and Lynchings*

1. Nathan Harris v. Mark Winn. Precipe for Execution filed June 15, 1865. All cases cited are found in the records of the Clerk of the District Court of Allen County, Kansas, at Iola, Kansas.

2. Territory of Kansas v. Henry Mitchell (1859) for the prosecution in the death of the Indian. William G. Cutler, *History of the State of Kansas* (Chicago: A.T. Andreas, 1883), 668.

3. State of Kansas v. Laborn Kingston (1861).

4. Territory of Kansas v. Madison Tye (1859).

5. Territory of Kansas v. Isaac C. Parker (1859).

6. Territory of Kansas v. Abram Coleman (1859).

7. Territory of Kansas v. Leonard Fuqua, Homer C. Leonard, Anderson C. Smith, Avery C. Spencer, Vinton Spencer, Henry Spencer, Edward Cushion, and William Fuqua (1858). The jury verdict appears in this file.

8. State of Kansas v. Amanda Sheppard (1863).

9. State of Kansas v. Stephen S. Trimble (1864).

10. Territory of Kansas v. Oliver Cox (1860).

11. State of Kansas v. L.L. Northrup, Case No. 114 (1865); State of Kansas v. L.L. Northrup, Case No. 115 (1865).

12. Territory of Kansas v. Charles Wade and Abram Coleman (1859).

13. State of Kansas v. Justin Johnson (1864).

14. State of Kansas v. Wm. J. Larimer (1864).

15. Territory of Kansas v. Wm. Vail, J.R. Stilwagon, and P.P. Phillips (1860).

16. Territory of Kansas v. A.S. Curtis (1860).

17. Territory of Kansas v. Samuel Crist, A.C. West, Andrew Crist, Alexander Steel, Samuel Howry (1859). Two of the defendants, A.C. West and Samuel Crist, were discharged when the prosecuting witness failed to appear at the appointed time before the court.

18. *The Weekly Free Press*, Atchison, Kansas, May 12, 1866.

19. State of Kansas v. _____ Cook, John Long, _____ Scott, Wm. Christy, and Stephen Cunningham (1866).

20. J.C. Norton, *Community Tales of Old*. This is a series of articles published in *The Moran Herald*, Moran, Kansas, under this title from February 17, 1927, to February 16, 1928. Typescript of these articles is at Iola Public Library and Allen County Historical Society, Inc.

21. [Allen County, Kansas] *Journal A (October 5, 1858 – Jan 22, 1872)*, 41-42. This is at the Allen County Historical Society, Inc.

22. "Figures Won't Lie," *The Allen County Courant*, July 18, 1868.

23. "Startling Growth—County Seat," *Neosho Valley Register*, August 5, 1868, quoting *The Humboldt Union* about the petition.

24. "Jail Bonds," *Neosho Valley Register*, August 19, 1868. This article quoted *The Humboldt Union*.

25. *Neosho Valley Register*, August 12, 1868.

26. "Jail Bonds," *Neosho Valley Register*, August 19, 1868.

27. "County Bonds," *Neosho Valley Register*, August 19, 1868. Since there were no negative votes cast in Deer Creek Township, and since Ed Funston (listed as E. A. Funston) voted in the election according to the poll records shown in the lawsuit filed after the election (see note 29 below), Ed clearly voted for the bonds.

28. "Local Matters," *Neosho Valley Register*, August 19, 1868.

29. Watson Stewart and William Wakefield v. The Board of County Commissioners for Allen County, Case No. 214, Seventh Judicial District Court, Allen County, Kansas (Office of the Clerk of the District Court of Allen County, Kansas).

30. "District Court," *Neosho Valley Register*, October 7, 1868.

31. "County Jail," *Neosho Valley Register*, January 27, 1869.

32. "The County Commissioners," *Neosho Valley Register*, October 13, 1869.

33. "Down the Neosho Valley," *Neosho Valley Register*, March 23, 1870.

34. "Broke Jail," *Neosho Valley Register*, July 20, 1870. Since 1962, the jail building has been a museum owned and operated by the Allen County Historical Society, Inc.

35. "The Story of Ladore," *Collections of the Kansas State Historical Society, 1911-1912* (Topeka: State Printing Office, 1912), Vol. XII, 450-451.

36. "Horrible Outrage," *Neosho Valley Register*, May 18, 1870.

37. J. H. Andrews, "Old Cofachique," *The Humboldt Union*, May 5, 1927. Andrews was a son of the Justice of the Peace, William H. Andrews, before whom Dolson had his first court appearance.

38. State of Kansas v. Elzy Dolson, Case No. 341. Signed statement of Elzy G. Dolson at Humboldt, Kansas, on June 26, 1870, before William H. Andrews, Justice of the Peace.

39. "Judge Lynch Again!" *Neosho Valley Register*, Wednesday, June 29, 1870.

40. *The Iola Daily Register*, June 26, 1911.

41. Andrews, "Old Cofachique."

42. Andrews, "Old Cofachique."

43. *Jail Record*, Allen County, Kansas, entry of June 27, 1870. Allen County Historical Society, Inc., Iola, Kansas.

44. State of Kansas v. Elzy Dolson.

45. State of Kansas v. Elzy Dolson.

46. Andrews, "Old Cofachique."

47. State of Kansas v. Elzy Dolson, Case no. 341. State warrant dated June 26, 1870.

48. Andrews, "Old Cofachique."

49. Andrews, "Old Cofachique."

50. "Judge Lynch Again!"

51. L. Wallace Duncan and Chas. F. Scott, *History of Allen and Woodson Counties Kansas* (Iola, Kansas: Iola Register, Printers and Binders, 1901), 62.

52. "The Stevens' Trial," *The Humboldt Union*, December 21, 1878.

53. "Lynch Is A Poor Judge," *Neosho Valley Register*, July 6, 1870.

His Excellency, President Rutherford B. Hayes, and the Neosho Valley District Fair

The obvious question asked by visitors to the small Kansas town of Neosho Falls is "Where are the falls?" A riffle in the nearby Neosho River is the source of the "Falls" name. A disappointing explanation, "[b]ut this gradual fall in the deliberate stream, just nine feet in two miles, was the determining factor in the genesis of the place [,] and because the men who founded it had the sense of euphony, Neosho Falls is a matter of natural right as well as verbal beauty."[1] Founded in 1857, Neosho Falls was designated the next year the county seat of Woodson County, which adjoins Allen County on its western border. In 1867, agitation began over the location of the county seat. Lasting nine years and including a half dozen elections, this controversy resulted in Neosho Falls losing the county seat in 1873 in the third election. The "final settlement of the vexed and vexing question" occurred in 1876 with the selection of Yates Center as county seat, but the prolonged fight over the county seat location created much bitterness among the "contesting sections of the county."[2]

In 1874, the annual Neosho Valley District Fair was established at Neosho Falls. The district comprised four counties: Allen, Anderson (adjoining Allen on its northern border), Woodson (adjoining Allen on its western border), and Coffey (adjoining Woodson on its northern border). A square was thus created by these four counties, and Neosho Falls, located in the northeast corner of Woodson County and thus nearly in the center of this square, was ideally situated to host the fair. The fair was always held the last full week in September, "the orchard of the year," as one newspaper described it, when "the trees bend their boughs to the earth, redolent of glowing fruit; ripened seeds rattle in their pods; apples drop in the stillest hours. The woods are thinner, so that we can see the heavens plainer... The time was well chosen—it could not be better. The year's work is nearly done."[3]

In 1879, the board of directors of the Neosho Valley District Fair Association decided to have a fair that would "outdo all former efforts." A letter of invitation was sent to the country's president, Rutherford B. Hayes, to visit Kansas during fair week and honor the fair with his attendance.[4] The efforts of Kansas state officials and of Kansas' U.S. senators and representatives were utilized in the challenge to secure an acceptance. In due course, President Hayes accepted the invitation, writing on August 10:

> My Dear Sir:—I have accepted the invitation to attend the Neosho Valley District Fair, Sept. 25th, '79. General Sherman and aids [sic] and Mrs. Hayes will accompany me, probably also Mr. Evarts the Secretary of State and one or two others, altogether about six or

eight persons. Our stay in Kansas will not exceed two or three days. I will leave Fremont, Ohio, Sept. 22nd, and go by most direct route to Neosho Falls.

Sincerely, R. B. Hayes[5]

The Association secured the services of Professor Worrall of Topeka to handle the fair decorations. He had been the "artistic decorator" responsible for the Kansas exhibit at the Centennial International Exhibition held in 1876 in Philadelphia. Those exhibits "excited the wonder of the world, and made the name of Kansas a household word in every corner of the earth." Worrall's grandest decoration at the district fair was at the entrance to the fairgrounds:

> A triumphal arch had been erected over the main entrance gate of the grounds, decorated with the productions of Woodson county. In this arch, Prof. Worrall, who designed and superintended its construction, accomplished the *chef d'oeuvre* of his life. The arch is a substantial frame work, latticed with broomcorn to about half way down from the top, bordered with heads of the sugarcane, the dark, rich color of which made a pleasing contrast to the green of the broomcorn. Sheafs of wheat in bas relief were on each side. The base was surrounded with stalks of corn. Festoons of the heads of millet hung in graceful curves, interspersed with hanging baskets of luscious fruit. The structure was surmounted with a battlemented top, the battlements being made of large ears of yellow corn. In the center of the top was the coat-of-arms of Kansas... In the center of the arch proper, on a blue background, was the word "Welcome," in letters of gold, made of chopped wheat straw. On the reverse side of the arch was the following:

KANSAS

1856:	1860:	1879:
BLEEDING.	DROUTHY.	BOOMING.

> Both sides were additionally ornamented with flags and shields, and the structure in its entirety was the most beautiful and unique thing we ever saw.

Although Thursday, September 25, the fourth day of the six day fair, would be the most important day with its presidential visit, this was still a traditional county fair with numerous exhibits. There were 710 exhibit entries processed before the Saturday evening preceding the fair's opening on Monday. More entries were submitted when the fair opened. Displayed were horses and cattle; grains and vegetables; fruits; agricultural implements, including "two plows of very ancient make," one purportedly having been purchased on the Nile River and the other obtained near Jerusalem; handiwork; sheep and swine; and poultry. On Monday and Tuesday not only were more exhibits entered, but locations for vendor booths were sold.

The appearance of the President of the United States at the fair was an immense attraction for people living for many miles around. "Excursion rates" were given by all the railroads in the state, and there were special trains to transport people to the fair.[6]

> There was a very respectable attendance on Tuesday—estimated at 2,500—but on Wednesday the crowds began to come in by every road, and at 3 o'clock in the afternoon there were probably 6,000 people on the fair grounds. Every available space for camping was taken up, and south of the racetrack there was a regular town of tents. It is estimated that fully 4,000 people camped on the fair grounds Wednesday night. ["Small colonies were present from Garnett, Iola, and other towns."[7]]

> All around Floral Hall and between the amphitheatre and the cattle pens, and extending almost to the secretary's office, every available space was occupied. The space under the amphitheatre seats was also taken up with booths.

> Including shows, photograph galleries, barber shops, hot candy stands, lunch counters, wheels of fortune, etc., there were 46 booths. Besides these there were 3 large dining halls. It was a town of itself, teeming with life and activity. Everything was hurry and bustle, and everybody was excited and still there was no disorder.

On Wednesday, Co. H, Sixteenth U.S. Infantry, arrived from Fort Riley, Kansas, accompanied by the Sixteenth's regimental band of twenty-seven pieces. Two napoleons, cannons which shot a twelve-pound shell, also arrived. "At last the long expected and anxiously-looked-for day arrived." President's Day! The sky had been cloudless all week, but on Thursday morning, "in honor of a Republican President upon its historic soil, Nature quickly changed the scene, and Republican Kansas put on a hazy look." On Wednesday night, the roads had been lined with vehicles of arriving attendees, and farmers living nearby had to wait for their chance to enter the procession.[8] The trains brought in carloads of passengers on Thursday, and from dawn to 11 o'clock this huge crowd passed through the gates to the fairgrounds.[9] At the main entrance gate, 20,000 tickets, at 25 cents per person per day, were sold as of 3 p.m. that day. Several thousand additional tickets were sold at two other entrances.[10] All were eager for a seat as close as possible to the speakers' stand.[11]

The fairgoers came from Allen, Anderson, Coffey, Lyon, Wilson, Neosho, Elk, Chautauqua, Butler, and other counties. "There are teams here from over a hundred miles away, all flocking in to see a real live President. It was the one chance of their lives, and they have made good use of it. The crowd today is not less than thirty thousand and many estimate it far above that figure."[12] This tremendous event was covered by between sixty and seventy Kansas newspapers. The presidential party itself included reporters from the *New York Herald* and from the *Chicago Tribune*.[13]

The presidential party, including the President and First Lady, Lucy (Webb) Hayes, their grown sons Birchard and Webb,[14] and General William Tecumseh Sherman, accompanied by Kansas Governor John P. St. John, arrived by palace car train at the Neosho Falls depot soon after 10 a.m. As a result of mismanagement, the train carrying the Capital Guards and its band from Topeka failed to arrive until twenty minutes after the presidential party's arrival. In the interim, the local reception committee visited with the distinguished guests, and there was handshaking and congratulations. "The President and Mrs. Hayes were in excellent spirits, but seemed somewhat disappointed at the smallness of the crowd awaiting them at the depot."

The editor of *The Yates Center News* was among those who greeted the distinguished guests. "It was at this time the President made a confidential communication to us regarding his impressions upon seeing the town for the first time. He said: 'Your town does not impress me very favorably; in fact it has the appearance of being a very small, one-horse town. But then you have a beautiful country, and, what is more, you have an unbounded amount of cheek.'" This was certainly a rude, impolitic statement, and, though made confidentially, that did not keep it out of the next issue of the newspaper.

With the other train having arrived, the procession of bands, distinguished visitors, Capital Guards, and others formed to proceed to the fair grounds. As the procession marched north on Main Street toward the Neosho River bridge, "[c]heer after cheer rent the air from the crowds of people who were on the streets witnessing the imposing spectacle."[15] On the opposite side of the river lay the fair grounds and the awaiting thousands of people. "On crossing the bridge, which was gaily decorated with flags, a beautiful sight burst upon the view of the distinguished guests." It was the magnificent triumphal arch created by Professor Worrall, only now, immediately behind the Kansas coat-of-arms on the top, "stood the beautiful Miss Emma [sic: Emily] Snow, representing the Goddess of Liberty. Her attitude was perfect, and persons not in the secret would not have known but that they were looking at a most beautiful piece of statuary." The President and Mrs. Hayes apparently recognized that the Goddess of Liberty was alive: "He took off his silk hat and bowed real low, and she waved her lace handkerchief, just a little, something special, like her smile."[16]

As President Hayes passed under this arch, the Sixteenth U.S. Infantry, using the two napoleons, fired a twenty-one-gun salute which lasted for 5¼ minutes.[17] "[S]uch a volume of cheers and shouts as went up from the assembled multitude was never before heard in the Neosho valley, and probably never will be again. Women waved their handkerchiefs, men threw their hats in the air, and all shouted till they were hoarse—even the little children lending their treble voices to swell the grand cry of welcome." Thirteen-year-old Fred Funston was in that vast, cheering crowd.[18]

When the presidential party had neared Neosho Falls, a town of approximately five hundred people, the President had asked, "Where is the town?" "But when he passed through the arch and saw the vast multitude assembled in that lovely grove on the banks of the beautiful Neosho, he inquired, 'Where did all these people come from?' It has been estimated by many that there were 40,000 people present. It is safe to say that there were at least 30,000 there." The distinguished visitors sat on a grandstand prepared for the occasion, and there followed various speeches. *The Humboldt Union* described the President's remarks as "happy and well chosen."[19] His Excellency then introduced General Sherman, "alluding to him as the man who led our armies from Atlanta to the sea. [Loud cheers]." When order had been restored, the idolized general spoke, concluding with these remarks:

> When we were invited to come to Neosho Falls, we did not know where it was and I had to look it up on the map. I have not found the Falls. [Laughter and cheers] When you get to Niagara Falls you don't have to ask where they are but you hear them. [Laughter] I have not seen nor heard the Neosho Falls yet. [Laughter]
>
> Now, ladies and gentlemen, I am overwhelmed and delighted with your presence today; which I regard as a testimony of your respect and appreciation of your chief magistrate. You have come here to celebrate a civil victory and you soldiers know perfectly well that there are civil victories as well as victories in wars. You have come here to celebrate the victory you have achieved over the soil.
>
> I want you to excuse me now and let me go and see your fair. I hope you have some good horses. The speaking is mainly, of course, to enable you to look at the people on this stand here, whom you have come to see. Now will you permit us to go to see the fair? If you will, I shall thank you very much indeed.

The crowd then gave three cheers for General Sherman.[20]

At the close of the proceeding, Hayes was presented, on behalf of the fair association, "a remarkable chair, without its like or equal in the world, manufactured from the horns of Kansas steers." This upholstered chair, with its very large steer horns forming the legs, arms, and back is still extant. The horns were pure Woodson County, the steers having been raised on the Warren Crandall ranch north of Yates Center.[21] "In accepting the handsome gift, the President pleasantly said that he thought he would now have no difficulty in introducing a 'horn' into the White House, and that, too, with Mrs. Hayes' consent." There were then calls for Mrs. Hayes. "Gov. St. John gallantly led the lady of the White House to the front of the stage. Her appearance was greeted with a perfect storm of cheers. Mrs. Hayes simply bowed her acknowledgement and retired." Hundreds then attempted to shake hands with the President. who was still on the grandstand. One young man, who pushed his way through the crowd, told the President that he had come thirty-five miles from his home. where his wife had given birth the prior week to twins, a boy and a girl. He requested the President to name them, which he did, naming the boy Rutherford and the girl Mary.

The thousands in the crowd were ripe to become crime victims. "The grounds were amply policed, but the thieves were a little more numerous than common. Hence, many mourn for wealth departed. Pickpockets and thieves abounded. Over forty pocket books were taken besides several watches and some miscellaneous property."[22] Two young men, alleged to have been pickpockets, shoved their way through the huge crowd, knocking people left and right, one of whom fell against two women and lodged at about a 45° angle, being unable to straighten up, yet having no room to fall. "People were everywhere, acres of them. A man afterward said that while in the jam of people he thought he would have died, but if he had, he would have died standing—there was no room to fall."[23]

The presidential party and invited guests, making about one hundred persons, dined at the Allen County Dining Hall, where an elegant lunch was served. Following this was a reunion of old soldiers on the fairgrounds at which the speakers included President Hayes and General Sherman. Civil War veteran Ed Funston and son Fred likely were present. The presidential party witnessed next a horse race and viewed the exhibits in Floral Hall.

Here was the opportunity for Emily Snow and her sister, Florence, to meet the three distinguished guests. Florence recalled what Mrs. Hayes said to them: "'Ah, the Goddess of Liberty, we congratulate you.' And to me, 'You must be very happy together,' giving her two hands to me, and then a marvelous kiss. The President was also very cordial. Then General William Tecumseh Sherman towered high above us and took our breath completely, saying, with a deep bow, 'I, also, salute you,' while the whole group applauded the additional honor. It detracted nothing at all from our exaltation when we read in the papers that he was in the habit of kissing all the attractive girls he met on the tour. The famous stubble beard was very scratchy, but we should probably never know the like again."[24]

Then, it was time for departure, and the distinguished guests entered their carriages to be taken to the railroad depot to travel to Fort Dodge, Kansas. As President Hayes passed again under the magnificent arch, he received a national salute of thirty-eight guns fired by the two napoleons. This final salute lasted nine and a half minutes.[25] "The crowd soon began to disperse, the sun sank to rest 'mid purple clouds descending, softly the moonbeams shone on the still branches of the shadowy trees, and the most memorable day ever known in the Neosho Valley had passed, without an accident occurring to mar the happiness of the occasion."

And what did His Excellency, President Hayes, think of his trip to Neosho Falls, Kansas? An inveterate diarist since he was twelve years old, he observed: "Thence into Kansas at Fort Scott, and to Parsons in the evening. Great interest and friendliness in Kansas everywhere, with large and enthusiastic crowds of laboring, intelligent Americans. Governor St. John and wife with us throughout. The Neosho Fair was in the newer part of southern Kansas but numerously attended and very interesting."[26] As for young Fred Funston, presumably he was thrilled to have seen the President of the United States and the great military hero, General William Tecumseh Sherman.

Chapter Six Notes, continued—*His Excellency, President Rutherford B. Hayes, and the Neosho Valley District Fair*

1. L. Wallace Duncan and Chas. F. Scott, *History of Allen and Woodson Counties Kansas* (Iola, Kansas: Iola Register, Printers and Binders, 1901), 610 ("Neosho Falls" by Miss Florence L. Snow).

2. Duncan and Scott, *History of Allen and Woodson Counties Kansas* (Iola, Kansas: Iola Register, Printers and Binders, 1901), 583.

3. "Labor Omnia Vincit," *The Yates Center News*, October 2, 1879. This local account of the events at the fair, and particularly of those that occurred on September 25, 1879, when President Hayes attended, is the principal source for the text in this chapter and will not be so identified again by use of subsequent notes. Subsequent notes, however, will be used to identify at the appropriate places in the text other sources used in the writing of this chapter.

4. The original of this letter from G. B. Inge et al. to R. B. Hayes, dated June 8, 1879, is at The Rutherford B. Hayes Presidential Library & Museum.

5. "Communicated," *The Iola Register*, September 5, 1879. For a shorter version of this letter, written apparently to another person, see Opal McCullough Henderson and Terri Lynn Henderson, *To-Day, Beginning, Yesterday A History of Neosho Falls, Kansas*, no publisher, no date, 80.

6. Neosho Valley District Fair poster (commencing September 22, 1879) www.kansasmemory.org/item/213007 (Kansas Memory is a service of the Kansas State Historical Society: kshs.org).

7. "N.V.D.F.," *The Iola Register*, October 3, 1879.

8. "When President Hayes Came to Neosho Falls," *The Neosho Falls Post*, July 13, 1933. Letter of E. B. Moore, who had attended the fair.

9. "N.V.D.F.," *The Iola Register*, October 3, 1879.

10. "Neosho Falls," *The Junction City Weekly Union*, September 27, 1879. The ticket cost was listed on the fair poster (see note 6).

11. "N.V.D.F.," *The Iola Register*, October 3, 1879.

12. "Labor Omnia Vincit," *The Yates Center News*, October 2, 1879. This quotation comes from another newspaper ("Special Dispatch to the Capital"), which *The Yates Center News* reprinted at the end of its own story about the fair.

13. "N.V.D.F.," *The Iola Register*, October 3, 1879.

14. "N.V.D.F.," *The Iola Register*, October 3, 1879. This is the only news account I read that listed Webb Hayes as one of the presidential party. Some accounts listed Birchard Hayes, and others did not, as traveling with his parents.

15. "The District Fair," *The Humboldt Union*, September 27, 1879. This bridge, one span from abutment to abutment, collapsed in 1898, under the weight of sixty head of cattle and two horsemen. The headline in *The Iola Daily Register* of July 15, 1898, was properly descriptive: "Falls Bridge Falls."

16. Florence L. Snow, *Pictures On My Wall: A Lifetime in Kansas* (Lawrence, Kansas: University of Kansas Press, 1945), 34.

17. *Junction City Daily Union*, September 30, 1879, for length of the salute (reprint at the end of the article "Labor Omnia Vincit"; see note 3).

18. Frederick Funston, *Memories of Two Wars: Cuban and Philippine Experiences* (New York: Charles Scribner's Sons, 1914), 5-6. "My own artillery experience consisted

in once having seen a salute fired to President Hayes at a country fair in Kansas." Presumably, not only Fred, but all of the members of his family were present to view this salute.

19. "The District Fair," *The Humboldt Union*, September 27, 1879.

20. "The President," *The Leavenworth Times*, September 26, 1879.

21. Bob Johnson, "Presidential chair featured," *The Iola Register*, May 5, 2009. This chair resides in the Rutherford B. Hayes Presidential Center, Fremont, Ohio.

22. "N.V.D.F.," *The Iola Register*, October 3, 1879.

23. "When President Hayes Came to Neosho Falls," *The Neosho Falls Post*, July 13, 1933. Letter of E. B. Moore who had attended the fair.

24. Florence L. Snow, *Pictures On My Wall: A Lifetime in Kansas* (Lawrence, Kansas: University of Kansas Press, 1945), 37.

25. *Junction City Daily Union*, September 30, 1879, for length of the salute (reprint at the end of the article "Labor Omnia Vincit"; see note 3).

26. *The Diary and Letters of Rutherford B. Hayes, Nineteenth President of the United States*, ed. by Charles Richard Williams (Columbus, Ohio: Ohio State Archeological and Historical Society, 1922), Vol. III, 572. The Rutherford B. Hayes Presidential Library and Museum's website: rhayes.org

The U.S. Naval Academy, the Allen County Normal Institute, and Teacher Examinations

In an 1896 newspaper article complimentary of Ed Funston, the problem of young men leaving the farm was dealt with head on:

> As a rule farmer boys when nearing manhood leave home and seek some other occupation. The father and mother's fond hopes of seeing their family settled around them are a disappointment. The boy can see but little before him but drudgery without honor of any kind. He sees the road to distinction leading only through some of the professions or business occupations. The father and mother could point him to no exception to the rule until Funston, the plain farmer of Allen County, forged to the front and forced all to acknowledge his ability. Farmers you owe it to yourselves and to your families, that you support Funston, for congress; and thus show your sons that they may be honored though they are farmers.[1]

In the case of Fred Funston, however, his desire to leave the family farm had nothing to do with following the "road to distinction" through a profession or business. Instead, there were two aspects of his personality that propelled him to seek a life away from the farm—his love of adventure and his restless nature.

With most of his country school education finished by the beginning of 1881, 15-year-old Fred Funston took a look beyond life on the farm and decided that a naval career was his future. Perhaps his apparent enjoyment of the book he had borrowed, *Cook's Voyage Around the World*, was a significant influence upon the young boy in making his decision. He may have viewed the navy as an opportunity to find adventure, just as Captain Cook had found adventure in his storied naval career. Also, Fred was of a restless disposition. In a 1914 conversation, he first acknowledged what he liked about the farm: "I was raised on a farm and I like the feel of the soil. It's good to hoe potatoes and radishes and plow corn." He further acknowledged how "restless" he had been living on the farm.[2] Fred had previously described himself as "a rover."[3] Perhaps he was best described by a soldier comrade, who characterized Fred quaintly: "Fred was born with a pair of wandering feet."[4] How Fred satisfied his desire for adventure and his restlessness is the subject of this trilogy.

An announcement on the front page of *The Iola Register* of December 17, 1880, likely precipitated Fred's decision to seek a naval career. Kansas Second Congressional District Congressman Dudley C. Haskell announced a vacancy from his district at the Naval School at Annapolis which he proposed to fill by a competitive examination among the boys ages fourteen to seventeen of the district. Each county of the district would conduct its own competitive examination with the "two who pass the best examination" eligible to compete at the final competition. These county finalists would appear before the Board of Education meeting at the State University in Lawrence, which would recommend the boy to receive the appointment as a Cadet Midshipman. The Allen County examination was set for Saturday, January 15, 1881, at "8½ o'clock A.M." at the schoolhouse in Iola.[5]

The recipient of the appointment of Cadet Midshipman would make a major commitment by accepting the appointment. "He will be required to sign articles binding himself to serve in the United States navy eight years (including his time of probation at the Academy) unless sooner discharged, and his pay will be $500 a year, commencing at the time of his admission."[6] That Fred was willing to make an eight-year commitment is a testament to his desire for the appointment with its presumed opportunity for an adventurous life.

Both Fred and his good friend, Roy Fetherngill, decided to compete for the two positions from Allen County. One wonders if they had any discussion between themselves as to how they would feel if only one of them were to be successful. If so, they need not have been concerned. On the day of the examination, they were the only two competitors. They took the examination, and were designated to attend the final examination. In announcing their selection, *The Iola Register*, which was not yet owned by Fred's friend Charlie Scott, paid the two boys this compliment: "They are both bright fellows, and we hope one of them may be the lucky fellow."[7]

Such was not to be. In fact, neither Fred nor Roy participated in the final competition. As Roy explained to Fred's sister, Ella (Funston) Eckdall, many years later, "Your father had seen something of life in the navy during the Civil War while he was an officer in the Union Army operating on the Lower Mississippi and had a very unfavorable impression of life in the U S Navy and talked us both out of the idea of taking the final test."[8] The cadet appointment went to 16-year-old Benjamin "Bennie" Jacobs of Lawrence, but he failed to graduate from the Naval Academy.[9]

With his plans for a naval career abandoned, Fred may have considered applying to the United States Military Academy at West Point. If so, he would have to wait to do so, since at age fifteen he was two years younger than the minimum age requirement of seventeen. Fred now reversed course and decided on a non-farm career that would keep him in Allen County. At least he took the necessary steps to become a schoolteacher, but whether he really wanted to pursue such a sedentary occupation is unknown. Fred may not have known himself. At a minimum, a teaching position away from the farm would provide him a different perspective on his life. In the meantime, as he took the necessary steps to become a teacher, he continued with his chores on the farm until September of 1884.

Attendance at the annual Allen County Normal Institutes, held during the years 1881, 1882, and 1883, became a regular part of Fred's life. The purpose of the several-week county Normal Institute was to train teachers and those who wanted to become teachers. The 1881 Normal Institute started in early July.[10] Undoubtedly, a major subject of conversation among the attendees was the shooting on July 2 of the country's president, James A. Garfield, at a railway station in Washington, D.C. He was to linger for over two months before dying on September 19. As to the Institute itself, an observer noted on July 12 that "[t]he Institute is getting down to business. The pupils are beginning to understand what is expected from them, and the professors are learning to not expect too much. The corps of instructors are full blooded workers... In short, if we were to be the judge, the verdict would be, good teachers, good scholars, and much good work."[11]

By the second day of classes the next year, the 1882 Institute's enrollment had reached 81.[12] There were three instructors that year, Olin, Hamm, and Young, and they taught a daily program of work as follows:[13]

PROGRAMME

OLIN.	Hamm.	Young.
7:55 School Management.		
8:25 A, mental science.	B1, Read.	B2, Arith.
8:55 B1, Grammar.	B2, Reading.	A, Methods.
9:25 A, Constitution.	B2, Geog.	B1, Arith.
9:55 Gymnastics (general).		
10:5 Recess.		
10:15 A, Philosophy.	B2, Gram.	B1, Consti'n.
10:45 A, Physiology.	Pensman'p	(B united)
11:15 B1, History.	A, Gram.	B2, History.
11:45 B2, Constitution.	B1, Geog.	A, History.
12:15 Roll call and dismissal.		

Fred was nearly 17 years old when he attended the 1882 Institute, which makes the following description of the typical male student particularly interesting:

The average male pedagogue this year is of an extraordinary type. He is about seventeen years old; his hands and feet are considerably in the way; just beneath his auricular appendage, on either side, there is a small field but whether of oats, wheat or flax we can not determine; the chinch bugs are evidently bad. Beneath his nose there is also an uprising that is apparently uttering a protest that "if it *nose* anything it will not be kept *down*." There is evidently a latent hankering in this specimen for the female pedagogue. It manifests itself now, in sly glances, small notes, etc., but by and by it will assume the form of boat rides, livery rigs, moonlight promenades and ice cream. Then it will be dangerous—to the pocket book.[14]

Along the same line is this report by an Institute attendee: "The Professors complain every Monday about poor lessons, and I think it incumbent upon me, as the oracle of the Normal, to rise and explain thusly: We always make it a point to study our lessons on Sunday evening so as to be sure and have them for Monday morning. It must be accident, but someway it always falls out that a male and female pedagogue study their lessons together, and they study them so hard, and protract them so long that their physical powers are so worn out that when Monday comes, although they know their lessons perfectly, they have not the necessary energy to make the correct answers. Professors, do you not know how it is yourselves? "[15]

The 1883 summer Institute saw its enrollment reach 135 pupils. This largest enrollment ever was caused by the attendance of "students of the Iola high school who are making a cramming institution out of the normal, to prepare themselves for examination this fall."[16] Unlike the 1881 and 1882 Institutes when *The Iola Register* had published a list of attendees, there was no published list in 1883. Fred most likely attended that year, since he took the teacher exam administered after the Institute ended. This was a two-day examination held on August 3 and 4, 1883, for those who sought to teach in the common schools of Allen County. At a teachers' examination the next year, the candidates were required to write an essay on the subject of the examination itself. One of the youngest teachers taking the examination wrote about the experience of taking the examination for the first time. *The Iola Register* published it in its entirety. Since the August 1883 exam was Fred's first experience taking the exam, it is apropos to reprint this essay here:

> The greatest "bug-bear" in a young teacher's life is his first examination. He looks forward to the fatal day with a feeling akin to fear. Many a man has faced the scaffold with better nerve than the average young pedagogue faces the examination. But after all, what is there to be afraid of? It is not a matter of life or death, and if we fail, we can try again. A teachers' examination, looked at in a sensible manner, should scare no one. The questions are put in the simplest manner possible, but if they are not understood we can soon call one of the examiners and have them explained. In fact, every possible chance is given us to succeed and all we have to do

is to keep cool and not get excited and to be perfectly oblivious to everything except our work.[17]

Seventeen-year-old Fred passed his first examination, and received a Third Grade Certificate, one of thirty-eight Third Grade Certificates awarded.[18]

The written public examination had been administered by a three member county board of examiners, which awarded with a teacher's certificate all those " who shall pass the requisite examination, and satisfy the board as to their good moral character and their ability to teach and govern school successfully." Under the Kansas laws of 1881, there were three grades of teacher certificates:

First Grade, which was good for two years, and for which the recipient had to be at least eighteen years of age and have "taught successfully twelve months."

Second Grade, which was good for one year, and for which the recipient had to be at least seventeen years of age and have "taught successfully not less than three months."

Third Grade, which was good for six months, and for which the recipient had to be at least sixteen years of age.

There were two additional requirements for each grade of certificate: (1) several subject areas for which proficiency was required, and (2) a minimum general average score. In the case of a Third Grade Certificate, the one received by Fred, he had to prove proficiency in orthography, reading, writing, English grammar, geography, arithmetic, and United States history, and he had to score a general average of not less than 70 percent, except he could not make less than 60 percent in any one branch of study. Unfortunately, the records from this 1883 examination are no longer extant, and though he did pass, Fred's scores are unknown. A final statutory provision was that "in no case shall a third-grade certificate be given a second time to the same person."[19] Despite this statute, and as we will see, Fred was to receive two additional Third Grade Certificates the following year.

What did the newly minted teachers do after receiving their certificates? The Carlyle correspondent for *The Iola Register* in August of 1889 described what occurred next: "The Normal has closed, the examination is over and the community is now being over-run by teachers in search of members of school boards, whom they may annoy for a few hours. Let us hope the annoyance will not be entirely fruitless."[20] Whether Fred was among those seeking a teaching position with one of the county's many rural schools is unknown. What is known is that he did not teach that fall. On November 9, 1883, Frederick Funston became 18 years of age, bringing to a close his childhood.

Chapter Six Notes, continued—*The U.S. Naval Academy, the Allen County Normal Institute, and Teacher Examinations*

1. "Farmer Boys," *Southern Kansas Horticulturalist*, Vol I–No. XI (March Number) [1896] (published at Iola, Kansas, by E.S. Davis, and edited by L. M. Pancoast). This was an "Extra Edition" and was devoted to the life and career of the Hon. E. H. Funston, "a successful farmer and horticulturalist."

2. "Funston Longs for A Farm," *Kansas City Times*, December 9, 1914 (Kansas State Historical Society, *Frederick Funston Clippings*, Vol. 1).

3. Frederick Funston to Ann E. Funston, Christmas Day, 1898. Written in Manila, Philippine Islands, Fred wrote his mother as follows: "Great a rover as I have been in my live [sic], I am now farther away from home than I have ever been before, as from Carlyle to Manila is a good 8,500 miles" (FFP Micro). This is a typescript, and thus the misspelling in the quoted reference may not have been made by Fred Funston.

4. "Funston's Abiding Fame Rests Securely On Four Events In Busy Career," *New York American* (date not shown) (FFP Micro).

5. *The Iola Register*, December 17, 1880, for all except the term "Cadet Midshipman," which is from the source immediately below.

6. "Which will Explain Itself," *The Lawrence Daily Journal*, December 19, 1880. This article contained Haskell's letter (sent to each county of the district), with an introduction by Sarah A. Brown, the Douglas County Superintendent of Instruction. It is from this introduction that this quotation comes.

7. "Local Matters," *The Iola Register*, Februar y 11, 1881.

8. Roy Fetherngill to Ella (Funston) Eckdall, November 8, 1925 (Eckdall Scrapbook III; loose letter).

9. "Birthday Party," *The Lawrence Daily Journal*, June 3, 1881. "City and County," Kansas Daily Tribune (Lawrence, Kansas), May 13, 1881. Telephone discussion by the author on October 12, 1999, with Gary LaValley, Archivist for the United States Naval Academy.

10. "Normal Institute," *The Iola Register*, July 8, 1881. This has a list of attendees to that date, including "Frederick Funston."

11. "Teachers Institute," *The Humboldt Union*, July 16, 1881. The observer is G. B. Welch.

12. "Normal Institute," *The Humboldt Union*, July 15, 1882.

13. "Normal Institute," *The Iola Register*, July 14, 1882. This has a list of attendees up to noon on July 11, including "Frederick Funston."

14. "Normal Notes," *The Iola Register*, July 28, 1882. This report was written by one of the Institute attendees, who is unidentified.15.

15. "Normal Notes," *The Humboldt Union*, July 28, 1883.

16. "Teachers' Examination," *The Iola Register*, February 8, 1884.

17. "Certificates Granted," *The Iola Register*, August 10, 1883.

19. State of Kansas, *Session Laws of 1881* (Topeka, Kansas: Geo. W. Marlin, Kansas Publishing House, 1881), Chapter CLI, 274-276.

20. "Carlyle Clippings," *The Iola Register*, August 9, 1889.

A U.S. Congressman, a Business College Student, and a Competitor for a West Point Cadetship

January – May 1884

Each Congressional District and Territory—also the District of Columbia—is entitled to have one Cadet at the academy. Ten are also appointed *at large*. The appointments (except those *at large*) are made by the Secretary of War at the request of the Representative, or Delegate, in Congress from the District or Territory; and the person appointed must be an actual resident of the District or Territory from which the appointment is made.

—"Information Relative to the Appointment and Admission of Cadets to the United States Military Academy" for June 1884[1]

As the year 1884 dawned, the death two weeks before of the Honorable Dudley C. Haskell likely was on the minds of many citizens of Kansas's Second Congressional District. Haskell had been first elected to the U.S. House of Representatives in 1876, and, at the time of his unexpected death at age forty-one, he was in his fourth term. His death was apparently caused by overwork.[2] At his death, he was chairman of the Committee on Indian Affairs, and his work had resulted in the establishment at Lawrence of the federal industrial training school for Indian boys and girls.[3] This school opened in 1884, and was named Haskell Institute.[4]

As a resident of the Second Congressional District, Ed Funston had a particular interest in this unexpected legislative vacancy. In 1880, Ed had been elected a Kansas State Senator, and, from that political base, two years later he made an unsuccessful attempt to be nominated for the position of Kansas congressman-at-large by the Republican State Convention in Topeka. At this convention held to nominate candidates for four Representative positions in Congress, one of which would be a congressman-at-large, 187 votes were required in order to be selected. On the first ballot, Ed received 113 votes out of the 1286 votes cast for twenty-one candidates. His 113 votes were the fifth highest number for any candidate, the highest being 156 votes. Since no candidates received the required 187 votes, a second ballot was taken. On this second ballot there were sixteen candidates, and Ed received 106 votes out of a total of 1421 votes, making him the sixth highest in votes received. This time, one candidate received the required 187 votes; he received 252 votes and thus was chosen as a congressional nominee. The third ballot was then taken, and of the seven candidates, three received the minimum 187 votes (282, 273, and 250 votes, respectively), and thus became the remaining three congressional nominees. Ed Funston with 88 votes received the most votes of the four unsuccessful candidates (the other votes were 54, 58, and 5).[5]

Haskell had died on December 16. In its next edition, *The Iola Register* remembered him with a laudatory front-page tribute, bordered in black at the top and bottom. Ed Funston quickly decided to implement one of his political ambitions, since in the next weekly issue, there appeared a large article reporting that he was a candidate for the Republican nomination for the vacant congressional seat. The 47-year-old state senator was in an enviable position. In assessing the status of various potential candidates to replace the recently deceased Haskell, *The Kansas City Times* reported that Ed was expected to "go into a convention with more followers than any other man, and unless the opposition should combine their united strength against him the nomination is his."[6]

The time period for campaigning in the fifteen counties of the district for the Republican party nomination for representative was short, lasting only from Haskell's death to the party convention on January 31, 1884. Held in Parsons, the crowd in the city for the convention was "very great," and hotel accommodations were unavailable for many. At one point during the convention, "the corner of the gallery broke under the weight of the immense crowd...," but no one was injured. "While it was generally conceded that Funston would be the successful man, it was evident that the friends of the other candidates were not going to give up without a struggle, and combinations were talked of in a manner so mysterious as to rather puzzle those who hoped for a short convention." When it came time to nominate candidates for the position of representative, the Douglas County delegation nominated Edward H. Funston. When the balloting was over, Ed had received 80 votes, far more than any of the other seven candidates, the next highest number being 29 out of a total of 154 votes. On motion, Ed was nominated by acclamation.[7]

The congressional election was scheduled for March 1, and two incidents during Ed's political campaign as the Republican candidate show the close relationship between Ed and his son, Fred. The first incident allowed Ed to benefit from his son's phenomenal memory and the knowledge he had acquired from all of his book and newspaper reading. During the campaign there was very limited time for Ed to prepare his speeches and, in doing so, he relied almost totally on the data Fred furnished to him. "One night the overworked candidate went to his son's bedside, awoke him and asked him what he knew about England's attitude toward her colonies in the matter of wool-growing. 'Instantly he gave me the facts, and the books and pages where they could be found in print.'"

The other incident displayed Fred's intelligence, sense of humor, and expertise as a public speaker. It also showed the strategic planning of father and son in skillfully utilizing Fred in his father's campaign:

> [Fred's] first charge against an enemy overwhelming in numbers occurred in 1884, before he rounded out his eighteenth year... [Ed's Democratic] opponent was an able campaigner named Riggs, who had, by his vigorous canvass of the district, thrown the adherents of the "Farmer," as he nicknamed Funston, into consternation. One night in February a rousing Riggs meeting was held in the opera house in Fort Scott. Enthusiasm had been aroused to a wild pitch by the last speaker, and the crowd was making ready to depart, when a smooth faced boy, a little chap of not more than five feet three inches, clambered upon the stage and shouted, "Sit down!"
>
> Every one turned to see what it was all about, and amazement was expressed in every face when the boy, without a trace of embarrassment in his attitude or voice, said:—"I am Frederick Funston, son of the 'Farmer.' I want you to listen to me."
>
> There were a few cries of "Put him out!" and one impatient democrat even suggested that "the boy should be spanked and put to bed." But the majority were pleased with the impudence of the lad, and, thinking to derive a choice bit of diversion at the expense of the son of the opposition candidate, sat down and demanded that he be heard.
>
> Young Funston looked into the faces of those men, and knew that nine out of ten were opposed to his father. Without flinching, he began with a short story of his father's life on the farm near Iola. He was witty, and as his anecdote turned upon a joke at his father's expense, he soon had his hearers in excellent humor. He told story after story, all worth listening to, but as each brought out in better light than the previous one the sturdy character of his parent, the democratic managers sought again to shut him off. By that time he

had friends who resented unfair treatment for him, and he was told to proceed.

In another moment Funston was well launched into a political speech, discussing the issues of the campaign with all the knowledge of a veteran. The crowd listened to him for thirty minutes, and when he ceased speaking the occasion had been turned into a republican love feast. From that moment the democrats were beaten, E. H. Funston being elected by the largest majority the district had ever given.[8]

The Democratic Party's candidate, Samuel A. Riggs, of Lawrence, was a lawyer and a member of the Kansas House of Representatives. Riggs, like Funston, was both Ohio-born and had received part of his education at Marietta College.[9] Ed trounced Riggs on election day by 6,212 votes, Ed receiving 24,116 and Riggs 17,904.[10] The city of Iola on the Monday after the Saturday election had "a regular Republican love feast." Editor Charlie Scott likely wrote the following front-page account under the heading "Rah For Funston!":

At an early hour Monday flags were displayed from the band stand and most of the stores, and when night came the brilliant illumination of every store in town, the huge bon fire and the flying fire balls, the crowds of cheering people and the music of the K.P. band made the scene one of the most lively and beautiful that Iola has witnessed for many a day. After playing two or three pieces the band adjourned to the Opera House and was followed by the crowd which filled the large hall from stage to stairway... Mr. Funston entered the room and was greeted with cheers which were redoubled when...he took his seat on the stage... Upon taking the chair Mr. Foust made a stirring address... The meeting was then addressed by [several] gentlemen... By this time the audience which had been calling for "Funston" at intervals all the evening would not be put off any longer, so the chairman introduced our congressman elect as the "annihilator of the eliminator." [Riggs had favored elimination of the country's high tariff.] Mr. Funston was evidently deeply touched by the reception given him and began by returning earnest thanks to his Iola and Allen county friends without whose substantial aid and support he could not have made the race.... The speech occupied about half a hour and was listened with the closest attention. At its close some one suggested "Three cheers for Hon. E. H. Funston" and they were given with a will.... Taken for all and all the meeting was a grand success and was a fitting finale to one of the most brilliant and hotly contested campaigns ever made in Kansas.[11]

Undoubtedly, Fred and other members of the Funston family were a part of the huge crowd on that glorious evening. The Honorable E. H. Funston was to serve the Second District as congressman for slightly more than ten years.

Campaigning for Congress was no easy task for any candidate, including incumbents. Iola attorney J. H. Richards owned several pacing horses which he often used "to haul congressional candidates considerable distances over rough dirt roads to rural political meetings...[which] were for most part held in country schoolhouses."[12] In those years, all candidates, including the incumbent congressmen, "had to put in practically as much time in the field during a campaign, appearing before the voters mile for mile, as is now generally required on duty in Washington serving a full term."[13]

On one such occasion, Richards took Congressman Ed Funston, a political figure named Hart, a corpulent country doctor, and the lady schoolteacher who unlocked the schoolhouse door for the political meeting and lit the lamp, "which last mentioned act really made the meeting possible." Funston "had a thunderous voice and at the height of his eloquence unintentionally blew out the lamp. Doctor Hart waddled forward and as he set his lantern on the teacher's desk yelled at orator of the day, 'Blow that out if you can.'"[14]

Ed's loud voice was legendary. A few years after his death in 1911, an article in the *Topeka Capital* described it this way: "It was said that when Congressman Funston was feeling right and his voice was in good trim, he could stand on a platform in the public square in Iola and make the windows rattle in Humboldt ten miles south of there." The same article also credited Ed as a skillful politician: "When he was in his prime Funston came nearer knowing the first and last names of every farmer in the Second District than any other man in Kansas."[15]

Both Ed's occupation and loud voice generated nicknames for him during his political career, and both his detractors and his supporters used these same nicknames but with different meanings. This phenomenon was explained in a biographical sketch of Ed, which appeared in a local specialist journal in 1896:

Mr. Funston certainly has had enough sobrequets [sic] attached to his name to crush the ordinary man. At first those who desired to get him out of the way declared he was nothing but a farmer and therefore could not possibly be qualified for a position so exalted as a member of Congress. "Why," they said, "he is nothing but a jake from Deer Creek who ought to be at home pulling weeds and feeding pigs instead of showing himself in the halls of Congress." But he held the even tenor of his way giving no attention to their slurs upon the farmers. When he entered the campaign after nomination

he proved to be one of the most interesting and logical speakers using good language and showing himself a thoroughly trained and
educated gentleman who could speak as well as plow. When those
who desired his place heard him and saw the crowd that gathered
to hear him, they had to abandon the "farmer" charge, for Funston
had made the slur of farmer honorable and his own friends were
delighted to so address him. Finding that Funston had made honorable the name of farmer, their next effort was to represent him as a
coarse bellowing fellow and, therefore, stealing an epithet that was
once applied to Gov. Allen of Ohio [for whom Allen County, Kansas,
is named], they called him Foghorn. All the narrow breasted, squal-
ing [sic], wheezing little fellows went about calling him Foghorn
Funston thus insinuating that he had neither brains nor education,
nothing but voice. "Foghorn" drew better than all else. The people
wanted to hear a man who could speak out like a man and whom
acres of them could hear. They came and filled up the space around
him and those who took outside seats heard all distinctly. The boys
began to wear miniature foghorns on the lapels of their coats and
many parents whose babes had good sound lungs gave their young
hopefuls the name of Funston having no objection to their being
called Foghorn.

Funston made the name of Foghorn honorable and when all the
old delegation in Congress but himself went down before the hosts
of Pops and Democrats, Funston's foghorn was heard rallying his
disconfited [sic: discomfited] party again to the contest and back to
victory. The next epithet applied to him by those who would make
us believe he had reached old age, and imbecility was that of "The
old man." Though in but his fifty ninth year Funston delights in the
appellation of "Old man," and his friends are beginning to apply it
as a term of endearment. To them it means maturity of mind and
a fully developed intellect and therefore the best days of his life for
the discharge of his duties as Congressman. Funston is making old
age not only honorable but desirable by setting an example unsur-
passed in purity of life and vigor of thought.[16]

What was Ed like as a congressman? The Leavenworth, Kansas, *Standard* in 1888 provided its readers this description: "His tall, thick set,
broad shouldered form, rosy face, and reddish hair are well knowned [sic]
in Washington... He has acquired a considerable reputation here as a
first-rate story teller. On the floor of the House he makes a good, unpre-
tentious, matter of fact speech, and in tilts with other members he generally comes out with flying colors, owing to the fact that he never gets
excited, never gets mad, and has the tact, so rare among Congressmen,
to ward off the shafts of his antagonists by maintaining a calm and col-

lected demeanor."[17]

During his ten years as a congressman, Ed served on the Committee on Agriculture, most of the time as a member only, but at least one year as its chairman. As a result of the work of the committee, the Agricultural Department was raised from a mere bureau to a cabinet department, with a secretary at its head.[18] As a congressman, Ed aided 944 old soldiers with their pension claims. Many of these pensions were granted by special acts of Congress.[19] Also as a congressman, Ed had at his disposal the appointment of local postmasters throughout the Second District. These were lucrative positions. For example, the postmasters at Kansas City and at Fort Scott each received a $2,500 annual salary; the one at Iola received $1,400.[20] The Funston farm was soon overrun with office seekers. Ella (Funston) Eckdall described many years later her father's congressional career and its effects upon the members of his family:

> Our home was fast becoming the Mecca of the politicians of the Second District. This district, located in the eastern half of Kansas, contained many of the larger cities and towns of the state, and produced many aspiring politicians. At a change in Presidential administrations, when all the post offices in the Second District became vacant, there was an influx of office seekers to our home, that completely disrupted the domestic routine of the family. Father was obliged to take rooms at the Pennsylvania House in Iola, to receive these office seekers and their retinue of supporters. They came up the highway in buggies and carts and by train from far and near. I have seen them seated with Father in the library arguing their qualifications for their respective offices; I have seen them resting beneath the shade of the maple tree beside the front gate, and perched upon the barn fence, awaiting their turns to present their credentials.
>
> Unfortunately for us, the schedule of the trains at Carlyle was not such that the callers might return the same day of their arrival, but must remain at our home until the following day. Carlyle was a "flag" station where trains stopped only when passengers arrived or departed. Two whistles indicated a passenger coming or going, and to us it usually meant coming to the Funston home. If the visitor was unannounced he was obliged to walk the distance of a mile and a quarter up the road to our farm. This gave us time to dust the "parlor," tidy up the "spare bedroom," and make preparations for a meal of country fried chicken with cream gravy, fluffy potatoes and deep-dish apple pie....
>
> During the many years of Father's incumbency in office, he found little or no time for leisure. He wrote thousands of letters, made many speeches on the tariff and silver questions and on farm

problems, as well, and he delivered numberless patriotic and other addresses. He subscribed for every Republican newspaper in the Second District, but for lack of time to peruse their pages, he delegated that task to Mother, who carefully clipped and preserved every item of interest to him.

At times Father pressed some of the older members of his family into his service in Washington, to assist him in his work. Occasionally some of his children left the farm for a winter of sight-seeing in the nation's capital. Oftentimes Mother took her small son, Edward Hogue, Jr. with her, who learned to walk on the "terra firma" of Franklin Park of that city.

Memory reflects the image of Father some sixty years ago, dressed in a neatly tailored Prince Albert suit, with derby hat and cane, as he walked with a firm step and dignified bearing down the broad and beautiful Pennsylvania Avenue of Washington, D.C. A handsome man of six feet, two, and well proportioned, he possessed the ruddy complexion, blue eyes and high forehead of his Scottish ancestors. Many times Mother accompanied him at receptions and dinners at the White House. She was a "petite" figure of five feet, two, beside her tall husband, as she stepped forth in her red plush evening gown with train and Duchess lace, carrying a large black ostrich feather fan. [The deep ruby red plush evening gown had a tapered bodice which emphasized 45-year-old Lida's 19-inch waistline and 26-inch bustline.[21]] She was living once again in the days of the green "watered silk" opera cape, the rosewood and mahogany of her dear old Ohio home.[22]

Ella noted her mother's contribution to her father's political career by Lida's clipping and preserving relevant newspaper articles. Her contribution, however, appears to have possibly been greater. In 1885, the Washington correspondent for the Pleasanton, Kansas, *Observer* reported that "[i]n my calls on Christmas day I included Mr. and Mrs. Funston, in connection with the mention of which I will take the liberty to say that the key to the solution of the secret of the enviable political success of the Kansas farmer was furnished me by the general appearance and deportment of his wife. A man may plan and study and pull the hair out of his head trying to catch hold of new and strange ideas, to make a success of life, but without the co-operation of his wife he will fail."[23]

Edward Funston's ten years in Congress ended in an unexpected manner in 1894. For now, however, we return to the year of 1884 when Ed Funston was flush with his smashing electoral victory. Ten days later, on March 11, he took the train headed for Washington, D.C., and his new position. He was accompanied by son Fred as far as Lawrence, where Fred entered the Lawrence Business College.[24] Before heading off to school, however, Fred had attended on March 4 the evening festival held by the Methodist Episcopal Church at the Opera House in Iola. In addition to the supper served by the church ladies, there was a spelling match in which Fred participated. A list of twenty names had been prepared, from which two leaders chose sides. After spelling a total of one hundred words, "the whole party stood up and had a 'spell down.' A great deal of amusement was caused by the way the crowd withered before the little word 'fice' (a small dog)...[Angelo] Scott had the good luck to be the last man standing and spelled it the only way there was left."[25]

Fred entered the Lawrence Business College on March 12. Not only did the college note this fact in its "Business College News" column in *The Lawrence Daily Journal*, the newspaper also reported it in its "Personal" column, describing him as the "son of Representative-elect Funston."[26] The new student wore a "very large derby hat," which he had borrowed from his father.[27] Established in 1869, the college in the year 1882-1883 had 350 students from thirteen states. There were five departments: business, penmanship, shorthand, telegraphy, and English. "It is the intention of the proprietor to furnish a strictly practical education—one can be immediately made available in the counting room, the bank, the manufactory, the railroad office, the telegraph room, at the reporter's table, or as instructor in plain and ornamental penmanship."[28]

As to the business department, in which Fred enrolled, "a thorough knowledge of recording the business transactions, wholesale and retail merchandising, banking, railroading, manufacturing, real estate and insurance is given. The students are thus qualified, upon graduation, to enter at once into actual business life."[29] The business courses offered were many: "Book-keeping (by Single and Double Entry), Commercial Arithmetic, Rapid Calculations, Actual Business Practice, Commercial Law, Business Penmanship, Letter Writing, Spelling and Grammar."[30]

The year prior to Fred's attendance, the college occupied the third story of the National Bank building located on Massachusetts Street.[31] By the time that Fred attended, the college had expanded beyond the bank's third floor to include "a large room opposite the opera house block," where the business department was located. One of the State University student newspapers offered this high praise of the business department: "Those who are prone to consider this part of the business course mere innocent play will quickly undeceive themselves in a few minutes look into this department."[32]

Why would Fred Funston undertake what appears to have been a demanding course of study, and one which, arguably, would lead to a life of sedentary work? At this point, Fred apparently knew that he was going to seek an appointment to a cadet vacancy at the United States Military Academy at West Point, and, perhaps, that is where our answer lies.

Since he had only a common school education, Fred may have undertaken his business studies as a way of preparing himself for the competitive academic exam for West Point that he would take a couple of months later. To succeed, he would have to receive the top score on the examination. Perhaps, he, and likely his father also, hoped that the concentrated business courses would provide him the edge that he would need to come out on top.

At the same time that *The Iola Register* was announcing the death of Congressman Haskell and lauding his many accomplishments, it was also running in the adjoining column a notification from him addressed to the "young men" of the congressional district. This notification alerted them to a vacancy at West Point to be filled by appointment from him, and advised that applications should be sent to him by letter. The successful applicant would be selected by "competition or other examination." At the end of this announcement was the *Register's* note: "The above was in type before Mr. Haskell's death was known. Further announcement in regard to the matter will be made in due time."[33]

About three months later, in early April 1884, the newly elected congressman, Ed Funston, published in newspapers of the congressional district his announcement of a "competitive examination of applicants for appointment as cadets to the United States Military Academy from the old Second District." The examination would be held at Iola on May 8, starting at 9 a.m. Each applicant would first be subjected to a physical examination by "physicians of good professional standing" designated by Funston, and for those who passed, they would then participate in the competitive examination supervised and scored by three County Superintendents of Public Instruction. Additional information could be found in the appropriate circular obtainable from the War Department.[34]

Eighteen-year-old Fred read the circular, and on April 9, using Lawrence Business College stationery, he wrote a letter to the Adjutant General of the War Department seeking clarification on one point. The circular noted that appointments are required to be made one year in advance of the date of admission to the academy. In the case of the current appointment, Fred stated that he understood that the successful candidate was to report at the Academy between June 10 and June 20, 1884, which would be less than a month after the examination. Fred, logically, inquired in his letter whether the cadet to be selected would report at the Academy in June of 1884, or June of 1885.[35] The Adjutant General replied three days later, advising that the cadet candidate would be required to report at West Point for examination on "the 14th day of June next."[36]

A few days later, Fred was at home for a visit. *The Iola Register* reported that "[h]e will be one of the competitors in the examination for the West Point cadetship."[37] A week before the examination and at the request of congressman Funston, two Iola residents selected by lot the three examiners, each being a County Superintendent of Public Instruction from counties of the district. None of the three selected was from Allen County.[38] Fred was one of eleven candidates in the required age range of seventeen to twenty-two years, with candidates coming from seven counties of the congressional district: Allen, Miami, Neosho, Douglas, Crawford, Anderson, and Bourbon.[39] The medical examination was first. Candidates, who had to be unmarried, were required to be at least five feet in height. Thus, Fred at five feet, four inches in height was not too short to be a candidate. Candidates had to be "free from any infections or immoral disorder, and generally, from any deformity, disease, or infirmity which may render them unfit for military service." The written examination followed. Candidates were expected to "be well versed in reading, in writing, including orthography, in arithmetic, and have a knowledge of the elements of English grammar, of descriptive geography, (particularly of our own country), and of the history of the United States."[40]

The Iola Register trumpeted the examination results: "Allen County again has the honor of furnishing the successful competitor for the West Point appointment." This was a reference to Allen Countian George T. Bartlett, who had graduated from West Point in 1881. In the 1884 competition, the highest score of an average of 88 4/7 was attained by Howard Lincoln Power of rural Iola. With an average score of 87 5/7, Charles Crawford of Paola in Miami County was less than a point behind Power and placed second. Fred Funston was third.[41] At twenty-one, Power was three years older than the 18-year-old Funston, while Crawford, at age seventeen, was a year younger than Fred.[42] *The Iola Register* named only the top two scorers while *Allen County Courant* reported the scores of all eleven candidates, including Fred's. His score was quite respectable, 86 3/7.[43] Thus, Fred came very close to success, being just over two points shy of the first-place competitor, but, close was not good enough. Fred's plans for a likely adventurous life elsewhere were to no avail. Interestingly, according to Fred's sister, Ella (Funston) Eckdall, Howard Power had been Fred's teacher at Maple Grove School.[44] Another competitive advantage that the older Power had over Fred was that he had attended the State University in Lawrence in the 1879-1880 school year.[45]

Howard Power went off to West Point where he passed both the physical and academic examinations, and was admitted to the Academy. There, he failed the mathematics course, and was discharged from the Academy the following January of 1885. Since Charles Crawford had scored the second highest on the competitive examination, he then received the appointment to the Academy.[46] Later that year, the Board of Regents of the State Normal School at Emporia chose Professor M.A. Bailey of Keene,

New Hampshire, to be the chair of mathematics. Bailey was regarded as an authority on mathematics, and the hope in selecting him was that the teachers turned out from the Normal would be able to teach mathematics with "still greater success; that in a few years one-half, at least, of the young men appointed to West Point military [sic] from Kansas, will be able to remain there and not be dismissed on account of being deficient in this branch of study, as has been the case up to this time."[47] Howard Power's failure at West Point had clearly reverberated through Kansas, including in the teaching profession.

During Fred's military service in the Philippines with the Twentieth Kansas in 1899, the foregoing sequence of events was distorted in a newspaper account to be found in the Frederick Funston Papers. This article, clipped from an unidentified newspaper, is dated from "Washington, May 1," and quoted "one of Funston's classmates at the Kansas State university [sic] after reading the dispatches from Manila." This anonymous source claimed that Fred "will never get over his disappointment at not going to West Point about fourteen years ago." Perhaps this was true, but this anonymous source, though credible on first blush, soon destroys all of his credibility with his allegations about Fred's actions after he was unsuccessful in the competitive examination. The anonymous source does not mention Howard Power as the successful competitor. Instead, this source states that "[w]hen the papers were examined Crawford was found to be the winner by a handsome margin, with Fred a poor second. The disappointment nearly broke Funston's heart, and he was as savage as a bulldog for months afterward. Fred was named as the alternate, and he had a gleam of hope that Crawford would be killed in a cyclone, or get struck by lightning, or get crippled in a railroad smashup, and that as alternate he would go to West Point after all."[48] (!)

The canard that Fred was the alternate West Point candidate was not limited to the anonymous, alleged classmate of Fred, since it was shared by at least one member of the Power family. Howard's sister, Maude Pearl (Power) Fonville, who was fifteen years his junior, claimed incorrectly that her brother had attended West Point for two years, but had been "hazed" by officers since Congressman Edward Funston wanted his son Fred to have the appointment. According to Maude, the only two who took the West Point examination were Howard Power and Fred Funston, and Power won. When Howard subsequently could no longer stand the hazing, he deliberately failed his studies, wrote Maude, and "Frederick Funston was appointed to fill the unexpired time at West Point."[49] (!) Between the unfounded erroneous assertions of the anonymous classmate of Fred and those of Howard Power's sister, one is left speechless. Howard Power will appear again, briefly, one more time in our story of Fred Funston's early life.

As for Charles Crawford, he graduated from West Point in 1889, and made the military his career. In the Spanish-American War, he participated in the battle of San Juan Hill, Cuba, and, in the war in the Philippines, he served three years. He later became a General, and in World War I he was in charge of the 6th Brigade, which was sent to Europe. Crawford died at age seventy-nine in 1945. At the time that Brigadier General Frederick Funston of the Volunteers captured Aguinaldo in March 1901, Charles Crawford was a Captain in the 20th Infantry, and upon learning of Funston's coup, Crawford cablegrammed him as follows: "Congratulations, except my self [sic] there is no one who I had rather seen capture Aguinaldo than you."[50]

Fred Funston Age 18 Years

Chapter Seven Notes—*A U.S. Congressman, a Business College Student, and a Competitor for a West Point Cadetship*

1. "Information Relative to the Appointment and Admission of Cadets to the United States Military Academy," *Official Register of the Officers and Cadets of the U. S. Military Academy 1884*, 33.

2. "Dudley C. Haskell," *The Iola Register*, December 21,1883.

3. "Haskell Indian Nations University," Kansapedia, Kansas Historical Society (internet website).

4. The year of 1884 comes from the issue of August 27, 1884, of *The Lawrence Gazette* which stated under "The City": "The Indian school will hereafter be known as the Haskell Institute." Thereafter, this newspaper consistently and frequently used that title. Today, the Institute is known as Haskell Indian Nations University.

5. "The Congressional Convention," *The Iola Register*, July 7, 1882.

6. "Hon. E. H. Funston," *The Iola Register*, December 28, 1883 (article about Funston's candidacy). "The Congressional Outlook," *Fort Scott Daily Monitor*, December 23, 1883 (reprint of "Special Dispatch to the *Kansas City Times*").

7. "Parsons Congressional Convention," *Fort Scott Daily Monitor*, February 1, 1884.

8. For the incident involving Fred's memory and knowledge, see Charles S. Gleed, "Romance and Reality In A Single Life. Gen. Frederick Funston," *The Cosmopolitan Illustrated Monthly Magazine*, July 1899. For the Fort Scott speech, see an untitled newspaper article, possibly from the New York *Herald* in 1899 (FFP Micro). For a similar version of this story, see "Little Colonel Funston," *The New York Times*, April 30, 1899 (FFP).

9. "Biographical," *Fort Scott Weekly Monitor*, January 24, 1884.

10. D. W. Wilder, *The Annals of Kansas New Edition*, 1541-1885 (Topeka: T. Dwight Thacher, Kansas Publishing House, 1886), 1050.

11. "Rah For Funston!" *The Iola Register*, March 7, 1884.

12. Ralph Richards, *A History of IOLA, KANSAS From the Beginning Up To These Times Called Modern* (no date or place), 19-20. Copy at Iola Public Library.

13. Richards, *A History of IOLA, KANSAS*, 20.

14. Richards, *A History of IOLA, KANSAS*, 20. Ralph Richards, the author and son of J.H. Richards, was born in 1871 and stated that he was "about nine years of age" when this event, which he attended, occurred. That would make the date of occurrence about 1880, four years before Ed Funston was elected to Congress. Thus, this event more likely occurred in connection with a state race, but since Richards has described Ed as Congressman at this time, I have inserted this campaign story in this chapter. Richards referred to "Doctor Hart" in the quotation, yet earlier he had said that Hart was a political figure, and that there was also present a "corpulent country doctor."

15. Tom McNeal, "A Bouquet of Sunflowers," *Topeka Capital*, February 26, 1915 (Kansas State Historical Society, *Allen County Clippings*, Vol. 1, 1875-1955).

16. "Farmer Funston, Foghorn Funston, Old Man Funston," *Southern Kansas Horticulturalist*, Vol I – No. XI (March Number) [1896] (published at Iola, Kansas, by E.S. Davis, and edited by L. M. Pancoast). This was an "Extra Edition" and was devoted to the life and career of the Hon. E. H. Funston, "a successful farmer and horticulturalist." Photocopy at Allen County Historical Society, Inc.

17. "Hon. E.H. Funston," *The Iola Register*, April 27, 1888 (reprint from Leavenworth *Standard*).

18. "What Has Funston Done?" *Southern Kansas Horticulturalist*.

19. "Pensions" and "A Friend to the Old Soldier in Need," *Southern Kansas Horticultur-alist*.

20. "Presidential Office in the Second Congressional Dist. Of Kansas" (Edward H. Funston Political Scrapbooks). Allen County Historical Society, Inc.

21. "Funston gown family treasure," unidentified newspaper (likely *The Iola Register*), March 5, 1981 (Allen County Historical Society, Inc.). This article tells the story of the red plush gown, and provides additional detail about it. A Washington, D.C., dressmaker was commissioned to fashion this gown. "Panels of ivory brocaded satin were inserted in the skirt back and front while the sleeves featured satin insets. Ivory Dutchess lace bordered the brocaded front panel and was gathered around the neckline. It was repeated at the sleeve edges." Wires, padding, and stays created the fashionable hourglass shape. Lida wore long, white kid gloves, and size one shoes! Having given birth to eight children, Lida's 19-inch waistline at age forty-five is, indeed, impressive.

    Lida wore this gown to the 1889 inaugural ball of President Benjamin Harrison, and again, in 1901, to President William McKinley's inauguration. In this gown, Lida danced with General William T. Sherman. The waistline and bust line measurements are from the gown itself, which is on display at the Funston Home Museum, Iola, Kansas.

22. Ella Funston Eckdall, *The Funston Homestead* (Emporia, Kansas: Raymond Lees, 1949), 26-29.

23. "Editorial Notes," *The Iola Register*, January 16, 1885 (reprint from Pleasanton, Kansas, *Observer*).

24. "Local Matters," *The Iola Register*, March 14, 1884.

25. "Local Matters," *The Iola Register*, March 7, 1884 (two articles).

26. "Business College News" and "Personal," *The Lawrence Daily Journal*, March 13, 1884.

27. A. L. Burney to Frederick Funston, November 17, 1914 (FFP Micro).

28. "A Flourishing Institution," *The Lawrence Gazette*, August 30, 1883.

29. "Lawrence Business College," *The Lawrence Gazette*, February 1, 1883.

30. "Lawrence Business College," *The Lawrence Gazette*, August 30, 1883 (advertisement).

31. "Lawrence Business College," *The Lawrence Gazette*, February 1, 1883.

32. "What the University Courier of February 11th Has to Say of the Lawrence Business College," *The Lawrence Daily Journal*, February 24, 1884.

33. "Editorial Notes," *The Iola Register*, December 21, 1883.

34. "West Point Appointment," *The Iola Register*, April 4, 1884.

35. Fred Funston to Adjutant General, April 9, 1884 (Records of the Adjutant General Office, 1780s-1917, United States Military Academy; Letters Received, 1874-1889 (Record Group 94), File 245-1884 (Frederick Funston)). National Archives.

36. Adjutant General to Fred Funston, April 12, 1884 (Records of the Adjutant General Office, 1780s-1917, United States Military Academy; Letters Received, 1874-1889 (Record Group 94), File 245-1884 (Frederick Funston)). National Archives.

37. "Local Matters," *The Iola Register*, April 18, 1884.

38. "Local Matters," *The Iola Register*, May 2, 1884.

39. "West Point Cadetship," *Fort Scott Weekly Monitor*, May 22, 1884.

40. "Information Relative to the Appointment and Admission of Cadets to the United States Military Academy," *Official Register of the Officers and Cadets of the U.S. Military Academy 1884*, 33.

41. "West Point Cadetship," *Fort Scott Weekly Monitor*, May 22, 1884. "Additional Locals," *The Iola Register*, May 16, 1884. *The Monitor* reported average score of 88 for Power and 87 for Crawford, and the *Register* reported 88 4/7 for Power and 86 3/7 for Crawford. This latter score was Fred Funston's, not Crawford's. *The Monitor* likely rounded the scores. The source at note 43 below states Crawford's score as 87 5/7.

42. Power was born on September 6, 1862; Funston on November 9, 1865; and Crawford on December 27, 1866. Power's date of birth from Records of the Adjutant General's Office, 1780s-1917, United States Military Academy; Letters Received, 1874-1889, Record Group 94, file 371-1884. Crawford's date of birth from the same source except his file is 283-1885. National Archives.

43. "Candidates for West Point," *Allen County Courant*, May 15, 1884. Fred Funston's scores: Spelling, 88; Reading, 87½; Writing, 80; Arithmetic, 75; Geography, 96; Grammar, 81; History, 98.

44. Statement by Ella (Funston) Eckdall in connection with her typed "Preface Page (2)" concerning the book *Scouting with General Funston* (Eckdall donation in 2003 to Allen County Historical Society, Inc.). I have been unable to ascertain when this would have been. The Maple Grove School quilt states that Power was the teacher in 1884, but that was not a year that Fred attended Maple Grove School. This teacher-pupil relationship undoubtedly did exist at one time, since Ella, as Fred's sister, would have known this fact of her own knowledge.

45. Howard Power's student enrollment card in the University of Kansas Archives shows his attendance in "Jr. Prep" for the 1879-1880 year (Becky Schulte of Spencer Research Library, University of Kansas, e-mail to author, November 3, 2014).

46. "A Retired General in Kansas Shows Ability as an Economist," *The Kansas City Star*, July 13, 1936 (Eckdall Scrapbook I, 254), and biography of Crawford in *Assembly Magazine*, October 1946. In *The Kansas City Star* article, which Ella (Funston) Eckdall included in her scrapbook, she not only wrote "correct" next to the text about how Crawford became a West Point cadet, but also summarized in her own handwriting these events.

47. "Professors Chosen," *Fort Scott Weekly Monitor*, August 6, 1885.

48. "Funston and Crawford," undated and from an unknown newspaper (Byline: "Washington, May 1") (FFP).

49. Genealogical notes about Howard Lincoln Power by his sister, Maude Pearl (Power) Fonville (1877-1972). Courtesy of Scott Jordan, a distant relative of Howard and Maude Power.

50. Crawford to Funston, April 1, 1901 (FFP Micro). Another cablegram dated March 28, 1901, was sent to Brigadier General Funston from the newspaper magnate, "W. R. Hearst, New York Journal," who wrote "Congratulations to the Newest Hero Of The Philippine War How Did you Do It" (FFP Micro).

CHAPTER EIGHT

The Schoolmaster and the Bully

September 22, 1884 – January 9, 1885

[T]he unruly big boy, who in most of the country districts make [sic] life a misery for the teacher on every possible occasion.

—"C.S.R.," who became intimately associated with Fred Funston when both were attending the Allen County Normal Institute.[1]

SONG OF THE SCHOOLMA'AM

Sixty little urchins
  Coming through the door,
Pushing, crowding, making
  A tremendous roar.
Why don't you keep quiet?
  Can't you mind the rule?
Bless me, this is pleasant
  Teaching public school.

Sixty little pilgrims
  On the road to fame,
If they fail to reach it
  Who will be to blame?
High and lowly station—
  Birds of every feather—
On a common level
  Here are brought together.

Dirty little faces,
  Loving little hearts,
Eyes brim full of mischief,
  Skilled in all its arts.
'That's a precious darling!
  What are you about?'
'May I pass the water?'
  'Please may I go out?'

> Boots and shoes are shuffling.
>   Slates and books are rattling—
> And, in the corner yonder,
>   Two pugilists are battling.
> Others cutting didoes.
>   What a botheration!
> No wonder we grow crusty
>   From such association!
>
> —*The Iola Register.*
>   February 26, 1876.[2]

While Ed Funston had been busy in January of 1884 campaigning for Haskell's vacant congressional seat, Fred Funston had been busy, at least part of the time, working toward a personal goal of his own: obtaining a new Third Grade Teacher's Certificate. Although the one he had qualified for the previous August was still valid for about another month, he apparently decided that he should qualify for an additional one, which would be good for six months from the date of issue.

As previously noted, Kansas law did not permit the holder of a Third Grade Certificate to receive a second one. It is difficult to understand the rationale behind this punitive law, since it meant that if a recipient, for whatever reason, failed to teach for at least three months, the recipient was barred from receiving a Second Grade Certificate, the next higher certificate, which required that the applicant had taught at least three months. Without having taught the minimum of three months, an individual could not move up to the next certificate, and, at the same time, since the law forbade his receiving a second Third Grade Certificate, the unlucky individual was effectively barred from the teaching profession.

In Fred's case, he had not used the certificate he had earned in August of 1883, yet he was to compete successfully twice for a Third Grade Certificate in 1884. He, and others in this situation, benefited from the Allen County examining board's practical approach to this problem. The board did not *issue* the certificate until the individual had secured a teaching position.[3] Thus, if a teaching position was not obtained, the individual could take the examination again, and, if successful, be eligible to receive a new Third Grade Certificate.

On January 26, 1884, Fred, age eighteen, took the teacher's examination, and scored an overall average of eighty-six, which was sufficient to obtain the Third Grade Certificate. His grades in the several subjects examined were as follows:

Orthography	70
Reading	89
Writing	85

Geography	90
Composition	98
Arithmetic	88
Grammar	81
Constitution	100[4]

In view of Fred's interest at the same time in attending West Point, perhaps he was hedging his bets by obtaining this second Teacher's Certificate, which was good for use in Allen County until July 26. In any event, after he was unsuccessful in the West Point competition, he did not teach; whether he sought a teaching position before his certificate expired is unknown.

The 1884 Allen County Normal Institute opened on August 4, and closed on August 29. A longtime teacher observed that "[a] large number of those attending the Normal are from the country, and it speaks well for our future as a people. When such interest is taken by the 'brown handed' farmer boys and girls in educational work we need not fear but our places will be well filled after we have passed away."[5]

There were at least 113 Institute attendees, but Fred was not one of them. Although *The Iola Register* did not publish a list of the attendees, *The Humboldt Union* did, and Fred was not listed.[6] Perhaps he enrolled late and thus his name did not appear in the newspaper, or, more likely, he believed that he did not need to attend in order to be prepared to take, once again, the teacher's examination. After all, he had been successful twice within a year's time in securing a Third Grade Certificate. On August 29 and 30, at the end of the Institute, Fred took the teacher's examination.[7] His score is unknown, but he received, once again, a Third Grade Certificate.[8]

This time Fred used his certificate. He quickly acquired a teaching position with School District No. 12. Known as Star Valley School District, it was located about five miles southwest of Iola, and thus a considerable distance from the Funston farm. The schoolhouse sat on a three-acre tract of land, which had been purchased for thirteen dollars in September of 1867.[9] A neighboring farmer and school board member, Samuel F. Hubbard, donated the funds to build the schoolhouse.[10] The building was situated at the north foot of Strosnider Hill, now known as Humboldt Hill, halfway between Iola and Humboldt.[11] Lying north of this hill was a beautiful valley, and a star was carved in a rock over the door of the schoolhouse, making it Star Valley School District.[12] The school building was constructed of native stone, and that fact and its isolated location at the foot of the high hill resulted in the popular nickname of Stoney Lonesome for the school.[13] The word "Stoney" is also spelled "Stony" in various sources. There is no local standard for the spelling of the school's nickname.

The rules in an 1883 architectural guide for selecting the proper site for a school building indicate that those who designed the stone building planned unwisely from the standpoint of "healthfulness." "In this State, every school-house should be so situated as to have access to the south wind during the summer season," observed the guide. "The north side or north foot of a hill is undesirable."[14] Stoney Lonesome failed on this score, but since school was usually not held during any summer months, its location at the north foot of a hill seems insignificant.

As to the best direction for a school building to face, Stoney Lonesome was designed correctly, using this 1883 guide, since it faced toward the east. According to the guide, the rear, west end of the building could then be unbroken by windows and thus occupied by the black board and the teacher's stand.[15] Then, the sides of the building could be cut up by windows through which the "prevailing south wind" could move during the summer season.[16] Since school was usually in session in the Star Valley School District during the early, warm part of the fall, this aspect would be a benefit for this stone building. A south front was not good, however, according to the guide, since it allowed the wind to sweep "through the entry along the aisles, whenever a door opens, thus continually blowing dust about the room and into the lungs of teacher and scholars."[17]

The one-room Stoney Lonesome school building was about twenty-two feet in width and about seventeen feet in length, thus being slightly wider than it was long. The schoolhouse was built just a few feet west of the Iola-Humboldt road, and had a well for drinking water located north of the door. Two windows were cut into the south wall and likely there were two comparable windows in the north wall. There were no windows on the west end of the box-like structure, which stood naked on the prairie.[18] Writing many years later, Ella (Funston) Eckdall noted that straying herds of cattle wandered at times near the unprotected school building.[19]

Children of District No. 12 may have attended classes before Stoney Lonesome was built in 1867, since a Mrs. Neville taught from September to December 1865.[20] The District's "Register of Teachers Employed" from September 1870 to June 19, 1885, has survived, and it shows both male and female teachers employed during those years.[21] One teacher, Thomas Bartlett, taught three years in succession and then another year a couple of years later. He possessed a First Grade Teacher's Certificate, and received a $40 monthly salary.[22] Bartlett (1821-1891) was both a minister and teacher.[23] Interestingly, Thomas Bartlett was the father of George T. Bartlett, Allen County's pride, who had graduated from West Point in 1881 and who became a Major General.[24] At the time Fred captured Aguinaldo in 1901, *The Humboldt Union* ran a brief article about Fred's having taught school "in the little old stone school house north of the 'Strosnider hill.'" Although the schoolhouse was tumbling down, "Fred keeps climbing up higher toward the top of the hill, and finally has captured a star. The Kansas motto 'ad astra per aspera' [to the stars through difficulties], must have been Fred's companion through life." *The Humboldt Union* then confused Bartlett père with Bartlett fils, claiming that "George W. [sic] Bartlett," who had graduated from West Point, had taught in the same building as Fred.[25]

On September 8, Fred signed a Teacher's Contract with School District No. 12, which called for a salary of $35 per month, for a total of $140 for four months. This was payable on or before February 1, 1885. The term he was to teach was four months, commencing on September 22.[26] The "Register of Teachers Employed" shows the final date of the term was January 14, 1885.[27] Fred, however, in his "Teacher's Term Report to District Clerk" listed the closing date as January 9. He reported that this term covered sixteen weeks and eighty school days.[28]

The fact that Fred was not to be paid his total salary of $140 until "on or before" February 1, 1885, a date after his term of employment had ended, may have been necessitated by the precarious financial situation of the school district. Star Valley School District began the fiscal year of August 1, 1884, through July 31, 1885, with a cash balance of a mere $2.96. Its only source of revenue was the tax funds distributed by Allen County, which amounted that fiscal year to $260.71.[29] The tax funds received annually from the county were based on the mill levy set by the legal voters of School District No. 12 at their Annual School Meeting held at the schoolhouse. At this meeting on August 14, 1884, those present voted a tax of 5 mills for teachers' wages and ½ mill for incidentals.[30] The 5½ mills were levied on the taxable property of the small district, and thus would not generate a large sum for the support of the school district's operation. At 5½ mills, the levy was significantly less than the average 12½ mill levy in all Allen County school districts for that 1884-1885 fiscal year.[31]

The Annual School Meeting had multiple purposes, including setting the mill levy; electing the district officers of director, clerk, and treasurer; determining which sex of teacher was to be employed; setting the length of the school term; etc. At the August 14, 1884, meeting, the sex of the teacher to be hired was not set by the legal voters, but the term of school for "the coming year" was set at six months.[32] In reality, it became a term of almost seven months. The Annual School Meeting five years later on July 25, 1889, directed the school board to "employ a teacher the best to be had regardless of sex." Perhaps based on a recent bad experience, the voters that year also instructed the board to hire the teacher subject to the "condition that if upon a unanimous verdict of the board or a majority of the patrons of the Dist. the school be decided not a success...," the teacher would immediately stop teaching. The teacher's contract would be canceled upon the district board's paying the teacher the wages due for services performed.[33]

The major Star Valley School District expense the year Fred taught was the salaries of the teachers. Fred taught only the winter term for $140. The spring term was taught by Oliver "Ollie" Adams, a son of the school district's director, William C. Adams. Young Adams had received a Second Grade Certificate at the end of August of 1884, but whether he taught at a school the subsequent winter term is unknown.[34] It is interesting that nepotism apparently did not exist in the Star Valley District, since Fred was hired for the winter term instead of the son of the school district's director.

The spring term was different, however, and Oliver Adams was employed as teacher to succeed Fred. He received a monthly salary of only $28, 20% less than that which had been paid to Fred.[35] Fred's $35 monthly salary was itself $5 less than that received by the teacher the prior year, who also had held a Third Grade Teacher's Certificate. At $28, however, Ollie Adams still received $3 more monthly than the female teacher with a Second Grade Certificate had received three years earlier.[36] The slim finances of the district may have determined the lower salary for each of the nearly three months that Adams taught (March 30, 1885 - June 19, 1885).[37] His total salary amounted to $84, and this, plus Fred's salary of $140 and "repairs and other incidentals" of $40.98, left the district in debt in the amount of $1.31 at the end of the 1884-1885 fiscal year.[38]

Although Oliver Adams' contract provided for him to be paid at the end of each month, that did not fully materialize.[39] He started teaching March 30, and did receive $28 on May 4, but it was not until June 20, the day after his term ended, that he received $56 for the balance due to him. As for Fred, in the end, he did receive his wages before February 1, 1885. He started teaching September 22, 1884, and received his first $35 payment about a month later on October 28. The next payment was for $70, two months' salary, which was paid on December 12, and the final $35 was paid on January 14, 1885, at the end of his teaching term.[40]

For that fiscal year ending July 31, 1885, during which Fred had taught, fifty-one men and sixty-four women taught in the Allen County schools. The average salary of the male teachers was $43.18, and the average salary of the female teachers was significantly less at $34.55.[41] Pay inequality, in today's terminology, was an integral part of the Allen County educational establishment.

The day came that September of 1884 for Fred to move from the Funston farm to the home of William C. Adams and his wife, Melissa Adams, where Fred was to room. The Adams family, former neighbors of the Funstons, lived in the vicinity of Stoney Lonesome. This was the same William C. Adams who served as the school district's director. Fred and his brother, Burt, hitched their father's best team of horses to his Studebaker wagon, and together made the twelve-mile trip to the Adams home.[42] Apparently, Fred would be afoot during his stay as a teacher, unless he was able to borrow a horse or wagon on occasion. Fred took with him a brand-new trunk, which contained his heavy winter wardrobe and a generous supply of books.[43] The books, likely, were to be utilized by Fred in connection with a plan of self-advancement that he and seven other young men, including Oliver Adams, had decided to pursue. *The Iola Register* announced that "[a] number of our young men who wish to prepare themselves for college, have prevailed upon Prof. Harris to organize a private school for the study of the higher branches."[44] Consequently, Fred was a student at the same time as he was a teacher, and clearly had higher ambition than being a country schoolteacher.

The small stone schoolhouse was filled with pupils—31. This was out of an eligible school population of 50 children between the ages of 5 and 21. Of these 50, there were 27 males and 23 females.[45] Of Fred's 31 pupils, they ranged in age from 4 through 18, and there were 17 males and 14 females. Twenty-one of the students were between the ages of 4 and 11; seven were ages 13 through 15; two boys age 17; and one boy age 18, the same age as Fred the teacher. According to Fred's report at the end of his term of teaching, "[q]uite a number of pupils" started school about a month late, and he took that into account in figuring averages. Perhaps the late starters were involved in the fall harvest. Of the thirty-one pupils, the males' average daily attendance was 10 4/6 and the females 10 34/60. There were 68 "tardinesses" but four students were neither absent nor tardy.[46]

A significant variety of textbooks was used because of the different educational levels of Fred's students:

> Writing—10 pupils
> Appleton's First Reader—11 pupils
> Appleton's Second Reader—4 pupils
> Appleton's Third Reader—4 pupils
> Appleton's Fourth Reader—1 pupil
> Fifth Reader—11 pupils
> Wilson's Speller—20 pupils
> Swinton's Language—1 pupil
> Swinton's Grammar—4 pupils
> Monteith's Primary Geography—1 pupil
> Monteith's Higher Geography—10 pupils
> French's 1st part Arithmetic—3 pupils

French's 2nd part Arithmetic—7 pupils

French's 3rd part Arithmetic—11 pupils

Scott's U.S. History—5 pupils [47]

Although Stoney Lonesome's classroom size seems small for thirty-one pupils, it may not have been unreasonably so under the standards of the time. The same 1883 "School Architecture" guide, cited previously, included a design for a schoolhouse for "Country Districts and Suburbs of Cities" in which the schoolroom was 20 feet, 10 inches by 27 feet, 4 inches and which was capable of seating forty pupils. Included in this one room were a vestibule and small, separate ward rooms for boys and girls, one on each side of the vestibule.[48] Comparing the square footage of Stoney Lonesome against the architect's plan, Stoney Lonesome had about twelve square feet for each of the thirty-one pupils but this is calculated by ignoring furniture and aisles. The architect's plan, in contrast, had about fourteen square feet for each of the forty pupils (ignoring the vestibule, ward rooms, furniture, and aisles). Although Stoney Lonesome was not unusually small for the time, it seems crowded, at least today.

A shocking contrast to Stoney Lonesome's small one room with thirty-one pupils was School District No. 25's one room which, in the spring of 1886, had sixty-one pupils in a room 18 feet by 24 feet. This is 432 square feet or only about 7 square feet per pupil (ignoring furniture and aisles). The school's, and teacher's, plight was spelled out in a school report published in *The Iola Register*. The obviously frustrated teacher reported 24 daily recitations; an average of 8 pupils in each class; 23 desks; 2 aisles; a 3 feet by 22 feet blackboard, "about one half of which can be used for the purpose intended." The teacher noted "[w]e have two [students] in all single seats and five in all combined seats, with a floating population of 12. One out of three can write, providing one-third of the school stand on the floor during that exercise."[49]

In 1928, the Humboldt Chapter of the Daughters of the American Revolution dedicated a memorial tablet to Fred at the remnant of Stoney Lonesome. Ella (Funston) Eckdall described teacher Fred as follows: "[We] see again in our mind's eye, the schoolmaster, quick and alert of step, performing his pedagogical duties with a cheerful air; a smile now and then lights up his determined face, and a twinkle of the eye betrays a keen sense of humor..."[50]

Ella later wrote, "In certain backwoods districts of that day, the presence of a schoolteacher with all his learning, was not as welcome as one might wish. To till the soil and draw a meagre living therefrom was all they needed or desired. Why bother with the difficulties of spelling and the perplexities of arithmetic when they could already count their bushels and sign their names? This was the high standard maintained at

Stony Lonesome when Fred undertook the education and culture of those country youths."[51] Ella also remembered what was, perhaps, the defining moment of Fred's teaching career:

> For some months all went well in the little school... But one day a brawny youth of some six feet, who was allergic to learning in general, decided that a little excitement would liven up the schoolroom and test the mettle of the teacher. Attracted by some confusion at the rear of the room, the teacher glanced quickly and saw a stream of amber-colored juice cut through the air and land with a splash in the center aisle.
>
> Walking back to the youth, who was shoving a plug of Horseshoe tobacco into the pocket of his blue jeans, the teacher said, "Young man, the place to spit is in the coal bucket." The teacher filled the coal scuttle with lumps of coal from an outside shed, returned and locked the door. As he placed the scuttle close beside the culprit, he observed the butt of a revolver protruding from the boy's pocket. The teacher reached for the weapon.
>
> The surprised bully lunged at the schoolmaster with a blow that fairly staggered him, but the fiery little teacher struck back with telling effect. Up and down the aisle they struggled and fought, blow upon blow, until the teacher outmaneuvered his antagonist and seized the revolver.
>
> The battle ended and the enemy subdued, the teacher looked about for the rest of his flock. They had vanished; the terrified children had opened the windows and leaped out. The cowed and crestfallen bully had stolen sulkily away, leaving behind only fragmentary bits of coal, slues of tobacco and a few strands of hair to tell the story of his inglorious defeat.[52]

Years later, after Fred had become a Major General, he was the guest of honor at a reception given by the Governor of California. A distinguished architect approached Fred, and asked if Fred remembered him. The General replied in the negative. Smiling broadly, the architect said, "General, I was one of your boys that jumped out of the window at Stony Lonesome, the day you licked the school's bully."[53]

Ella recounted in later years that, though the bully had been vanquished, "it was decidedly evident from the lack of cooperation by their [sic: the] illustrious school board—the representatives of law and order—that they resented the downfall of the school's hero—the pride of the rural community. With them, brawn was far more useful than brains."[54] The school district had three officers who constituted the school board: Director William C. Adams, Clerk Robert L. Thompson, and Treasurer George W. Grissom.[55] Both Adams and Grissom had children in Fred's classroom. Thompson (1860-1952), age twenty-four, did not, but his wife had a niece, Jennie Kelso, enrolled in the school. Thompson's role in this episode is of particular interest to this author, since he was my great-grandfather. How fascinating it would be to hear his version! The relationship between Fred and Director Adams must have been difficult after the episode with the bully, since this was the same Adams at whose home Fred boarded.

Although Fred's disagreement with his employer was obviously not good for him, the consequences of his subduing the bully could have been much worse for Fred. In 1891, seven years later, a young teacher at the Iola High School faced criminal charges for his conduct with a difficult pupil:

> The trial of Mr. Grant Billbe for "unlawfully wounding and beating Rad. Parkinson," a pupil under his charge, was held before Justice Cummings and a jury of six men last Saturday and drew a crowded house.... A large number of witnesses were examined and the facts in the case, as gathered from their evidence, seemed to be about as follows: Mr. Billbe was conducting an algebra recitation and Rad. had put a problem on the board. Some of the class questioned the correctness of the solution and considerable time was spent discussing it. Finally Mr. Billbe said that no more time could now be taken up with it, but that Rad. could bring it up in the form of a question the next day. Rad. then asked another question about it, to which Mr. Billbe paid no attention, whereupon Rad. said: "Did you hear my question?" Mr. B. replied, "I did, but I don't think it necessary to answer it." Rad. said, "But that is what you are here for. You are paid to answer my questions." At this Mr. B. ordered him to go to the chemistry room. Rad. refused, whereupon Mr. B. took hold of him to make him go. Rad. caught hold of his seat and there was quite a struggle. The testimony as to the details of this struggle was rather conflicting, some of the witnesses stating that Mr. Billbe threw his forearm around Rad's neck in such a way as to choke him, while others stated that he dragged him from his seat by the collar of his clothing. Rad's own testimony was that he was choked until he was semi-unconscious. The outcome was that he was taken into the chemistry room, where he had been first ordered to go. The testimony made it clear that if the pupil had obeyed the teacher's orders in the first place there would have been no violence used. The question for the jury to decide was whether the teacher used undue violence in enforcing his commands. The case went to the jury at twelve o'clock Saturday night, and in ten minutes a verdict was returned declaring Mr. Billbe not guilty. The verdict was received with applause by the large audience that had crowded the courthouse during the entire day.[56]

Fred was fortunate to have escaped a comparable ordeal.

Fred's successful fight with the school bully reflects well on his character. He had a job to do as teacher—enforce classroom discipline—and he did not shirk from the task, when he easily could have done so. Instead, he upheld his position as teacher, even at the price of likely some minor bodily injury to himself. It was a good test of the mettle of the future soldier and leader of his troops.

During his term as teacher, life had not been all work for Fred, since there was his courtship of Anna Pickell. Judging from a photograph of her, she was a strikingly pretty young woman. The family surname Pickell had been pronounced "pickle," but when family members became socially prominent in Iola, they changed the pronunciation to put the accent on the second syllable. It was thus pronounced Pĭ-kell'.[57]

Anna, age sixteen, lived in Iola, and, on occasion, Fred walked to town to see her. Anna, who was also known as Annie, was the daughter of Moses Pickell and Mary (Mark) Pickell. The parents were Canadian, and Moses was both a millwright and a blacksmith. In 1861, the family settled in northern Indiana where Anna was born in 1868. The following year, they arrived in Allen County, where Moses purchased five hundred acres of land five miles east of Iola. That fall Anna's mother died at age forty-two, and two years later Anna's father died at age forty-four. Orphaned at age three, Anna lived with older siblings, in 1884 living with her sister, Elizabeth Beck, and her husband and family in Iola.

Fred and Anna started going together in the winter of 1884. How many times that winter, and perhaps also during the fall, Fred traveled to town to see Anna is unknown. As a result of walking on the dirt roads, Fred's boots usually were dusty when he arrived at the Beck home to see Anna. That did not please her, since she thought he should polish them before he came to see her. Apparently, Fred wore a sidearm of some kind when he visited Anna, and he would take it off and place it on a bookcase out of reach of young children in the Beck household. These children thought it was funny that when Fred sat to the back on a couch, his feet would not touch the floor. Thus, they made a show out of getting a footstool and taking it over and pushing it under his feet. "[T]hey would giggle and carry on that he was not as tall as he ought to be."

At Christmas that year there was a community Christmas tree at the Opera House, where people hung gifts on the tree for named persons. On Christmas Eve, Fred and Anna attended the exercises there. She had previously hinted to him that she would like a silver pin, which was a silver rose, sold at a local jewelry store. The wrapped gift for her on the tree was larger than a silver pin would be, and, when Anna opened it, she found that Fred's gift was a red velvet photo album with a silver rose on the front. He had mistakenly thought when she said that there was a silver rose at the jewelry store that she would love to have, that she meant the album with the silver rose on the cover and not the silver rose pin. Inside the album was a photograph of Fred. Anna claimed, many years after Fred's death, not only to be surprised by Fred's gift, but also "chagrined" by it, since she had no money to buy him a gift. To solve this problem, she sold her elocution book and bought Fred a gold toothpick to carry on his watch chain.

Anna's grandniece, Winifred "Petey" Bicknell, speculated long after Anna's death that perhaps Fred's purchase of the wrong silver rose put the "quietus" on the romance. Even if this was one of the reasons that the romance floundered, Anna evidently treasured the photo album, since she would never let her only child play with it when she was growing up. Fred's short height was a definite impediment to a successful romance. In fact, he was shorter than Anna by about an inch. The fundamental problem in their relationship was Anna's criteria for a husband. "She wanted a tall, handsome hero," remembered Petey, "and he wasn't a tall, handsome hero."

It is unknown whether Fred actually proposed marriage and was rejected by Anna, or whether she discouraged a proposal before Fred made one. Petey did not know for certain which was the case, but "he definitely was in the market for a bride." Presumably, Fred was broken-hearted by the rejection. As for Anna, she got half of her wish, marrying seven years later Lewis Henry Wishard, who was several inches taller than she; had a full head of hair; and stood ramrod straight. The other half of her wish did not materialize: her husband was a schoolteacher.[58] As for Fred, though he remained short, he did become a hero.

Fred also made visits home during his time as a teacher. At the end of November he "was home to his old resorts Sunday [November 30]."[59] This visit likely was precipitated by his parents' impending departure by train for Washington, D.C., for the legislative session of Congress. In their absence, the farm was left to the care of Burt Funston, and Ed's niece, Julia Krug, managed the household duties.[60]

The day after his parents' departure, Fred hosted a festive event: "A merry party of young folks, a dozen couples or more, accompanied Fred Funston up to his home on the farm last Friday evening [December 5], where they had a jolly time for nearly half of the night."[61] Fred returned home again a little over a week later: "Eugene Whitaker came up home with Fred Funston last Sunday [December 14] and took dinner with him."[62] Perhaps they participated in an unusual competition. "The young men of Carlyle are going to have what they call a rabbit ear supper. The side that gets the least number of scalps pays for the supper of both sides .... The boys are killing lots of rabbits, but there will be enough left for stock."[63]

Likely, the end of Fred's term as teacher in early January of 1885 was welcomed by all involved with the school. Ella recalled that their brother, Pogue, brought a wagon to the Adams house to pick up Fred and his belongings. Unbeknownst to Fred, Pogue had placed a gun in the wagon so that the boys could shoot rabbits on the way home. Mrs. Adams placed a huge pumpkin in the wagon, a present for the boys' mother. After having traveled some distance with Fred in the wagon seat, a dog jumped from the bushes beside the road and stampeded the wagon's horses. A shot rang out from the rear of the wagon where Pogue was sitting with his gun and guarding Fred's trunk and the pumpkin. "Fred, startled, shouted, 'That's that school board after me.' The terrified horses ran pell-mell down the road, through the streets of Iola, and slackened their speed only when they reached the town's limits." There, a neighbor boy, Lee Gilkerson, who was a practical joker, asked Fred what was happening, and after hearing his response, pretended alarm while looking down the road. He "called out, 'Speed up, Fred, I see them still coming away off yonder.'" The prize pumpkin was destroyed by being dashed from side to side in the wagon.[64] Writing to Fred's widow, Eda, some years after Fred's death, his brother, Aldo, succinctly summarized Fred's pedagogical career: "You know he only taught one school and that was enough for him."[65]

Freed from his teaching job, Fred soon traveled to Emporia, Topeka and Leavenworth, Kansas, "to visit relatives and renew old friendships; after which he resumes his course of study."[66] While teaching was no longer in his plans, Fred still pursued his private study to prepare himself to attend college. Living at home again, Fred would have resumed his responsibilities in connection with the farm.

At some point, Fred decided that his next step would be to attend the Iola High School where classes started in September. A great advantage to graduating from the Iola High School was its status in relationship to the State University. As of 1881, it was designated a "State High School" of Kansas and its graduates were permitted to enter the State University, without an examination in the branches taught in Iola, "by presenting their accredited standing and examination papers."[67] Starting in the spring of 1885 graduates of the Iola High School were permitted to enter the freshman class at the State University without any examination. "As there are very few schools in the state that are recognized in this way, it proves that our school has reached a pretty high standing," noted the two student columnists for *The Iola Register*.[68] Thus, Fred, by graduating from Iola High School, would be in a solid position for admission to the State University.

With the advent of summer, Fred and other residents of Allen County presumably looked forward to the elaborate celebration planned for the Fourth of July. Ed Funston was to be the "President of the day." In the morning, a Comic Cavalcade would parade through the streets of Iola. The participants would be "a large number of men and boys mounted on horses, with masked faces and fantastically dressed." Additional activities were planned to occur at Horville's grove northwest of Iola. Events included a free swimming match in the Neosho River, and climbing a greased pole, at the top of which would be the reward of a five-dollar gold piece. Events were scheduled to conclude in Iola.[69] Unfortunately, massive flooding of the Neosho River and Elm Creek occurred, starting on the evening of July 1.[70] On the 4th, Horville's grove was covered by four to ten feet of water, and, according to one reporter, "the Fourth at Iola was a little less Glorious than usual." A large number of people, however, still came to Iola for the day. The parade did occur, and there were events held at the Opera House. The day ended with a display of fireworks, so all was not lost.[71]

A more somber event occurred in August following the death on July 23 of the great Civil War commander and former U. S. president, Ulysses S. Grant. "In company with all the world Iola observed the funeral day of Gen. Grant with appropriate ceremonies." Most business buildings and offices were draped in mourning. "Firing of anvils was begun in the park at seven o'clock and continued at intervals of ten minutes during the day." That evening, formal ceremonies were held on a platform erected in front of the Opera House corner. After they concluded, "the crowd quietly dispersed through the twilight, and the last public testimonial of gratitude and affection of the people for him who is now indeed 'the silent man,' was ended."[72]

Fred Funston
Age probably about 19 or 20 Years

Abandoned "Stoney Lonesome" school building

South side

West and South sides

Front (East side)

Chapter Eight Notes—*The Schoolmaster and the Bully*

1. "Letters From The People," *The Iola Daily Register*, May 28, 1917. Letter from "C.S.R."

2. *The Iola Register*, February 26, 1876.

3. *Allen County Courant*, September 18, 1884. Perhaps in response to protests, this law was re-examined by the Kansas Legislature in the 1885 legislative session, and amended to provide that "[i]n no case shall a third-grade certificate be given a third time to the same person." State of Kansas, *Session Laws of 1885* (Topeka, Kansas: Kansas Publishing House: T.D. Thacher, State Printer, 1885), Chapter CLXX, 274.

4. Aldo Funston to Eda B. Funston, May 27, 1931 (FFP). Aldo enclosed the record of Fred Funston's grades which Aldo's wife, Maude Funston, had copied from the Allen County Superintendent of Public Instruction's records. She listed the January 26, 1884, exam results, and the "July 10, 1885" exam results. The latter date should have been written, when she copied it, as 1886 instead of 1885, since it was July 10, 1886, after graduating from Iola High School, that Fred took the examination.

5. "The Institute," *The Humboldt Union*, August 23, 1884. Letter written by Mrs. H.M. McCorkle.

6. "Normal Institute," *The Humboldt Union*, August 9, 1884. A higher number of attendees —117—was noted by a visitor to the Allen County Normal Institute. In the issue of August 16, 1884, of *The Humboldt Union* under the heading "Insti-Toots," this visitor to the Institute made this observation: "There are one hundred and seventeen pupils enrolled, and if the old maxim that 'school marms are destined to be old maids' is correct, we must admit that the prospects for happy homes of large and loving families, in Allen county, for the future, are not the most flattering."

7. "Teacher's Examination," *The Iola Register*, August 15, 1884.

8. "Certificates Granted," *The Iola Register*, September 12, 1884. This article does not identify the grade of certificate received by each of the many persons listed, including Fred, but other records show that his was a Third Grade Certificate. See Frederick Funston's "Teacher's Term Report to District Clerk" (note 28). During the fiscal year of August 1, 1884, through July 31, 1885, a total of 144 certificates were granted: first grade, 21; second grade, 65; third grade, 57; temporary, 1. The number of applicants who failed the test was 39. The total number of applicants was 183, and the average age of the persons receiving certificates was 23 years ("Report," *The Iola Register*, October 23, 1885).

9. Samuel F. Hubbard and Pamelia [sic: Permelia] C. Hubbard, his wife, to School District Number Twelve, Allen County, Kansas, deed dated September 14, 1867 (Deed Record C, 199, Office of Register of Deeds, Allen County, Kansas).

   The legal description is: Commencing at a point 46 rods north of the Southeast corner of the Southwest ¼ of Section 16, Township 25, Range 18, thence west 14 rods, thence north 34 rods, thence east 14 rods, thence south 34 rods to the place of beginning, containing 3 acres, more or less.

10. Clyde W. Toland, *Samuel Franklin Hubbard and Permelia Caroline (Spencer) Hubbard: Pioneer Settlers in 1857 of Allen County, Kansas Territory, and Their Descendants* (Iola, Kansas, 1985), 12. Samuel and Permelia Hubbard are my great-great-grandparents.

11. "Funston's First School." Undated newspaper clipping from *The Humboldt Union*. This is not the actual news article from *The Humboldt Union*, but quoted from it (*Frederick Funston: Adventurer, Explorer, and Soldier*) (scrapbook of newspaper clippings, Spencer Research Library, University of Kansas).

The high hill is much steeper on the north slope than on the south slope. It has been known as Humboldt Hill for many years. The Strosnider name apparently came from a family who lived in the area at one time. For many years now, Humboldt Hill has had an aura of mystery to it among many Allen Countians. About fifty years ago, the engines of several cars driving on the highway going over the hill quit running without notice. After a short time, the engines restarted, and the motorists proceeded in their travels. Those who reported this experience had reputations for truthfulness. "In the 1950s, strange lights sometimes were seen on the hill...and never with a source found" (Bob Johnson, "Incident adds to intrigue about Humboldt Hill," *The Iola Register*, March 17, 2007). No sightings of a spectral Fred Funston have been reported.

12. "Star Valley H.D.U.," *The Iola Register*, June 2, 1955. Report on program given at the Star Valley Home Demonstration Unit by Mrs. Belle Crook. This incorrectly stated that Stoney Lonesome was built in 1863.

13. L. Wallace Duncan and Charles F. Scott, *History of Allen and Woodson Counties Kansas* (Iola, Kansas: Iola Register, Printers and Binders, 1901), 520.

14. "School Architecture" guide is contained in P. McVicar, *Official School District Clerk's Record Book Revised* (Topeka, Kansas: Geo. W. Crane & Co., 1883), 115. McVicar was the "Ex-State Superintendent of Public Instruction." This copy is in the possession of this author and contains various records of School District No. 12, Allen County, Kansas.

15. "School Architecture" guide, 115.

16. "School Architecture" guide, 115.

17. "School Architecture" guide, 115.

18. For many years now, only the northeast corner of Stoney Lonesome has survived. On December 5, 1998, this author and his daughter, Elizabeth Toland, now Elizabeth (Toland) Smith, measured that wall remnant from its north corner south to where the doorway had been, and measured the height of the north wall where it had joined the east wall (we could see where the top of the wall had joined the northeast corner of the building). Then, comparing these measurements with photographs of the original building, I was able to calculate the approximate dimensions of the building. One of these photos at the Allen County Historical Society, Inc., provides the evidence that there were two windows in the south wall and none on the west wall.

In 1924, the Kiwanis Club of Iola constructed a stone memorial in memory of Fred Funston at the site of Stoney Lonesome, including building up the walls around the well about three feet above the ground. The stone memorial was destroyed some years later by an automobile running into it, I have been told, thus leaving only the corner of the structure and the well to mark the site of Fred's experience as a teacher.

19. Ella (Funston) Eckdall, "Stony Lonesome." This is a five-page typed manuscript containing handwritten additions made by its author, Ella (Funston) Eckdall. Original is at the Allen County Historical Society, Inc. in Eckdall materials donated in 2003. This document appears to be the basis for a shorter version published in an unidentified newspaper (undated copy of this article at the same location as the typed manuscript but in other Funston materials). Written also by Ella (Funston) Eckdall, this article was titled "Teaching School Had Its Thrills." Reference in the text is from the manuscript.

In both the manuscript and the published article, Ella mistakenly stated that Fred had already graduated from high school, even though she does have the date of his commencement of teaching correct—the fall of 1884. Ella spelled the school nickname "Stony" and I have used "Stoney." There is no local uniformity in the spelling of the school's nickname.

20. "Star Valley H.D.U."

21. "Register of Teachers Employed," Oliver Adams, *District School Record For District No. Twelve, County of Allen, and State of Kansas* (Chicago: Adams, Blackmer, & Lyon, Publishers, 1870). This was a generic record book utilized by many school districts. Handwritten in the front is this: "District Clerk's Record of School Business. R. L. Thompson Dist. Clerk." Thus, while Oliver Adams was the author of the form of this record book, the content of the book was provided by the school district's clerk (original in my possession). This Oliver Adams is not the same Oliver Adams who succeeded Fred as the teacher at Stoney Lonesome.

22. "Register of Teachers Employed."

23. "Rev. Thomas Bartlett," *The Iola Register*, December 25, 1891. This is his obituary. Arriving in Allen County in 1866, Bartlett "settled on a farm, but he believed he could accomplish more good by teaching than by preaching, so while he labored much with his hands he taught in the district schools of Allen County, the greater part of the time in his own district [Star Valley] until 1876, when he was attacked with a severe inflammation of the eyes which troubled him the remainder of his life."

24. "Gen. Bartlett is Retired," *The Iola Daily Register*, October 15, 1918, and "A Former Allen County Resident Is Oldest Living West Pointer," *The Iola Register*, July 26, 1948.

25. "Funston's First School."

26. Fred's signature on this contract does not match his signature on his Teacher's Term Report to District Clerk. The handwriting of his signature on the contract is similar to the handwriting of the signatures of W. C. Adams, Director, and R. L. Thompson, District Clerk, who also executed the contract. I suspect that this is a conformed copy of the executed Teacher's Contract. This copy is found in the District No. 12's copy of Oliver Adams, *District School Record For District No. Twelve, County of Allen, and State of Kansas*. See note 21.

27. "Register of Teachers Employed."

28. "Teacher's Term Report to District Clerk." This detailed report was completed by Frederick Funston at the end of his term of teaching. Original at Allen County Historical Society, Inc.

29. Adams, *District School Record For District No. Twelve, County of Allen, and State of Kansas*. See note 21.

30. Adams, *District School Record For District No. Twelve, County of Allen, and State of Kansas*.

31. "Report," *The Iola Register*, October 23, 1885. This is a summary of the Annual Report of the County Superintendent for the year ending July 31, 1885.

32. Adams, *District School Record For District No. Twelve, County of Allen, and State of Kansas*.

33. Adams, *District School Record For District No. Twelve, County of Allen, and State of Kansas*.

34. "Certificates Granted," *The Iola Register*, September 12, 1884. See also source at note 35.

35. "Register of Teachers Employed."

36. "Register of Teachers Employed."

37. "Register of Teachers Employed."

38. Adams, *District School Record For District No. Twelve, County of Allen, and State of Kansas.*

39. "Teacher's Contract" of O.O. Adams. Oliver Adams, *District School Record For District No. Twelve, County of Allen, and State of Kansas* (Chicago: Adams, Blackmer, & Lyon, Publishers, 1870). Oliver Adams the teacher is not the same Oliver Adams who prepared the *District School Record For District No. Twelve.* See note 21.

40. Adams, *District School Record For District No. Twelve, County of Allen, and State of Kansas.*

41. "Report."

42. Ella (Funston) Eckdall, "Stony Lonesome." Ella mentioned only Melissa Adams, but the family also included her husband, William, and several children, including Adda Adams.

43. Eckdall, "Stony Lonesome."

44. "Local Matters," *The Iola Register*, September 26, 1884.

45. School District No. 12, *Annual Report* for the year ending July 31, 1884 (Office of Register of Deeds of Allen County, Kansas). Unfortunately, the report ending July 31, 1885, which covered the year during which Fred taught, is missing from the records. Excerpts from this report appeared in *The Iola Register*, however. See note 8.

46. "Teacher's Term Report to District Clerk." This detailed report was completed by Frederick Funston at the end of his term of teaching, and the original is at the Allen County Historical Society, Inc., Iola, Kansas. Since Fred's students have the distinction of having been his students, their names are as follows (the first number after each child's name is his or her age, and the second is the number of days of attendance): Addie Adams 15 65 Samuel Adams 18 83 Lulu Adams 11 72 Elsie Adams 9 62 Ethel Adams 6 49 Charles Buchanan 6 35 Thomas Fiser 8 24 Benton Fiser 11 24 Ida Gibson 14 60 Frank Gibson 15 66 Leonard Gibson 10 65 Wm. Grissem 13 68 Mary Grissem 11 38 Jessie Green 8 42 Phebe Hodgson 13 60 Anna Hodgson 11 60 Jennie Kelso 8 14 John Kelly 13 27 Sammie Kelly 7 55 John Meek 10 55 Gertie Meek 9 41 Janie Meek 7 30 Elmer Moore 14 21 Walter Moore 10 51 Otis Stigenwalt 17 38 Eugene Stephens 17 33 Lily Stephens 11 29 Roscoe Stephens 7 49 George Thornton 11 15 Otis Young 4 19 Frank Young 6 19.

47. "Teacher's Term Report to District Clerk."

48. "School Architecture" guide, 116.

49. "School Reports," *The Iola Register*, March 5, 1886. Report For School District No. 25 by "H. Tallentire, Teacher." District No. 25 was known as Spring Valley.

50. Ella (Funston) Eckdall, "Tribute to 'Stony Lonesome.'" Three-page manuscript by Ella (Funston) Eckdall, which is typed and with handwritten changes made by her. Original at Allen County Historical Society, Inc. in Eckdall materials donated in 2003. Ella delivered these remarks at the time of the unveiling by her of a memorial tablet to Fred at Stoney Lonesome. The tablet was furnished by the Frederick Funston Chapter of the Daughters of the American Revolution located in Humboldt, Kansas ("D.A.R. Present Funston Memorial Tablet," *The Humboldt Union*, October 17, 1928). The tablet inscription read "In memory of General Frederick Funston" and then identified the donor.

51. Eckdall, "Stony Lonesome." Quotation from manuscript.

52. Eckdall, "Stony Lonesome." Quotation from published article, except for the last sentence, which is from the manuscript.

53. Eckdall, "Stony Lonesome." Quotation from manuscript.

54. Eckdall, "Stony Lonesome." Quotation from manuscript.

55. School District No. 12, *Annual Report* for the year ending July 31, 1884.

56. "Local Matters," *The Iola Register*, April 3, 1891.

57. June (Thompson) Toland (1914-2013), this author's mother. Mother was a lifelong Iola resident, and grew up in a prominent family. A highly intelligent, warm and gracious person, Mother was interested in people and local history, and was a wonderful storehouse of knowledge about local people and history. She was a founder in 1954 of what became the Allen County Historical Society, Inc., and served on its Board of Directors for more than twenty years.

58. Interview by author of Winifred "Petey" Bicknell (1924-1992) on September 22, 1992. Petey was a grandniece of Anna Pickell, Petey's grandmother, Elizabeth (Pickell) Beck, having been Anna's oldest sister, and with whom Anna lived at least part of the time as a child. Petey was knowledgeable about the Beck and Pickell family history. Her grandparents, Elizabeth and A. W. Beck, were two of Iola's most prominent citizens in the late 1800s and early 1900s.

The account in the chapter text of the courtship of Anna Pickell by Fred Funston is based on this interview, the details of which track closely with a short written statement given in 1955 by Anna (Pickell) Wishard. This statement appeared in *The Topeka Daily Capital Sunday Magazine*, October 9, 1955, in an article by Alan J. Stewart, "Funston Homestead Will Become Park." That statement is the source for when Anna and Fred started going together; the location of the community Christmas tree; when the gifts were distributed from the tree; that the photo album contained a photograph of Fred; and her being "surprised and chagrined." Anna stated nothing about the silver rose aspect of Fred's gift nor anything about Fred possibly being interested in marriage.

Petey Bicknell told me that her mother, Bess (Beck) Taylor, told her these stories about "the little man who wasn't a hero." The only error that I perceive in what Petey told me is that she said that it was her mother, Bess, and Bess' little brother, Rusty, who were the two children at the Beck house with the footstool. That is not possible, since in 1884 neither was born yet. I do not know who these children would have been, but believe this part of the story is still correct as is the balance of the story told me by Petey.

The detail about Moses and Mary (Mark) Pickell comes from L. Wallace Duncan and Chas. F. Scott, *History of Allen and Woodson Counties Kansas* (Iola, Kansas: Iola Register, Printers and Binders, 1901), 333 (biographical sketch of William J. Pickell, Anna's brother), and 484 (biographical sketch of Lewis Henry Wishard).

59. "Carlyle Correspondence," *The Iola Register*, December 5, 1884.

60. "Carlyle Correspondence," *The Iola Register*, November 27, 1884.

61. "Local Matters," *The Iola Register*, December 12, 1884.

62. "Carlyle Correspondence," *The Iola Register*, December 19, 1884.

63. "Carlyle Correspondence," *The Iola Register*, December 19, 1884.

64. Eckdall, "Stony Lonesome" (manuscript and published article). Writing many years after Fred had taught at Stoney Lonesome, Ella mistakenly described his term as teacher as ending in the spring, and gave a generic description of the end of the year

activities that would have occurred. This description was likely based on her own experiences as a student at Maple Grove School.

65. Aldo Funston to Eda B. Funston, May 27, 1931 (FFP). Stoney Lonesome, as a school, did not long outlast Fred's departure. A more modern building was needed, and, in 1886, a new frame building was constructed less than a mile northeast of Stoney Lonesome (Lease dated November 4, 1886, to J. S. Perry et al. as Board of Directors of School District Number Twelve; Misc. Record Book 2, 419, Office of Register of Deeds of Allen County, Kansas). In 1950, the Star Valley School District consolidated with the Prairie Dell School District, and in 1953 the building and contents were sold at public auction. See note 12 for source.

The building was later razed, and a house built on the site. As for Stoney Lonesome, "the old stone school house" and the three acre tract on which it was situated were sold at public auction ("Notice," *The Iola Register*, December 24, 1886) for $40 in January 1887 (School District Number Twelve to James Perry, January 6, 1887; Deed Record Book 8, 63, Office of Register of Deeds, Allen County, Kansas).

66. "Carlyle Correspondence," *The Iola Register*, January 30, 1885.

67. "Local Matters," *The Iola Register*, February 18, 1881.

68. "High School Jottings," *The Iola Register*, April 3, 1885.

69. "An Attractive Program," *The Iola Register*, June 12, 1885. Also, "Our Fourth," *The Iola Register*, July 10, 1885.

70. "The Flood," *The Iola Register*, July 3, 1885. Also, "More About the Flood," *The Iola Register*, July 10, 1885.

71. "Our Fourth," *The Iola Register*, July 10, 1885.

72. "The Memorial Service," *The Iola Register*, August 14, 1885.

CHAPTER NINE

Iola High School

September 14, 1885 – May 14, 1886
Willing Workers Win
— Motto of Iola High School Class of 1886[1]

Even before the founding of Iola in 1859, there were a couple of small private schools for the children of nearby settlers. One of these schools existed in the summer of 1858 when 19-year-old William Hart taught school in a little log house about 12-feet by 14-feet, and which had two windows, each 2-feet by 2-feet.[2]

In the fall of 1859, Miss E. Y. Hancock organized a private school in her home located in the newly laid out town site. She had come west from Massachusetts to teach among the Choctaw Indians, and eventually came to Iola where she had approximately twenty students at a charge of five cents per day per student. At night, she conducted a grammar school which was attended by numerous adults, many of whom were married. The only available textbook was the Bible.

In 1861, the Iola school district, District No. 10, was organized, and a term of school was held which started about December 1 that year. This was the first public school in Iola. Hester Walters, who had taught in Wisconsin for some years, was the first teacher at a salary of $13.50 per month. The term was three months of twenty-two days each month, but the district treasurer refused to pay her the full salary because she had not taught full-time, the treasurer insisting that she must teach every day of each month except on Sunday. The county superintendent over-rode the treasurer's decision, and Hester Walters was paid her full sala-ry, which was little more than sixty-one cents per day. School enrollment was 103 pupils, who had an average attendance of eighty-five.[3]

As Iola grew in population during the next seven years, the district's frame schoolhouse became inadequate. It was sold for $349, and bonds totaling $7,000, drawing ten percent interest, were issued to build a two-towered stone structure in 1868.[4] Unfortunately, the bonds could not be negotiated; consequently, local banker Levi L. Northrup (L.L. Northrup), who was also a school board member, cashed them. It was due to his "active efforts and financial assistance the success of the enterprise was mainly due." Native lumber was used in the new building whenever possible, since all the pine lumber had to be hauled in wagons from Kansas City, located approximately a hundred miles to the northeast. Except for the stone for the building, all other material also had to be transported from Kansas City. The building cost $6,000.[5]

For about fifteen years, the new building was considered "very handsome and commodious," but as Iola's population grew, the stone building became inadequate in size. To accommodate the primary pupils, the school board bought from Allen County, and moved next to the towered stone building, the old frame court house building no longer in use as a courthouse.[6] "Aside from the towers the most distinguishing feature of this [original stone] building was the malicious way the chimneys had of smoking. Many holidays were thus obtained, and the remembrance of those [holidays] not obtained when the teachers sternly refused to dismiss, though the smoke hung in clouds, brings the tears afresh to the eyes of many [in 1903]."[7]

The stone building had two classrooms and two recitation rooms so that four teachers could be employed if necessary. School was held for ten months each year. A school for "colored children" was taught in one of the recitation rooms, but the school year of 1872-1873 was the last one in which white and colored children were taught in separate classrooms. In 1878, the school became graded rather than having all students in one grade. Two years later the first class, consisting of three members, graduated.[8]

The school year of 1884-1885 was unusual, since the students were scattered among several non-school buildings after the towered stone building was razed to be replaced by a much larger stone and brick building. The cost of this large, two-story building was funded by $17,000 in bonds which were voted in the spring of 1884.[9] "Considering the magnitude of the question at issue, there was remarkable little interest exhibited in the district bond election." Of the 258 votes, only thirty-six were against the bonds. "The ladies who voted were unanimously in favor, about eighty casting their ballots for the bonds."[10]

The new building had hot air for heat, presumably a tremendous improvement over the smoking chimneys of the old stone school building, and a total of nine rooms, five on the first floor and four on the second floor. Although the building was to have been completed by November of 1884, this did not occur, and classes could not be held in it until the start of the fall semester of 1885.[11] There were classes in the new building for students in first and second grammar; first, second, and third intermediate; and first, second, and third primary.[12] Also included were the high school students who were in the seventh, eighth, ninth, and tenth grades.

School opened on Monday, September 14, 1885, in both Iola and Humboldt. The Iola enrollment in the new building was 410 while that of the Humboldt school was sixty-nine fewer. The Iola High School enrollment was ninety-five, and one of those students was Fred Funston. He was one of the nine members of the 10th or Senior Grade, about six of whom were expected to complete the course of study that school year.[13] One of the nine members, Beulah Reimert, left school by the end of the first month.[14] The following May she took a position as a pianist—"a pleasant and profitable position"—at the Insane Asylum in Topeka.[15] Fred was nearly 20-years-old when he started high school. Prior to the opening of school, examinations for classification of new pupils were held.[16] Presumably, Fred took this exam, and, for his one year as a high school student, he was classified as a senior. Perhaps his studies in the private school of Professor Harris beginning the year before had provided him with the knowledge necessary to qualify him to enter the senior grade.

Sixteen of the pupils in the school were from other school districts, including Fred, who was listed as being from Carlyle.[17] Fred lived at home, and Charlie Gleed recollected that he daily made the approximate ten-mile round trip to attend school by riding "a Mexican pony of most volcanic disposition. No boy ever had a better horseback training than the young man got on the hurricane deck of this 'genuine Mexican plug.'"[18] Another description of the challenge for Fred of riding this pony, named Tom, was given in 1899: "He went mounted on a buckskin broncho. It was a vicious little pony from the plains of Texas. No one else on the farm could ride it, but Funston would mount it in the stable yard every morning, and every morning it would cavort around for awhile in a frantic effort to dislodge him. Then when it would find it couldn't get him out of the saddle it would go off on a run, never slacking its pace until it had carried him to school. On the return trip it would cover the distance as if it were being run in a race, and the next morning it would be as eager as ever to throw its master in the stable yard. But it never threw him."[19] In future years, when Fred described his 1893 experience in the deadly rushing waters of Miles Cañon of the Yukon River as "akin to that of riding a bucking broncho," he truly knew of what he wrote.

Although Fred was attending school fulltime, he still had his daily farm chores to do when he returned home from school. In the evening, he consequently was too tired to study, resulting in his usually arising at 4 a.m. the next day to study before riding his pony to school.[20]

At the end of the first month of school, all scholars were re-seated according to deportment and scholarship. Those who had one hundred in deportment occupied the back seats. In Fred's tenth grade, there was 97.4 percent attendance. There were no tardies. Of the 468 students in all grades, attendance was 94.2 percent.[21]

Throughout the school year, two students using the name of "Two Jotters" wrote frequent accounts of school activities for *The Iola Register*. In their first column of the 1885-1886 school year, they noted that "[t]he majority of the scholars regret that arrangements could not have been made for having nine months school instead of eight." "Two Jotters" ended their first column by observing that "[i]t is quite amusing to see the number of scholars wandering about the hall, with perplexed faces, looking for their rooms."[22] A rule forbidding whispering in the halls by the students was "rigidly enforced."[23]

Occasionally, the "Two Jotters" specifically referenced the work of the tenth grade. "The 10th grade completed the 1st Oration of Cicero against Cataline on Wednesday [October 7] and will study Latin composition hereafter, in connection with the other Latin work."[24] "The 10th grade have completed the second book in geometry and the second Oration of Cicero." [October 30, 1885][25] "The 10th grade Cicero class are now reading a page a day." [November 6, 1885][26]

"The 10th grade complete the fourth oration of Cicero this week [of November 30], having read about fifty pages in less than three months."[27] "The tenth grade find the translating of Virgil much more interesting than their former Latin studies." [January 29, 1886][28] "The Virgil class are now reading thirty-five lines a day." [February 19, 1886][29] "The tenth grade complete the 7th book of geometry to-day, this finishing their year's work." [April 2, 1886][30] At the end of the school year, "Two Jotters" observed that "[t]he work in the Latin classes this year has been more thorough and extensive than ever before... Within the last four months the tenth grade has read 4 books of Virgil."[31]

The schoolwork was challenging. "An essay on Wm. E. Gladstone is on the high school program for today [March 12]. It is to be written in half an hour without any reference whatever to notes. The subject is certainly an interesting one and the exercise ought to be profitable both for gaining facility in composition and information on the subject itself."[32] "Two Jotters" began their February 26 column with this great news: "Hereafter there will be but two examinations a month. Hurrah!"[33]

On Friday evening, December 11, 1885, the high school presented an entertainment for the public. The purpose of the event was to raise funds to purchase "philosophical apparatus" and inside blinds. The admission cost was fifteen cents, twenty cents for reserved seats. "It's cheaper to go than to stay at home," opined the *Register's* Charlie Scott.[34] The seven students on the program included one eighth grader, two ninth graders, and four tenth graders. Tenth graders Fred Funston and May Ewing were included. May Ewing was later to marry Fred's good friend, Charlie Scott. Fred recited, undoubtedly from memory in view of his outstanding memory, the lengthy Irish ballad "Shamus O'Brien."[35] Scott, in his review of "The School Entertainment," wrote that Fred "told the story of 'Shamus O'Brien' in a very effective and entertaining manner. Fred handles the Irish as though to the manner born, and his renditien [sic] of the difficult piece was creditable throughout."[36]

Due to bad weather, wrote the "Two Jotters," there was "a rather small audience." Those attending "seemed very appreciative, however, and gave their best attention." Gross receipts were $14.45 with a net of $7.20 which, with the net proceeds from the prior spring's entertainment, were to be used for the purchase of a number of instruments needed by the philosophy class to make simple experiments.[37] A portion of the funds was quickly spent for subscriptions to several leading magazines and newspapers. "The scholars will be at liberty to use these when not engaged in regular school work, and will also be allowed to take them to their houses for a short time on certain conditions."[38]

At least five monthly Honor Rolls were published in *The Iola Register*. Fred was the sole senior to appear in the Honor Roll published on December 25, 1885, and he and his close friend and fellow senior, Schuyler Brewster, both appeared on the Honor Roll for the sixth month, published April 16, 1886.[39]

Schuyler Brewster was a member of a prominent and well-to-do Iola family. His late father, Brinkerhoff "Brink" Brewster, had been an early-day Iola resident and had died in early 1878 when Schuyler was only nine. Schuyler was nearly three years younger than Fred. In his last will and testament written two years before his death, Brink left all of his estate to his wife, Maria L. Brewster, except for a $2,000 cash bequest to each of his children, payable to each upon "becoming of age," i.e., upon turning twenty-one years of age. He also made this direction to Maria: "It is my wish that my wife move back within a reasonable time to some place in the state of New York for the purpose of educating our children and that each receive a good Liberal Education if capable of receiving such."[40] The Brewster family had lived some years in New York, where Schuyler had been born and where Maria took her husband's body for burial.[41] For now unknown reason or reasons, Maria did not comply with this precatory direction of her late husband, and she and her five minor children, ages three to thirteen years, remained in Iola.

Maria was a wealthy widow.[42] She was also a cultured woman. Later in that year of her husband's death, Maria purchased a piano "which is probably one of the finest, if not the finest, in this part of the state. It is a Steinway upright—valued at about a thousand dollars. Our musical folks now hold their soirees at Mrs. Brewster's—one of the most pleasant places imaginable to spend an evening," according to *The Iola Register*.[43] Many years later, Charlie Scott paid tribute to Maria Brewster following her death: "In many ways Mrs. Brewster was a very remarkable woman. She came from a family distinguished for strong intellectuality and great force of character and she exemplified in a marked degree both of these characteristics...she...educated and cultivated herself to a degree that made her a welcome member of any intellectual circle."[44]

In 1882, Maria built a house for herself and her children worthy of their social position. North of the small town of Iola the ground slopes northward to the top of a hill, a hill noticeable from the town because of the lack of buildings on the hillside. It was on this hilltop that Maria purchased the site for her new home.[45] *The Iola Register* noted in June that she had let the contract for "a magnificent house" which would be 30-feet by 32-feet with a 12-feet by 30-feet addition. The cost was "upwards" of $2,000.[46]

As the residence neared completion, *The Iola Register* complimented it and its location: "It is 'placed on a hill' from whence a magnificent view can be had in all directions. When completed it will indeed be a beautiful and commodious residence."[47] From Iola the new house presented "an imposing appearance."[48] In the end, the two-story house was 30-feet by 40-feet and its addition was 12-feet by 24-feet. The cost was "upwards of $2,500."[49]

Schuyler Brewster was a handsome man, judging from photographs of him, but he "never had robust health." That would not deter him from following his friend, Fred Funston, in the Twentieth Kansas when the Spanish-American War broke out in 1898, and then serving in the war in the Philippines the next year. Many of his friends doubted that he would be able to handle "the hardship and exposure of army life," but he did his full duty in the "bullet department" in the arduous five-month Philippine military campaign during February to July 1899.[50] Schuyler was apparently physically tougher than others thought him to be, just as Fred, small though he was, possessed a tremendous physical strength not to be expected in one so diminutive.

The new school building was not without drawbacks. Charlie Scott, in February 1886, noted that "[o]ur experiment with hot air has certainly not been satisfactory." This was in response to the suggestion of installing a steam-heating system. Although Charlie agreed that such a change would be of "great advantage," it would be expensive to make this change.[51] The condition of the grounds surrounding the newly constructed building was a concern to the school board. In the spring of 1886, the school yard was sown with bluegrass seed, thus depriving the students of their playgrounds.[52] In connection with Arbor Day on April 1, about eighty trees were set out on the school grounds.[53]

According to the reporter for *The Chicago Sunday Tribune*, Fred's "adventurous spirit" was well known to the young men of Iola who were his classmates.

They knew some of the inner workings of his mind. They say that as a youth in those days he was every ready to create "a stir" and seeking to make adventures in the peace loving village, which was hard to do. One night he gathered a crowd of his companions around him and suggested that they go under the cover of darkness and bombard with stones a "joint" that had just opened in the town.

A "joint" is a Kansas saloon. It is an unlicensed institution whose whereabouts is known to everybody but the officers of the law. The only purpose young Fred Funston had in mind in throwing bricks against the windows of the "joint" was to make adventure. The other young fellows followed him, and they came nearly demolishing the "joint" and were rewarded by the excitement that followed. The jointkeeper had no recourse at law, even if he could find the offenders, but he had a large, horny hand which he could use without legal aid, but Fred Funston didn't mind the danger of getting into the hands of the jointkeeper so long as he had rested his mind with the diverting excitement. Even in doing this he was not malicious. He cautioned the other boys not to hurt anybody, but to make as much of a tumult as possible, so as to arouse the whole town. He was mischievous but not malicious.[54]

At the end of the 1885-1886 school year, "Two Jotters" concluded their final column with an assessment of the year's success:

Quite a number of our brightest and most faithful pupils this term have been those living outside of the district. We hope they will be able to attend until they complete the course.

All things taken together, the Jotters do not remember a more happy and successful school year than the one has been that closes today. Throughout the entire year there have been no jars worth speaking of. Teachers and pupils have worked harmoniously, the latter being as ambitious, apparently, for their own advancement and for the good name of the school as the former. Even down to the lowest grades the greatest interest and enthusiasm has prevailed during the entire year, and more and better work has been done than ever before.[55]

Commencement exercises for Fred's class were held on Friday evening, May 14. In order to defray expenses, adults were charged fifteen cents, children ten cents.[56] Even though there had been heavy rain in the afternoon which continued late into the evening, every seat in the Opera House was occupied when exercises began, and standing room was at a premium by the time the exercises concluded. The class motto, "Willing Workers Win," appeared in large evergreen letters across the top of the stage, while below and back of the footlights, there was a bank of roses across the stage with large stands of house plants at both ends. The exercises opened with an invocation followed by a double quartette of singers, including Charlie Scott. Then, each graduate read, in turn, the essay which he or she had written, the order being interspersed at times with musical numbers. Fred's essay was described in *The Iola Register* by Scott: "Following the music was an oration by Mr. Frederick Funston on 'Intellectual Liberty.' The oration was marked by unusual maturity of thought and energy of composition, and was delivered with a great deal of force. Although quite long it was listened to with close attention to the end and was heartily applauded. It was certainly a most creditable production."

After the presentation of the diplomas, the audience rose and joined in singing the doxology. Scott noted that they were dismissed with a benediction. "Thus was ended the Fourth Annual Commencement of the Iola High School, and the occasion is certainly one to be long remembered not only by those who made the programme but by those who heard it as well....We doubt if any other high school in the State will send out this year a class that will average as high as this, in maturity of thought, as evinced by their essays, and in grace of delivery and general comportment. We can assure every one of the class of '86 that their friends are proud of them, although such assurance seems unnecessary in view of the deluge of flowers with which they were each overwhelmed. The *REGISTER* certainly congratulates the class, collectively and individually, and hopes, with Rip Van Winkle, that they, 'may all lif and prosper.'"[57]

Charlie Scott later summarized for Eda Funston her husband's high school career: "[H]is favorite studies were English, History, and Geography; that he was noted among his schoolmates as an omnivorous reader; that he was always gay, full of pranks, fond of practical jokes with a rare gift for narrating his own experiences, particularly when a humorous turn could be given to them..."[58] In his eulogy to Fred, Charlie expanded on his description of Fred's sense of humor in high school, as a student at the State University, and as a reporter: "[H]e was eternally 'breaking out' in some unexpected fashion—getting into some sort of predicament that usually had a ludicrous ending or falling into some embarrassing situation, and then telling the story of it in picturesque and vivid and humorous phrases that stuck like burrs in the memory of those who heard him. He never spared himself in these recitals, for he never committed the sin of taking himself too seriously. It was this rare combination of a sense of humor, along with his innate modesty, that was one of his greatest charms."[59]

As a result of his studies at Iola High School, Fred had accumulated significant entrance credits for admission to the State University at Lawrence. His entrance credits included Arithmetic, U.S. History, Desc. Geography, English Grammar, Geometry, Essentials of English, Algebra, Outlines of History, U. S. Constitution, English Composition, Physics,

German, 3 terms, and Latin: Grammar, Reader, Caesar, Composition, Archias and Aeneid.[60] According to Fred's mother when interviewed in 1899, Fred "took Spanish as an extra."[61] Perhaps Spanish did not qualify as an entrance credit.

The summer started with the significant national news of the wedding of the President of the United States, a Democrat. Republican Charlie Scott reported the nuptials with this brief front-page account:

MARRIED.: On Wednesday, June 2, 1886, at 7 o'clock p.m., in the White House, Washington, D. C., Grover Cleveland, aged 49, and Frances Folsom, aged 22. The REGISTER congratulates—the country, that it will now have a chance to read and talk about something else. It hopes also that Mr. and Mrs. Cleveland will live long and happily; but it cannot help wondering whether they ever read lines that run something as follows:
> Crabbed age and youth,
> Cannot live together;
> Youth is full of pleasance,
> Age is full of care;...
Etc., Etc., Etc.[62]

As for Fred Funston's life, he was apparently still undecided about his future, since, starting on June 14, he attended, once again, the Allen County Normal Institute for teachers. Other attendees included his former love, Anna Pickell, and his old rival for West Point, Howard Power.[63] *The Iola Register* welcomed the more than ninety attendees: "The REGISTER extends to the teachers, now students, at the Normal, its usual cordial greeting and hopes they will have a jolly time in addition to laying up tons of petrified knowledge."[64]

The physiology class had much to interest the students, notably "[a] fine folding chart, showing the structure of the human body, in all its parts..." This chart "much increased the interest in that branch."[65] Another subject in the physiology class was "the study of alcohol in its various forms and its effect on the human system."[66]

Howard Power called much attention to himself, on one occasion, as reported by *The Iola Register*: "On Wednesday Howard Power, a member of the 'A' class, covered himself with immortal glory by rising in the presence of the entire Institute and saying that 'any young lady in need of an escort for the lecture should call on him and her wishes would be granted.' At this writing there have been no takers but serious results are looked for in the future."[67] Rather than teaching that fall of 1886, Howard Power in September went to Chicago to attend Rush Medical College.[68] He completed his medical course in the spring of 1888.[69] Dr. Power practiced medicine in Texas and died of typhoid fever in Marlin, Texas, in 1908.[70]

The Normal concluded its work on July 8, and the next two days the teacher examination occurred.[71] "The questions propounded at the Teachers' examination last week were unusual [sic] difficult, and nearly fifty per cent of those applying for certificates failed to obtain them." Nine received first grade certificates, and forty-five received either second or third grade certificates. Included in this latter group were Anna Pickell, Howard Power, and Fred Funston.[72]

Fred received a second-grade certificate based upon having taught four months and having the following quite respectable grades:

Orthography	87
Reading	88
Writing	90
English Grammar	86
Composition	94
Geography	96
Arithmetic	80
U.S. History	95
Physiology	76
Constitution	91
Didactics	90
Average Standing	88[73]

Physiology may have been a popular class with the students, but the subject was not one in which Fred excelled—at least on this exam. At this point, Fred may have settled on teaching for his occupation, or he may have remained undecided on his future career plans, though contemplating a teaching career. In any event, by late August Fred had made his decision. *The Iola Register* correspondent for Carlyle-area news reported as follows: "Mr. Fred Funston announces his intention to go to the Kansas State University this fall. May success go with him."[74]

The correspondent also noted recent experiences of "Farmer" Ed Funston and farmer Fred Funston. "Hon. E.H. Funston, although he has been enjoying the luxuries of Washington for some time, has not forgotten how to be a 'granger.' We notice him in the hayfield [in late August] enjoying the healthy exercise of pitching hay."[75] Putting up the hay was more challenging by then, since "the windy season is upon us."[76] Also, beginning August 16, Allen County experienced, for at least three days, an "intense heat" not previously known. Incredible consequences resulted, including the burning of the ends of the mustache on the face of a man, "the reflections of the sun from [his] cheek having set them on fire."[77]

As for Fred the farmer, "[w]hile at work in the hayfield last Monday [August 23], Fred Funston received a slight sunstroke. He was immediately taken home, where he revived only to faint away again. He is, however, able to be about, and, in fact, to go back to the hayfield."[78] Less than a week later, Fred was off to matriculate at Kansas State University at Lawrence.

Iola's only school building when Fred Funston
attended the high school portion, 1885-1886

Chapter Nine Notes—*Iola High School*

1. "High School Jottings," *The Iola Register*, May 7, 1886.

2. Kate Thrasher Cooper, "Forty Years," *The Iola Daily Register*, May 10.1898.

3. "Historical," *The Iolian*, Vol. 1, No. 1, November 1903, 3-4. Located at Iola Public Library.

4. "Historical," 5.

5. "The Old and the New," *The Iola Register*, undated clipping; photocopy in my possession.

6. "The Old and the New."

7. "Historical," 5.

8. "Historical," 5-6, 8.

9. "Historical," 9, and "The Old and the New."

10. "Local Matters," *The Iola Register*, April 18, 1884.

11. "The Old and the New."

12. "Early High School Graduates Were Given Two-Year Diplomas," *Centennial Edition, The Iola Register*, May 30, 1955, 2-B.

13. "High School Jottings," *The Iola Register*, September 18, 1885.

14. "High School Jottings," *The Iola Register*, October 9, 1885.

15. "Personal," *The Iola Register*, May 21, 1886.

16. "Public School Examination," *The Iola Register*, September 4, 1885.

17. "High School Jottings," *The Iola Register*, October 2, 1885.

18. Charles S. Gleed, "Romance and Reality in a Single Life. Gen. Frederick Funston," *The Cosmopolitan Illustrated Monthly Magazine*, July 1899.

19. "Fred Funston's Restless Life of Adventure," *The Chicago Sunday Tribune*, May 7, 1899 (FFP). The pony's name is provided in Ella Funston Eckdall, *The Funston Homestead* (Emporia, Kansas: Raymond Lees, 1949), 12.

20. Alan J. Stewart, "Maj.-Gen. Fredrick [sic] Funston Brought Glory to Kansas with His Victories," *The Topeka Daily Capital Sunday Magazine*, March 13, 1955.

21. "High School Jottings," *The Iola Register*, October 23, 1885.

22. "High School Jottings," *The Iola Register*, September 18, 1885.

23. "High School Jottings," *The Iola Register*, November 6, 1885.

24. "High School Jottings," *The Iola Register*, October 9, 1885.

25. "High School Jottings," *The Iola Register*, October 30, 1885.

26. "High School Jottings," *The Iola Register*, November 6, 1885.

27. "High School Jottings," *The Iola Register*, December 4, 1885.

28. "High School Jottings," *The Iola Register*, January 29, 1886.

29. "High School Jottings," *The Iola Register*, February 19, 1886.

30. "High School Jottings," *The Iola Register*, April 2, 1886.

31. "High School Jottings," *The Iola Register*, May 7, 1886.

32. "High School Jottings," *The Iola Register*, March 12, 1886.

33. "High School Jottings," *The Iola Register*, February 26, 1886.

34. "Local Matters," *The Iola Register*, December 11, 1885 (two short items).

35. "High School Jottings," *The Iola Register*, December 4, 1885.

36. "The School Entertainment," *The Iola Register*, December 18, 1885.

37. "High School Jottings," *The Iola Register*, December 18, 1885.

38. "High School Jottings," *The Iola Register*, January 8, 1886.

39. "Monthly School Report," *The Iola Register*, December 25, 1885, and "High School Jottings," *The Iola Register*, April 16, 1886.

40. In the Matter of the Estate of Brinkerhoff Brewster, Probate Court of Allen County, Kansas, Case No. 345.

41. "Personal Mention," *The Iola Register*, February 23, 1878.

42. In the Matter of the Estate of Brinkerhoff Brewster, Probate Court of Allen County, Kansas, Case No. 345. See Inventory and Valuation.

43. *The Iola Register*, October 19, 1878.

44. "Mrs. Brewster Died on Monday," *The Iola Daily Register*, March 30, 1927.

45. *The Iola Register*, April 2, 1880.

46. "Boom! Facts and Figures Going To Show The Actual Prosperity of Iola," *The Iola Register*, June 25, 1880.

47. *The Iola Register*, July 23, 1880.

48. "Local Matters," *The Iola Register*, November 19, 1880.

49. "Booming! Facts and Figures Going to Show the Actual Prosperity of Iola," *The Iola Register*, April 21, 1882.

50. "Schuyler Brewster For District Clerk," *The Iola Daily Register*, March 26, 1900.

51. "Local Matters," *The Iola Register*, February 12, 1886.

52. "High School Jottings," *The Iola Register*, February 12, 1886, and "Local Matters," *The Iola Register*, April 9, 1886.

53. "Arbor Day In Iola," *The Iola Register*, March 26, 1886, and "Local Matters," *The Iola Register*, April 9, 1886.

54. "Fred Funston's Restless Life of Adventure."

55. "High School Jottings," *The Iola Register*, May 14, 1886.

56. "Local Matters," *The Iola Register*, May 14, 1886.

57. "Commencement," *The Iola Register*, May 21, 1886. At the Allen County Historical Society, Inc., Iola, Kansas, there is a group photograph titled "Iola High School Graduates and Faculty, 1885-1886." The title, and the identities of those in the photograph, are typed on a piece of paper pasted on the reverse. The six 1886 female graduates are identified, as are the two female graduates from the prior year of 1885: Medea Brewster and Alice Hendricks. Also identified are two teachers and Anna "Pickle" Wishard, who was to be in the following year's class of 1887. Thus, the photograph's title is incorrect.

Two young men are identified as Frederick Funston and Schuyler Brewster, respectively. This is incorrect. Not only does neither look like the person claimed, the putative Frederick Funston is several inches taller than Anna Pickell, who is standing in the row in front of him. In reality, Anna was slightly taller than Fred. See Chapter Eight.

58. Charles F. Scott to Mrs. Frederick Funston, December 29, 1924 (FFP).

59. Charles F. Scott, eulogy, "Report of Select Committee," *Journal of the House*, Hall of the House of Representatives, Topeka, Kansas, February 26, 1917 (FFP).

60. George O. Foster, Registrar, University of Kansas to Mrs. Frederick Funston, February 14, 1931 (FFP).

61. Ode C. Nichols, "Funston, From Babyhood to Present Day as His Mother Knows Him," *The World*, May 21, 1899 (FFP).

62. *The Iola Register*, June 4, 1886.

63. "Normal Students," *The Iola Register*, June 18, 1886.

64. "Local Matters," *The Iola Register*, June 18, 1886.

65. "Normal Notes," *The Iola Register* June 25, 1886.

66. "Normal Notes," *The Iola Register* July 2, 1886.

67. "Normal Notes," *The Iola Register*, July 2, 1886.

68. "Personal," *The Iola Register*, September 10, 1886.

69. "Personal," *The Iola Register*, March 2, 1888.

70. "Dr. Powers [sic] Is Dead," *The Iola Register*, October 21, 1908.

71. "Local Matters," *The Iola Register*, July 9, 1886.

72. "The Successful Teachers," *The Iola Register*, July 16, 1886.

73. *County Superintendent's Complete Record No. 1, Allen County* [1884-1890]. Located at Office of Register of Deeds, Allen County, Kansas.

74. "Carlyle Correspondence," *The Iola Register*, August 27, 1886.

75. "Carlyle Correspondence," *The Iola Register*, August 27, 1886.

76. "Carlyle Correspondence," *The Iola Register*, August 20, 1886.

77. "Local Matters," *The Iola Register*, August 20, 1886.

78. "Carlyle Correspondence," *The Iola Register*, August 27, 1886.

CHAPTER TEN

State University

September 1886 – May 1887

The State University of Kansas is the first institute of learning in the West, with the possible exception of Ann Arbor [Michigan].

—President Eliot of Harvard University

"The ascending, and descending, that hill is what first impresses itself upon the brain, but that is not all that it does for it oppresses the lungs, and weakens, (or strengthens) the knees; anyhow it reminds one of mounting Pike's Peak."[1] Thus was described, in 1890, the tall, steep hill, grandly called Mount Oread, upon which the State University sits in Lawrence. The climb is no less steep today. The author continued: "But when the summit is reached and the mammoth University building is seen for the first time, as well as the modern edifice 'Snow Hall' then a Kansan feels proud of his state and realizes that she need not hide this institution in the valley or under the 'half-bushel' but is justified in placing it upon the apex of University hill or a mountain, as emblematical of the grand system of education prevailing in our state."[2]

September of 1886, the month freshmen Fred Funston and Schuyler Brewster arrived on campus, marked the twentieth anniversary of the university's opening on September 12, 1866. The lone building, called the North College, was completed that September of 1866, with the carpenters putting the finishing touches to the building's stairway on the morning of the opening day.[3] Forty students enrolled that first day, and this number grew to fifty-five for the year's enrollment. Of the forty students, twenty-two were male and eighteen were female.[4] The Kansas law establishing the university provided for two separate branches, one for men and one for women, the two branches to be educated in separate buildings. This provision was never executed, and, from the beginning of the university, there has been no separation of the sexes into separate educational facilities.[5]

None of these first students was qualified educationally to do college level work. Opportunities to obtain such an education did not exist in

235

frontier Kansas. Accordingly, a preparatory department was established to prepare students to be admitted as freshmen to the university. It was to be twenty-five years before this preparatory department was entirely abolished, and this occurred only when Kansas high schools succeeded in preparing their students for university level work. The course of study leading to a bachelor's degree took seven years, which included three years of preparatory work, and thus there was not a graduating class until 1873 when there were four graduates, three men and one woman.[6]

Since the university was the state university, it was commonly referred to as the State University or as Kansas State University (K.S.U.), even though Kansas legislation in 1864 designated it The University of Kansas.[7] This was in contrast to the agricultural educational institution at Manhattan, Kansas, the Kansas State Agricultural College. Today, this is Kansas State University (KSU), and the State University at Lawrence is the University of Kansas (KU).

The State University of Kansas was the educational institution attended by "the sons and daughters of some of the best blood of this country."[8] There were three young men in attendance from Allen County that fall of 1886: Fred Funston, Schuyler Brewster, and Alva Christian of the prosperous Christian family, which lived on a farm down the road north of the Funston farm.[9] Charlie Scott, himself an 1881 State University graduate, through his *Iola Register*, wished Fred and Schuyler well: "We are glad Allen county is to have two such bright representatives at our *Alma Mater*."[10]

The three Allen County boys were part of 105 freshmen that fall of 1886. The freshmen were divided between 71 men and 34 women. Total university enrollment was 491 students, 438 of whom came from sixty-two Kansas counties. The next largest number of students—20—came from the adjoining state of Missouri, and there was a scattering of students from eleven other states and four territories. The actual attendance of students was 316 men and 173 women, and the average age of all students was 19.5 years.[11] Fred was nearly 21 years old.

Professor James H. Canfield remembered years later Fred's appearance his first day at the university: "He was below the average height, and slight in frame—the very antipodes of his father, who is a perfect giant. He had light-brown hair—not 'red hair,' as it has been so often described in the press of late; a keen eye, which generally looked out between half-closed lids; an erect stature, with a slight swing in his walk which at first gave the impression of a swagger, than which, however, nothing was more foreign to the man."[12]

During the years of 1886-1890, Fred was to be a student for only 2½ years: the school terms of 1886-1887, spring 1889, and 1889-1890. He never graduated. He "was an erratic man in his school work...," observed the school librarian not long after Fred's death.[13] During his time as a student, Fred took fourteen courses in the Latin Scientific course of study. From the university's records, it is not clear when Fred took any particular class during that time period. As to the academic classes he took, there were three classes of grades given: 1st class (I) for grades of 90 and upwards; 2nd class (II) for grades between 80 and 90; and 3rd class (III) for grades between 70 and 80. Any grade below 70 was not a passing grade.[14] Fred scored about an equal number of grades in the three classes of grades: Class I – Not surprisingly, these grades were in Greek and Roman History, Political Economy, American History, and American History (again); Class II – in Elocution, Trigonometry, Botany (b), German, and Advanced Political Economy; and Class III – in German, Goethe; Algebra (b); Geometry (a); Chemistry (a); and Shakespere [sic].[15] Billy White also had a less than sterling academic record, which included failing solid geometry. When Fred became famous in 1899, Billy was quick to point out that if it had not been for him, Fred would have been at the foot of the class, and that it was "a close race."[16] In his *Autobiography* many years later, Billy made the same claim.[17]

Fred's academic record was provided to Eda Funston by the university's registrar in 1931. Examination of the original university records reveals that the registrar omitted one class and grade: rhetoric in which Fred scored an "F."[18] There is no record of why Fred did so poorly, particularly in a subject which would seem to be a natural for a writer like himself (Billy White said that Fred wrote "beautifully" at the university[19]). After his death, one of the faculty members observed that Fred "would not perform routine work in the college." Although Fred did not fail chemistry as this professor alleged (Fred received a III), the professor observed that the low grade was probably caused by Fred's willingness to take "a flunk in chemistry rather than go to class every day and perform the experiments. In rhetoric he was a failure. But he was one of those keen-minded men who, although perfectly capable of getting his work, would not do it. The love of adventure was too great."[20]

Billy White, in his usual descriptive prose, characterized Fred as "of the type that instructors yearn to strangle for the levity that he bred in the classroom." He was also "the maker of nick-names [sic], the dictionary of mirth." He called the Greek professor "Zeus."[21] Another professor was "old purple whiskers." A third was "sunset whiskers."[22] Fred's delight in giving nicknames extended to Richard Cordley, the pastor of the Congregational Church in Lawrence, whom he called "One-eyed Dick." As for the church itself, Fred dubbed it "One-Eyed Dick's Joss House." It is noteworthy that Fred's distance from home did not adversely affect his religious bent, since he was "a prominent member of Captain John's Sunday School class..." at the Congregational Church. Fred also attended the church socials in Lawrence.[23]

Fred's friend and fellow soldier, Major D. P. Quinlan, described Fred's approach to religion at the time of his death thirty years later:

> Freddy Funston had the most divine conception of the purpose for which God created him of any man I ever have known.
>
> General Funston was in tune with the infinite. He taught me my philosophy of life. He understood more than any one I ever have known the lot of the other fellow. He believed that 50 per cent of the sorrows of this world, the tribulations of mankind, were due to the fact that you and I didn't get the viewpoint of yourself and me.
>
> That, he used to say to me, puts 100 per cent responsibility on every man for the sorrows of this world. His idea was that if men would get to an understanding with each other and forget the petty things of life the world would be much happier.
>
> While General Funston was not religious as we understand religion, he was intensely spiritual. He had mental faculties which, combined with the spiritual, raised him above the ordinary man and soldier. The average civilian didn't understand Freddy Funston. The General believed that the acme of perfection in the army was harmony and that the life of every man should be devoted to harmony among mankind. And so he lived out his life.[24]

Professor Canfield taught Fred American history and economics, in which Fred had an intense interest, and left this description of Fred's performance: "I well recall him in the classroom—attentive, alert, always ready to take part in a discussion, but not over-talkative; with a keen sense of humor and with no little wit; apparently mastering with ease fundamental principles, though not always careful as to details in application; with rare good sense, holding tenaciously to his own opinion—and I always thought because he had formed it carefully—but always amenable to reason."[25] Not surprisingly, in view of Fred's constant reading while growing up, Canfield found Fred to be an omnivorous reader who "soon seemed to have mastered the resources that our comparatively small library furnished, and he had this matter at his fingers' ends." Canfield specifically recalled what happened one day when Fred came to the lecture room with an armful of authorities which he put on the table in front of him:

> [A]t the proper time, with perfectly respectful manner but with a triumphant note in his voice, [Fred] presented a brief, backed by his texts, which I immediately confessed set aside a statement and a proposition which I had made on the previous day. It was peculiarly gratifying to myself to know that already a youngster had come up in my classes who could master his instructor, even on a

comparatively minor and technical point. As an illustration of his humor may be quoted his reply to a question which I put one day, in the oratorical sense rather than expecting an answer. Speaking of the tremendous advance in land values which had come in all parts of Kansas during the "boom," I said: "What service have the owners of these lands rendered to the community for which they can expect such extraordinary returns as may possibly be theirs because of this assumed advance in value?" Instantly he interrupted: "Don't you really think, professor, that the Kansas man is entitled to something for standing on top of the fence and waving his hat and shouting so long for the rest of the world to come on?" There was some shrewd philosophy underlying this retort—philosophy which I came to know he clearly appreciated.[26]

Professor Canfield's classes sat around a U-shaped, calico-covered, pine table. Canfield sat at the head with the students along the sides. Included were not only Fred and Billy White, but also their friends, Vernon Kellogg, brothers Ed and Will Franklin, Herbert Hadley, and William Borah, later the famous United States Senator from Idaho.[27] It is not clear whether all of these friends were in the same classes at the same time.[28]

Canfield encouraged "the freest discussion" among his students. Canfield himself was a rebel in Republican Kansas—an independent politically and a devoted believer in free trade, unlike Fred's father and other Kansas Republicans who favored a high tariff.[29] Canfield was a tremendous influence on Fred, Billy White, and William Borah. Billy characterized the professor as "a free man who preached freedom and nurtured independent thinking and made us more or less rebels, all of us." The result of Canfield's preaching and nurturing, Billy concluded, was that the "thing that we all had, and Funston more than any of us, was a tremendous desire to be free. Looking back in those days it was obvious that we all were battling against conventions." Billy noted that neither he nor Fred ever graduated, even after several years (he incorrectly claimed that Fred was a student "six or seven years"). "[W]e were militant in our letch to be free. The university never fired either of us. But neither was it able to brand us." Billy further noted that both he and Fred did not always take the prescribed courses—they had an "irregular" education. "And it was because I didn't subscribe, I didn't conform: I took what I wanted to. The same thing is true of Funston." Billy concluded "that it was the love of freedom, the thing called independence, that we got out of K.U."[30]

This, I believe, is the key to understanding Frederick Funston. His desire to be his own master was to drive Fred the rest of his life. Combined with his restlessness and love of adventure, this desire took him to Death

Valley, twice to Alaska, and to Cuba as a volunteer revolutionary soldier. This desire even drove his career as a United States Army soldier, since he started his career as the officer commanding the Twentieth Kansas. Thereafter, as a very high-ranking officer, he always had substantial control over what he and his soldiers did. He was his own boss, a lasting legacy of his days on Mount Oread.

Many years later a faculty member gave this insightful description of Fred, to which I have added in brackets the words of another:

> We knew he would never be a student. He was always on the lookout for something unusual, and whenever he heard a scuffling of feet he was in the middle of the crowd, to see what the fight was going to be about ["fights were common with him"[31]]. He was never unruly, but he loved adventure. He was aggressive, persistent, and he had a good head that got him out of many scrapes with the faculty. He was never afraid of anybody or anything, and "impossible" was not in his vocabulary. That was the spirit that put him in his prominent position in the army. He was a leader of men here in the University, and his temperament when he was young showed he would always be a leader. He was abrupt, never loving a big talker, and a man of firm convictions.[32]

The university librarian described Fred as "a likeable young man and [he] made many friends in the student body and faculty in spite of his perpetual practical joking."[33]

This leads to the non-academic, and perhaps more important, part of Fred's college life. He quickly pledged Phi Delta Theta social fraternity, a wise decision in view of the lifelong close friendships that he formed with several of his fraternity brothers.[34] Amazingly, he and these brothers all were to become nationally prominent. There were the Franklin brothers, Edward ("Ed") (1862-1937), who became an internationally known chemist who was an authority on ammonia and liquid air, and William ("Will") (1863-1930), who later studied at the University of Berlin and became an internationally known physicist. Vernon L. Kellogg (1867-1937), known as V. L., subsequently studied at the University of Leipzig and acquired renown as a biologist and science administrator. A fourth friend was, of course, William Allen "Billy" White (1868-1944), Emporia, Kansas, newspaper editor of national fame. Of these four, Fred's "two most intimate friends" were Ed Franklin and V. L. Kellogg, according to Ella (Funston) Eckdall though Billy White and Fred were certainly also close.[35] Billy's assessment of Fred in his *Autobiography* was that he was "a pudgy, apple-cheeked young fellow," who clowned to overcome his short height. He "had absolutely no sense of fear, physical or spiritual...was methodical and rather meticulous in his habits, affectionate by nature..." Fred was loved by all in the fraternity, and Billy "clave to him like a brother."[36]

Membership in Phi Delta Theta brought Fred two nicknames, Gric and Timmy. In tribute to Fred's father, "Farmer" Funston, Fred was called Agricola, the Latin word for farmer, and this was shortened to Gric.[37] After Fred was initiated into the fraternity in the early fall of 1886, a chapter member reported the list of initiates to the national organization. Since the reporter wrote a "wretched hand," according to fellow initiate Amos Plumb, *The Scroll* magazine of Phi Delta Theta listed Fred as "Frederick Timiston." His fraternity brothers started calling him Timiston for fun, and this was soon abbreviated to Timmie or Timmy.[38] As a result of the misspelling in *The Scroll*, Fred apparently was re-initiated, since the February 1887 issue of *The Scroll* reported as an initiate Frederick Funston.[39] Initiates endured at least one ordeal, which Ed Franklin recalled many years later. A "dapper little man" was the first initiate "to undergo the ordeal of being rolled the length of the hall in an iron cylinder while playful initiators pounded on the outside of it. He came out smiling. General Funston, next to go, came out in a dead faint. And he is the man who led the Philippine and Mexican expeditions," observed Ed Franklin.[40]

One of Fred's fraternity brothers in 1901 described him as he had been in the fraternity: "In the few instances in college life when he was called upon, he never proved cowardly, but always defended himself or his cause ably. He was naturally quiet and unassuming and was the butt of his whole circle of friends, which included a great many besides Phi Delta Thetas." Physically, "[h]e is under size in stature and has remarkably small feet and hands, and these peculiarities, together with that of always whistling, were the subject of many more or less humorous remarks around our club boarding house." Always the whistler! "In the fraternity meetings Funston contributed ably in the way of speeches or mock-heroic lectures or ridiculous recitations of some sort, and his efforts were always applauded. His language was at that time characteristic and frequently lurid, and he enjoyed nothing better than a quiet evening with a party of good listeners."[41]

In that day, no fraternity had a house so the members rented available rooms for sleeping. Each fraternity had an eating-club where they ate three times a day.[42] The Phi Delts boarded at the Johnson boarding house on Kentucky Street.[43] Fred served as the steward, whose responsibility was to keep the cost below $2.50 per man per week.[44] Stories have survived about Fred and his experiences at the Johnson house. Fred and Frank Craig, who is the same fraternity member that Fred refers to in the next chapter about a dispute between themselves, had a difference of opinion about some other matter. In that case, a committee of fraternity members visited "each of the belligerents." Craig, whose nickname was "Cassowary" because of his ostrich-like swagger, "was unresponsive, indefinite and glum." In contrast, Fred "broke out in a hearty laugh and agreed to everything proposed." At the next meeting at the Johnson house, Cassowary arrived first. Then, Fred arrived. He walked half the length of the room, turned on his heel, saluted, and exclaimed, "A, ha, greetings: Oh, my darling blue eyed Cassowary, how I love thee." "A roar of laughter followed, in which Craig joined, the entente cordiale was restored and the incident closed."[45]

At mealtimes, "[o]ne of the regular amusements was to watch Funston burn his mouth on the hot dessert." Unlike the other boys, who would first investigate the dish put before them, Fred "always attacked the pudding recklessly and with unhappy results."[46]

Another episode at the Johnson house involving Fred occurred one evening when a cattle man rode by carrying a long whip. He let two or three of the boys crack the whip to show their skill as cow men. While they were doing so, Fred came hurrying in late for supper. Culver, the most skillful with the whip, and the others decided that Fred should be chastised for his tardiness, and Culver cracked the whip close to Fred's feet. Fred jumped high, and then "went through some performance that made a great deal of fun..." for the others, including the boys of the Beta fraternity, who also ate there. With about twenty-five boys standing in a circle around Culver and Fred, Fred fell to his knees before Culver, "and holding his hands in an attitude of prayer and supplication, begged him for mercy." Suddenly, "a woman dashed through the crowd, grabbed a handful of Culver's blue flannel shirt, and raising her right hand, cried out: 'How dare you strike this man.'...Culver was speechless and humiliated beyond measure." As the woman disappeared, she was recognized as Nellie Franklin, sister of the two Franklin brothers.[47]

Fred's education at the State University was basically paid for by his father. Ed always encouraged his children to educate themselves, and, as a result of his insistence, his children "early had it instilled into our minds that an education was the first duty we owed to ourselves," remembered Ella (Funston) Eckdall. Ed also "believed it was best for a boy to earn something for himself if he could...rather than to depend upon his father for every cent. It makes a man of him and father knew it and besides Fred was energetic and ambitious and wanted to do something for himself."[48]

Fred, thus, supplemented his father's financial support by his work as steward at the Johnson house in order to pay for his board.[49] He also had a second job. During his student years he served as a university guide, and, as such, showed "visitors through the different museums and other 'showplaces' of the university..."[50] One of these showplaces was the

Main Building, later called Fraser Hall. Built at a cost of $175,000, this three-story, double-towered building stretched nearly 250 feet and had fifty-four rooms, including a main audience room which seated approximately 1,200 people.[51] In September 1879, President and Mrs. Rutherford B. Hayes and General William Tecumseh Sherman had ascended to the building's observatory and taken a view from its summit. "Mrs. Hayes, at first thought she would not go up, but Gen. Sherman said to her, you will regret it all of your life if you do not. She acknowledged the correctness of the remark when she took in the landscape. The party were delighted, as everybody is, with the noble view [of the Kaw Valley]."[52] This was a view which actually extended for miles and miles.[53] The presidential party had stopped in Lawrence after attending the Neosho Valley District Fair only days earlier.

Since the campus fraternities lacked houses, they leased downtown halls for chapter meetings and for frequent dances, which were not chaperoned. Few of the young men, and only some of the young women, could dance when they arrived on campus, but they readily learned from their classmates.[54] Since Fred was eager to do his part at the monthly "hops," he learned how to dance. According to one of his fraternity brothers, "there was no fellow in the University more absolutely awkward on the dancing floor than Funston. Try as hard as he might he could not master the terpsichorean art, but he had a queer idea that the best way for him to learn the 'light fantastic' was to have a large girl for a teacher. So if anyone went to a dance and wanted to see Funston they would at once find the largest woman in the room and under her protecting care would be 'Timmy.'"[55] According to Billy White, Fred broke four chairs while learning to waltz with them.[56] Fred had been curious about the word "scherzo" and one of his fraternity brothers, either Ed Franklin or Cassowary Craig, took advantage of him by letting him believe that it was a form of dance and then instructing him in its mysteries.[57]

As for Fred's amours on campus, Billy White reported that "[Fred] fell desperately in love every six months with a new girl..."[58] These love affairs were both "generally short lived and enthusiastic" and were also "most innocent."[59] Billy claimed that because of Fred's short physical stature "he could never hold the kind he loved."[60] I believe, instead, that Fred lacked the self-confidence to woo successfully any of the women that he fell in love with. When he called at night on a young woman, he began to get restless about 9 o'clock, and would soon thereafter say good night, even though 10 o'clock was the conservative and correct time for departure. When asked about his unusual behavior, his explanation was characteristically modest: "Well, to tell the truth, as soon as I get comfortably settled for a nice talk with a girl I begin to suspect that she is being bored and wants me to go home, and I am uneasy until I get my hat on."[61]

Fred exhibited two prominent behavioral traits while at the university. One he may have had when he arrived on campus, but the other he undoubtedly acquired only once he was living away from home. As to the first, Billy White described Fred's swearing succinctly: He had "a wide eclectic Spanish-Texan-Kansan-and-Old English collection of oaths which he loved to juggle with in emotional moments. For he was an emotional creature."[62] Fred was not alone in swearing, however; Billy White also indulged in "emphatic language." On one occasion, probably about 1890-1891, Fred and Billy were visiting together in *The El Dorado Republican* newspaper office where Billy worked. They were overheard. The listener recalled that oaths were the larger part of the words the two young men used, and that the listener had the desire to "wash out their mouths."[63]

On at least one occasion, however, during a night on the mountains while on the 1889 Estes Park outing, Fred used profanity effectively for the benefit of himself and the others in his camping party. Fred was so widely known on campus for his swearing that in November 1889 one of the campus newspapers observed as follows: "Funston claims to have stopped swearing and Voorhis never smokes now except on Saturday. What powerful influence is this which is at work amongst us?"[64] Fred apparently never renounced swearing, which a fellow military officer regarded as a positive trait: "The dignity of the eagles [Fred's rank as general] did not take from him the prerogative of his fine, old-fashioned anger-purging profanity. He believes, I think, in the virtue of that vice, as many another man has. This human quality was, in the first days, seen the most often in his frank boyishness."[65]

White's discussion in his *Autobiography* of Fred's second behavioral trait—drinking of liquor—is what enraged Fred's sister, Ella. In her apparently unpublished rebuttal, she wrote the following:

> I knew Fred Funston and I knew him well. We were born of the same parents, reared in the same home and trained in the same strict school of honesty, sobriety and decency. I knew him in his boyhood day throughout his college career, and was at all times in close contact with him in his later years through his numerous letters and frequent visits home. And this is the first time in all these years that his friends and family have learned that he was a drunken sot, a frequenter of negro hovels, that he delighted in tearing up sidewalks, and that he was a poor student who lowered the high scholastic standing of his fraternity to disgraceful levels. His record does not bear out these false accusations.[66]

In my opinion, this is one time that Ella is wrong. She would not have known all of the details of Fred's years at the State University, including his discovery of alcoholic drink, and thus Billy White's claims about Fred would have come as a surprise and shock to her. As to Fred's drinking in college, while I accept that this behavior occurred, I note that only Billy has placed this of record; I have found no other contemporary sources on this subject. Incidentally, Billy's comments on Fred's drinking are at times somewhat inconsistent between his other writings and his *Autobiography*. I am reminded of Billy's warning at the start of his *Autobiography* that it is "necessarily fiction," and "not to confuse this story with reality."[67]

According to Billy White, Fred could not carry his liquor; in fact, Billy claimed that even the smell of a rotten apple would launch Fred into tearing up the board sidewalks of Lawrence, which he did in "terrible earnest," since he regarded their presence as dangerous to "the public welfare."[68] Consequently, the fraternity brothers kept rotten apples, hard cider, and homemade wine away from Fred.[69] Also, according to Billy's *Autobiography*, after two drinks, it took three men to hold Fred.[70] And yet, according to Billy in another writing, once Fred had had three drinks, he was the "funniest man I ever knew." In order to enjoy him, Billy stayed sober, he claimed.[71] In his *Autobiography*, however, Billy stated that he "never saw him tight..."[72] Fred did not necessarily drink alone, since he and Billy, recollected Billy, started down the path of excessive drinking together when they were young newspapermen in Kansas City in October 1891. Billy was saved from a life of drinking by his future wife, Sallie Lindsay, who refused to marry him unless he gave up drinking, which he did.[73] According to Billy, Fred never gave up drink.[74]

Although now living away from home, Fred maintained his family contacts. In mid-October 1886, his father visited him.[75] Thanksgiving found both Fred and Schuyler Brewster back home. Charlie Scott reported to his newspaper readers: "They are much pleased with the University, and we are glad to learn, from other sources, that they are both regarded as exceptionally good students."[76] Fred spent the Christmas vacation differently, however, working in Topeka for the *Topeka Capital* newspaper as its Lawrence correspondent and agent.[77] A Lawrence newspaper reported that Fred was "meeting with considerable success, working for the *Capital*. He is getting quite a list of subscribers."[78] Unless Fred had worked on one of the student newspapers that fall, this was his first exposure to an occupation that he would return to from time to time in the future.

Two notable, but very different, events occurred just before the Christmas vacation. First, Fred was one of 125 signers of a letter addressed to the Chancellor and to the Regents of the State University about the "very limited library facilities." Lacking were both additional books and sufficient copies of books that were in constant demand. "We feel we are given poor facilities to do our work, especially when we see how much is asked for and given in some directions." This letter was published on the front page of one of the student newspapers.[79]

On the second page of the same issue was the report of "A Jolly Time." Four fraternities, including the Phi Delts, after their regular fraternity meetings, met in the halls of two of the fraternities in the Opera House block in Lawrence "to celebrate in a fitting manner the closing of the year." Refreshments of nuts and candy, fruits, cigars, and cider were furnished by the fraternities. "A gigantic tin horn capable of creating a deafening noise was at hand, to assist in the swelling of the din which arose from the throats of the sixty-five boys who were present." Presumably, Fred was one of them. "Quite a number of the gentlemen assumed the part of ladies, and wore costumes in accordance with the part which they represented."

About ten o'clock "the merry making was at its highest...and the roof of the building was rising and falling, in its endeavor to accommodate itself to the noise." Suddenly, Lawrence's City Marshal Prentice appeared and advised the celebrating boys that in the nearby Opera House, where a play was being performed, "the noise by the frats was so great that nothing could be heard by the audience." In fact, "in the most affecting part of the play, just as the audience was about to burst into tears,...'that horn went ka-bloo, ka-bloo, ka-bloo,' and knocked the sentiment higher than a kite." The upshot of this confrontation of the boys by the marshal and another officer was that the two lawmen grabbed one of the boys. The other students grabbed him at the same moment. Each side pulled on the unlucky boy. "It was a battle for the student, and now in the hall, in the corridor, half way down the steps, back again in the corridor, in the hall again, the battle raged fiercely." The subject of this tug of war had his feminine costume torn completely off and was "almost torn to pieces, himself." Ultimately, the unfortunate boy was taken to a nearby office where, after "an explanation," he was released.

"After this episode, the fun raged higher than ever before." This included composing, and then singing, songs about Prentice; performing "takeoffs" on the University professors; making speeches; and enacting "the great 'bear act.'" Every student assisted in "making things lively" before the celebration broke up just before Sunday morning.[80] What a way for Fred to celebrate the closing of his first term at the State University.

The spring of 1887 brought two events of note, one sartorial, the other adversarial. *The Weekly University Courier* of March 18 pegged Fred as follows: "That Funston in a seersucker is the greatest 'ham' of the season, and takes them all in."[81] Likely, this is the light gray summer suit that Fred had purchased. His fraternity brother, A. L. Burney, had also purchased such a suit, and both had bought them earlier than any of the others who boarded at Johnson house. Although the two boys were subjected to "the taunts and jibes" of the others, the warm weather justified their wearing of the light-colored suits. The "chill of winter" returned, however, forcing them to resume wearing darker garb and resulting in a severe roasting from the other boys. When the weather soon warmed up, Burney encouraged Fred to resume wearing the summer clothes, provided, Burney said, the "weather remains warm and it is clear." Burney reminded Fred years later of his response: "You looked very sober, ran your hands down into your pockets, and in a very positive tone said: 'Well, I'll tell you Burney, it's got to be damned clear if I put on those light clothes again.'"[82] Billy White recollected that Fred liked good clothes, but could not afford to buy them.[83] One item Fred did buy was waistcoats called "explosions," which were known for their "brilliancy in color design."[84]

The other event of note occurred about the same time as the seersucker suit episode. *The Weekly University Courier* of March 25 warned its readers on the front page: "Beware of Funston for he is on the war path."[85] George Bivins, a large Black man weighing nearly 200 pounds and armed with a razor, and having served time in the penitentiary for "carving a man up," had been terrorizing the town.[86] Fred applied to the city council for permission to carry firearms. "One day Dr. Snow after class asked Funston if it was true that he was a walking arsenal. Funston promptly reached under his coat tails and hauled forth two murderous looking forty-fours to show the Doctor he spoke rightly."[87] Fred was on the outlook for Bivins, and what happened on the previous Saturday, March 19, was observed and reported in the commonly used racist language of the time in the same issue of the campus newspaper that carried the front-page warning about Fred's being on the warpath:

Our "David"

Saturday afternoon,—and down the dusty thoroughfare of our booming city, a small compact, and square built figure was seen wending its sturdy way. As it approached our point of observation, it developed into the form of a young man with a mildly ferocious cast of countenance and a very familiar swagger. He seemed to be on the lookout for some one, for his small eyes snapped restlessly and his glances were directed continually to the right and left. Suddenly, without a moments' warning and with no apparent hesitation, he stepped up to a strapping negro and accosting him with, "I believe you are the man I'm looking for," seized him by the third button of his coat with one hand and with the other, holding a pistol a foot long under the terrified darkey's nose, turned half around, saying "move and you're a dead man!"

The negro, scared to death, the young man gradually realizing the presence in his hand, of a black, "white elephant," growing every second blacker and more formidable, formed an interesting center to a crowd of admiring Athenians.

"Brocklesby, oh Brocklesby, I've got him, I've got him!" rang out in the oppressive air from the lungs of the small young man and that august minion [officer] of Lawrence culture, starting from his slumbers on a dry goods box, hastened across the street that he might relieve the "David" of his darkey-ed Goliath. "To the dungeon—t'was in vain he sought for mercy" the mighty man of valor with stern and rigid step marched off with growing pallor, the man of dusky hue, t'was done, and David with placid mien, walked calmly through the crowd, the cynosure of all eyes. Verily, we do envy him in his deed and wish for him, that he may never feel the cutting edge of razor, knife or tongue.[88]

The following day, in Judge Howard's court, George Bivins pled guilty to disturbing the peace of Fred Funston and paid a one dollar fine and costs.[89] *The Weekly University Courier*, which had carried the "Our David" story, reported in its next issue that "Funston wanted to buy up our entire last week's edition. Negotiations pended so long that the issue was delayed."[90]

The Bivins incident shows young Fred at his best. He was willing, despite his small size, to confront a much larger armed man who was threatening the community. Others apparently shirked from such a challenge. If Fred felt fear, and he may not have, it did not deter him from the challenge. "Fearless" Fred he was, indeed. When Fred became nationally famous in the spring of 1899, Billy White was soon writing about this incident for the national press, including in an article reprinted in *The New York Times*.[91] It undoubtedly was the Bivins incident that Fred was referring to when he wrote Billy on July 1, 1899, from the Philippines— "And then raking up the old rows of my college and train collector days was bad, awfully bad."[92]

Both the spring and Fred's stay in the ivory tower were rapidly ending. In mid-March, a student newspaper reported that Fred had applied for a position with Pinkerton, a famous detective agency.[93] In mid-April, he and Schuyler Brewster spent spring vacation at their respective homes.[94] In mid-May, Fred went to nearby Topeka, where he took the civil service examination.[95] The results are unknown, but, clearly, Fred was looking for his next landing place after the academic term was over. Academic life was not for him, and so he left for adventures in the larger world. This decision may have been influenced by a physical problem that he was experiencing. According to one credible account, Fred was unable to "study at night on account of his eyes..."[96] There is no detail of record about this so the precise problem is unknown. Whether Fred intended to return to the State University some day is unknown.

Fred Funston Age 21 Years

KANSAS ALPHA, 1887

This is probably the greatest chapter in the history of Phi Delta Theta—or any other fraternity—from the standpoint of the life records of its members. A high percentage of the college boys pictured here became prominent leaders in their lines of endeavor, and at least five of them achieved international fame. In the back row are Leland D. Henshaw, '90; Amos H. Plumb, '90; Joseph T. Dickerson, '87; William S. Franklin, '87; John Shawl, '90; William E. Higgins, '88; Edward C. Franklin, '88 and Edward L. Glasgow, '90. In the second row are Frederick Funston, '90; Orley C. Billings, '91; Jeptha D. Davis, '87; George S. Lewis, '90; Charles S. McFarland, '90; Edward A. Wheeler, '88 and Julius M. Liepman, '89. In the front are Fred H. Kellogg, '90; Hansford E. Finney, '89; James W. O'Bryon, '89; Vernon L. Kellogg, '89 and William Allen White, '90. The Franklin brothers won world fame as scientists at Stanford and M.I.T.; Funston became a famed U. S. Army general; Vernon Kellogg gained international repute as head of the National Research Council and White was known across the world as the "Sage of Emporia." The Phis did not have all the good men at Kansas University, however, for at the same time the Beta Theta Pi chapter there claimed the late great Senator William E. Borah.

University Hall (Fraser Hall)

(Frank Leslie's Illustrated Newspaper, July 16, 1887)

"Now, by the grace of God, we have a building nearly completed that has not its peer in the land." Chancellor John Fraser, 1872

Chapter Ten Notes—*State University*

Epigraph: Quoted in "The State University," *The Iola Register*, July 9, 1886

1. "A Students' [sic] First Impressions," *The University Courier*, September 26, 1890.

2. "A Students' [sic] First Impressions."

3. F. H. Snow, "The Beginnings of the University of Kansas," *Transactions of the Kansas State Historical Society, 1897-1900* (Topeka, Kansas: W.Y. Morgan, State Printer, 1900), Vol. VI, 70.

4. Snow, "The Beginnings of the University of Kansas," 70.

5. Snow, "The Beginnings of the University of Kansas," 70.

6. Snow, "The Beginnings of the University of Kansas," 70.

7. *Twenty-First Annual Catalogue of the Officers and Students of the University of Kansas For The Collegiate Year of 1886-7* (Topeka, Kansas: Kansas Publishing House, 1887), 5.

8. James H. Canfield, "Funston: A Kansas Product," *The American Monthly Review of Reviews*, May 1901. James H. Canfield (1847-1909) had a distinguished career. After he left the Kansas State University, he was chancellor of the University of Nebraska, then president of Ohio State University, and, finally, a librarian at Columbia University. He was the father of Dorothy Canfield Fisher, famous author and social activist.

9. *Twenty-First Annual Catalogue of the Officers and Students*, 15.

10. "Personals," *The Iola Register*, September 5, 1886.

11. *Twenty-First Annual Catalogue of the Officers and Students*, 32-33.

12. Canfield, "Funston: A Kansas Product."

13. "General Frederick Funston Dies Of Heart Disease Following Dinner In San Antonio," *University Daily Kansan*, February 20, 1917, quoting Miss Carrie Watson, K.U. librarian.

14. Telephone conversation on December 3, 1998, between the author and Barry Bunch of University Archives of the University of Kansas.

15. George O. Foster, Registrar, to Mrs. Frederick Funston, February 14, 1931 (FFP).

16. "Daring Little Col. Funston," *The New York Times*, April 30, 1899 (FFP). As to White's own grades, he made a I in three courses (two rhetoric and one history); a III in three courses (two mathematics and one Latin); and a II in all other courses except the one course he failed (Everett Rich, *William Allen White The Man from Emporia* (New York: Farrar & Rinehart, Inc., 1941), Chapter IV, "footnote" 1).

17. William Allen White, *The Autobiography of William Allen White* (New York: The Macmillan Company, 1946), 143. White is in error about the subjects Fred excelled in. He claimed that Fred's only "A" grades were in "English composition," which he never took. White also stated that Fred was "excellent" in mathematics, yet he received only a II in trigonometry and a III in geometry.

18. *Register Kansas State University*, 228 ("Funston, Frederick"). These ledgers are confusing to understand many years later, and the ledgers have no dates inscribed on them as to when specific classes were taken.

19. White, *The Autobiography of William Allen White*, 143.

20. "General Funston Was Only 'Just a Kansan,'" *University Daily Kansan*, February 21, 1917, quoting Professor M. W. Sterling.

21. William Allen White, "The Hero Of The Philippines," *The St. Louis Republic Magazine Section*, May 21, 1899.

22. "Another Funston Story," *The Iola Daily Register*, October 16, 1923. These are reminiscences by Edward Franklin.

23. "Another Funston Story" for the Cordley story. A. L. Burney to General Frederick Funston, November 17, 1914 (FFP Micro) about Fred's religious bent. Burney and Fred were fraternity brothers together.

24. "General Funston Was Philosopher, Says Army Officer," *The San Francisco Examiner*, February 24,1917.

25. Canfield, "Funston: A Kansas Product."

26. Canfield, "Funston: A Kansas Product."

27. David Hinshaw, *A Man From Kansas: The Story of William Allen White* (New York: G. P. Putnam's Sons, 1945), 39.

28. White, *The Autobiography of William Allen White*, 144. White does identify Borah and Herbert Hadley by name as sitting at the table with White.

29. Walter Johnson, *William Allen White's America* (New York: Henry Holt and Company, 1947), 37.

30. William Allen White to Paul Jones, January 29, 1940 (William Allen White Collection, Container C-359, Manuscript Division, Library of Congress).

31. "General Funston Was Only 'Just a Kansan,'" *University Daily Kansan*, February 21, 1917, quoting Professor M. W. Sterling.

32. "General Frederick Funston Dies Of Heart Disease Following Dinner In San Antonio," quoting Dean Olin Templin, who knew Fred both as a friend and a student.

33. "General Frederick Funston Dies Of Heart Disease Following Dinner In San Antonio," quoting Miss Carrie Watson, K.U. librarian.

34. "University Notes," *Lawrence Daily Journal*, September 21, 1886.

35. Eckdall Scrapbook II, 261, handwritten note of Ella (Funston) Eckdall next to photographs of Ed Franklin and Vernon Kellogg.

36. White, *The Autobiography of William Allen White*, 142.

37. Paul Wilkinson, "Frederick Funston In The Chapter," *The Scroll of Phi Delta Theta*, Volume XXV, October, 1900-June, 1901, 430.

38. "Plumb Of Kansas Talks About Fighting Fred Funston," unknown newspaper and undated clipping (FFP). Amos Plumb was initiated into the fraternity at the same time as Fred. This story of the origin of the nickname "Timmy" is confirmed by Paul Wilkinson, except he wrote that the Funston surname was misspelled as Timson (see note 37), and confirmed by William Allen White in his *Autobiography* (143). The applicable issue of *The Scroll* confirms the misspelling but shows Fred's surname as Timston (*The Scroll of Phi Delta Theta*, Volume XI, October 1886-June 1887, 127, chapter report dated November 14, 1886).

39. *The Scroll of Phi Delta Theta*, Issue No. 5-February 1887, 226. "Kansas Alpha Initiates."

40. "Another Funston Story."

41. Wilkinson, "Frederick Funston In The Chapter,"430-431.

42. Everett Rich, *William Allen White: The Man from Emporia* (New York: Farrar & Rinehart, Inc., 1941), 38.

43. A. L. Burney to General Frederick Funston, November 17, 1914 (FFP Micro).

44. Thornton Cooke, "And When I Came to K.U.," *The Graduate Magazine*, September 1938.

45. A. L. Burney to General Frederick Funston, November 17, 1914 (FFP Micro).

46. "Funston In Student Days," unidentified newspaper clipping dated May 12 (probably 1902) (*Frederick Funston: Adventurer, Explorer, and Soldier*) (scrapbook of newspaper clippings, Spencer Research Library, University of Kansas).

47. A. L. Burney to General Frederick Funston, November 17, 1914 (FFP Micro).

48. Ella (Funston) Eckdall to Eda B. Funston, October 25, 1925 (FFP).

49. "Another Funston Story."

50. Canfield, "Funston: A Kansas Product." Canfield erroneously believed that Fred was "entirely dependent upon his own resources." Canfield apparently was not alone in this opinion. Ed Funston "resented...very bitterly" that people believed this, since he could and did largely pay for his son's education (Ella (Funston) Eckdall to Eda B. Funston, October 25, 1925) (FFP).

51. "University of Kansas," *The Weekly University Courier*, July 19, 1889.

52. "The President In Lawrence," *The Lawrence Daily Journal*, September 28, 1879.

53. White, *The Autobiography of William Allen White*, 140.

54. Rich, *William Allen White: The Man from Emporia*, 38.

55. "General Funston's Visit," *The University Daily Kansan*, March 25, 1905. W. H. Higgins, who was one of Fred's fraternity brothers when they attended the university, told this story at a welcome meeting given by the students to Brigadier General Frederick Funston.

56. White, "The Hero Of The Philippines."

57. Wilkinson, "Frederick Funston In The Chapter," 431.

58. White, *The Autobiography of William Allen White*, 142.

59. On December 12, 1942, William Allen White wrote a letter describing each of the 1889 Estes Park photographs (William Allen White Collection, RH MS929, Spencer Research Library, University of Kansas, Lawrence, Kansas).

60. White, *The Autobiography of William Allen White*, 142.

61. "Funston In Student Days," unidentified newspaper clipping dated May 12 (probably 1902) (*Frederick Funston: Adventurer, Explorer, and Soldier*) (scrapbook of newspaper clippings, Spencer Research Library, University of Kansas).

62. White, *The Autobiography of William Allen White*, 143.

63. Johnson, *William Allen White's America* (New York: Henry Holt and Company, 1947), 55. Quoted is the correspondence between the unidentified writer and White in 1912. White acknowledged that he "must have been highly offensive to a lot of decent fellows."

64. *The Weekly University Courier*, November 1, 1889.

65. Louis Stanley Young and Henry Davenport Northrop, *Life and Heroic Deeds of Admiral Dewey* (Philadelphia: Globe Bible Publishing Co., 1899), 348. Quoted is Wil-

liam A. DeFord, the first commissioned officer appointed in Kansas at the outbreak of the Spanish-American War. As adjutant, he recruited the entire Twentieth Kansas Regiment.

66. Original draft in possession of the late Frank Funston Eckdall (photocopy in possession of this author).

67. See Chapter Two.

68. White, *The Autobiography of William Allen White,* 1946), 142, as to "even the smell of a rotten apple." The description of how and why Fred tore up the board sidewalks from White, "The Hero Of The Philippines."

69. White, *The Autobiography of William Allen White,* 142.

70. White, *The Autobiography of William Allen White,* 142.

71. Johnson, *William Allen White's America,* 59. Johnson quoted White, but the endnote does not appear to pertain to the subject. Johnson cited White to S.P. Aber, March 9, 1933, and Walter Armstrong to writer, September 18, 1944. The former letter, which does not pertain to the subject, is in the William Allen White Collection, Container C205, Manuscript Division, Library of Congress. The latter letter I have not located.

72. White, *The Autobiography of William Allen White,* 169.

73. Hinshaw, *A Man From Kansas: The Story of William Allen White,* 33-34.

74. Johnson, *William Allen White's America,* 59.

75. "Personal," *The Weekly University Courier,* October 22, 1886.

76. "Personal," *The Iola Register,* December 3, 1886.

77. "Personal," *The Iola Register,* December 31, 1886, and "News Around Town," *The Lawrence Daily Journal,* December 23, 1886.

78. "News Around Town," *The Lawrence Daily Journal,* December 26, 1886.

79. "To The Chancellor And Regents Of The State University," *The Weekly University Courier,* December 17, 1886.

80. "A Jolly Time," *The Weekly University Courier,* December 17, 1886.

81. "Personal," *The Weekly University Courier,* March 18, 1887.

82. A. L. Burney to General Frederick Funston, November 17, 1914 (FFP Micro).

83. White, *The Autobiography of William Allen White,* 142.

84. "Funston Bought 'Explosions,'" *The Iola Daily Register,* August 24, 1908.

85. "Personal," *The Weekly University Courier,* March 25, 1887.

86. "Daring Little Col. Funston," *The New York Times,* April 30, 1899, quoting William Allen White (FFP); William Allen White to Paul Jones, January 20, 1940, William Allen White Collection, Container C-359, Manuscript Division, Library of Congress; Frederick W. Webber, "General Fred. Funston—A Character Sketch," *Metropolitan Magazine,* June 1901.

87. "General Funston's Visit."

88. "Our David," *The Weekly University Courier,* March 25, 1887.

89. "Judge Howard's Court," *The Lawrence Daily Journal,* March 20, 1887. The surname Bivins is misspelled as Blevins in the newspaper report.

90. "Personal," *The Weekly University Courier,* April 1, 1887.

91. "Daring Little Col. Funston," *The New York Times*, April 30, 1899, quoting William Allen White (FFP).

92. Frederick Funston to William Allen White, July 1, 1899 (FFP Micro). See discussion about this in Chapter Two.

93. "Personal," *The Weekly University Courier*, March 25, 1887.

94. "Personal," *The Iola Register*, April 28, 1887.

95. "Personal," *The Lawrence Daily Journal*, May 19, 1887.

96. "Funston In Student Days," unidentified newspaper clipping dated May 12 (probably 1902) (*Frederick Funston: Adventurer, Explorer, and Soldier*) (scrapbook of newspaper clippings, Spencer Research Library, University of Kansas).

    The entire article clearly is based on information from an unnamed person who knew Fred. This article does not state when, during his academic career, Fred had his vision problem. I believe this occurred during his first year in view of Fred's letter to his mother at the end of 1888 just before Fred resumed his studies at the State University (see Chapter Twelve).

CHAPTER ELEVEN

"General Funston's Reminiscences of the University"

The State University at Lawrence was a place of both education and fun for the high-spirited Fred Funston. In his 1909 reminiscences of his time as a university student, Fred provided in his own words an overview of his student experiences. The following account was originally published in *Kansas Magazine*, April 1909, and thereafter republished in *The Graduate Magazine of the University of Kansas*, Volume XIV, No. 3, December 1915, 67-72.

***

In looking back to the time nearly twenty-three years ago when I entered the University of Kansas, and recalling the incidents of the four years during which, off and on, I was an alleged student at the institution, I find that my principal recollection is of the humorous happenings and of the boyish pranks in which some of us from time to time indulged.

Almost gone is the memory of the weary hours that I struggled over Caesar's Commentaries, wondering how in one short life a man could find time to kill so many people and to write about it so voluminously. And how often, as I came into the German class with a badly prepared lesson, I wished Schiller's mother had dropped him into a well in early childhood, and thus relieved future generations of Kansans from the painful necessity of reading his productions in the original. And how often the thought occurred that the old Arabs who invented algebra would have been in better business grooming their camels or raising garden truck for the subsistence of their families. But it was a condition and not a theory that confronted those of us who had come to Lawrence with the idea that we would find ample time for baseball, swimming in the Kaw, and making up to the pretty co-eds. The faculty, individually and *en masse*, had some definite ideas as to why we were there and why they were set over us. But, although painful recollections on these subjects have all but faded, vivid indeed is the memory of the practical jokes and of the harmless escapades that added zest to life, even if they did interfere to a certain extent with the day's work.

There were in those days among the students a number of men who in their various spheres of life have become widely known. Especially well, do I recall William Allen White, who is now prosperous and famous. We entered in the same year, 1886, were members of the same fraternity, and were as we are today, particularly close friends. My first impression of him was unfavorable. He was fat, freckle faced and flippant, and wrote "pieces" for the *El Dorado Republican*, which when copied in the Lawrence papers made cold waves chase themselves up and down the spines of the faculty and other proper folk. I made a mental prediction in those early days that White would come to some bad end, mayhap on the gallows, but instead he is a moulder of public opinion, incidentally writing fat checks for the Y.M.C.A. with one hand, and at the same time cuffing the legislature with the other. And there were the two Franklins, W.S. and E. C. known as "Cap" and "Buck," both hard students, but with time and disposition to enjoy life, notwithstanding. The former is a member of the faculty of Lehigh University, and the latter of Stanford. William Harvey Brown was a leader among the students, and has had a life of unusual interest. He went on Hornaday's expedition after buffalo in the Yellowstone country, was a member of the eclipse expedition sent to Africa on the old warship Pensacola, in 1889, was with Frederick Selous when he invaded Mashonaland, fought in the Matabele War as a trooper, and is now a prominent resident of Rhodesia. Vernon L. Kellogg, now of Stanford University, and well known as investigator and writer on biological subjects, was a student, and for one year we roomed together. Another, who came a couple of years later, was Herbert S. Hadley who was destined to tame the Standard Oil company so that it would eat out of one's hand, and is now the widely known governor of Missouri. Space does not permit mention of dozens of other students of those days who have made good in the intervening years. The majority of those in attendance were a hard working and earnest lot, but managed to mix a good deal of harmless fun with their work. I do not know how it is now, but in those days the "rah rah boy," who turns up his trousers in order to exhibit vari-colored hosiery, and who by his conduct makes the plain and quiet-loving citizens long for open season on students, had not yet invaded the University of Kansas. A few crept in before the "nineties," but a process of elimination at the close of the semi-annual examinations sent the most of them to their homes. We were a pretty plain lot, and the most of us showed by gait and appearance the results of assiduously following the cultivator up and down the sweltering corn rows and wielding the pitchfork in haying time. Some few owned evening dress suits, but wore them apologetically and uneasily, as if afraid they would come off. The "Phi

Gams," who came from Atchison and Topeka, were currently reported to sleep in pajamas, and to scorn the homely but comfortable "nighty," and so were looked up to as beings apart.

I early joined the Phi Delta, one of the nine fraternities then existing among the students and found in it congenial companionship and opportunity for social enjoyment. Well conducted college fraternities are an undoubted benefit to those who belong to them, but unfortunately there is a tendency for all the social life of an educational institution where they exist to center around them, thus leaving out in the cold many worthy young men and women who in consequence have nothing to break the monotony of hard work over their books. This result of the fraternity system always seemed regrettable to me, and does to this day.

The great mass of the students from outside of Lawrence were scattered though boarding houses, which were really private families that took in from one to half a dozen boarders or roomers. A few fraternities had clubs, which were really messes. (Mess is a horrible word, suggestive of the pig-sty, but unfortunately has no synonym in our poor language.) For years I served gratuitously as steward of the Phi Delta mess, and kept the price of table board down to $2.50 a week, thereby acquiring a reputation as a financier that I have not been able to keep in later life. One of my fraternity brothers was J.F. Craig, now a lawyer in Oklahoma. He had from time to time dropped deprecatory remarks regarding the lack of variety in the food served at our table, and kept up this form of amusement until one day just after dinner we strolled out into the street and without any preliminaries entered into a kicking and slugging match which quickly filled the windows of near by residences with the faces of scandalized spectators. This encounter settled nothing, but after that anyone who felt moved to reflect on the quality of canned goods or coffee purchased for our mess, relieved himself of his feelings in the secrecy of his closet. One summer when about a dozen of us students spent several months on an outing in Colorado, I had the pleasure of witnessing a fight between Craig and William Allen White, in which the former used a dull butcher knife and the latter a loaded valise. This row, too, arose over a culinary matter.

An incident that created much merriment at the time, and the recollection of which even now, after the lapse of twenty years, is a source of positive joy, occurred one Sunday afternoon when about a dozen of us, including V. L. and F. H. Kellogg, White, E. C. Franklin, Paul Wilkinson and myself were foregathered in Kellogg's and my room, and with the aid of a mandolin in the hands of Wilkinson were making more noise than was seemly on that particular day. While we were thus engaged W.E. Higgins, now a member of the faculty of the University dropped in to urge us to attend some special service to be held at the Y.M.C.A. that afternoon and was listened to somewhat disrespectfully. At this juncture feminine footsteps were heard on the stairway, and all realized that our landlady, the long suffering and estimable Mrs. H——— was coming up to remonstrate with us for our boisterous conduct. With a wild impulse all except Higgins dashed madly through the door and into an unoccupied bed room, and locked the door. Higgins was begged to save himself in like manner, but bestowed on us a withering glance and replied, "I have done no wrong. I scorn to fly." So the poor man remained and faced Mrs. H———alone. The good lady was astonished that one of the pillars of the Young Men's Christian Association would participate in revelries in her house on the Sabbath. Higgins, strong and calm in the knowledge of his own virtue, cleared his throat and started out, "Madam, you do me a grave injustice. I assure you that—," but the indignant lady swept from the room, while the dozen real culprits who had been listening intently through the door, howled with derision. It was many a year before the unfortunate man got over the name, "Grave Injustice Higgins."

Higgins was a prominent actor in a somewhat more exciting drama a few years later. The students in returning to town from the athletic ground were in the habit of making a short cut across the spacious and well kept grounds of a certain prominent resident who was the father of a couple of hot tempered boys. It had been from time to time suggested that the streets and sidewalks were for the use of pedestrians, but without effect, and one day the usual crowd of trespassers swarmed across the premises, whereupon one of the dutiful sons emerged from the house armed with the family fowling piece. Higgins being tall and of dignified carriage, was the most promising target and the easiest to hit. The contents of the first barrel were quite evenly distributed over his person from head to waist, while the second looked after the remaining portions of his anatomy. At the conclusion of the function Higgins constituted what would be called in mining circles an "unusually uniform body of ore," the metal being not in pockets or streaks, but well distributed through the rock. The surgeons of Lawrence had a busy and interesting night picking quail shot from the person of the unfortunate collegian, but were able to find and extract only a portion thereof. In due time the victim appeared on the streets, but greatly embarrassed his friends and himself by from time to time exuding bird shot, and always at the most inappropriate moment. It got to be a saying that Higgins could not even laugh without an accompaniment of the tell tale rattle on the sidewalk. A suggestion that he be sent to a smelter to get rid of his surplus metal was not kindly received.

One of the joyous incidents of these years was the visit to Lawrence of a young man whom we shall call Tweed, because that was not his name, but sounds very much like it. He was from Ohio, and had recently won oratorical honors at an institution in that state, and was not inclined to hide his light under a bushel. He was the guest of a relative in town, but at once made himself known in University circles. It was at once reported that he was "easy game," and then the fun began. A committee, on which served the now dignified governor of Missouri, took charge of him and presented him to those of us who were in the secret. We had all heard of his fame as an orator in Ohio, and hoped that we could have the pleasure of hearing him while in town. All of us were introduced as the sons of various rich or powerful men, and offered him all sorts of courtesies. I was the son of the president of the Santa Fe Road, and insisted on his taking a trip over the system in my father's private car. Invitations came thick and fast, and the enthusiasm over the presence in our midst of so distinguished a man showed no signs of abatement. Everything was so easy that finally it was suggested that he might go on a "snipe hunt," that time worn practical joke that has been played on generations of men. The committee discreetly broached the subject and their invitation was most cordially accepted. So that night a number of us drove out with him to a point near Blue Mound, seven miles south of town. As he was the guest of the evening, it was insisted that he take the post of honor, holding the sack while the rest of us beat up the snipe and drove them toward him. He was cautioned to stand perfectly noiseless, holding in the mouth of the bag a lighted lantern that had been brought for the purpose. It was a damp night and the birds might not begin to enter the trap until late, but when they did come it would be a sport fit for a king. So we left him and scattered, presumably to beat up the doomed birds in the surrounding fields, but really to meet at the point where we had hitched the teams and drive back to town. Just before daylight Tweed walked into town, mildly wondering why he had seen nothing more of his fellow sportsmen. During the day he was told that the teams had been frightened and had broken loose and that we had chased them back to town in the hope of overtaking them. This was satisfactory, but the almost unbelievable thing is that he was taken out the next night. But on this occasion the tables were turned to a certain extent by several students who followed the party from town on horseback, and just as soon as the teams had been left drove back to town with them, leaving not only Tweed but his tormentors to measure the distance by pacing the seven miles back to Lawrence.

Two nights later our visitor was tendered a grand reception in one of the city parks. All the male students were invited by the committee in charge and each one directed to bring some musical instrument well concealed about his clothing. I recollect obtaining from my landlady the loan of a tin pan, which it was a nuisance to have to keep under my coat. It was quite noticeable that all of the four hundred students in attendance moved about stiffly and carefully and held their arms closely against their sides. William Harvey Brown presided with dignity; "Cap" Franklin delivered an address of welcome in which he fairly covered our guest with glucose. As he finished there was a wild yell for Tweed, and he came forward and lifting his right arm impressively began, "Fellow searchers in the field of knowledge—." From four hundred throats arose cries of "Hear, hear," and "Magnificent." He tried it again, but was drowned in the roar of applause punctured by the blowing of horns and the vigorous beating of tin pans. A third attempt had a like result, and it was explained to him that the boys were so overcome by enthusiasm over his presence that they could not restrain themselves, which came mighty near being true. However, we would have a parade, and started up Massachusetts street in column. Student parades had been prohibited by the town authorities, and at the psychological moment Marshal Prentice and his legion bore down on us. There was a wild scattering into side streets, and all escaped except Tweed, who not being familiar with the geography of the town, was cut off and captured, but obtained his release on assuring the officers that he was a stranger. Of course, looking back over twenty years, I realize that we could have been in better business, but we did our victim no harm. In fact he had brought these adventures upon himself by his pompous egotism.

But it was not all "horse play," and there was plenty of good, honest hard work done. The faculty consisted of a body of able and painstaking men and women, several of whom are still with the institution. As to our milder pranks, they were indulgent, but when we went too far they knew how to bring us up standing. With liberal support from the legislature, they have built up an institution of which the state may well be proud and which I feel sure has no more loyal friends than those of us who were in attendance in the "Eighties."

Rodman, Rebellious Reporter, and Railroad Ticket Collector

June 1887 – December 1888

Ft. Smith is a great place for hangings, and clover for newspaper men.

—*The Lawrence Daily Journal,* October 23, 1887[1]

One thing you did was to bring your train in on time.

—George T. Nicholson, Fred Funston's
Santa Fe Railway co-worker[2]

Having left the State University after only a year of studies, the question was, what would Fred Funston do. He chose not to return to either farming or teaching. If he had not already decided on his course of action before he left the State University, he quickly made his decision after leaving the university. On June 10, Charlie Scott reported Fred's status in *The Iola Register*: "A card from Fred Funston informs us that he is roughing it this summer with a Santa Fe [Railway] surveying corps. His present address is Jetmore,"[3] a small town located in western Kansas. The same *Register* issue reported that Fred's close friend, Schuyler Brewster, had returned to Iola, "having concluded a very successful year at the State University."[4] Academia clearly suited Schuyler better than it did Fred.

Fred's position on the surveying corps was as a rodman, and the corps worked that summer surveying the Larned branch of the railroad between the towns of Burdett and Jetmore, Kansas.[5] Perhaps the surveying corps also was at times in eastern Colorado. Fred's mother, in 1899, mentioned that he was in Colorado with a "Government surveying party."[6] This must be the Santa Fe crew, not a government crew.

The surveying position was probably only a summer job, and "roughing it" and a paycheck were likely the reasons Fred assumed the role of rodman. Fred successfully sought other work at the end of the summer, and the September 2 issue of *The Iola Register* reported his latest employment: "A card from Fred Funston informs us that he had accepted a 'sit' as a reporter on the Kansas City *Evening News*. He will 'do' the humorous route,—coroner, undertaker, hospitals, morgue etc. The REGISTER wishes him success in his new career."[7] Noting Fred's new position with the *Evening News, The Lawrence Daily Journal* complimented him: "Fred is a rustler and will make an excellent newspaper man."[8] Two years later, in 1889, *The Iola Register* encouraged its readers to subscribe to the *Evening News,* and in doing so, noted that it "is not the oldest nor the largest paper in the west, and these facts we think are largely in its favor. It is young in years and for that reason is active, aggressive and fearless. It is small in dimensions... The thirty-two columns...are completely filled with condensed news from which all the chaff and 'slush' is carefully eliminated by experienced writers."[9] If the *Evening News* was in that "active, aggressive and fearless" mold when Fred was there as a reporter, it would appear to have been a perfect fit for him.

Why journalism? Fred's close friend, Charlie Gleed, in his eulogy for Fred in 1917 reminisced:

> My first distinct recollection of him was when he consulted me as to what his life work should be. I was then a member of the board of regents of the University, and I must have acquired some knowledge of his capabilities—some opinion as to what his temperament and his talent indicated that he ought to do. I remember I assured him that he could be a lawyer and make a good income. I assured him that his talent for knowing things accurately, for reading diligently and for contending valiantly would insure for him success as a lawyer; but I said to him that I thought his temperament was such as to indicate his desire for a calling less sedentary, something more active, something having about it more change and variety, and I told him I felt sure he could become a journalist of the very highest class. I do not know it to be true, but it is possible that this advice resulted in his trying journalism.[10]

Charlie Scott provided insight into both Fred's abilities and career plans at this time. First, Fred "had a peculiar aptitude" for the newspaper business, and, second, he "firmly believed [that the newspaper business] would be his life work."[11] If Charlie was correct, and he knew Fred well enough at this point in 1887 to know his thinking about his life work, then Fred was a more settled person in his career plans than is frequently believed. As will be noted, after Fred abruptly ended his newspaper job in Fort Smith, Arkansas, it was only because of "[a]nother opening in the newspaper business not appearing immediately..." that he became a railroad employee.[12] If there had been a newspaper opening available, one wonders how differently Fred's life might have been.

Fred's "sit" as an *Evening News* reporter was short, since before the end of the next month, he had accepted employment on the *Tribune* newspaper at Fort Smith, Arkansas. Billy White explained several years later the reasons both for Fred's being hired by the *Evening News* and, then, for his taking the position with the *Tribune*: "He had never been in a city newspaper office, when by force of sheer audacity he struck a Kanas City city editor for a place and got a probational job. Luck brought him a beat which the first day convinced the city editor that Funston was a phenomenal reporter. When a letter came from a man in Fort Smith to the newspaper office asking the city editor to send him a first-class man to take care of a country daily, Funston went. He didn't know any more about a country daily than he knew about the climate of Mars, but he tackled it."[13]

The attraction of the *Tribune* for Fred may have been two-fold. He would be the "local editor" instead of simply a reporter, and Fort Smith was a place of adventure and excitement. *The Lawrence Daily Journal* of October 23 reported: "Fred Funston started for Ft. Smith, Ark., yesterday to accept the position of local editor of the daily *Tribune* of that city. Ft. Smith is a great place for hangings, and clover for newspaper men."[14]

Fred's stay in Fort Smith was brief. There are several stories concerning his activities there, where he also served as a reporter. "His 'beat,'" wrote Charlie Scott, "was the police and other criminal courts, the jails, prisons and hanging yards, and he used to observe that he had more thieves, murderers and other outlaws on his visiting list than any other man in America."[15] A few years later, Charlie Gleed provided the details of Fred's relationship with the notorious Judge Isaac Parker, District Judge for the Western District of Arkansas at Fort Smith, who served twenty-one years until his death in 1896.[16]

> Probably the most important feature of [Fred's] experience in Fort Smith was his close acquaintance with Judge Parker, whose record as a criminal judge has no equal in the history of this country. Judge Parker's special mission was to exterminate crime and criminals in the Indian Territory [now Oklahoma], over which his court had jurisdiction. To this end, in his judicial career of twenty-one years and a half, he condemned to death one hundred and fifty-nine murderers, of whom seventy-eight were hanged, and gave prison sentences in like proportion. Funston reported the proceedings in Judge Parker's court and discussed at great length with the Judge the relations of the United States to the Indian tribes, and to the outlaws from everywhere who took refuge in one way or another among the Indians. In this way he began the study of unusual peo-

ples whose ways are not our ways, and whose habits and customs are incompatible with the civilization of the day.[17]

In Gleed's eulogy for Fred, he characterized the relationship of the two men this way: "Funston and Judge Parker were close friends—at least as close as an elderly judge and a young reporter could be…"[18]

Billy White's account of the Parker-Funston relationship differed significantly from Gleed's: "When the United States District Court met at Fort Smith, Funston started in to take sides in a murder case, and Judge Parker, the famous hanging Judge, who has sentenced over a hundred murderers to death, called Funston into his study one evening, ostensibly to talk about the case in question. The Judge opened the conversation by telling Mr. Funston in confidence, that journalism wasn't his profession, and closed the incident by intimating that the climate of Arkansas was very, very unhealthy at that particular season. Not desiring to go to jail for contempt Funston got out of town on a night train, and the owner of the paper found a new man the next morning."[19] Whatever the relationship may have been, his involvement with Judge Parker was only one part of the story of Fred's brief stay in Fort Smith.

The other part is Fred's actual work as local editor of the *Tribune*. Charlie Scott, about a decade later, recounted what Fred had done one day in the absence of the newspaper's editor, W. S. Murphy: "The Tribune was a hard shell Democratic paper, and in the course of duty its editor went away to attend a state convention, leaving the young man from Kansas in charge. The next day there was a double leaded [sic: headed] leader on the editorial page stating that the Tribune had supported the Democracy of Arkansaw [sic] and Pulaski county [in] the past in spite of its blunders and corruptions and crimes, but that its patience was at last exhausted. It hereby and herewith shook the whole rotten gang, and would give its support hereafter to the Republican party, the party that had sustained the Union, freed the slaves, paid the national debt, etc., etc."[20]

Editor Murphy later told of his reaction when he learned of this editorial reversal by his own newspaper: "One day I was called to Little Rock to attend a consultation of stockholders of the paper. I named Funston to act for me in my absence. I arrived in Little Rock in the morning. Pretty soon came the morning edition of the Times [sic]. Everything in it was familiar except a double headed, two-column editorial headed 'Conscience vs. Coin.' I could scarcely believe myself awake as I read it. The writer, [sic] apologized for the previous course of the paper. He stated that the Times [sic] was and would be henceforth Republican; that it had been Democratic only for the money there was in it and that conscience had outweighed coin in the scales."[21]

Charlie Scott noted, succinctly, what occurred the day the newspaper with its editorial reversal was published: "It was very warm in Ft. Smith all that day." According to one secondary account, the enraged citizens of Fort Smith planned to burn the *Tribune* building, and "[Fred] gathered his staff about him and prepared to defend the place..."[22] Scott continued: "And the day afterward, when the editor returned—having been summoned by wire—there was a vacancy on the Tribune staff. 'I thought likely it might come out that way,' Fred explained to his Kansas friends when he came back, 'but I didn't like the town and I didn't like my boarding house, and I didn't like the job and I thought I might as well let them know I had been there before I quit.'"[23]

Editor Murphy described his actions upon reading the dramatically altered *Tribune*: "I took the next train to Fort Smith, sweating blood. When I reached the office, Funston had gone. He left this note:

'Please accept my resignation. FRED FUNSTON' He was gone; so was the Times [sic]. I never could explain away that editorial. The paper failed."[24]

Fred's stay in Fort Smith had been less than a month. Charlie Scott reported in *The Iola Register* of November 25 that "Fred Funston dropped into town yesterday from Ft. Smith, Arkansas, where he has been doing newspaper work for the past few weeks. The paper on which he was engaged 'defuncted,' hence his return."[25] In view of editor Murphy's independent account and the detail provided by Charlie Scott, I find the *Tribune* episode to be more believable as to why Fred left Fort Smith than Billy White's claim that Judge Parker was responsible for Fred's decision to leave. Of course, possibly Fred and Parker had come to a parting of the ways at the same time as Fred's bombshell editorial, and, if so, then Fred had absolutely no reason to remain in Fort Smith.

Another newspaper job did not immediately appear.[26] Thus, by January of 1888 Fred had begun a one-year stint as a ticket collector on the Santa Fe. *The Iola Register* of January 13 chronicled this new, and different, employment by reprinting the brief notice in *The Lawrence Daily Journal* that "Fred Funston has a position as collector on the Santa Fe."[27] Charlie Scott recalled, years later, Fred's early days as a ticket collector:

> The next job was collector on the Santa Fe. He was still very young [and was "standing very erect and feeling very proud in his new uniform..."[28]] and the braid and brass buttons of his first uniform were very pleasing to his eye. But they caught the eye of an enfant terrible as the train was pulling out of Kansas City one day, and in the dead silence that pervaded the car as the train stopped at the Turkey creek bridge the youngster drawled out, 'Maw look at the little sawed-off conductor!' Fred was sensitive about his five feet three in those days—he has gotten bravely over it since—and besides the pretty girl whose ticket he was about to take, laughed. And he never liked the job very much after that.[29]

"'I could have wrung the brat's neck,' [Fred] said, 'but I didn't; I merely shrunk to my normal size and was properly humble for the rest of the trip.'"[30] Charlie Scott remembered "with what enjoyment" Fred told this story, since "[h]e never spared himself in these recitals, for he never committed the sin of taking himself too seriously."[31]

At least during the month of March of 1888, Fred served as a ticket collector on a passenger train running from Albuquerque, New Mexico, to La Junta, Colorado. A Dr. Metcalf of Colony, the small town a few miles north of the Funston farm, saw Fred when Dr. Metcalf was returning from California. "[Dr. Metcalf] reports Fred having a good position as collector...and as being well and contented."[32] Part of Fred's "contentment" may have originated from the adventures he had as a ticket collector:

> One day a cowboy full of rum became rampageous in his car, and, lying down on his back in the aisle, began to shoot holes in the ceiling. The little conductor kicked the revolver out of his hand, yanked him along the aisle, and threw him off the back platform. The cowboy got up and hurled a piece of ballast, which broke an end window, then started and ran down the track, with Funston in hot pursuit, flinging ballast as he ran, until the fugitive distanced him. By the time he got back to his train, sweating and breathless, half an hour had been dropped on the schedule. The Superintendent made inquiry about it, and the conductor explained.
>
> "It was all right to throw him off," said the Superintendent, "but what did you go and chase him for?"
>
> "I suppose I was mad," said Funston. "Wouldn't you be mad if a man threw a rock through your window?"
>
> "Probably; but don't do it again," said the Superintendent.[33]

Perhaps another version of this story appeared in the little magazine *Pull*, published by a window shade company, shortly after Fred's death. Fred's sister, Ella (Funston) Eckdall, owned a copy, and she not only X'ed the story out, she also wrote next to it "Wrong," "No," "a lie," and "No" (again). This account read as follows: "Funston's first public notice came as a result of his knocking down and disarming a notorious drunken cowboy and afterward chasing him two miles across the Arizona Desert."[34] Perhaps Ella is correct that this account is untrue, but I am not convinced that she is right. We know from Fred's own words that he had "rows" as a train collector. Additionally, I do not believe that Fred would necessarily have told stories, such as this one, to his sister, since she might not have approved of his actions. If Ella had never heard this story from Fred, then she easily would believe that it was "a lie." This is the type of story, if true, that Fred more likely shared with one of his buddies, such as Billy White, Ed Franklin, or V. L. Kellogg.

A second story involved Fred's attempt to collect a ticket from another cowboy. In response to Fred's request, the cowboy pulled his revolver and responded, "I ride on this." Fred's response was laconic: "That's good, that's good." Later, he returned with a large bore-rifle and announced that he had come to "punch that ticket."[35] The cowboy presumably complied.

In January of 1904, *The Saturday Evening Post* magazine carried a story titled "Kansas Fakes" written by a former Kansas City newspaperman, Phillip Eastman. By "fakes" he meant stories that were not true, and he included one about Fred Funston. Charlie Scott quoted the following part of the *Post* article in *The Iola Register*:

When Frederick Funston became prominent the writers were busy hunting up his past career. For a time, events in his life furnished a varied assortment of startling stories. When everything truthful about him had been printed the fakirs [sic] took their turn. The most startling was the tale of how Funston captured a runaway locomotive. This train was being made up at Downs, Osborne county, Kansas, on the Missouri Pacific, for the daily trip to Atchison [Kansas]. The engine that was to pull the train had not been coupled to the coaches. The engineer and fireman left the cab for a few moments. Suddenly the engine gave a puff and started off toward Atchison. The operator at Downs telegraphed to Cawker City, the next station east: "Runaway engine. Throw the derailing switch." Funston "happened" to be in the depot at Cawker. As the operator ran toward the switch he shouted to Funston that a runaway engine was coming from Downs. One hundred [feet?] west of the station was a water tank. Funston ran to the tank, climbed up to where he would be even with the top of the engine, calculated the distance and, when the engine came thundering along, jumped on to the pile of coal in the tender, climbed into the cab, shoved over the throttle, put on the airbrakes and brought the engine to a stop. He was supposed to have said, when it was all over, "It wasn't much. Even if the old kettle had jumped the track I could have got off all right." The Missouri Pacific Company rewarded Funston by issuing him an annual pass, which was renewed each year, in the story. The Missouri Pacific has no record of any runaway engine at Downs nor of Funston having been rewarded, and the oldest inhabitant of Cawker cannot remember that the hero of the story was even in the town.[36]

I find unconvincing Eastman's "proof" that this story is untrue. The fact that the Missouri Pacific did not have a record of a runaway engine or of an annual pass because of Fred's successful involvement, and the fact that the "oldest inhabitant" of Cawker cannot remember that Funston was ever in the town, is weak evidence at best. There is no indication as to what records were checked or whether the account of this runaway engine would have been noted in them. No detail is furnished about the "oldest inhabitant," including whether the "oldest inhabitant" had even lived there in 1888, and thus there is no way to test the veracity of his or her claim that Fred was never in town. In contrast, I find this story highly believable, since it shows Fred's customary nerve, resourcefulness, and modesty ("It wasn't much."). Thus, I accept it as a part of the Fred Funston life story.

When I first read this account of Fred's actions in successfully boarding the runaway train, I immediately thought of the great silent film star Buster Keaton's exploits, in his role as the train engineer Johnnie Gray, in Keaton's masterpiece, "The General." Keaton was only an inch taller than Fred, and like Fred, possessed great physical strength. Interestingly, Buster Keaton was almost a native of Allen County, Kansas, having been born in 1895 seven miles west of Iola in the small town of Piqua, which is located across the county line in Woodson County.

Billy White recounted his version of Fred's railroad days in a lengthy biographical sketch published in *The Saint Louis Republic Magazine Section* of May 21, 1899. In it, White described Fred as a "train bouncer" in his capacity of train collector. "He weighed little more than 100 pounds then, but that didn't stand in the way of his success as a bouncer." White then made this ridiculous assertion: "The record of his grit is still in the clogged Supreme Court of Kansas, where damage suits against the Santa Fe are 'awaiting the judgment day.'" White concluded his brief account of Fred's railroad days with this striking image of the little guy: "And among the greasers and cowboys of New Mexico, Colorado and Western Kansas there is a myth to the effect that the Santa Fe once put a human marmot on its trains, who concealed death in his right hand and lingering illness in his left."[37]

Charlie Gleed, in his eulogy, challenged the idea that Fred had been a conductor for the Santa Fe, describing his role as "cashier." By this, Gleed may mean ticket collector. "Much nonsense has been printed about his work in that line. He was not a 'bouncer.' That work belonged to the conductor in charge of the train. The man who would not pay fare or whose conduct was otherwise improper was designated to the conductor, and he took care of the trouble."[38]

Although Fred may not have been the conductor, by his own words he was, in reality, a bouncer in his role of ticket collector. In upbraiding Billy White for what he had written about him in early 1899, Fred wrote—"And then raking up the old rows of my college and train collector days was bad, awfully bad."[39] Fourteen years later, in 1902, Fred described the significance of his days in the employ of the Santa Fe, and, in the process, confirmed the nature of his railroad duties: "The Santa Fe was a great training school. Punching tickets and ejecting tramps who didn't have the price gave me a physique that stood me in good stead in Cuba and the Philippines."[40]

Fred's remark occurred in conversation with his former co-worker, George T. Nicholson, who had been in charge of the Santa Fe's Kansas lines. Nicholson complimented Fred, saying that one thing he had done "was to bring your train in on time." In response, Fred gave this assessment of his own abilities: "I believe I could take out a train today and run it all right. It's a good business, but I wouldn't like to go back to it; it has its limitations."[41] The newspaper article recounting the conversation described Fred as a conductor, and it would appear that he, indeed, had those responsibilities, if not the title, since, based on his own words and those of his former co-worker, he was in charge of the train. A mere ticket collector would not have been responsible for bringing the train in.

In this same 1902 newspaper article, Fred recounted the experience of one of his novice brakemen:

> There was one brakeman, a new hand, that General Funston had. Some wag had told him that the rear lights, red, on a train should never be shown unless there were more than fifty passengers aboard. Should there be any Chinamen a lantern showing a white light should be suspended from the railing on the last coach. He was told that it was a portion of his duty to count the number of cars and to suspend red lanterns from the rear platform, one for each car, all these signals to be for the guidance of the operators and station agents as the train rushed by, so, if by any chance the dispatchers should want information, the train would not have to stop and report.
>
> The "green" brakeman did as he was told. It is a mystery how the train was allowed to leave the depot yards, but it was not long before operators along the road began to wonder. At the first stopping place Funston, who had been busily collecting fares, received this message:
>
> "What in the devil is the matter? Are you running a train or a rainbow?"
>
> The "green" brakeman turned red when it dawned on him he had been the victim of a joke. He silently stole away and disappeared.[42]

In June of 1888, Fred had a nearly fatal accident when the train he was collecting on was leaving the Kansas town of Marion, which is located near Emporia. "As the 6:30 train pulled out Friday evening Mr.

Funston was standing on the steps of a car and was struck with a trunk which stood on a track close to the train. He fainted and was caught in time by Sheriff Davis and D. F. Myers and prevented from falling under the cars."[43] Once again, Fred Funston's lucky star was with him, as it would be so often throughout his life. On another occasion, Fred fell off the platform of a passenger train on the plains of Colorado. He landed uninjured on the railroad right of way.[44]

As a railroad employee, Fred apparently was based in Kansas City.[45] Two days after Fred's death, *The Kansas City Star* published this interview:

"Remember Fred Funston?" said A. Lindeman, chief usher at the Union Station. "Why, of course I do. We worked together a couple of years at the old station. No, sir, he wasn't at all the kind of fellow in those days you'd think he must have been, judging by what he was afterward. He was a kind of sissy then. Small, you know, anyway, and he was possessed to grow one of those durned little messes of whiskers. Color was sort of dirty straw. I was sorry he did that, for I liked him.

"He was an awful quiet cuss, never had anything to say to most of the fellows. Wasn't popular at all, result of his sissified looks and not having much to say, I guess. Hadn't any nickname then. Nobody paid any attention to him then. He was a collector for the Santa Fe, you know. Assistant collector, I mean. Always would have been if he had stayed, I guess, for he hadn't any ambition. Never saw a fellow with less get-up-and-git to him than Fred Funston had in those days.

"Then he got the idea in his head of starting off somewhere. That was in the spring of '87. He'd come to us in '86, I believe it was. Went off to Alaska first. Then he began to be in this place and that. I sure was surprised to hear of his tearing around so. I remember how taken back Fred's own father was at the boy's waking up. Yes sir, he certainly was a live one when he once got started. Always used to drop in and see me when he was by this way. Always said he was going to write to me. One time he told me to look for a postal from Honolulu from him. Well, it ain't come yet, and I don't expect it now."[46]

That Lindeman and other train workers found Fred to be a quiet cuss tells me that Fred was not close friends with them. Fred was usually quiet and reticent with those that he did not know well, but fully engaged and bubbling with his intimates. As a result, Lindeman would have had no idea as to Fred's ambitions, and, accordingly, underestimated him.

In January of 1889, all ticket collectors were to be taken off of the Santa Fe.[47] The "ticket business" was again to be turned over to the conductors.[48] Perhaps Fred knew before the year of 1888 ended that this would happen, or perhaps he had simply decided that it was time to try academic life again at the State University. Whatever the reason, Fred's days as a collector ended in late November or early December of 1888, when he resigned his position and announced that he would resume his studies after the holidays.[49] He returned home on December 5, after first stopping in Lawrence, probably to see friends there.[50] Shortly before Christmas "Fred Funston dropped in [on Charlie Scott]...for a little chat over old railroad experiences and to order the *Register* sent to him in Lawrence."[51]

Fred's parents and their youngest son, Edward Jr., a 1-year-old baby, were not at home, being in Washington, D.C., in connection with his father's duties as a congressman. The day after Christmas, Fred wrote his mother:

> Dear Ma – I have just recovered from Christmas and will try my hand at writing a letter. Burt came home [from the State University] for his vacation about 3 days ago so the Funston boys are all together now except E. H. F. Jr.
>
> The weather is rather bad now as we had a snow and it is just melting off now and makes it very muddy. Everything is getting along very well about the place. We are going to kill hogs tomorrow.
>
> We got the Christmas presents you sent us and all think them very nice.
>
> There was an entertainment at the church a few nights ago and we all went.
>
> I see considerable change in the people here in the past two years, more than a person would think who has been staying here that time.
>
> Geo Kerr and Mattie Riggs were married a few days ago and are going to live on the Riggs place while the old folks live in town.
>
> Alva Christian shipped some cattle to Chicago last week and managed to lose some money on them.
>
> Burt and I are going up to Lawrence in a week or two. I may not go until a few days after he does. I think of getting glasses for my eyes instead of goggles as I used to wear. They are rather weak but I believe I can get through by being careful with them.
>
> Hope I will hear from you soon.
>
> Your son
Fred Funston[52]

The "entertainment" at the Presbyterian Church in Carlyle was a vocal concert given by the young people of the church on December 18.[53]

Fred had clearly experienced vision difficulties in view of his reference to wearing glasses. This is the only reference I have ever seen to glasses or goggles other than when Fred was in Alaska and wore goggles to protect his eyes from the sun. Perhaps he did not have to wear glasses very long. In any event, Fred's days of adventure in the non-academic world had ended for now, and January of 1889 saw him back in Lawrence as a university student.

Fred Funston, Santa Fe Railway Survey Team, Jetmore, Kansas, June 13, 1887

Chapter Twelve Notes—*Rodman, Rebellious Reporter, and Railroad Ticket Collector*

1. "Personal," *The Lawrence Daily Journal*, October 23, 1887 (reprint in T*he Iola Register*, October 28, 1887).

2. "Funny Tales of Funston," *Denver Post*, September 29, 1902.

3. "Local Matters," T*he Iola Register*, June 10, 1887.

4. "Personal," T*he Iola Register*, June 10, 1887.

5. Major H. H. Llewellyn, "The Santa Fe, Its Men and the Spanish-American War," *Santa Fe Employes' Magazine* (Railway Exchange, Chicago), September 1910 (FFP Micro).

6. Ode C. Nichols, "Funston, From Babyhood to Present Day as His Mother Knows Him," *The World*, May 21, 1899 (FFP). Nichols was from Iola and had served as a lieutenant in Troop M, First Volunteer Cavalry (Rough Riders).

7. "Local Matters," T*he Iola Register*, September 2, 1887.

8. "News Around Town," *The Lawrence Daily Journal*, August 31, 1887.

9. "A Great Offer," T*he Iola Register*, March 22, 1889.

10. C. S. Gleed, eulogy, "Report of Select Committee," *Journal of the House*, Hall of the House of Representatives, Topeka, Kansas, February 26, 1917 (FFP).

11. Charles F. Scott, "Frederick Funston," *The Independent*, April 11, 1901.

12. Scott, "Frederick Funston."

13. William Allen White, "The Hero Of The Philippines," *The Saint Louis Republic Magazine Section*, May 21, 1899.

14. "Personal," *The Lawrence Daily Journal*, October 23, 1887.

15. Scott, "Frederick Funston."

16. Chas. B. Sornborger (Department of Justice Appointment Clerk) to David Potter, May 26, 1932 (FFP Micro).

17. Charles S. Gleed, "Romance and Reality In A Single Life. Gen. Frederick Funston," *The Cosmopolitan Illustrated Monthly Magazine*, July 1899.

18. Gleed, eulogy.

19. White, "The Hero Of The Philippines."

20. Chas. F. Scott, "Remarkable Career of a Kansas Boy," *Mail and Breeze* (about March 20, 1898) (FFP).

21. Ode C. Nichols, "Funston, From Babyhood to Present Day as His Mother Knows Him," *The World*, May 21, 1899 (FFP). Nichols was from Iola and stated that he and Murphy had been in the same troop (Troop M, First Volunteer Cavalry (Rough Riders)), and that Murphy had told him about "a prank played by Funston."

22. Chas. F. Scott, "Remarkable Career of a Kansas Boy," *Mail and Breeze* (about March 20, 1898) (FFP) for Scott's quotation, and "Daring Little Col. Funston," *The New York Times*, April 30, 1899 (reprint from *New York Sun*, April 29, 1899) (FFP) for the secondary account.

23. Scott, "Remarkable Career of a Kansas Boy."

24. Nichols, "Funston."

25. "Local Matters," T*he Iola Register*, November 25, 1887.

26. Scott, "Frederick Funston."

27. "Personal," *The Lawrence Daily Journal*, January 10, 1888 (reprint in *The Iola Register*, January 13, 1888).

28. "Frederick Funston" (editorial), *The Iola Register*, February 24, 1917 (Kansas State Historical Society, *Frederick Funston Clippings*, Vol. 1).

29. Scott, "Remarkable Career of a Kansas Boy."

30. "Frederick Funston" (editorial).

31. "Frederick Funston" (editorial).

32. "Local Matters," *The Iola Register*, March 23, 1888 (reprint from *Colony Free Press*).

33. "Daring Little Col. Funston," *The New York Times*, April 30, 1899 (reprint from *New York Sun*, April 29, 1899) (FFP).

34. "The Story of General Funston," *Pull* (The Western Shade Cloth Co., 1917), Vol. I, No. 6 (April 1917). A photocopy of Ella Eckdall's copy is at the Allen County Historical Society, Inc.

35. David Hinshaw, *A Man From Kansas: The Story of William Allen White* (New York: G.P. Putnam's Sons, 1945), 38.

36. "Fake Stories from Kansas," *The Iola Register*, January 15, 1904.

37. White, "The Hero Of The Philippines."

38. Gleed, eulogy.

39. Fred Funston to William Allen White, San Fernando, Luzon, Philippines, July 1, 1899 (FFP Micro).

40. "Funny Tales of Funston," *Denver Post*, September 29, 1902.

41. "Funny Tales of Funston."

42. "Funny Tales of Funston."

43. *Cottonwood Valley Times,* Marion, Kansas, June 21, 1888. Gilson Files containing Frederick Funston materials, Lyon County History Center & Historical Society, Emporia, Kansas.

44. Fred Funston to Charles F. Scott, August 3, 1893 (published in *The Iola Register*, November 10, 1893).

45. "Hotel Arrivals," *Newton Daily Republican*, September 21, 1888. Fred was listed as a guest from Kansas City registered at the Arcade Hotel.

46. "When Funston Was Lazy," *Kansas City Star*, February 21, 1917 (Kansas State Historical Society, *Frederick Funston Clippings*, Vol. 1).

47. Llewellyn, "The Santa Fe, Its Men and the Spanish-American War."

48. "Local Matters," *The Iola Register*, January 11, 1889.

49. "Lawrence News," *Topeka Daily Capital*, December 5, 1888.

50. "House on the Hill," *The Lawrence Daily Journal*, December 5, 1888.

51. "Local Matters," *The Iola Register*, December 28, 1888.

52. Eckdall collection of letters. Allen County Historical Society, Inc.

53. "Local Matters," *The Iola Register*, December 14, 1888 (announcement that the concert will be held December 18).

CHAPTER THIRTEEN

State University Again and Camps Jayhawk and Phi Delt

January 1889 – June 1890

Two of the pleasantest summers of my life were spent roaming through the mountains in the vicinity of Estes Park. I doubt if there is a better place in Colorado to spend the summer.

—General Frederick Funston (1902)[1]

Our crowd is an especially jolly one. Will Franklin and Harry Riggs are both in for fun and Funston keeps the whole crowd laughing most of the time.

—Herbert S. Hadley to J. M. Hadley,
June 26, 1889, Camp Jayhawk[2]

Before leaving for Lawrence to resume his studies, Fred was one of a merry company of ladies and gentlemen who, the evening of January 2, 1889, filled the elegant parlors of the Richards mansion in Iola, the home of a former Iola High School friend, Maude Richards. The twenty-five young men and women enjoyed fruits and confections, music, and dancing.[3] Once back at the State University, Fred resumed academics and the pleasures of his fraternity. The Phi Delts, at the end of January, entertained their many lady friends with card playing, conversation, and dancing. Elaborate refreshments were served about midnight, and then a few hours were spent in "solid amusement."[4] What a night it must have been for the nearly forty present! That spring Fred put his budding journalism skills to use as one of ten assistant editors of one of the student newspapers.[5]

At a Sunday dinner in May 1889, the Franklin brothers, Ed and Will, and Harry Riggs conceived the idea of a summer adventure in Estes Park, Colorado. Will Franklin was confident that a party of seven could live there for two months for $500. The three selected four other young men: Fred Funston, Billy White, V.L. Kellogg, and Cassowary Craig. Of this original gang, all were members of Phi Delta Theta social fraternity except Riggs, who was a member of Phi Gamma Delta. Each put up $75 to cover round trip railroad fare, cabin rent, jackass rent (to "'tote' for us"), subsistence, and photographic supplies. The calculation was correct—$75 each proved to be sufficient.[6]

Incidentally, all seven young men in future years were biographees in *Who's Who in America*, and three of them, the scientist Kellogg, the editor White, and the soldier Funston, were to have ships named for them in World War II: Liberty cargo ships *S.S. Vernon L. Kellogg* and *S.S. William Allen White*, and the *U.S.S. Frederick Funston*, respectively. Fred received additional posthumous recognition: Braniff Airways named one of its big Douglas airliners for him, and a fort and boulevard are his namesakes in his beloved San Francisco. He was the subject of two books written for young boys. As one author observed, "The character of Major General Frederick Funston is one that appeals strongly to the heroic element in every American boy. The 'Little Guy,' as his soldiers affectionately called him, was the personification of daring."[7]

Another party of young men made their own plans and joined the first group: Schuyler Brewster, his younger brother "Willie" Brewster, who had just graduated from Iola High School, Alvin Wilmoth, and Herbert Hadley, who was later Governor of Missouri.[8] Briefly with the party in Colorado was one more K.S.U. man—Amos Plumb, a Phi Delt. Plumb, son of a U.S. Senator from Kansas, made unpalatable biscuits one day for the campers. Funston asked where Plumb had gotten his recipe. He responded that it was from his father's army cookbook. Fred observed, "Well, I understand now why there were so many desertions from the Union army. I always wondered about it."[9] Because of health problems, Plumb was a camping participant for only a short time.[10]

Before leaving for Colorado, White and Kellogg needed to finish earning funds to pay for their roundtrip railroad ticket.[11] Nearly all of the campers, however, left by train from Lawrence headed to Denver on Monday, June 17.[12] The trip was uneventful, except for sighting two wolves and numerous prairie dog towns.[13] Fred made a sartorial impression upon friends who saw him when the party arrived in Denver: "He wore an old slouch hat of his father's, a flannel shirt and a pair of blue overalls, evidently borrowed from the hired man on the farm, which fitted fairly well around the waist but had to be turned up about six inches at the bottom. Serenely unconscious of his clothes, he bore himself with his usual dignified and pompous gait, which always suggests a man six feet tall and weighing 200 pounds."[14]

After a fifteen-cent meal at a lunch counter, the boys took the train to Loveland, Colorado, where they disembarked and walked the thirty-three miles, upgrade, to near Estes Park. This "long tramp" was a great physical challenge. Hadley wrote his father, "I tell you we roughed it in dead earnest during that tramp. I never did have things quite so rough before. But that is what I came for and I am getting it."[15] Hadley also noted: "It was a comical sight to see us on our tramp from Loveland out here and we were taken for a band of Utes by one man."[16] Fred was not yet toughened for the uphill tramp, and another in the party carried Fred's rifle for him the last ten or twelve miles. A night's rest, however, restored him.[17]

Although the camping party was referred to as being in Estes Park, they actually settled in a nearby valley known both as Willow Park and Moraine Park. In the Rocky Mountains, the title "park" is applied to the small, treeless, grassy valleys. Willow Park is about two-and-a-half miles long by three quarters of a mile wide. With an elevation of approximately 8,000 feet, the park is surrounded by mountains, beyond which lies the Snowy Range from which rises Long's Peak, with an elevation of 14,271 feet. Willow Park was owned by a Mr. Sprague who farmed it. Most of his living came, however, from tourists who boarded in his cabins at the Sprague Ranch. Others, like the K.S.U. Phi Delt group, rented a cabin in the valley while the Phi Psi fellows pitched their tent nearby without having to pay a ground rent. "It is a place to go and wear your old clothes and do and look as you please," wrote Charlie Scott, who later built a cottage there.[18]

The adventurers named their site Camp Jayhawk and called themselves the Estes Park Camping out Party.[19] The rented log cabin was 17-feet by 20-feet; unplastered without a ceiling; a good floor; three windows; some chinks between the logs of the walls; plenty of nails in the walls to hang items on; and cracker boxes for cupboards. There were a stove, a pine table, and rough pine chairs.[20] All campers stayed initially in this cabin near the Big Thompson River, but when White and Kellogg arrived on July 3, Hadley and the Brewster brothers moved into the 8-feet by 10-feet tent that they had purchased for $6.50.[21] At $2.20 apiece, the cost was less than that for those who stayed in the cabin. At some point, Alvin Wilmoth arrived at Camp Jayhawk and joined them in the tent. When the boys all lived together in the cabin, they cooked by turns, two by two, and washed dishes based on alphabetical order of the boys' names. Fred was one of the boys who could throw a flapjack toward the roof while swiping the griddle with a greased rag, and then catch the "flapjack with the pasty side down with an ease and airy grace that betrays the professional 'batches' at a glance."[22]

Once both the cabin and tent were in use, each had its own mess. The cabin mess was the Phi Delt mess; the tent mess the Phi Psi mess.[23] All of the tent occupants, except young Willie Brewster, called by his fellow campers Petit Brewster, were members of Phi Kappa Psi social fraternity. There was also a third mess—an all-female one—the Pi Phi mess, named for the social fraternity Pi Beta Phi to which several of the young women belonged, and located in a cabin down the Big Thompson River a mile from the boys' cabin. The Pi Phi cabin was occupied by friends from Lawrence: Mrs. Sutliff and her university student daughters Helen and Jennie; Nellie (Nell) Franklin, the sister of Ed and Will Franklin; and Nellie's friend from Iowa, Eva Fleming.[24] These university boys and girls socialized together, including making mountain-climbing trips.

The next two months were idyllic—fishing, hunting, and mountain climbing. There were only two rules: "every man should clean his own fish and there should be no razor in the camp."[25] The cabin served only as a home camp and starting point for numerous trips into the surrounding mountains and was deserted much of the time. Members of the party slept from fifteen to thirty-two nights away from the base camp, with only blankets for shelter.[26] Trout were plentiful, and quickly caught by various members of the party, except for Billy White, who did not fish. By June 26, Herbert Hadley had caught the most trout to date—twenty-two, and Fred had caught about five.[27] Two weeks later, Hadley's trout catch was a total of 236.[28]

Although an energetic fisherman, Fred was not a skilled one. He had a "great natural awkwardness," according to Hadley. When a trout took Fred's hook, Fred yanked the fish out just like he would yank a catfish back in Kansas. The result was that the trout often landed in the willow branches above his head, and the line became tangled in the trees. More than once, Fred tumbled into the river in his efforts to untangle his line.[29] One day, while fishing alone, Fred climbed the tree in which his trout had landed. According to one of his fellow campers, the tree was unable to support Fred's weight, and he came crashing down, landing with his head on the river bank and his body in the water. Unconscious, he remained there for several hours before awakening to discover his perilous position. "Cold, bruised and weary he dragged himself into camp, where his absence was causing considerable concern."[30]

On one occasion, Fred and one of his friends caught 312 trout in three hours. They accomplished this feat at a place in the Big Thompson River where a short fall formed a pool beneath it. As the fish went upstream, they jumped this fall, with the result that more than a dozen were in the air at the same time. The two boys cleverly used a net, which they attached to an old tennis racquet, to score so many trout. During the summer's outing, according to one of the campers, they caught a total of 6,000 fish, all of which were eaten.[31]

For the 4th of July, the campers, who now included White and Kellogg, obtained a case of beer from Loveland. They "had a great celebration," Hadley wrote his father. "Several good speeches were made. The programme was interspersed with appropriate songs and stories. Altogether we had a fine time."[32] Three or four days later, the young men posed for a photograph with Kellogg and White pretending to be "tight," though no one got tight because there was not enough beer to do so. As Billy White later wrote, "[t]he picture was posed to show that we were hard-boiled young blades."[33] When various members of the group became famous, this photograph was printed in many magazines and newspapers, thus freezing them "as the young devils we were not."[34] The handwritten legend by one of the campers on a copy of this photograph was Les Compagnons Bon Vivants—Eine lustige Gesellschaft. Incidentally, this was the only case of beer in the camp during the two months.[35]

Specimen Mountain, across the main mountain ridge about twenty-five miles from the boys' cabin, was to be the site for one of Fred's most satisfying adventures. The mountain was the home of the Rocky Mountain sheep, a prize for any hunter to bag. Herbert Hadley was the first of the party to do so. As he wrote his father, "I can hardly realize that I have actually killed [a] Wild Rocky Mt. sheep, and that with a shot gun. I remember reading stories when a small boy about how these sheep were killed and how very difficult a task it was. The boys say they believe I was born under a lucky star or in the right quarter of the moon."[36]

Fred had his own lucky star, and on this same outing killed a mountain sheep at the salt lick in the crater of an extinct volcano. He proudly came into camp with the sheep's legs trussed together around his neck and with his "faithful Betsy Jane" rifle over one of his shoulders. Billy White helped Fred clean the sheep. They jerked as much of the meat as possible and took a hind quarter twenty miles back to the cabin. For two days, they cooked it in a big iron kettle in order to soften the meat. One evening, when the pot was boiling and "stinking up the atmosphere," the boys spotted the game wardens a half mile below the cabin by the Big Thompson River. The killing of a mountain sheep was a penitentiary offense, and the boys had prepared for "that awful hour" of potential discovery. Billy White took the pot from the stove, and, lifting up two previously loosened floorboards, lowered the pot under the cabin. He then replaced the floorboards. The air both inside and outside the cabin stank from the fumes of the boiling kettle. The wardens accused the boys; they denied it. The wardens failed to find the concealed pot, "[b]ut it was a tense high half hour when they were looking for that sheep and finally rode away. When they left we had a whooping, howling celebration," Billy remembered many years later.[37]

Fred frequently tramped alone over the mountains. One day, about noon, he was standing on a rocky height when he saw a gaunt mountain lion eyeing him. As the beast leapt for him, Fred discharged his rifle. The lion "quivered a second in midair and landed on Funston's chest, bowling him over to the edge of a precipe [sic]." A brief struggle ensued before Fred fell over the edge, landing on a ledge twelve feet below. He regained consciousness only as the sun was setting. Although weakened by the loss of blood and from the fall, Fred still succeeded in climbing back up to where the struggle had occurred. Covered with bruises, he slowly made his way back to his companions, who presumably were waiting at the cabin. Perhaps for the first time, he was called "Fearless Fred," a popular sobriquet for him during his military career.[38]

Fred was not alone in encountering a beast of the forest. Ed Franklin saw a deer and remained motionless with "buck fever." His companions soon nicknamed him "Buck," and he was thereafter Buck Franklin to them all, including Fred.[39] Herbert Hadley peppered the bottom of a bear cub with bird shot, only to have the cub's enraged mother, with teeth bared and standing on her hind feet, lunge at him. Mama bear chased Hadley through the woods to a steep ledge, from which Hadley jumped down twenty feet. Limping and "paler than a sheet," Hadley made it to the camp, where he promptly fainted. "It was a close call."[40]

In one respect, Fred was, perhaps, an early day conservationist. One day, he took his rifle and chased off sign painters who were desecrating the rocks by painting advertising on them.[41] Unfortunately, the damage was already done, and now, more than a century later, the painted sign "Drink Denver Soda" remains.[42]

Fred was often alone when he set out for a day's hunting or fishing. Elsewhere in this book is a photograph taken of him on one such day. In Billy White's words more than a half century later, "[n]o better picture of Funston anywhere is extant than..." this photo. It shows the bedroll, the tin cup, and Fred's gun, which he always took with him. "It was the only sign or symbol that any of us had of what he was to be," wrote Billy White. Fred's gun was a rifle, which he affectionately called Betsy Jane. White is inconsistent in his assessment of Fred's marksmanship. On one occasion, he described Fred as "not a particularly good shot."[43] In White's *Autobiography*, however, he stated that Fred was "a good rifle shot."[44]

Billy described his friend Timmy as "clumsy but nimble;" walking "swiftly but not too steadily;" and unable "to walk a log across a creek," and thus had "to coon" it. All of this is in White's *Autobiography*.[45] Elsewhere, however, he wrote that Fred's inability to walk a log was because he got dizzy. "But he was intrepid. I never knew a braver man," Billy wrote.[46] Fred's lack of agility would make his friends wonder about some of his later physical exploits, for which he would appear to be incapable. As an example of his lack of agility on the Estes Park outing, when the trail led through a forest of fallen logs, "poor 'Gric' could not jump from one log to the other, but had to clamber painfully down from one and up on the next."[47] One wonders if his short legs played a role in his inability to jump from log to log.

A fun experience for the boys was playing baseball. "We have a ball club in our camp and a fine ball club it is," wrote Herbert Hadley.[48] The "opposing nine were from Hotels in that part of the Park."[49] V.L. was the pitcher, and "Little Brewster, or as he is called Petite," was the catcher. Schuyler Brewster, known as "Brewster major," played third base. Billy and Fred, along with Ed Franklin and Cassowary Craig, were "scattered promiscuously about the field."[50] This is particularly interesting since Billy in his *Autobiography* claimed that both he and Fred did not participate in any athletic sports. That may have been true as far as playing organized ball on campus was concerned, but the above account refutes the absoluteness of Billy's assertion. Fred's own words years later are also relevant. He referred to "those of us who had come to Lawrence with the idea that we would find ample time for baseball, swimming..."[51]

Late in life, William Allen White drafted his autobiography in preliminary form, but died in 1944 before completing the project. The editing of the manuscript was done by others, including Billy White's widow, Sallie White, his son, William Lindsay White, and the editors at The Macmillan Company.[52] Examination of earlier drafts of White's autobiography reveals two stories about Fred Funston not included in the 1946 edition. These earlier drafts also disclose that Billy White included in his account the presence of Mrs. Sutliff, her two daughters and their friends, Nellie Franklin and Eva Fleming, in Estes Park at the same time that the young university men, including White, were there. All of these references to the presence of women that summer have been omitted from the published *Autobiography*, having been edited out prior to publication.[53]

Billy White's first unpublished story about Fred involved a bear encountered a thousand feet above timberline by Fred, Billy, and Ed and Will Franklin. Fred, "swift as a rabbit," chased the bear as it ran down the hill into the timber. Running close behind the bear, Fred thought it had disappeared into a hole under a rock. He promptly dove into the hole. White with fear, the Franklin brothers ran "screaming and cursing at Funston for his temerity," and by each of them pulling on one of Fred's legs, they pulled him out of the bear's presumed cave. Then, they "threw the little devil as far as they could..., damning him and his ancestors to the third and fourth generation for his folly."[54] Fred truly was without fear. In Billy's words, "He didn't know he had done anything particularly brave."[55]

V.L. Kellogg many years later told of a similar encounter with a bear. This time the three men involved were Fred, V. L., and one of the Franklin brothers, likely Ed. The three saw a "rather small bear" on its way toward the mountain summit. The adventurers gave chase, and the bear made it to a nearby rock ridge, where it disappeared. Arriving there, the fellows found the only cave or hole that the bear could have gone into. After waiting fruitlessly for the bear to come out, Fred made the "rather startling proposal" that he would crawl into the hole and stir up the bear, which would then chase him out. When the bear appeared second, it would be shot by the waiting Kellogg and Franklin. V.L. recorded their response: "After careful consideration of this proposition, entirely generous on Funston's part, as one must admit, Franklin and I finally declined it, on the ground that in our excitement we should be almost certain to shoot at the first creature that appeared from the hole, and if this were Funston,—as it probably would be if he came out at all,—and we should hit him, we should have to answer to his parents. As his father was a Congressman, these parents seemed formidable. Also, if Funston, by any rub of the green, did not come out at all, we should have to help the burro carry Funston's pack back to camp. The final vote, therefore, was two to one against the proposal of the future general."[56] Although it seems improbable that Fred would have had in one summer two similar experiences with a disappearing bear, his knack for experiencing the most unlikely adventures apparently happened here.

The second of Billy White's unpublished stories about Fred involved the young university women, the two Sutliff sisters and their friend, Nellie Franklin. White, Fred and two other young men took the "girls" up Long's Peak and camped with them at the timberline overnight. On their way down the mountain the next day, they had been late starting. Eventually, Jennie Sutliff "gave out," and she was placed on the burro, which carried the party's bedding. At midnight, the little group was six miles from the Sutliff cabin and still in the woods when the burro balked and refused to go farther. Jennie was still on board the burro. Beating him; yelling at him; and twisting his tail were all to no avail in getting him to move. The language used in yelling was "chaste and proper," since there were women present.

What was lacking to make the "old devil" move was for Fred to curse him in that "razor edged voice," using all the English obscenity he knew plus a bit of Spanish. A consultation was held by Billy, Fred, V.L. Kellogg, and Franklin (White does not identify which brother), and then they told the girls that the only way to get the burro moving again was for Fred, in his "harrowing voice and indecent language" to verbally blast the burro. It was the girls' turn to hold a long consultation with each other. The upshot was that the girls approved the plan but wanted Fred to speak as softly as possible. Fred went to work, and the burro sullenly moved on down the mountain though the darkness. It was nearly daybreak when the undoubtedly exhausted party arrived at the Sutliff cabin, where Mrs. Sutliff had kept a "frightened vigil" during the night.[57]

One of the original professors at the State University was Francis H. Snow. He was the botany instructor for Fred and the other boys and it was on his behalf Fred and other students at the university went on collecting expeditions for plants and insects. On the first of August Professor Snow arrived from Lawrence to spend a month "botanizing." He wrote his family the next day:

> After a long stage ride of 32 miles (Loveland to Moraine) from 11:30 am [sic] to 8 pm [sic], I was put down at the cabin of the "Kansas boys," as they are now quite widely known in this region. I found them just returned from a ten days trip to "Specimen mountain," and came in upon them with a Rock Chalk, Jay Hawk just as they

had seated themselves to the supper table. Kellogg & Ed. Franklin did not return from this trip with the rest but they will be here to-night. The boys, having lived 10 days on oatmeal + corn-cake, were ravenously hungry. Supper consisted of roast mountain sheep (two of which were killed by Funston and Hadley) fried trout, biscuit + coffee. There is no butter in camp, but milk in abundance. The cake was much enjoyed and I had to unpack my trunk to get it out to round off the supper in becoming style. The boys are strictly enforc-ing the rule of "no razors in camp," and you would be amused to see the different stages in the evolution of beard illustrated by the various members of the party. Will Franklin + Harry Riggs have a patriarchal aspect, Funston Wilmoth + Brewster have a less ad-vanced development, while Hadley, Craig + the younger Brewster exhibit the incipient stages of hirsute adolescence. Hadley's panta-loons have been repaired successfully with cloth of another color but most of the rest exhibit a decided need of repairs in the fundamen-tal portion of their attire. Funston was hard at work with his pants off this forenoon in the act of resealing them, when two young ladies from the Sutliff cabin put in an appearance and he was compelled to suspend operations rather hurriedly. Being the cook today he was however forced to exhibit to them his rent arrearages as he opened the stove door to examine the roasting wild mutton.

I slept last night on the cabin floor with W.S. Franklin for a bedfellow, and found him a very quiet non-calcitrant partner. When Kellogg gets back I will put up the fine new tent I bought in Denver. This is a nice lot of boys. The two Brewsters, Hadley + Wilmoth occupy a tent by themselves and have a separate mess, and I am with the 7 boys in the cabin, messing with them. They take turns as cooks, each of the 7 holding office for one day each week and they will not allow me to share the work, which is good of them. So I can collect at my pleasure. This is a fine locality for botanizing and I hope to make a large collection of plants as well as insects.[58]

A few days later Snow wrote his family again, telling them about at-tending a campfire at Sprague's Ranch, half a mile away, to which the campers were invited. "Our K.S.U. boys and girls entertained the east-ern tourists by singing the round of university songs..." There followed a notable dance in the hotel dining room. Participants included the Sut-liff sisters, Nellie Franklin, Eva Fleming, Fred, V.L., Hadley, Schuyler Brewster, and Will Franklin. "It was a killing sight (and sound) to watch Hadley and Funston attempt the light fantastic with heavy *hob-nailed shoes.* The landlady hastily hunted up some slippers, and Hadley was in his element at once, but Funston's slippers were so large that they kept coming off, when the landlady again came to the rescue by producing a pair of her own garters with which to fasten them on, but one of these broke almost immediately and Funston was obliged to give it up." Professor Snow also noted in his letter that the day before Fred had picked about four quarts of "nice red raspberries, at which occupation he was surprised by a bear which seemed equally surprised and beat a rapid retreat."[59]

By about mid-August it was time to end an idyllic summer and return to Lawrence. In 1906, one member summarized the finale:

At the end of the summer the young Kansans were as lean and hard and brown as Indians, and felt fit for a little detour of 150 miles by way of reaching a railroad station. Over the range, across Middle park, up the Frazer river, across Berthaud pass to Georgetown, and then to Golden, they tramped nonchalantly, recalling with scorn the fact that they had found wearisome the thirty-two miles' walk into the park at the beginning of the summer. The summer had done great things for them physically and deserves, no doubt, some credit in the making of their careers; partly because it gave them a generous draught of vigor then in their early manhood, partly because it begot in them a love of manly outings which has borne fruit in many wholesome vacation trips.[60]

Fred arrived in Lawrence on August 31, and *The Lawrence Daily Journal* duly reported that he and the others had returned from "two months hunting giraff [sic], hippopotomi, wild Injuns and other mountain game..." Fred reported that the party had caught 3,000 trout, 500 grouse, and ptarmigan, a deer, and three mountain sheep. With all of their walking, the boys had averaged 739 miles apiece on foot in Colorado.[61]

This 1889 Estes Park trip was the most famous of several composed of the Kansas State University students. The trip was "a liberal education," remembered Billy White, who believed that "[i]t represented more to me than any other ten weeks in my life—more in the way of stimulation—spiritual, emotional, physical—than anything that ever happened."[62] The two-month experience was equally pivotal for Fred Funston, I believe, since it represented freedom and independence, and thus helped him to decide that formal education no longer was of benefit to him. It was this "thing called independence" that Billy White and Fred Funston had learned from Professor Canfield at the university.[63] Two months of total freedom in Estes Park settled it for Fred, I believe—it was time to move on to the larger world rather than remain in the halls of academia. His mother explained his decision simply: "Fred concluded that it wasn't worth his while to finish his college course. The fact is he wanted to travel, to see wild life and meet adventures."[64] Fred was twenty-four when he left the university at the end of the spring term of 1890. Fifteen years later, in a brief speech to KU students "he remarked that he regretted that he had not pursued his college course until graduation."[65] If he said why he felt this way, it was not reported in the newspaper account of his speech, but a man at nearly forty generally sees life differently than one at twenty-four.

In the meantime, Fred was home to the farm for Christmas holidays, and Charlie Scott reported in *The Iola Register* that Fred would take a trip to South America in February.[66] Charlie's understanding was correct. In January 1890, near the end of the university's academic term, one of the campus student newspapers asked "that pleasant gentleman" about his plans to leave for South America shortly after the close of the term. From an article titled "Fearless Fred," we learn Fred's ambitions in his own words:

> "How long do you intend to stay, and what have you in view"? was the next very modest (?) question.
>
> "Well, it is pretty hard to tell how long I will stay. That will depend a great deal upon circumstances and the course of events. And what have I in view? Well, nothing more than what will turn up. My visit you know is one of pleasure, business and adventure, and should I find any of these things in anything like agreeable quantities, there is no telling when I shall return. I want to see the world and I propose to go if I am compelled to rest a part of my happiness on luck."
>
> And as Fred stopped the *COURIER* wished him an immeasurable amount of it. We also proceeded to the conclusion that fellows as determined and fearless as Fred are not as numerous as they might be.[67]

What could be more free than traveling the world in search of pleasure, business, and adventure? Fred clearly was still in search of his purpose in life, and it is interesting that, in addition to pleasure and adventure, Fred identified the potential aspect of business, meaning a livelihood for himself. Mystifyingly, Fred did not travel to South America, instead staying in school one final term. There appears to be no record explaining why he changed course so abruptly.

Academics and the fraternity presumably were Fred's primary focus that last semester. Described as "one of our most popular students," he attended in early February 1890 a Phi Delt party where dancing was the principal amusement.[68] In April, Fred had a curious experience when he attended a "most interesting and instructive entertainment" given by a local mesmerist and hypnotist. Fred was an audience member who accepted the hypnotist's invitation to sit on the front row and be hypnotized. The hypnotist was "remarkably successful in obtaining influence over several persons," and Fred and another student "were especially susceptible, and their subjection to the suggestion of Mr. Smith was noted with wonder by the audience."[69] One wonders about the details of Fred's hypnotic experience.

On the evening of May 23, Fred attended the Phi Delt's annual spring reception for nearly seventy men and women, which included a supper and dancing.[70] The next day he wrote his mother, informing her of his plans:

Dear Ma,

Can you send to me by express immediately my old blue railroad coat and vest which I left at home after my return from Colo. last summer. Also [sic] I wish you would let me have that blanket again and if you have a [sic] similar other blankets like it send them too.

V.L. Kellogg and I have been employed to get natural history specimens for the University and will be gone about a month. We will leave here about the 6th of June and am not sure yet where we will go. We will have to rough it and sleep out after night so that any blankets will come very handy except yellow bed blankets which are no good.

As soon as we get back I shall come down home on a small visit but will not have time to come down before leaving. Please send me the things right away.

Your Son

Fred Funston

As soon as I know what our address will be I will let you know.[71]

Fred was never again to attend the State University. At some point, he went to see Professor Canfield to tell him goodbye. Canfield had felt that Fred's nature was one "that might be cramped or warped by the methods and restrictions necessary in a university course." Canfield was glad that Fred "undertook to work out his own salvation."

"We had a long talk together about the future," wrote Canfield, "a future which he was facing without very clear ideas about what it contained for him, and without what might be called a definite ambition. In fact, he is a good example of the truth that most men and women find their true places in this world by trying several places. He was in no particular hurry to do any particular thing; but he felt he ought to be up and doing something rather than loitering in what seemed to him a somewhat hungry land of theories and dreams."[72]

Fred and V.L. Kellogg were undoubtedly delighted when they were told that their destination was the Estes Park area, the site of such pleasure the prior summer. They were not to go alone; three other Phi Delts, V.L.'s brother Fred, Jack Schall, and Amos Plumb, joined them. The plan was to "hunt, fish, shoot, and tramp to their hearts' content."[73] Before the group left by train for Colorado on June 4, an unusual incident occurred: "A desperate looking character, attired in a dark flannel shirt, black trousers, a slouch hat, carrying a double-barreled shot gun, and looking like a veritable tough, came into the *JOURNAL-TRIBUNE* office this morning and inquired for the fighting editor. When that personage had mustered courage enough to peep out from his place of concealment he recognized Fred Funston, who had stopped in to bid him good-bye before starting for

Estes Park, Colorado. A pleasant trip, Fred."[74]

After arriving in Willow Park, the five Phi Delt campers settled into the cabin that had been used by the Phi Delts the prior summer. Not surprisingly, they named their abode Camp Phi Delt, and from there, on June 12, V.L. wrote Helen Sutliff. He did not mention his and Fred's job, describing instead more recreational events. V.L. wrote about the burro they had rented: "Timmy and I have put in the forenoon capturing 'Billy the Mule'—we are jubilant over our success in stalking and 'roping' the sad eyed humorist of the mountains and as I sit here in the boys' cabin and gaze with my left eye...on William the Conquered, I gloat, as Mr. White would say, several large and audible gloats." V.L. also wrote about the cabin occupied by Helen and the other women the prior summer: "Le 'Chateau' is quite deserted, and Timmy and I feel lonesome when in its sight." He also noted: "Miss the jeans and bedticking dressed figures a deal," possibly referring by their attire to the young women, including Helen. Perhaps a reflection of Fred's attempting to decide his future was that he and V.L. "think of buying" the nearby Sprague ranch. "We always did have very lively 'thinkers,'" V. L. concluded.[75]

The next day Fred, V.L., and Billy the burro set out for Flat Top Mountain with the plan to work their way northward along the mountain range and ending at the big mountain at the head of Thompson Cañon; "thence down and home."[76] This climb was to prove nearly fatal to the two intrepid adventurers. First, however, was their experience with a mountain lion.

They climbed up into the Great Spruce Forest on the flanks of Flat Top Mountain and Hollet's Peak. V.L. later remembered that they were deer hunting in the hope of varying the camp diet of bacon and trout. They made a hasty camp in the forest the first day, turning Billy the burro loose to nibble on what he found to be edible. The two boys then found in the forest positions they each believed to be advantageous in spotting a deer. After several hours, a "great mountain lion" came silently padding along the trail by which V.L. had posted himself. Just as it disappeared out of V.L.'s sight, the lion emitted "a blood-curdling cry, half-bestial, half-human." V.L. hastened to their camp, only to be surprised to find a "great, roaring fire," on which Fred was piling even more fuel. Fred blurted out, "I have just seen the biggest cougar in Colorado." Protected by this fire, the boys ate supper and then rolled up in their blankets near the fire.

During the night and after the fire had gone down, V.L. was awakened by a blow on his chest, which he surmised was caused by the lion. But it was Fred, who whispered hoarsely, "That cat is prowling around the camp. I have heard it several times. We must build up the fire." This was promptly done, and then the boys fell into an uneasy sleep. V.L. was again awakened by a blow from Fred, who was really excited. "He's still around," he said. "There, you can hear him now." Daylight was just starting to break the darkness, and it became light enough to see Billy the burro grazing on brush a couple of rods away. With great relief, Fred and V.L. "rolled over for a real nap..." as they listened to the "rippling call" of several hermit thrush. "It was the most beautiful, most thrilling bird-song I have ever heard," wrote V.L. many years later. "We lay entranced. And then Funston, sitting up in his blankets to glance around the echoing forest, stretched out again with a grunt of comfort, and murmuring, 'Say, it's damn religious up here,' drew his blankets up to his eyes for the needed nap."[77] The rest of the day was to be one of trial and suffering.

Fred Funston
"No better picture of Funston anywhere is extant... He often set out
alone for a day's hunting or fishing,
accoutered as he is here. Note the
gun, the bedroll, the tin cup."
("Billy" White)

Camp Jayhawk Cabin (L to R) "Billy" White, Frank Craig, V.L. Kellogg,
Fred Funston, "Buck" Franklin, Harry Riggs, Will Franklin

Inside the cabin

4th of July 1889 posed celebration photograph
Left at top: Harry Riggs
Next to him: Frank Craig
(L to R): V. L. Kellogg, "Billy" White, Herbert Hadley, Will Franklin, "Buck" Frankin, Fred Funston, Schuyler Brewster

"Buck" Franklin, Billy the burro, and Fred Funston

Fred Funston and his mountain sheep

Crossing the boulder field. Fred Funston at the end of the procession.

Taken on the brink of the peak of Deer Mountain and "romantically posed"*(L to R):*
"Billy" White, Jennie Sutliff, Harry Riggs, Eva Fleming, Fred Funston, Nell Franklin

State University of Kansas
"as we were when we dressed in our Sunday best in Lawrence, after we had returned
from the mountains." ("Billy" White)
Front row (L to R): Harry Riggs, Professor Francis Snow, V. L. Kellogg, Nell Franklin,
"Billy" White
Back row (L to R): Schuyler Brewster, "Buck" Franklin, Frank Craig, Fred Funston

Enlargement of Fred Funston with his rifle, Betsy Jane

Enlargement of Fred Funston as he appears in the 4th of July 1889 posed photograph. Note the handkerchief protruding from his back pocket.

Chapter Thirteen Notes—*State University Again and Camps Jayhawk and Phi Delt*

1. "Funston in the Mountains of Colorado," *The Denver Times*, May 18, 1902.

2. Herbert S. Hadley to J. M. Hadley, June 26, 1889, from Camp Jawhawk, Colorado (Typescript of Hadley's letters in Herbert S. Hadley Misc in Archives Division, Kansas State Historical Society). Henry E. "Harry" Riggs was the son of Samuel A. Riggs, whom Ed Funston had defeated in the March 1, 1884, election for congress.

3. "Local Matters," *The Iola Register*, January 4, 1889.

4. "Phi Delta Theta," *The University Courier*, February 1, 1889.

5. *University Times*, April 12, 1889, 2

6. Henry E. Riggs, May 24, 1944, note on back of photograph of the original seven men taken in front of their Estes Park cabin (Spencer Research Library, University of Kansas).

7. For Kellogg and White, see Harold J. Henderson, comp. "Ships in World War II Bearing Kansas Names," *Kansas Historical Quarterly*, May 1947, 113; *USS Frederick Funston* (APA-89) (Wikipedia). "General Funston Paid High Honor By Braniff Line," *Wichita Eagle*, January 21, 1939 (Eckdall materials donated in 2004). Allen County Historical Society, Inc.

   Frank Fowler, *The Broncho Rider Boys With Funston at Vera Cruz Or Upholding the Honor of the Stars and Stripes* (New York: A.L. Burt Company, 1916), and Everett T. Tomlinson, *Scouting With General Funston* (New York: Grosset & Dunlap, Publisher, 1917). Quotation in chapter from Tomlinson, v.

   I wonder if Fred would approve the posthumous naming for him of Funston Boulevard in San Francisco. He certainly did not approve of naming a street for him in 1906. "Gen. Frederick Funston is not ambitious of being immortalized by having a San Francisco thoroughfare named after him. Learning that there was a movement afoot to call Devisadero street Funston, the general declared that he had no acquaintance living on that street and not above 30 in the whole city. He thinks the 'project inadvisable on the broad ground that it is not customary to honor living men in this fashion'" ("Funston Is Modest," *Parsons* (Kansas) *Palladium*, November 21, 1906). On reflection, I believe Fred would appreciate the honor of Funston Boulevard but would regard it as a totally unnecessary action.

8. Henry E. Riggs, May 24, 1944. See "The Class of '89," *The Iola Register*, June 7, 1889, for the graduation of "Fred W. Brewster."

9. "Funston In Student Days," unknown newspaper, datelined Lawrence, Kansas, May 13 (probably 1902) (*Frederick Funston: Adventurer, Explorer, and Soldier*) (scrapbook of newspaper clippings, Spencer Research Library, University of Kansas).

10. "Funston in the Mountains of Colorado."

11. William Allen White, *The Autobiography of William Allen White* (New York: The Macmillan Company, 1946), 172.

12. It is not clear as to the names of all men who traveled on June 17, 1889. "Local News Briefs," *The Lawrence Daily Journal*, June 14, 1889; "Local Matters," *The Iola Register*, June 14, 1889; and "Personal," *The Iola Register*, June 21, 1889.

13. Herbert S. Hadley to J. M. Hadley, June 21, 1889, from Moraine, Colorado (Typescript of Hadley's letters in Herbert S. Hadley Misc).

14. "Funston In Student Days," unknown newspaper, datelined Lawrence, Kansas, May 13 (probably 1902) (*Frederick Funston: Adventurer, Explorer, and Soldier*) (scrapbook of newspaper clippings, Spencer Research Library, University of Kansas).

15. Herbert S. Hadley to J. M. Hadley, June 21, 1889, from Moraine, Colorado (Typescript of Hadley's letters in Herbert S. Hadley Misc).

16. Herbert S. Hadley to J. M. Hadley, June 26, 1889, from Camp Jayhawk, Colorado (Typescript of Hadley's letters in Herbert S. Hadley Misc).

17. "Funston In Student Days."

18. [Charles F. Scott,] "A Little Journey," *The Iola Register*, August 30, 1895.

19. Herbert S. Hadley to J. M. Hadley, June 26, 1889, from Camp Jayhawk, Colorado (Typescript of Hadley's letters in Herbert S. Hadley Misc).

20. "When Life Is Worth Living," *The Lawrence Daily Journal*, June 14, 1890. This is a letter dated June 12, 1890, at Camp Phi Delt, Willow Park, Colorado, written by Vernon Kellogg. He described the cabin that the five campers were using that June of 1890, and since it was the same cabin as the one used on the 1889 outing, the description is applicable here.

21. Herbert S. Hadley to J. M. Hadley, June 21, 1889, from Moraine, Colorado (Typescript of Hadley's letters in Herbert S. Hadley Misc). William Allen White letter, December 12, 1942, identifying photographs in a collection of 1889 Estes Park photographs (William Allen White Collection, RH MS 929, Spencer Research Library, University of Kansas).

22. Herbert S. Hadley to J. M. Hadley, June 26, 1889, from Camp Jayhawk, Colorado (Typescript of Hadley's letters in Herbert S. Hadley Misc). The flapjack story is from "When Life Is Worth Living."

23. William Allen White letter, December 12, 1942, identifying photographs in a collection of 1889 Estes Park photographs (William Allen White Collection, RH MS 929, Spencer Research Library, University of Kansas).

24. William Allen White letter, December 12, 1942. Eva Fleming is identified in Francis H. Snow's letter published in the *University Kansan*, September 13, 1889 (see note 59).

25. William Allen White letter, December 12, 1942.

26. "Before They Were Famous," *The Kansas City Star*, July 8, 1906. This was written by an unidentified member of the camping party.

27. Herbert S. Hadley to J. M. Hadley, June 26, 1889, from Camp Jayhawk, Colorado (Typescript of Hadley's letters in Herbert S. Hadley Misc).

28. Herbert S. Hadley to J. M. Hadley, July 13, 1889, from Moraine, Colorado (Typescript of Hadley's letters in Herbert S. Hadley Misc).

29. "Funston In Student Days." The description of Fred having a "great natural awkwardness" is from Herbert S. Hadley to J. M. Hadley, July 13, 1889, from Moraine, Colorado (Typescript of Hadley's letters in Herbert S. Hadley Misc).

30. "Before They Were Famous."

31. "Funston In Student Days." "Before They Were Famous" for the 6,000 fish.

32. Herbert S. Hadley to J. M. Hadley, July 13, 1889, from Moraine, Colorado (Typescript of Hadley's letters in Herbert S. Hadley Misc).

33. William Allen White letter, December 12, 1942.

34. White, *The Autobiography of William Allen White*, 174.

35. "Before They Were Famous."

36. Herbert S. Hadley to J. M. Hadley, August 14, 1889, from Moraine, Colorado (Typescript of Hadley's letters in Herbert S. Hadley Misc).

37. William Allen White's draft of his autobiography, Chapter 24, 9-10 (Papers of William Lindsay White, RH MS268, Box 6, Spencer Research Library, University of Kansas).

38. "Gained Title In Fight With Lion," *Kansas City Journal*, February 25, 1917 (Kansas State Historical Society, *Frederick Funston Clippings*, Vol. 1) This account stated that Fred fired a revolver at the lion, but the only firearm he would have had would have been his constant companion, his rifle. This article recounted stories told by Dr. Ernest F. Robinson, then of Kansas City, who was a university friend of Funston. It is not clear, from the way this article is written, that this story of the lion is one of those stories instead of coming from an unnamed source.

39. Clyde Kenneth Hyder, *Snow of Kansas: The Life of Francis Huntington Snow with Extracts from his Journals and Letters* (Lawrence: University of Kansas Press, 1953), 167.

40. William Allen White's draft of his autobiography, Chapter 24, 9.

41. William Allen White to Paul A. Jones, January 29, 1940 (William Allen White Papers, Container C-359, Library of Congress).

42. James H. Pickering and Nancy P. Thomas, *"If I Ever Grew Up and Became a Man": William Allen White's Moraine Park Years* (Estes Park, Colorado: The Estes Park Museum Friends & Foundation, Inc. Press, 2010), 19.

43. William Allen White letter, December 12, 1942.

44. White, *The Autobiography of William Allen White*, 142.

45. White, *The Autobiography of William Allen White*, 142, 173.

46. William Allen White letter, December 12, 1942.

47. "Funston In Student Days."

48. Herbert S. Hadley to J. M. Hadley, July 21, 1889, from Moraine, Colorado (Typescript of Hadley's letters in Herbert S. Hadley Misc).

49. Herbert S. Hadley to J. M. Hadley, July 19, 1889, from Moraine, Colorado (Typescript of Hadley's letters in Herbert S. Hadley Misc).

50. Herbert S. Hadley to J. M. Hadley, July 21, 1889, from Moraine, Colorado (Typescript of Hadley's letters in Herbert S. Hadley Misc).

51. White, *The Autobiography of William Allen White*, 142, 168. See Chapter Eleven for "General Funston's Reminiscences of the University."

52. Sally Foreman Griffith, ed., *The Autobiography of William Allen White* (Lawrence: University Press of Kansas, 1990), xix.

53. These earlier drafts are at Kenneth Spencer Research Library at the University of Kansas, and at the William Allen White Memorial Library at Emporia State University. The Spencer copies of these drafts have been used in writing this chapter.

54. William Allen White's draft of his autobiography, Chapter 24, 8.

55. William Allen White to Paul A. Jones, January 29, 1940 (William Allen White Papers, Container C-359, Library of Congress).

56. Vernon Kellogg, "Mountaineering in America," *The Atlantic Monthly*, October 1921.

57. William Allen White's draft of his autobiography, Chapter 24, 13.

58. Charles S. Gleed in his "Romance and Reality In A Single Life. Gen. Frederick Funston" is the source that Funston participated in many of Snow's collecting expeditions. It is my speculation that Fred's collecting was of both plants and insects, two of Snow's favorite collecting subjects for the natural history collections of the university. As to Snow's letter, Francis H. Snow to his family, Estes Park, Colorado, August 2, 1889 (Snow correspondence at Spencer Research Library, University of Kansas).

59. Francis H. Snow to his family, Estes Park, Colorado, date of letter not disclosed in reprint in *University Kansan*, September 13, 1889.

60. "Before They Were Famous."

61. "K.S.U. In Colorado," *The Lawrence Daily Journal*, September 1, 1889.

62. William Allen White letter, December 12, 1942.

63. William Allen White to Paul A. Jones, January 29, 1940.

64. Ode C. Nichols, "Funston, From Babyhood to Present Day as His Mother Knows Him," *The World*, May 21, 1899 (FFP). Nichols was from Iola and had served as a lieutenant in Troop M, First Volunteer Cavalry (Rough Riders).

65. "University of Kansas," *The Lawrence Daily Journal*, March 23, 1905.

66. "Local Matters," *The Iola Register*, December 27, 1889.

67. "Fearless Fred," *The Weekly University Courier*, January 17, 1890. *The Lawrence City Directory And Douglas County Gazetteer 1890-91*, 74, shows that Fred roomed at 1325 Kentucky. Likely, he was there also in 1889.

68. "Personal Mention," *The University Kansan*, December 6, 1889. "Phi Delta Theta," *The Lawrence Daily Journal*, February 9, 1890.

69. "Hypnotisni [sic] and Fun," *The Lawrence Daily Journal*, April 12, 1890.

70. "Phi Delta Theta," *The Lawrence Daily Journal*, May 24, 1890.

71. Eckdall collection of letters. Allen County Historical Society, Inc.

72. James H. Canfield, "Funston: A Product of Kansas," *The American Monthly Review of Reviews*, May 1901, 577.

73. "City News In Brief," *The Lawrence Daily Journal*, June 4, 1890.

74. "City News In Brief," *The Lawrence Daily Journal*, June 4, 1890.

75. Letter, From Kellogg, Vernon Lyman, To: Miss Sutliff, Moraine, Colo, Re: The Moraine, Larimer County, 1890 June 12, William Allen White Collection, Special Collections and Archives, Emporia State University, Emporia, Kansas.

76. Letter, From Kellogg, Vernon Lyman, To: Miss Sutliff, Moraine, Colo, Re: The Moraine, Larimer County, 1890 June 12.

77. Vernon Kellogg, "Mountaineering In America," *The Atlantic Monthly*, October 1921. Kellogg did not identify whether this occurred on the 1889 or 1890 expedition. Funston answered this question in his 1891 article, "Storm Bound above the Clouds," which pertains to the 1890 expedition. There, he referred to the night being passed in "a state of mild terror" caused by a mountain lion which prowled about their camp and was kept away by a blazing fire. Fred did not disclose in this article that, in reality, the prowler proved to be the burro, Billy.

CHAPTER FOURTEEN

"Storm Bound above the Clouds"

by **Frederick Funston**

June 1890
[Published in the July 1891 issue of *St. Nicholas Magazine*]

Extending north from Long's Peak, in Colorado, the Front Range or Continental Divide comprises a chain of stupendous peaks reaching into the clouds, and covered even in summer with great fields of snow and ice. This range, cut up by gorges and chasms thousands of feet in depth, which reach into it from the valleys on both sides, presents views of rugged grandeur excelled by none in the entire Rocky Mountain region. Many have compared them favorably with the world-famed glories of the Alps and Caucasus.

Below "timber-line," which in this region is at about eleven thousand feet elevation, the sides of the mountains are covered with a dense growth of spruce, which gives way in the lower valleys to the yellow-pine and quaking-ash. These grand forests have never been ravaged by fires nor marred by the woodman's ax; and in their gloomy depths the mule-deer, mountain-lion, and cinnamon-bear roam undisturbed by fear of man.

Above timber-line the mountains rise from two to three thousand feet more—in some places gentle slopes covered with huge granite boulders, and in others cliffs and crags rising almost sheer for hundreds of feet. Here and there are masses of hard packed snow, while in a sheltered spot on the south side of some cliff grow tiny alpine flowers and dwarf grasses—the food of the wary big-horn sheep, which still frequent this range in considerable numbers.

Comparatively few persons have explored these, the grandest of all the Rockies. Distance from railroads and the total absence of the precious metals have left the range uninhabited, the nearest settlers being the scattered ranchmen in Estes Park.

But few tourists have had the hardihood to scale the great peaks of this chain and risk life by exposure to the storms which almost constantly sweep them; though notably one, Mr. Frederick H. Chapin of Hartford, Conn., spent several summers in this region, and has given us his experiences in a charming book.*

Great peaks thirteen thousand feet in height have never been scaled, dark chasms and gorges are yet unexplored, and mountains higher than Mount Katahdin piled upon Mount Washington have never been deemed worthy of a name.

It was only a few years ago that the writer and a single companion, Mr. V. L. Kellogg, now an associate professor in the University of Kansas, stood on the summit of Table Mountain, a great elevation about six miles north of Long's Peak. Gazing down into the awful gorge which separates the mountain we were on from Stone's Peak, we marveled at its awful depths and precipitous sides, and resolved some day to explore it together, and to follow to its source the turbulent little stream that flowed at the bottom.

The wished-for opportunity came sooner than we dared to hope, and May [sic: June], 1890, found us again in Estes Park prepared to attack the Front Range.

The winter of 1889-90 will be long remembered by the inhabitants of the Rocky Mountain region for its great severity and unusual snowfall. The mild spring sunshine had made little impression on the great drifts which covered the mountains and filled the upper forests; and gazing on them from the valley on a bright May [sic: June] morning, it seemed to us that mountains had never looked grander. Long's Peak, rearing his great cap fourteen thousand three hundred feet in air, was a mass of immaculate glittering white, broken only by the black cliff on the northeast front; the perfect cone of Mount Hallett was as white as the drifting cloud through which it peered; while Stone's Peak, a beautiful mountain thirteen thousand eight hundred feet in height, showed not a speck of brown through its wintry covering.

Despite the arctic surroundings, Kellogg and I determined to explore the great chasm without delay, though the old stage-driver to whom we broached our project shook his head ominously and said:

"Boys, wait until the sun has hammered that snow for six weeks longer; even then it won't be any picnic."

But we were not to be scared out by a little snow. We had roamed over those mountains before, and more than once had been brought face to face with death by exposure or starvation but had always come out with little harm.

We soon procured the obstinate, mouse-colored little mule that had carried our packs on previous occasions; put "on board" blankets, cooking utensils, and three days' provisions, and immediately after dinner set out on an expedition, the recollection of which, as I look back on it, seems more a horrible nightmare than a reality.

It is needless to tell the story of the first afternoon's tramp—of the fruitless efforts of "Billy," the burro, to throw off his pack, and his almost

---

*Mountaineering in Colorado. University Press, Cambridge, 1889.

human shamming of lameness when the steep ascent began.

Suffice it to say that for six long hours we plodded up the lonely trail and, just before the daylight began to fade, found a suitable camping place among the dense spruces near the entrance to the great chasm which was to be the scene of the next day's trials and sufferings.

The night was passed in a state of mild terror, caused by the presence of a mountain-lion, which prowled about camp for several hours, and was kept at a safe distance only by a blazing fire.

The next morning, at five o'clock, we crawled out of our blankets, and an hour later resumed the journey, leaving Billy to watch the camp and meditate upon the follies of his past life. With no encumbrance but our guns, we made good progress, and soon reached the entrance of the gorge, and for two hours followed up the little rivulet at the bottom. It was a weird, uncanny place. The growth of spruce was so dense that it seemed the damp, mossy ground could never have had a good look at the sunlight.

Here and there we passed little banks of last winter's snow, and soon crossed the base of a great field which we could see extended up the sloping sides of Table Mountain almost to the summit. Of this snow-field more anon.

Onward and upward we pushed, crossing and recrossing the noisy little stream, now and then walking over the crust of a big snow-drift, and occasionally falling in waist-deep when we came to a soft place.

As we ascended, the gorge narrowed to about three hundred yards and the sides became much steeper. The spruce-trees here were dwarfed and gnarled old fellows that had battled bravely for years against the snow and ice of their storm-beaten home, and had not yet given up the struggle. We were now only a short distance below timber-line, and a few hundred feet above us not a green sprig showed above the glittering white of the snow or the somber brown of the granite.

A little higher we followed the bottom of the gorge; but there were now no rocks to walk on, nothing but snow from ten to twenty feet deep—acres and acres of it. The direct rays of the sun, which was now high in the heavens, had softened the crust, and we broke through at nearly every step.

The fatigue of floundering through the snow, together with the rarity of the atmosphere, for we were now eleven thousand feet up, was beginning to tell on our strength. We determined to leave the gorge and push up to the left on the sides of Table Mountain, where we judged, and, as it proved, correctly, that the crust of the snow would be stronger.

A sharp, hard struggle of ten minutes brought us above the stunted growth at timber-line, where we sat down to recover wind and strength, and eat our noon lunch.

Up to this time not a cloud had crossed the sky; but now, as we looked toward Stone's Peak, Kellogg called my attention to a feathery, foamy mass which had rolled up over the range and, dropping almost to a level with us, scudded down the chasm before the rising wind. It was an ominous sign, and we finished our meal in nervous haste. Presently another and larger cloud came boiling over the pass at the head of the chasm, and followed closely in its leader's wake. For only a moment we watched the dark shadows they cast moving over the spruce forest, and rose to our feet just as two more clouds came over into the gorge.

The wind, which had been rising for an hour, moaned and whistled among the crags; and the mutterings of distant thunder could be heard from the west side of the range.

By this time, though little had been said, both realized full well the meaning of this turmoil: we were to be caught among the clouds in a mountain storm.

There was no further thought of exploring the gorge. All our strength and time must now be used in reaching camp.

Should we go down into the gorge and get out the way we had come in, or should we go farther up and avoid the tangle of fallen trees and the treacherous drifts below? Higher up on the mountain the snow was packed harder and would afford better footing; and that way we started without delay, our object being to work around the north side of the mountain and reach the old trail on the east side. Up and up we scrambled over the snow and rocks.

The wind was now blowing a terrific gale, and above us, below us, and around us, the clouds were being driven before it.

The storm was gathering over the whole range. Mummy Mountain and Hague's Peak, fifteen miles away, were enveloped in a mass of gray mist; while the thunder boomed and rolled over Estes Park from a black cloud which was deluging the lower valleys with rain. Stone's Peak, looming up through an occasional rift in the clouds, was a sight of awe-inspiring grandeur.

Despite the difficulties of the way and the surrounding storm, we made good progress upward, and in half an hour turned to the left and began working along the side of the mountain.

Here our trials began in earnest. The storm was upon us in all its fury. The wind blew almost a hurricane, and the air was so filled with sleet and fine snow that it was impossible to see more than twenty yards in any direction. There would be an occasional lull in the tumult, when we could take in our surroundings for a moment, but another cloud would envelop us and fill the air with driving torrents of frozen mist.

Hour after hour we struggled on with the nervous, frantic energy born of desperation.

The rocks and snow were covered with ice thin as tissue paper, which caused many a hard fall, and made every step a source of peril. The force of the wind, too, threw us down continually, and we were bruised from head to foot. If we had carried steel-pointed poles instead of guns, they would have been of great service; the latter were now as much hindrance as help, though we were soon to find them useful.

Our hands and faces suffered terribly from the bitter cold, and the former were so numb that we dropped our guns repeatedly. Hair and clothing were matted with ice like a coat of mail. We realized that our progress was very slow, as we had not yet reached the great snow-field extending from timber-line to the summit, the base of which we had crossed in ascending the gorge. On and on we staggered, feeling our way over the slippery surface, and becoming weaker every moment from the hard struggle in the rarefied air of the mountain tops.

While stumbling over a mass of ice-covered boulders, I heard an excited exclamation and, looking up, saw Kellogg sink down behind a rock which afforded a slight shelter from the icy blast.

When I reached him he looked up and said, "Old boy, this is the worst box we were ever in. I guess we're at the end of our rope!" Both realized that the situation was desperate, almost hopeless. There was no sign of abatement of the storm, and weakened and enfeebled as we were by the long struggle, if we should not be able to cross the steep snowfield when we reached it, death from exhaustion and exposure would be a matter of only a few hours.

We dreaded to think of that snow-field, remembering how steep it had looked as we gazed upward from the bottom that morning, and knowing the condition it must be in now with the newly formed ice on the surface. However, it was thought best to rest a short time, and I lay down by Kellogg.

After a rest of about fifteen minutes we resumed the struggle, weak as before and much colder; but we had recovered our wind, a hard thing to keep at this altitude.

It was now four o'clock—ten hours since we left camp, and four since the struggle with the storm began. The battle for life could not last much longer.

Slowly and painfully we pushed forward, crawling on all-fours most of the time. I chewed savagely on a piece of tough grouse, the only remains of our dinner.

Would we ever reach the snow-field? A horrible thought crossed my mind. What if we had lost the direction and were going the wrong way? I did not mention my fears to Kellogg. What was the use?

Every few moments we sank down on our faces to recover our breath. At such times I found my mind wandering and could not think clearly. Kellogg made several remarks without any particular meaning, and his face had a vacant, sullen look. Almost the last ray of hope was gone. There was no complaining, no whining, only a sort of mad desperation which made us resolve to keep moving to the last.

Finally, through a rift in the clouds not fifty yards ahead, we saw the spotless white of the long-looked-for snow-field.

With a feeble shout we pushed forward, but when we reached its edge our worst fears were realized. It was terribly steep, being at an angle of about forty degrees, and the crust was a coating of hard, slippery ice, the thickness of pasteboard. Through a break in the clouds we saw that it extended downward to timber-line, fully 1500 feet, as steep as the roof of a house and smoother than the smoothest glass. How broad it was we could only conjecture.

As we came up, Kellogg struck the crust with the butt of his gun, and I threw a rock upon the surface, which went sliding and bounding down the steep face with terrific velocity.

We looked at each other in despair. "It's no use," I said.

"Not a bit," was the answer.

We sat down and talked it over. To retrace our steps was out of the question, and we could not climb to the top of the field, probably a thousand feet, in our weakened condition.

Suddenly Kellogg leaped to his feet and rushed toward the slippery mass, crying out, "Come on, we've got to do it. I'll take mine this way." Without a second thought, in my hopeless desperation I followed. By using his gun as a brace Kellogg kept his feet; but I slipped and fell on all-fours and began sliding down. In a wild frenzy I tried to drive my bare fingers through the crust, but only succeeded in tearing the skin off them.

Luckily, I had retained my rifle, and by a frantic effort drove it muzzle first through the hard crust and came to a stop, having gone about twenty feet. Had it not been for this fortunate move my body would have been hurled to the bottom of the gorge more than a thousand feet below, and mangled beyond all semblance of human form.

Looking up at my companion I saw that he had turned away his head, unwilling to be a witness of my horrible fate; but as I called out to him he looked around, and I saw a face so white and horror-stricken that I can never forget it. Cold beads of sweat stood on my forehead, and I felt that my courage was all gone. The experience of that awful moment almost unnerved me, and I was weak and helpless as a little child.

Lying on my face I held on tightly to the rifle driven deep through the crust. How to regain my footing was a puzzle. Kellogg started to come down to me, and it was with difficulty that I persuaded him to desist.

At last I hit on a plan. Holding on to the rifle with one hand, with the other I drew my pocket-knife, and, opening it with my teeth, cut two holes in the crust for my feet, and after much effort stood upright. But we were still in a bad fix. Kellogg called out to me to break holes through the crust for my feet with the butt of the gun. Although not more than twenty feet distant he could hardly make himself heard above the roar of the storm.

But the suggestion was a good one and proved our salvation. We moved slowly forward, breaking a hole in the ice for each step. It was severe treatment to give valuable guns, but they had to suffer in the best interests of their owners.

Slowly and carefully we moved forward, occasionally stopping to rest and speak words of encouragement to each other, for now we had the first gleam of hope for five long, terrible hours.

Although very weak physically, our minds were much clearer than an hour before, and we even went so far as to chaff each other a little. But we had plenty of fears yet. Once my heart leaped as Kellogg slipped and came down on both knees, clawing frantically at the air; but he regained his feet without difficulty, and we pushed on. Would we ever get across? Every minute seemed an hour.

Kellogg said that, as nearly as he could calculate, we had been floundering about on that man-trap for a week!

But we kept going; the end must come some time, and sure enough it did; and at six o'clock we stepped on the granite boulders again, having been just one hour and ten minutes on that terrible, inclined snow-field. Neither of us was much given to demonstration, but there was a hearty hand-shake and a few things said which sounded all right up there, but might look a little foolish in print.

The wind had moderated, and the clouds had now settled far below us, while the sun, nearly down, lighted up the surrounding mountains and snow-fields with a sort of radiant glory. But the grandest picture was in the east: Below us, over the spruce forest, over Willow Park, and far away Estes Park, was a tossing, rolling ocean of foamy clouds, their upper sides glistening in creamy and golden light from the rays of the setting sun. To the right the great mass of Long's Peak and the shattered crags of Lily Mountain towered above the burnished sea.

It was a grand picture—such as only those who have the hardihood to climb the highest mountains can hope to look upon. Any attempt of art to imitate them can be but mere mockery.

But it was not to last long. The clouds drifted off over the foot-hills, and there were none to take their places; and then we saw, far below, the world that we had almost given up forever; and as we stood there it looked to us grander than any picture of sun-burnished clouds and snow-covered peaks. We were glad to have another chance at it. But we were not there yet. After a good rest we started again just as the sun was sinking below the horizon.

Compared with what we had been in before, the walking was good, though a discriminating person would not have preferred it to asphalt pavement.

Just as darkness was setting over the range we reached the head of the trail at timber-line. Here, there was some more hard floundering through snow-drifts and plenty of falling over prostrate tree-trunks. But we soon left behind the last snow-drift and ice-covered boulder, and hurried through the forest down the trail—easy to keep even in the darkness. Once we heard the long-drawn scream of a mountain-lion, but only slipped cartridges into our guns and kept on. We were in no mood now to be frightened by such small fry as a mountain-lion.

Finally, at nine o'clock, weary, hungry, and bruised, we staggered into the camp that we had left fifteen hours before—a terrible day in which we had more real experience than many people get in a lifetime.

Our great equine freak, Billy, was on the alert, and greeted us with such a series of whinnies that we feared he was trying something new in solos.

We built a fire and prepared supper with the usual accessory of strong coffee, and at eleven o'clock were asleep under wet blankets. But it was a glorious sleep, and when the sunshine woke us the next morning we felt greatly refreshed, though still very weak and stiff.

After breakfast we repacked the burro, and started for camp in Estes Park. Billy did not need any urging now and showed great enthusiasm in jumping over fallen trees; so much, in fact, that he threw himself down continually.

At eleven o'clock we reached camp, and spent the next few days in resting and eating with commendable energy.

We determined hereafter to heed the advice of the old stage-driver and "let the sun hammer that snow six weeks longer" before we tried any more mountain climbing.

For my own part, I am willing to let him hammer it six centuries longer before repeating that experience.

CHAPTER FIFTEEN

Collecting Native Grass Seeds of North Dakota: A Warm-up for Death Valley

August 14, 1890 – November 13, 1890

His mission here is to supervise the collection of all species of native grasses for the department.

—*Grand Forks Herald*, August 19, 1890[1]

After returning home on June 28 from his several week Colorado outing, Fred appeared to have settled on a career. His editor friend, Charlie Scott, duly reported the news to his *Iola Register* readers: "He has decided to adopt journalism as his profession, and will probably find his first job on the Hutchinson *News*. Fred. is eminently fitted for newspaper work, being a close observer, a ready and picturesque writer, having a level head and capacity for eighteen hours work a day. We are glad he is going into the business and predict for him gratifying success."[2]

Six weeks later, Fred was on his way to North Dakota as a special agent for the United States Department of Agriculture. Why the abrupt change of career? No written record appears to exist explaining his decision, but one suspects that Fred's restlessness and desire for adventure triumphed over the more confining life of a journalist bound to one town. Earlier in that year of 1890, Fred's father was named Chairman of the Committee on Agriculture of the House of Representatives.[3] According to Charlie Scott, the congressman secured for his son a place in a party to be sent by the Department of Agriculture to gather grasses in Dakota for scientific purposes. Also according to Charlie, this was "the only position" that Fred ever held due to "influence" rather than proven merit.[4]

On August 14, Fred began his employment with the Department of Agriculture. It was a short-term employment, since it lasted only three months. His salary was $100 per month. He received payment for both salary and expenses for August 14-31 in the amount of $81.51; for September he received $126; for October, $141; and $42.30 for only salary for his final days, November 1-13.[5]

The geographical extent of Fred's mission has been incorrectly described in the past. Steele in his *Official History of the Operations of the Twentieth Kansas Infantry* mistakenly identified Fred's collector partner, Dr. William Patten, as a professor of natural history at the University of South Dakota, and claimed that the collecting of wild grasses was done in that state.[6] In reality, Patten was a professor in North Dakota at Grand Forks, and North Dakota was the state of collecting, not Montana, as claimed by some sources.[7]

Fred's arrival in Grand Forks as a special agent for the U. S. Department of Agriculture was noted in the local newspaper on August 19. His mission, according to the article, was to "supervise the collecting of all species of native grasses..."[8] Presumably, Fred went to Grand Forks to meet Professor Patten who was also a special agent of the Department of Agriculture. At a salary of $150 per month, he had a two-month appointment lasting from August 14 to October 13. Fred and Patten "were commissioned to make a collection of the grass seeds in the State of North Dakota, to be used in experiments carried on by the Department of Agriculture at Garden City, Kans., and at other points."[9]

Fred and Patten worked with C. B. Waldron, an arboriculturalist at the North Dakota Agricultural Experiment Station in Fargo. The station had been established pursuant to an 1887 act of Congress, which had become effective in North Dakota with the required assent of the Legislative Assembly of North Dakota on March 8, 1890. The station's purpose was to conduct experiments in agriculture for the benefit of the farming community.[10]

On July 17, Professor Waldron "began the collecting and classifying of portions of the local flora under an engagement with the station authorities."[11] Special attention in collecting and classifying was "given to the native grasses and to the weeds likely to prove injurious..."[12] This collecting of native grasses by the station continued for the next two years. During that first year of 1890, special agents Fred Funston and William Patten collected native grass seeds for the Department of Agriculture, while their companion, Waldron, collected native grasses for his experiment station. Waldron reported the areas where he collected. These are likely the areas where Funston and Patten also did their work as the party traveled on horseback or in wagons.[13] These areas were in the Red River Valley on the eastern side of North Dakota, where both Grand Forks and Fargo are located; in the vicinity of Devil's Lake in northeastern North Dakota; the Turtle Mountain region in north central North Dakota; and the Missouri River Valley north of Bismarck, North Dakota.[14]

The arrival of the three men in Bismarck was noted in the local press on October 10 under the heading "Hunting for Specimens." "The midnight train brought a trio of distinguished gentlemen to the capital." The article identified by name and place of work the two professors as well as "Fred Funston, special agent of the department at Washington." Professor Patten, however, was not identified as also a special agent for the department. They "are now in the city, and their mission is to gather seeds of the native grasses for experimental purposes and to collect specimens of animal and vegetable life on the slope." This claimed latter part of the mission was not correct, at least in the case of Fred and Patten, who gathered only seeds. "They will remain in the city a week or more and will make a thorough inspection of the country."[15]

Although Waldron may have made a "thorough inspection of the country," neither of the special agents could have done so. Patten's employment ended on October 13, three days after the news article appeared. On October 18, eight days after the article, Fred was back home on the Funston farm. *The Iola Register* noted his return "from North Dakota where he has been gathering specimens of indigenous grass seeds under the direction of the Department of Agriculture."[16] Fred's first three months of employment by the U. S. Department of Agriculture officially ended soon thereafter on November 13. What he did in the interim between his return to the farm and the end of his employment is unknown.

A few days later, Fred had the opportunity to gainfully employ his skills as a journalist. In mid-November, Charlie Scott traveled from Iola to Oklahoma Territory to visit his brothers, leaving Fred in charge of *The Iola Register* for the weekly issue of Friday, November 21.[17] In that issue, Fred reviewed the second and third nights of the entertainment at the Opera House furnished by the Library Association and the Ladies Cornet Band. The program was "of the very best quality," he wrote. The second evening, "[a] tableau, 'The President's Cabinet in 1990,' showed how things will be done in Washington when female suffrage spreads its pall over a once peaceful land." The third evening's presentation of this same tableau closed the program by showing the husbands of the cabinet of 1990. "Take it all in all, the entertainment was a great success...," and the two organizations split the net proceeds of $95.60.

Fred continued his review with this criticism:

> The only drawback to a thorough enjoyment of the entertainment at the Opera House last week was the whistling, yelling and caterwauling of a lot of fresh youths at the close of every number of the program. Iola is afflicted with a lot of boys who in their efforts to be bold, bad men before they are out of knee pants, are in the habit of making a holy show of themselves on every public occasion. This is becoming very monotonous. People are not saying much but they are thinking a great deal. We have a very promising field for a little efficient home missionary work with a rawhide and a ball bat, and if it were carefully worked over there would be a few more people grow up to manhood knowing that there is a very appreciable difference between an opera house and a race track.[18]

Another example of Fred's sense of humor appeared in the same *Reg-*

ister issue, and was about a different performance at the Opera House. "Every seat in the opera house was filled Wednesday evening to hear the popular comedian, John Dillon, in 'Wanted, the Earth.' It was the best show that has struck Iola for many a long year, and the size of the audience proves that we can patronize a good performance once in a while. It was a good chance for one to stretch the wrinkles out of his face with a good laugh and forget the politics and the weather for two hours at least."[19]

Less than a month later, on December 12, Fred resumed employment with the U. S. Department of Agriculture.[20] By the following New Year's Day, 1891, special agent and assistant botanist Fred Funston was riding horseback toward the fabled, mysterious, deadly Death Valley. His adventures there and subsequently in the Arctic cold of Alaska and the British Northwest Territory are the subject of the next volume of this trilogy.

Chapter Fifteen Notes—*Collecting Native Grass Seeds of North Dakota: A Warm-up for Death Valley, August 14, 1890- November 13, 1890*

1. "Briefs," *Grand Forks Herald*, August 19, 1890.

2. "Local Matters," *The Iola Register*, July 4, 1890.

3. *The Humboldt Union*, January 4, 1890.

4. Chas. F. Scott, "Remarkable Career of a Kansas Boy," *Mail and Breeze* (about March 20, 1898) (Fredrick Funston Papers, hereafter FFP) (Archives Division, Kansas State Historical Society).

5. *Expenditures in the Department of Agriculture. Letter From The Secretary Of Agriculture, Transmitting A detailed statement of all expenditures of appropriations for the Department of Agriculture for the year ending June 30, 1891.* House of Representatives, 52d Congress, 1st Session, Ex. Doc. No. 55, 72.

6. John M. Steele, *Official History of the Operations of the Twentieth Kansas Infantry, U.S.V.,* located inside *Campaigning in the Philippines* by Karl Irving Faust (San Francisco: Hicks-Judd Company Publishers, 1899), 44.

7. "Funston, Brig. Gen., U.S.V.," *The Kansas City Star*, May 7, 1899 (FFP).

8. "Briefs," *Grand Forks Herald*, August 19, 1890.

9. *Special Agents, Etc., Department of Agriculture. Letter From The Secretary Of Agriculture, Transmitting, In response to the resolution of the House of Representatives of January 22, 1894, a list of the special agents of the Department, together with a statement of their work and the salaries received, for the four years and six months ending December 31, 1893.* House of Representatives, 53d Congress, 2d Session, Ex. Doc. No. 243, 3,14.

10. *Second Annual Report of the North Dakota Agricultural Experiment Station, Fargo N.D.,* January 30, 1892, 16.

11. *First Annual Report of the North Dakota Agricultural Experiment Station, Fargo N.D.,* February 1st, 1891, 9.

12. *First Annual Report of the North Dakota Agricultural Experiment Station,* 9.

13. Steele, *Official History of the Operations of the Twentieth Kansas Infantry, U.S.V.,* 44.

14. *First Annual Report of the North Dakota Agricultural Experiment Station,* 9.

15. "Hunting for Specimens," *Bismarck Weekly Tribune*, October 10, 1890.

16. "Local Matters," *The Iola Register*, October 24, 1890.

17. "Local Matters," *The Iola Register*, November 14, 1890.

18. "Local Matters," *The Iola Register*, November 21, 1890.

19. "Local Matters," *The Iola Register*, November 21, 1890.

20. *Expenditures in the Department of Agriculture,* 72.

AFTERWORD

At age twenty-five, Fred Funston was not an aimless young man. Yet he lacked any settled ambition for his life. In his words, when he had planned to travel to South America: "And what have I in view? Well, nothing more than what will turn up. My visit you know is one of pleasure, business and adventure, and should I find any of these things in anything like agreeable quantities, there is no telling when I shall return. I want to see the world and I propose to go if I am compelled to rest a part of my happiness on luck."

Although Fred did not know what he wanted to do, his upbringing in rural, post-pioneer Kansas significantly affected him. The daily hard physical work of a farm laborer and stock handler, in all weather and in all seasons, created a great muscular strength and endurance for him. He had been born with an innate strength which was enhanced by this strenuous physical farm labor. His frequent swimming added to his strength. The wholesome outdoor life provided a favorable environment for good, vigorous health.

This physical strength went with his mental attitude of fearlessness. Whether it was daily riding his bucking bronco to school; riding a pig while holding on to its tail; trouncing the school and Lawrence bullies; or enjoying frequent fist fights, he was fearless. Fred's physical strength contributed to this mental toughness. All of this was despite his short height and his natural awkwardness and clumsiness.

Fred's short height bothered him but did not prevent his love of humor, telling jokes, and playing practical jokes. In fact, he possessed a self-deprecating humor and never took himself too seriously. He was cheerful and uncomplaining and was a hard worker. His keen mind absorbed knowledge like a sponge, whether from the books in his father's impressive and extensive library; from Allen County's emphasis on education in rural Maple Grove and Iola High schools; and from the growing state's high educational ambitions exemplified by the quality State University at Lawrence. Kansas helped provide Fred with an amazingly broad education and knowledge.

And, of course, Professor Canfield of the State University imbued in him the defining quality that he showed through his life—the desire for freedom and independence. His desire to be his own master was to drive Fred the rest of his life. Combined with his restlessness and love of adventure, this desire took him to Death Valley, usually alone twice to Alaska, and to Cuba as a volunteer revolutionary soldier. This desire even drove his career as a United States Army soldier, since he started his career as the officer commanding the Twentieth Kansas. Thereafter,

313

as a very high-ranking officer, he always had substantial control over what he and his soldiers did. He was his own boss, a lasting legacy of his studies at the State University.

The spirit of adventure went hand-in-hand with Fred's fearlessness and independent attitude. He was ambitious and willing to leave the security of the family farm and seek his own living, whether as a schoolteacher, newspaper reporter, or ticket collector on the Santa Fe Railway. But no job was permanent for Fred with his wandering feet and uncertainty about exactly what he wanted to do. It took a return to academia for Fred to verify for himself that his life was destined for the non-academic world.

Fred had no set goal and was in no particular hurry, but out-of-doors adventures attracted him. First, North Dakota briefly, and then the unexplored and dangerous Death Valley, the next step on the road to self-discovery. Although Kansas would never be his permanent home again, it helped to shape him for his experiences in the much larger world, which would ultimately make him an American hero.

APPENDIX A

Frederick Funston's cousin, Maude Minrow, was spending the winter of 1916-1917 in San Antonio, Texas, as the guest of friends. In a letter to her aunt, Fannie Mitchell, dated Wednesday morning, February 21, 1917, Maude wrote about Fred's death on the evening of February 19. The first part of this letter is missing. The original letter is among the miscellaneous materials gifted to the Allen County Historical Society, Inc., by Deborah (Eckdall) Helmken in 2003. Generally, Maude's punctuation, or lack thereof, is shown below as she wrote it.

* * *

Monday morning I talked to Fred over the phone. He said he was feeling fine that he had been a guest at a ranch with Capt. + Mrs. Lee Sat. night and all day Sunday had rested and was feeling fine. His voice sounded happy and I knew he was in good spirits. We invited him out for dinner for some evening this week and he seemed pleased. Said that he had no engagements except for dinner Feb. 20. Told me to call him up and let him know the day. We said good bye. Little did either one of us think it would be the last time we would ever talk together.

Monday night I was tired and went to bed early [.] [At] 11 o'clock Mary came to my bed and said that Capt. Lee and Capt. Drum were at the door and wanted to see me. I hurriedly slipped on my slippers kimona and cap and rushed out. Fred had told Capt. Drum of my being here and the chauffer had remembered bringing Fred out here. They told me that Fred had been having dinner at the St. Anthony hotel with Mayor Miller, Mayor of Corpus Christi who was a hunting chum of Freds [sic]. He ordered a heavy dinner but Fred a light one saying he was on a straw diet. After leaving the table they went to the lobby and were talking when a little girl came out and Fred played with her for a while. As she ran off the orchestra in the dance hall began to play The Blue Danube and Fred remarked how beautiful it was and how he always enjoyed it. He threw back his head, the leg which had been crossed dropped to the floor. Mayor Miller thought he was relaxing to better enjoy the music when he heard a queer sound in the nose and realized something was wrong, rushed over to the desk and an army physician was there. When he got to him the pulse beat was very slight three other Drs. were summoned but it was useless the heart that had done the work of a hundred years in the ordinary man refused to work longer and Fred's life went out in the very height of his fame, loved by all who knew him and worked under him. This last statement is no exaggeration if the testimony of the people who talked to me is of any value. Mrs. Drum told me she had never seen the

Capt. shed tear [sic] until that morning. As I walked out of the room at one time the guard who stood on duty at the head of casket brushed the tears from his eyes. One was a personal friend, the other had probably never spoken to him in his life. I have wandered a little. After they told me they asked for the addresses of his family. I gave them Dr. Eckdall, Aldo Funston. Burt Funston Uncle Asa and Burt Mitchell. I regretted afterward that I did not give them Cliffie and Florence for I knew how terrible it would be to read it in the paper. I did not know Edwards [sic] but knew someone would communicate with him. I did not know where Aunt Lida was but would not have sent the message direct to her. Ah! it is all so terrible. It is needless to say that I did not get a wink of sleep. I thought of you all as you received the message and especially Aunt Lida. But to be the mother of a man like Fred is worth all the struggles and tears of a life time. We who are related to him and have known him personally do not appreciate him. Capt. Allen said next to Pres. Wilson he is the biggest man in America today. But as I looked at him he was only Fred. Many lovely things are said of people after they are gone but to know that they are genuine is a comfort that does not come to all.

Tuesday morning Capt. Lee sent a car for me and I was there when they brought him home [from the mortuary]. Flowers kept coming and were perfectly beautiful. He was dressed in full dress uniform, the sash across the front white gloves, the major's sword on the casket which was entirely covered by a large American flag. He looked as if he could speak! There was a look around the mouth that made me think of the picture of grandpa Mitchell. The expression around the eyes was as if he had just told a joke and finished laughing. There was a twinkle there that we have all seen so many times. The services were very simple the chaplain read a few verses of scripture and a prayer, two ladies sang "Lead kindly light" the band played before and after the service. The details of the procession you will get in the papers which I am sending you. He was taken [to] the Alamo where he lay from 5-8 o'clock. This is the greatest honor Texas could pay and Fred is the first man to whom this honor was extended. He has surely won the Texas people. At 8:50 the train left for California. Mary and I went to the station. The chauffeur took us thru the baggage room to avoid the crowd. I stood there behind a pillar until the train pulled out and felt he was safely on his way to his family. How little he knew that so soon he would join them. It was an awful hard day the hardest I have had since I laid [my brother] John away and my heart aches for Ella and Aunt Lida.

Yours with love
Maude

Wed. morning Feb. 21-1917

Note: Lida Funston did not long survive her famous son, dying on April 26, 1917, at the home of her daughter, Ella (Funston) Eckdall. Ella spoke of her mother's death: "It seemed impossible for her to get her mind away from Fred. She thought of him and talked of him and grieved for him continually—and died because her heart was broken" ("The Funeral Of Mrs. Funston," *The Iola Daily Register*, April 30, 1917).

* * *

San Francisco Examiner
February 25, 1917

THOUSANDS DEFY STORM TO PAY FUNSTON LAST TRIBUTE
BODY IS BURIED IN NATIONAL CEMETERY

Throngs in the City Hall, on Van Ness Avenue, at the Church and at the Burying Place Bare Heads and Stand at Attention

Simplicity Marks Ceremonies That Attend Funeral; Guard of Honor Will Keep Day and Night Vigil at the Grave

---

TAPS!

That final but eloquent goodnight of the army to its dead has been sounded above the grave of Major General Frederick Funston at the National Cemetery of the Presidio.

The stormy skies echoed yesterday with the artillery's final salute to the brave commander.

On the hill overlooking the Golden Gate, through which he sailed to fame in 1898, and within the post where, in 1906, he sheltered San Francisco's destitute, General Funston was buried at noon yesterday as troops fired the parting three volleys and the bugler sounded taps.

Rain and wind added materially to the sadness of the scene. The elements were at their worst. Yet a thousand citizens braved storm and mud to stand around the grave for their mute farewell to a man whom all Americans admired, and all San Franciscans revered.

SIDEWALKS CROWDED

It was a repetition of what had occurred earlier in the day along the streets upon which the cortege had passed. Men stood hatless in the downpour; women, unable to hold umbrellas in the gale, defied the weather.

Van Ness avenue, from the City Hall to Union street, and Lombard, from Van Ness to the Presidio, had been lined all morning with men, women and children, who waited to get a glimpse of the funeral procession. There were thousands of them, and they stood for hours in the season's most violent storm.

Many automobiles went to the Presidio, and only the carrying capacity of the municipal cars limited the number of those less fortunately equipped who journeyed to the burying place.

Every element was represented—rich and poor, young and old, robust and decrepit, native and alien born. There were many men in many types of uniforms, representing the various veteran societies. Men they were, in many instances, who had seen service with General Funston, or under his command. Some were there who had followed him from Kansas to the Philippines as volunteers, and others who had obeyed his orders in the later days of the regular army.

SIMPLICITY AT GRAVE

At the grave military simplicity marked the ceremony. Soldiers lined up at attention as the body was carried from the caisson to its place of final repose. Minute guns had boomed the major general's salute as the procession wound its way to the cemetery.

Then the volleys were fired, taps sounded, the final salute given, flags went from half-mast to the top of the staff, and the last and greatest honor that the living can pay to the departed had been bestowed.

A guard of honor will keep vigil day and night at the grave for several days.

Equal simplicity attended the funeral service at the First Presbyterian Church.

Long before the body arrived the floral pieces sent by many individual organizations had been arranged in a semicircle in front of the pulpit. Representatives of many military and civic bodies had been seated by army officers acting as ushers, and the public had been admitted.

ALL STAND AT ATTENTION

Just before the body was carried in the mourners were led to their seats in the front row of pews. There was Mrs. Frederick Funston, the widow, supported by Colonel Benjamin Alvord; Frederick Funston Jr., clinging to his mother's hand; Mrs. E. H. Funston, the mother, on the arm of her youngest son, and the sisters and other relatives of the general's widow.

As the coffin bearers entered the church everybody stood at attention. Behind them were the pall bearers, followed closely by Major General J. Franklin Bell and members of his staff.

Rev. William Kirk Guthrie, pastor of the Frist Presbyterian Church, where the Funston family worship, repeated the Lord's Prayer. The choir sang "Lead, Kindly Light." Then followed a scriptural reading by Dr. Guthrie, and a bass solo, "Just For Today," by Godfrey Price.

DR. GUTHRIE'S SERMON

The funeral sermon was preached by Dr. Guthrie. He said:

I think it was Dr. Jowett of New York who, in a recent sermon, said the most impressive part of the great coronation ceremonies in Westminster Abbey was after the King and Queen had been crowned and received homage from the nobility of the empire, they stepped down from the throne and went to the communion table, and kneeling before the altar, they took their crowns from their heads and laid them on the ground, in token that their honor and dignity was as nothing to that of their Lord and King, and that, simply as a poor man and woman, they besought His grace and blessing, humbly and thankfully taking the sacrament—the oath of allegiance to Jesus, saviour of the world.

It is not possible for us all to be great and famous rulers of empires, princes in commerce, orators, statesmen, or as was he whose body rests so peacefull [sic] beneath the flag he loved and served, and whose glory both in peace and war he so steadfastly maintained—a master of arms.

LIFE OF HAPPY SERVICE

But we all, even the poorest and weakest among us, may be worthy of that honor which shall endure when earth's glory has passed away, if we so live that the Lord can say to us: "Well done, good and faithful servant; enter thou into the joy of the Lord."

And the joy of our Lord is not Nirvana, nor a Mohammedan and sensual Paradise;.it is a continued life of happy service—love of God and toward men, wrought out in obedience to His holy will, and brotherly kindness to one another. This is a future life worth believing in, where those things which we have sought and prayed and striven for on earth shall be realized in heaven.

When the news of General Funston's death was flashed across the country, from the President to the humblest citizen we were shocked and stunned, and said surely a great man has fallen among us, and we have lost a leader when we need leadership so much. We do not know what trials and disciplines await us as a people, but we do know that if we shall stand for and serve the right, we cannot fail.

SYMPATHY FOR KANSAS

We sorrow with and extend our sympathy to the great State of Kansas, who has lost one of her most famous sons, but we in California feel that we also have been stricken, for he was dear to us also. And we citizens of San Francisco, who went through trying days learned to know his worth, when his genius and his manhood brought order out of confusion, confidence out of fear, and much comfort in our distress. And this he did, not counting the cost to himself, and risking more than we can understand, that he might help the needy.

His varied and interesting life of preparation, his career in the army, is known to you all, and while no man goes forward in this world of so many little jealousies, without being criticized by those he leaves behind, yet I think the final verdict must be that the honors he received, he deserved, and the high position he achieved, he earned.

MAN OF DEEDS

He was a man of deeds, not words, and to say more about him would be displeasing to his soul. We know his worth and service, and he will not soon be forgotten among us.

Death is always sad, because it means a parting from those we love, and I know your hearts are throbbing in sympathy with the little family he leaves behind. May God keep and comfort them, and give them faith to trust in Him that all is well.

At the conclusion of this address, Dr. Guthrie offered a prayer. He asked guidance for the bereaved family, for the American people, who had lost a great leader, for President Wilson, deprived of an able lieutenant, and for the Nation as a whole, facing a future full of uncertainties.

LED BY GENERAL BELL

The voices of the choir rose in Tennyson's "Crossing the Bar." Benediction was pronounced, and the audience rose as the body of the general started on its last march.

Outside the church, as the casket was carried to the caisson, the Coast Artillery band played "Nearer, My God, to Thee," and the assembled populace along the avenue for half a dozen blocks uncovered.

The funeral procession was led by General Bell and his staff, flanked by the two-starred guidon of a major-general. Behind them marched two provisional regiments of the Coast Artillery. Next came the caisson, bearing the casket. General Funston's black-draped charger, with the empty boots within the stirrups, walked behind.

Pallbearers, mourners, and Major Rolph and other officials in automobiles followed. After them marched officers and members of the National Guard, led by Colonel Henry G. Mathewson. The United Spanish War Veterans and the Veterans of Foreign Wars were next in line, with the Boy Scouts bringing up the rear.

All night, as the general's body lay in state, the people had moved in a melancholy procession through the City Hall, paying their individual respect to the dead. And all night, motionless sentries had stood guard over the coffin beneath the dome of the big municipal building.

Early in the morning the number of citizens in the City Hall began to increase, and by the time the funeral procession started at 10 o'clock, galleries, corridors and main floor were jammed with silent onlookers.

Just as the coffin-bearers approached to remove the casket, Major-General Bell and his staff, Mayor Rolph, and a group of public officials, including Mayor John L. Davie of Oakland and Secretary Skelton of the Sacramento Chamber of Commerce, advanced slowly down the main stairway toward the catafalque.

The double file of soldiers presented arms, and silently the non-commissioned officers in olive drab, who had accompanied the body from the Texas border, lifted it from its place of honor, and bore it out to Van Ness avenue for the march to the grave.

* * *

APPENDIX B

The introductory paragraphs of William Allen White's "Gen. Frederick Funston," *Harper's Weekly*, May 20, 1899 (see Chapter Two for discussion):

The child of civilized parents is a savage: probably the male of the species is more nearly a wild creature than the female. And because he is a savage a boy is brave just so long as he holds to the traditions of savagery. When he begins to regard his raiment and to fear dirt, when he begins to take account of personal comfort — which, although "scorned of devils," is cherished in polite society — the boy begins to lose his valor and becomes a well-regulated member of society, with an ambition to sit at a desk and to avoid doing anything unusual. Now the key to the character of Frederick Funston, recently appointed Brigadier-General of Volunteers for gallant conduct, is the fact that in the thirty-three years of his romantic, adventurous, and eventful life he has never passed a period when he thought the second time about the dirt on his clothes. He wandered into the fringe of civilization in the years of his adolescence, and all his life it has been of more importance to him to accomplish his ends than it has been to keep his cuffs clean. Many a heroic deed in this world has been left undone because it would soil a shirt; but with Funston the deed, not the shirt, has been of primary importance, as it is with every boy. Funston is still a boy —a devil-may care, earnest, honest, patriotic boy, who will not be impressed with his gold braid and his star too deeply. He has lived all of his life out-of-doors, in lands of danger and amid alarms. The visions that boys see have come true in Funston's daily life, and he has never awakened from his dream to find his feet chained to a desk, and his mind the slave of a column of capricious figures which will not obey the reasonable requirements of a balance. His mind has grown with experience and with the culture that comes from wide reading. He has the keen intelligence of a scholar and a gentleman, and writes as well as he fights, having contributed to *Harper's Weekly* and to *Scribner's Magazine* and to *St. Nicholas*. But his body is a boy's body, that does not shiver nor falter at hardships and his eyes are a boy's eyes. They see expedients which reason and sage logic would hoot at. It was a boy who swam the Bagbag; a boy who charged the Filipinos from a raft. For a man would have thought of fever germs and rheumatism, and would have been a cautious colonel. But the boy in Funston put the star upon his shoulder, and the boy in the heart of all the world rouses to throw up its hat at these splendid achievements.

Now the foregoing remarks, being written by way of introduction, may be thrown out as irrelevant, incompetent, immaterial, and not the best evidence. Yet to comprehend the facts of Funston's career some explanatory words seem necessary.

* * *

The following is my transcription of William Allen White's response to Fred Funston's letter of July 1, 1899, (see Chapter Two for discussion). White kept carbon copies of his typed letters, which I reviewed in 2002: *Letter Books*, container B1, pt. 1, William Allen White Papers, Manuscript Division, Library of Congress, Washington, D.C. Starting on page 82 of *Letter Book* B1, pt.1, June 27, 1899 - Dec. 22, 1899, is the carbon copy of Billy's letter to Fred, but the blue type is so faded in places as to be totally illegible. The letter's beginning exists only in part, so this letter is identified as being addressed to Fred solely by the index at the front of this *Letter Book*. The date of the letter is illegible, but the letter copy immediately preceding is dated August 9, 1899, and the first letter copy that this author can read after the Funston letter is dated August 11, 1899.

Since the carbon copy likely will continue to fade over time and in order to preserve the currently legible portions of this document, the following is my transcription of the legible portions of White's response, with blanks for those words that are illegible:

Manila, Phillipine [sic] Islands, August _____

My Dear _____,

You are a good boy, and as you say of <u>me</u>, you mean well; but you are several thousand miles from Deer Creek, and your head isn't working. You are all right when you are alone; there is not a clearer eye on God's footstool than yours when you are away from the maddening throngs, ignoble strife; but down there in the Phillipines [sic] you seem to have absorbed the point of view of the regular army man who is a poor, benighted heathen about most things of this world, even if he is a first class fighting man.

[End of p. 82 text]

[First half of p. 83 text totally faded out; there are about 11 lines of text; then there are a few words before the text is completely legible.]

_____ though tempted by many hundreds _____ offer to write for the "Cosmopolitan" _____ and I refused offers starting at several hundred dollars to write about you, because it seems to me that I had written all that I could in justice to you; that is, all that I could write well, and in justice to myself, for I had almost a thousand dollars worth of other orders, at a very much higher price than I could get for writing about you. I did what I did as a labor of love, and I am infinitely sorry if it has not been satisfactory. There was just one paper in the United States that criticized the Harper [sic] Weekly article, and that was the "New York Sun," and I have a letter from the New York Sun apologizing for their criticism [?] [Rest is illegible: end of the line and the next line.]

[End of p. 83 text]

[p. 84 starts]

[On the first one-half of page, I can find only a few words that are legible as follows below:]

. _____ from the bottom of my heart the experience that had made me be [?] _____ as yours, and regret to learn at this late day, that my admiration and my envy came from a base and lamentable spirit which cannot receive your commendation. I am pained to learn that I have become one of the "mob" as you call it. American citizens who love courage, be it displayed however humble a walk and circumstance; who love high purposes, be their manifestation however lowly; who worship heroes, be their work "in Greenlands icy mountains, or by India _____ strands [?]"_____ on the traits that I admired in you Timmy, I shall

[End of p. 84 text]

[p. 85 starts] always admire [next 3 lines illegible]

[4th line] and thereafter_____ with rooster feathers, and the gilt braid of pomp and circumstance with which you have so recently became enamored by association and environment. I shall always thrill, when I think of the boy who bluffed Bivins the coon,

Though I still shut the door of my closet lest he should be associated with the hero of Culumpit. I shall ever cherish the memory of the youth, who is the hero of many charming incidents of my college days, though I shall forbear _____ the _____ of shame [?] be the Brigadier by _____ them in his name.

I do not in any way, sympathize with you in your reference to what you call the "damn newspapers" and their attitude towards you. I have seen several amusing pieces of fiction in the newspapers notably one which told of your ventures on an ice berg among the Indians of as but they were too ridiculous to be annoying and too palpabally [sic] absurd to inspire anything but a laugh! [?] but as a rule the "damn newspapers" are edited by gentlemen, who have not the distinction of your acquaintance, but who has [sic] allowed love for your heroism to inspire them to treat you with signal kindness, and it seems to me, with the utmost generosity, all over the land. The editors of the "damn newspapers" have glorified Fred Funston and prepared to enjoy him forever. It is a fad among the prigs of the regular army to sniff at these things, but it is all a hollow pretense; they enjoy it as much as any

[End of p. 85 text]

[p. 86 starts]

one _____ they are jealous, and they seek _____. Away the real fighters of the regular army, _____ America has made heroes, there has been a _____ different attitude toward the "damn newspapers." Governor Roosevelt [one word illegible] takes an entirely opposite view from you, and when the "damn newspapers" of Kansas mention him for President, was so far given over to the news of what you call the "mob" that he lowered himself, and absolutely wrote letters expressing his gratitude to the editors of the "damn newspapers" a half [?] a thousand or so of them _____ him. These same "damn newspapers" in a burst of national feeling which would be distinctly repulsive to the _____ of the _____, have mentioned you humorously and to my mind _____. These newspapers _____ from _____ to California; you _____ your feet on American soil, and get back your touch [?], with the plain, every day, honest, earnest, American, with his horse sense, that the [circumstances?] of your present environment will be strong enough, to hold you to your present opinion about the "damn newspapers."

[About three words are illegible] nests [?] which have been proposed for you, I have not been one of the proposers, because I knew of your sincere distaste for these things; neither have I suggested you for any office, nor have I encouraged those who have suggested you, because I knew of your temperament in that direction. I did wire to a number of politicians, and I

[End of p. 86 text]

[p. 87 Top half-plus of this last page is illegible; seems to be one long paragraph.]

I have made these remarks my son, in sorrow and not in anger. I have not intended to wound you, but rather to open your eyes to what seemed to me to be some important facts. I do not want you to get mad about this [two words illegible] I did not get mad when you suggested that I would lie to sell [a few words illegible] get mad when you [one word illegible] my _____ffles [?] _____ we will call it "horse and horse," and [one word illegible] we will always be to each other "Billie and Timmy" [about 10 words illegible.]

Sincerely yours,

* * *

326

ACKNOWLEDGMENTS
for *Becoming Frederick Funston Trilogy*

My great thanks to the following:

Members of the Funston family: first and foremost for their invaluable assistance and friendship, the late Frank Funston Eckdall and his daughter, Deborah (Eckdall) Helmken. Also, Martine Funston, Ellen (Lees) Stolte, the late Don Funston, Dale Funston, and the late Greta Funston. Each of these assisted me in one or more essential ways. Although she died long before I started work on this trilogy in 1995, I am grateful to Fred Funston's sister, Ella (Funston) Eckdall, whose writings and scrapbooks on her brother's life provided much important material and, at times, information that otherwise would have been lost forever.

Mitchell family: Burt Bowlus, grandnephew of Lida (Mitchell) Funston, mother of Fred Funston.

Brenda Cash, Resource Sharing Head, Southeast Kansas Library System, performed great work obtaining through interlibrary loan numerous essential materials. Also, Roger Carswell, Director of Iola Public Library, for an essential item that he obtained.

In 2010, a "fluke" stroke left me with only one functioning hand and mobility challenges. My longtime friend, Bill Crowe, made innumerable trips to the Kansas State Historical Society, Topeka, Kansas, to review various collections and to obtain copies of needed materials for this trilogy.

Rick Danley worked for me part-time from 2016-2019. He helped me organize and use my ever-growing collection of materials; checked microfilm at the Iola Public Library; and read and helpfully critiqued the entire trilogy manuscript after its completion.

John E. Miller, historian, professor, and author, who died unexpectedly in 2020, my friend since graduate school days in history at the University of Wisconsin-Madison. John read several years ago the manuscript as completed to that date and validated the worthwhileness of this work.

Jarrett Robinson, my comrade-in-arms for more than twenty-five years in our belief in the importance of preserving and publicizing the details of the life of a worthy man, Fred Funston. Among other help, Jarrett shared with me helpful "finds" on the early years of Funston's life.

Members of my family helped in various ways: Nancy, my wife, in multiple ways; David Toland, our son, and his wife, Beth Toland; Elizabeth (Toland) Smith, our daughter, and her husband, Bart Smith; and our granddaughter, Caroline Toland.

Bob Hawk prepared the excellent map showing Fred Funston's route through Alaska and British Northwest Territory and the map of Cuba, and assisted with the technical aspects of numerous photographs. Bob, long an admirer of Fred Funston, played an essential role in the creation of the Funston Home Museum and the Funston Museum and Visitors' Center.

American Hero, Kansas Heritage was made possible in part by the Center for Kansas Studies, Washburn University, Topeka, Kansas, which funded formatting and design costs. Carol Yoho used her valuable computer and design skills on this book. And special thanks to Thomas Fox Averill, noted Kansas author and emeritus professor of English at Washburn University, whose belief in this book made its publication a reality and who provided great editorial assistance.

Andres Rabinovich translated Prats-Lerma's crucial account about Funston's Cuban military experiences.

Barbara Diehl faithfully typed nearly all of my manuscript from my handwritten draft, and made changes and corrections in the typed draft, and Terri Jackman faithfully typed the balance and made needed changes and corrections throughout the typed draft.

For their help: Sally Huskey, Richard Zahn, Ed Fitzpatrick, Margaret Robb, the late Dorothy (Carnine) Scott, the late Emerson and Mickey Lynn, the late Winifred Bicknell, Scott Jordan, the late Ed Kelly, William Berry, Donna and the late Ray Houser, Katherine Crowe, Curator of Special Collections & Archives at University of Denver Libraries, Gary LaValley, Archivist for the United States Naval Academy, Kurtis Russell, Executive Director of Allen County Historical Society, Inc., and Allen County Register of Deeds Jacque Webb and her successor, Cara Barkdoll.

The excellent staff at Kenneth Spencer Research Library, including Becky Schulte, Sherry Williams, the late Mary Hawkins, and Kathy Lafferty; Barry Bunch of University Archives; Kevin L. Smith, Director of Libraries, all at the University of Kansas. The excellent staffs at Manuscript Division of the Library of Congress; Kansas State Historical Society; Special Collections and Archives at Emporia State University; Lyon County History Center & Historical Society; Elwyn B. Robinson Department of Special Collections in Chester Fritz Library at the University of North Dakota; Government Documents at North Dakota State University; Department of Rare Books and Special Collections at Princeton University Library; The Rutherford B. Hayes Presidential Library and Museum; and the Kansas Supreme Court Law Library.

My parents, the late June and Stanley Toland, encouraged and supported my interest in history starting in my childhood. I am definitely a product of that influence, and I shall always be grateful to them.

BIBLIOGRAPHY

Collections

Allen County Historical Society, Inc., Iola, Kansas

    Eckdall collection of letters

Kansas State Historical Society

    Frederick Funston Papers (Manuscript Collection 33, and Microfilm: MS75 – MS77)

    Herbert S. Hadley Misc

    Homer M. Limbird Papers

Library of Congress, Manuscript Division

    William Allen White Collection

Spencer Research Library, University of Kansas

    Papers of William Lindsay White

Scrapbooks

Allen County Historical Society, Inc., Iola, Kansas

    Eckdall Scrapbooks I, II, III, and IV (all photocopies)

    Funston Political Scrapbooks (photocopy)

Iola Public Library, Iola, Kansas

    Untitled scrapbook about Frederick Funston

Spencer Research Library, University of Kansas

    Frederick Funston: Adventurer, Explorer, and Soldier

    Wilder Stevens Metcalf and Frederick Funston With the Twentieth Kansas in the Philippines During the Spanish-American War

Manuscript

Potter, David, *Frederick Funston: A First Class Fighting Man: A Biography* (Department of Rare Books and Special Collections, Princeton University Library).

Selected Newspapers and Census Records

The Iola (Kansas) *Register* and its predecessors, including *The Iola Register, The Iola Daily Register, Neosho Valley Register, Kansas State Register,* and *Allen County Courant.* Microfilm at Iola Public Library, Iola, Kansas, and at Kansas State Historical Society, Topeka, Kansas. The Kansas State Historical Society has a wonderful and extensive collection on microfilm of many other Kansas newspapers and of *The Kansas City Star*, a Missouri newspaper.

The Iola Public Library has microfilm of the federal and Kansas Census records for Allen County, Kansas, in the 1870s and 1880s.

Interviews

Winifred Bicknell

Burton Bowlus

Frank Funston Eckdall

Greta Funston

Edwin Kelly

Ellen (Lees) Stolte

Selected Other Sources

(Some of these are located in the collections and scrapbooks, and others are located in the designated depositories.)

A Brief History of the Carlyle Church and Community (pamphlet). (Allen County Historical Society, Inc.).

"A Kansas Cuban Soldier," *The Iola Register*, December 25, 1896 (reprint from *The Kansas City Star*, December 13, 1896).

Accounts and Transactions of County Superintendent of Public Instruction for Allen County, Journals A, B, and C. (Allen County Historical Society, Inc.).

Adams, Adda Sophronia, *"Pioneering In Kansas" 1869 David Caldwell Adams, wife Delilah Smick Adams, and family* (no publisher, no date). (Iola Public Library).

[Allen County, Kansas, District Court] *Journal A (October 5, 1858 – Jan 22, 1872).* (Allen County Historical Society, Inc.).

Andrews, J. H., "Old Cofachique," *The Humboldt Union*, May 5, 1927.

Bain, David Haward, *Sitting in Darkness: Americans in the Philippines* (Boston: Houghton Mifflin Company, 1984).

Beadle, J. H., *The Undeveloped West, OR, Five Years in the Territories* (Philadelphia: National Publishing Company, 1873).

"Brigadier-General Frederick Funston," *The Literary Digest*, Vol. XVIII, No. 19 (May 13, 1899).

Canfield, James H., "Funston: A Kansas Product," *The American Monthly Review of Reviews*, May 1901.

Carnes, Mark C., "Little Colonel Funston," *American Heritage*, September 1998.

Centennial Edition, The Iola Register, May 30, 1955.

Church, Olin, *Lone Elm Days* (no publisher, no date) (pamphlet).

Crouch, Thomas W., "Frederick Funston of Kansas: His Formative Years, 1865-1891," *The Kansas Historical Quarterly*, Summer 1974.

Cutler, William G., *History of the State of Kansas* (Chicago: A.T. Andreas, 1883).

Duncan, L. Wallace and Chas. F. Scott, *History of Allen and Woodson Counties Kansas* (Iola, Kansas: Iola Register, Printers and Binders, 1901).

Eckdall, Ella Funston, *The Funston Homestead* (Emporia, Kansas: Raymond Lees, 1949).

Eckdall, Frank F., "'Fighting' Fred Funston of Kansas," *The Kansas Historical Quarterly*, Spring 1956.

"Emporia Girl, Niece of Funston, Writes of 'Incidents' in His Life," *Emporia Gazette*, October 9, 1928.

"Fred Funston's Restless Life of Adventure," *The Chicago Sunday Tribune*, May 7, 1899.

"Funston, Brig. Gen., U.S.V.," *The Kansas City Star*, May 7, 1899.

Funston, Frederick, "General Funston's Reminiscences of the University," *The Graduate Magazine of the University of Kansas*, Volume XIV, No. 3, December 1915.

Funston, Frederick, *Memories of Two Wars: Cuban and Philippine Experiences* (New York: Charles Scribner's Sons, 1914).

Funston, Frederick, "Over The Chilkoot Pass To The Yukon," *Scribner's Magazine*, November 1896.

Funston, Stanley Steele, *Paul Calvin Funston and Some of His Descendants, Including Major General Fredrick [sic] Funston and His Family* (Cedar Rapids, Iowa, by author, 2002).

Gleed, C. S., eulogy, "Report of Select Committee," *Journal of the House*, Hall of the House of Representatives, Topeka, Kansas, February 26, 1917.

Gleed, Charles S., "Romance And Reality In A Single Life. Gen. Frederick Funston," *The Cosmopolitan Illustrated Monthly Magazine*, July 1899.

Griffith, Sally Foreman, ed., *The Autobiography of William Allen White* (Lawrence: University Press of Kansas, 1990).

Henderson, Opal McCullough and Terri Lynn Henderson, *To-Day, Beginning, Yesterday: A History of Neosho Falls, Kansas* (no publisher, no date).

Hinshaw, David, *A Man From Kansas: The Story of William Allen White* (New York: G. P. Putnam's Sons, 1945).

"Historical," *The Iolian*, Vol. 1, No. 1, November 1903. (Iola Public Library).

History of the Sixteenth Battery of Ohio Volunteer Light Artillery U.S.A. (no publisher, 1906).

Hyder, Clyde Kenneth, *Snow of Kansas: The Life of Francis Huntington Snow with Extracts from his Journals and Letters* (Lawrence: University of Kansas Press, 1953).

Johnson, Bob, "Presidential chair featured," *The Iola Register*, May 5, 2009.

Johnson, Walter, *William Allen White's America* (New York: Henry Holt and Company, 1947).

Johnson, William E., "The Making of Brigadier Funston," *The New Voice*, May 13, 1899.

Kansas State Historical Society, *Frederick Funston Clippings*, Vol. 1

Kansapedia, Kansas Historical Society (www.kshs.org).

Kellogg, Vernon, "Mountaineering In America," *The Atlantic Monthly*, October 1921.

Llewellyn, Major H. H., "The Santa Fe, Its Men and the Spanish-American War," *Santa Fe Employes' Magazine* (Railway Exchange, Chicago), September 1910.

McCoy, Sondra Van Meter and Jan Hults, *1001 Kansas Place Names* (Lawrence: University Press of Kansas, 1989).

McGuffey's Third Eclectic Reader, Revised edition (New York: American Book Company, orig. 1879).

Nichols, Ode C., "Funston, From Babyhood to Present Day as His Mother Knows Him," *The World*, May 21, 1899.

Norton, J.C., *Community Tales of Old*. (Iola Public Library).

Peters, Alvin, "Fences and Settlers," *The Law and Lawyers in Kansas* (Topeka, Kansas: Kansas State Historical Society, 1992).

Pickering, James H. and Nancy P. Thomas, *"If I Ever Grew Up and Became a Man": William Allen White's Moraine Park Years* (Estes Park, Colorado: The Estes Park Museum Friends & Foundation, Inc. Press, 2010).

Portrait And Biographical Album of Washington County, Iowa (Chicago: Acme Publishing Company, 1887).

Rice, Cyrus R., "Experiences of a Pioneer Missionary," *Collections of the Kansas State Historical Society, 1913-1914*, Vol. XIII (Topeka, Kansas, 1915).

Rich, Everett, *William Allen White: The Man from Emporia* (New York: Farrar & Rinehart, Inc., 1941).

Richards, Ralph, *A History of IOLA, KANSAS From the Beginning Up To These Times Called Modern* (no publisher, no date). (Iola Public Library).

Richardson, Albert D., *Beyond the Mississippi* (Hartford, Conn.: American Publishing Company, 1867).

Richmond, Robert W., *Kansas: A Land of Contrasts* (Saint Charles, Missouri: Forum Press, 1974).

Ruggles, R. M., "Leaves From The Diary of Gen. Funston's Eventful Life" (unknown newspaper), datelined May 11 [1899].

Rydjord, John, *Kansas Place-Names* (Norman, Okla.: University of Oklahoma Press, 1972).

Scott, Angelo C., *A Boyhood in Old Carlyle* (Oklahoma City, 1940) (pamphlet). (Allen County Historical Society, Inc.).

Scott, Charles F., eulogy, "Report of Select Committee," *Journal of the House*, Hall of the House of Representatives, Topeka, Kansas, February 26, 1917.

Scott, Charles F., "Frederick Funston," *The Independent*, April 11, 1901.

Scott, Chas. F., "Remarkable Career of a Kansas Boy," *Mail and Breeze* (about March 20, 1898).

Smith, Lloyd F., "Farm Woodlot Management in Kansas" (Manhattan, Kansas: Kansas State College of Agriculture and Applied Science, Agricultural Experiment Station, Department of Horticulture, October 1940, Circular 201).

Snow, F. H., "The Beginnings of the University of Kansas," *Transactions of the Kansas State Historical Society, 1897-1900* (Topeka, Kansas: W. Y. Morgan, State Printer, 1900), Vol. VI.

Southern Kansas Horticulturalist, Vol I–No. XI (March Number) [1896] (published at Iola, Kansas, by E.S. Davis, and edited by L. M. Pancoast).

Steele, John M., *Official History of the Operations of the Twentieth Kansas Infantry, U.S.V.* located inside *Campaigning In the Philippines*, by Karl Irving Faust (San Francisco: Hicks-Judd Company Publishers, 1899).

Stewart, Alan J., "Funston Homestead Will Become Park," *The Topeka Daily Capital Sunday Magazine*, October 9, 1955.

Stewart, Alan J., "Maj.– Gen. Fredrick [sic] Funston Brought Glory to Kansas With His Victories," *The Topeka Daily Capital Sunday Magazine*, March 13, 1955.

"The Story of General Funston," *Pull* (The Western Shade Cloth Co., 1917), Vol. I, No. 6 (April 1917).

Thomas, Henry W., *Walter Johnson: Baseball's Big Train* (Washington, D.C.: Phenom Press, 1995).

Toland, Clyde W., *Samuel Franklin Hubbard and Permelia Caroline (Spencer) Hubbard: Pioneer Settlers in 1857 of Allen County, Kansas Territory, and Their Descendants* (Iola, Kansas, by author, 1985).

Trussell, John B.B., Jr., "The Man destiny just missed," *Military Review*, June 1973.

Tuttle, Charles R., *A New Centennial History of The State of Kansas* (Madison, Wisc.: Inter-State Book Company, 1876).

Twain, Mark, "A Defence of General Funston," *The North American Review*, Vol. CLXXIV (May 1902).

Watkins, W.I. and W. H. Metzger and J. R. Latta, *Soil Survey Allen County Kansas* (United States Department of Agriculture Bureau of Chemistry and Soils: Series 1935, No. 2. Issued November 1938).

West, S. H., *Life and Times of S. H. West* (LeRoy, Ill.: S.H. West, 1908).

"What the Little General Said in New York," *The Topeka State Journal*, March 14, 1902.

White, William Allen, "Frederick Funston's Alaskan Trip," *Harper's Weekly*, May 25, 1895.

White, William Allen, "Funston — the Man from Kansas," *The Saturday Evening Post*, May 18, 1901.

White, William Allen, "Gen. Frederick Funston," *Harper's Weekly*, May 20, 1899.

White, William Allen, *The Autobiography of William Allen White* (New York: The Macmillan Company, 1946).

White, William Allen, "The Hero Of The Philippines," *The St. Louis Republic Magazine Section*, May 21, 1899.

Wilder, D. W., *The Annals of Kansas New Edition, 1541-1885* (Topeka: T. Dwight Thacher, Kansas Publishing House, 1886).

Wilkinson, Paul, "Frederick Funston In The Chapter," *The Scroll of Phi Delta Theta*, Vol. XXV, October 1900-June 1901.

Williams, Elihu S., "Gen. Fred Funston," *The Buckeye*, Troy, Ohio, April 4, 1901.

Wood, Norman B., *Lives of Famous Indian Chiefs* (Aurora, Ill.: American Indian Historical Publishing Company, 1906).

Young, Louis Stanley, and Henry Davenport Northrop, *Life and Heroic Deeds of Admiral Dewey* (Philadelphia: Globe Publishing Co., 1899).